Deviants
and the Abandoned
in French Society

Other volumes in the Series

The Johns Hopkins University Press • Baltimore and London

Deviants and the Abandoned in French Society

Selections from the

Annales

Economies, Sociétés, Civilisations

Volume IV

Edited by

Robert Forster

and

Orest Ranum

Translated by

Elborg Forster

and

Patricia M. Ranum

This book has been brought to publication with the
generous assistance of the Andrew W. Mellon Foundation.

Manufactured in the United States of America

The Johns Hopkins University Press, Baltimore, Maryland 21218
The Johns Hopkins Press Ltd., London

Library of Congress Catalog Number 77–17253
ISBN 0–8018–1991–1 (hardcover)
ISBN 0–8018–1992–X (paperback)

Library of Congress Cataloging in Publication data
will be found on the last printed page of this book.

Contents

Introduction

What are the deviant or abandoned groups of society? At first glance the answer seems obvious. Vagrants and tramps, prostitutes, abandoned children, convicts, arsonists, the insane. Still other marginal groups come to mind. But where do the terms for deviant behavior come from? They are found in law codes, learned works on medicine and jurisprudence, and works of piety exhorting the faithful to charitable activities, and in novels, plays, and etchings.

Behind these terms for behavior are people. Their whole history can scarcely be subsumed under the heading of a single term such as "prostitute" or "tramp." Do the deviant or marginal groups in society have a history all their own? Would the people masked by such terms accept them as accurate or complete designations for their behavior and place in society? In this volume of articles selected from the *Annales,* the deviant groups are counted, their behavior is defined, and above all their roles in society are delineated.

To study deviants, historians have had to decipher hitherto neglected sources—usually volume upon volume of names, dates, places of birth, and occupations. These sources—usually compiled by a law court, prison, hospital, or other institution—constitute the first level of definition for marginal groups. A criminal record or the name and age of a child abandoned by his parents may be the only data that permit historians to assign an individual to a marginal group. The records have an uncanny similarity regardless of the particular deviant behavior: name, date of birth, place of birth, parish, height, and physical deformities file by in column after column of the registers—perfect evidence of the bureaucratic mind at work in the courts, hospitals, and prisons.

The marginal groups of society rarely contribute directly to political and social history as it is conventionally written and taught. An uneasiness develops among political historians when it is suggested that prostitutes and the insane be included in the syllabus or textbook of a history course. From the perspective of these historians, deviants do not count; they caused no ministry to fall (except, perhaps, through reactions to sex scandals among elite voters) and do not easily fit into studies of voting behavior. In short, deviants and outcasts have no place in what Lucien Febvre rather derisively called *grande histoire.*

Social historians, too, are often reluctant to embrace the study of marginal groups. Often eager to bring evidence to bear on some theory of society or community or to build toward an analysis of behavior on the basis of the study of occupations, incomes, and social mobility, they find it difficult to fit deviants into social history as it has been classically defined. They are almost obsessed with the search for typicality. Thus, historians who study the history of prostitutes and tramps, for example, have—politely—been accused by their colleagues in social history as erring on the side of the arcane, lewd, and antiquarian.*

As a result, the standard procedure for sneaking the study of marginal groups into history has been to assert that knowledge about them sheds light on the aspirations, fears, and conditions of the mainstream or dominant groups of society. In other words, the study of arsonists and abandoned children is important not for what they are, but for what they may tell us about family life, social structure, mentalities, mental derangement, as a whole. This approach yields results. The moral and social values of a society, especially on the level of collective mentalities and community behavior, are clarified by the study of those who reject those values and are cast out of society. Changes in the attitudes of dominant groups—the governing elites who pay for hospitals and prisons and who write the laws and render justice—may be discerned almost graphically by counting the number of delinquents and their crimes.

As Michelle Perrot's article reveals, the changes in the patterns of criminal activity during the nineteenth century have a rhythm that corresponds to political changes and to the articulation and instrumentation of "bourgeois values" in the law code and courts. Indeed, life in a nineteenth-century prison involved a level of coercive asceticism and desexualization rarely achieved in the most zealous of monastic orders. Once incarcerated, the deviant had to demonstrate even purer behavior than those outside the prison wall.

Asylums, in some instances model asylums for the insane, were built across the road from the prisons. Gérard Bleandonu and Guy Le Gaufey explore the scientific and bureaucratic dynamisms that culminated in the construction of vast institutions and expanded professional schools to confine and care for the insane. The scientific zeal to categorize different types of aberrant behavior was occurring simultaneously with the efforts of legislators and the courts to refine and make more specific the types of crime that required imprisonment. Local administrations ceded before the experts from medical schools and the Parisian bureaucrats and provided costly facilities that may not have been

* Examples of this type of criticism may be found in reviews of Richard Cobb's recent works. See J. Joll, *Times Literary Supplement*, "Commentary," 16 July 1976, and Robert Darnton, "French History: The Case of the Wandering Eye," *New York Review of Books*, 5 April 1973.

wanted by society at large. The doctors and the bureaucrats were builders; their energies provided careers for a burgeoning and increasingly well-educated elite. Upright, efficient, and scientific, were the Dr. Girards of nineteenth-century France perceiving illness in all cases or were they focusing their attention upon the behavior of deviants from an impoverished and threatening popular culture? It is clear that an unwillingness to work became, if not a crime, at least a symptom of illness in the eyes of the educated notables of the nineteenth century. But there is more to the study of deviants than the knowledge of the dominant social and moral values of a society.

Any history that claims to be *histoire totale,* as the school of the *Annales* does, must include the study of all groups in society, whether in the mainstream or at the periphery. Those individuals who remain "parasitic," who are too weak to fend for themselves, or who fail to conform and are rejected and imprisoned are part of that "total history." The articles in this volume elucidate the history of some key deviant groups. Arsonists, as André Abbiateci shows, have characteristics or backgrounds that evoke, or are part of patterns of behavior of, society as a whole. Is he more rural than urban, that man who sets fire to his own dwelling or that of his employer, carrying out the verbal threats about the use of fire that were so often expressed in moments of peasant fear and rage in the countryside? These articles reveal in what ways abandoned children, prostitutes, vagrants, galley rowers, arsonists, and to an appreciable extent even the insane, have histories that make their lives an integral part of society.

The study of isolated cases does not reveal this; but when all the entries in the registers have been copied and fed into the computer—which in turn prints out the age patterns and geographic origins—the history of deviant groups becomes an essential part of total history. Perhaps the most telling example of this is Claude Delasselle's analysis of the statistics regarding abandoned children. When the numbers are transferred to a graph and compared to bread prices, it becomes evident that parents throughout the Seine basin were forced to abandon children out of intense poverty, indeed, the threat of starvation. When deciding (the word is probably too strong because it evokes rational thought) that a child or newborn baby would have to be turned over to public care or left exposed before church doors, these parents could only believe that theirs was an individual action. They could not know that their personal decision was, in a sense, determined by conditions of dire necessity and that thousands of other parents were making the same decision.

Yet we ask, How could they possibly believe that their infants and children would survive the endemic contagion in foundling hospitals? They must have known that their offspring were going to die on the road, in the box on the back of the *meneur* who hauled babies to orphanages. As we read further, however, and learn that parents pinned little ribbons or medals to the clothing of infants, tokens to be kept with the child to insure its future identification, we are faced with a kind of devastating evidence that the abandonment of children was often an act of utter desperation. Didn't parents have to believe that they could one day recover their children? Some of the medals and little notes pinned to their clothes have survived in the archives, a testimony to the strong, very strong, parental affection in the traditional family. Fictions and perhaps little rituals developed when approaching death could not be accepted or faced straight on—a phenomenon not unknown in twentieth-century Western societies.

Ranging beyond each deviant group, as we read further, there is the sense that the margins of society—in the Ancien Régime and certainly down to the nineteenth century—are little more than administrative categories, legal jargon, and scientific speculations imposed upon a vast social complex of literally millions of largely inarticulate people. The person who steals and is caught, tried, and sent to row in the galleys becomes a member of a marginal group; but the person who steals and is *not* caught never does move to the fringes of society. A disconcerting thought. One wonders what one is really studying when concentrating on "deviant groups" identified by an "administration" of one kind or another.

Are these marginal groups really some sort of arbitrarily developed statistical sample—passed down to us in archives—of a much greater world of chronic hunger, aberrant speech and behavior, and helpless and indigent people? The legal system and the asylums, hospitals, and other institutions have produced an almost "controlled" sample for study. The particular marginal group into which individuals fell as a result of their behavior seems to have been determined by judges, parents, and physicians. Might not a particular individual have been assigned almost randomly to a different deviant group? From the vast population of rural France and the slums of its cities, the courts and hospitals would suck people up and categorize their behavior. A turn of phrase, a lack of connections or neighbors willing to testify in his or her behalf, even physical features, might determine an individual's assignment to a particular deviant group. And medicolegal procedures were constantly changing. The thief had a greater chance of being relegated to the galleys if tried by a *prévôt* than by a *parlement;* in some communities people were officially described as insane in order that they might be turned over to the care of the central government, thereby reducing costs at the local level. And clearly all thieves and all the "insane" in any period are not caught or reported to the "authorities."

As one reads article after article, the grid of social values and behavior patterns, or range of acceptable behavior, becomes apparent. This grid is ever-changing. A prostitute in a southern French town during the fifteenth century seems scarcely at the periphery of society, since brothels were officially administered and the girls virtually recruited and, upon reaching their thirties, married.* The town fathers who oversaw the brothels, and who occasionally visited them, would seem to have very little in common with those administrators and judges of the nineteenth century who dramatically increased the number of people imprisoned for sexual offenses. Excessive drinking also had not been a cause for indictment earlier, but became so in the nineteenth century. Note these changes, indeed, the extension of what is defined as "criminal behavior," when excessive drinking is added to disorderly conduct.

The historian must be skeptical and very cautious in reading these sources. This is what Perrot suggests when she distinguishes the "positivistic" way of reading the sources from the cautious, tentative approach she uses. For in one sense the statistics about criminals reveal what the legal system, judges, and lawyers deemed to be crime. And, as Nicole Castan shows, the comparison of these statistics over time, and for different regions, suggests both changing levels of crime and changing social conditions. Beneath this literal way of reading the sources, however, lies the more fundamental problem of discerning the nature of deviant behavior in any given society without the ideological and cultural presuppositions of those who tried the criminals and recorded them in the registers now being read by historians.

Michel Foucault has developed a general analysis of the increasingly restrictive, indeed repressive, tendencies of the medical and legal authorities during the period of transition from traditional to bourgeois society. What he has called the *Grand Renfermement*—that is, the "Great Confinement," a movement to remove "undesirables" from society—can be discerned in many of the articles here. And again it is apparent that general hospitals, asylums, and prisons constituted a much more effective apparatus for the control and isolation of deviant members of society than did incarceration and the galleys of earlier centuries.

It is also important to note that, wherever possible, great attention has been paid to the social status of individuals found in marginal groups. The various kinds of artisans are carefully distinguished, and the various categories in every other group are examined. The most important conclusion to be reached from all these studies is that rich Frenchmen and those of higher social status only rarely ended up in marginal groups. This is not surprising, of course, since all the known literary evidence points to this conclusion. But it further suggests that early-modern and nineteenth-century society was divided more by such categories as poor/rich and low status/high status than by the more

---

*For a general introduction to the study of sexuality in medieval times, see Jean-Louis Flandrin, "Contraception, Marriage, and Sexual Relations in the Christian West," in *Biology of Man in History, Selections from the "Annales, Economies, Sociétés, Civilisations,"* ed. Robert Forster and Orest Ranum, trans. Elborg Forster and Patricia M. Ranum (Baltimore, 1975) (the first volume of this series), pp. 23–47.

precise occupational and professional characteristics of social groups. Though the categories of artisans, *laboureurs,* and other lesser groups on the "poor" side are carefully counted and distinguished, no discernible patterns emerge. Here the study of deviant groups has obvious links with social history, for each of these historians has searched for possible correlations between social status and behavior. However, the inference that status and behavior are revealed in their fullness by occupation has not been born out in these studies.

The task of the future is to attempt to integrate such disparate and hitherto unexplained findings as the changing patterns of offenses by ages in the male criminal population. Those under forty, according to André Zysberg, were more frequently found guilty of theft, violence, or sexual offenses than those over forty, whereas smuggling was the most frequently tried crime among the older age group. As of now, this seems to be just a curious fact. So does Castan's evidence that many of the vagrants charged by the *prévôt* with criminal activity were several inches taller than the average Frenchman. It is tempting to dismiss these conclusions as merely interesting, because historians are too often unfamiliar with the biological, criminological, and even actuarial statistics that might shed light on them. As we read all these articles, we can perhaps put together the pieces of the puzzle more coherently than the individual authors and discern more precisely some of the fundamental dynamics of French society that have hitherto been known to us only through literary evidence.

Robert Forster
Orest Ranum

Deviants and
the Abandoned in
French Society

1
Prostitution, Youth, and Society in the Towns of Southeastern France in the Fifteenth Century

Jacques Rossiaud

The history of prostitution has received scant attention from the medievalists. Such studies as we do have are outdated and local in character. Their authors, usually physicians or jurists who dabbled in History, were rather too fond of anecdotes. For the most part, their works are little more than the curiosa of learned literature.[1] More recently, to be sure, historians have ceased to overlook the existence of prostitution, but they frequently use it as evidence to bolster a historiographical conception and a current of thought that attributes phenomena of this kind to the calamities of the late Middle Ages and to a general climate of moral disorder. How tempting to associate whore and roaming soldier, fornication and turpitude, *prostibulum* [house of prostitution] and court of miracles.[2]

Yet if we want to understand the scope and the social significance of prostitution, we must first define it in relation to the demographic structures, the patterns of marriage, the normal and deviant patterns of sexuality, and the cultural values and collective mentality of the social groups that did, or did not, tolerate it. This is an ambitious undertaking, but it is the only way to explore the vast, obscure zone that lies between the two areas treated hitherto by historians of sexuality, namely, ideology and moral codes on the one hand, and demographic behavior on the other.

In this essay I outline the contours of such a global explanation. The examples I use are the towns of southeastern France, from Burgundy to Provence. This choice was a natural outcome of my research on the people of

Annales, E. S. C. 31 (March–April 1976): 289–325. Translated by Elborg Forster.

the Rhône Valley, for in every town along the river I found dens of prostitution in the neighborhoods close to the water. Between 1440 and 1490, this
geographical area was almost untouched by war; it was a time when the cities
were convalescing or indeed prospering. Therefore, the analysis can be carried out for a period of relative economic and social stability.[3]

Structure and scope of urban prostitution

It would be a mistake to view the city as the only place favorable to the
development of venal love. The passing allusions occasionally encountered in
urban documents indicate that rural prostitution flourished as well. Even aside
from those times when great waves of poverty caused increasing numbers of
women to offer themselves along every roadside, roaming harlots, with or
without their pimps, went from village to village, here and there reinforcing
the small groups of prostitutes "common to many." They adapted their
itinerary to the calendar of fairs and markets, to pilgrimages, or to the high
seasons of the agricultural year. In outlying granges, the field hands and
mowers who lived together often kept and shared a whore for a few days or
weeks. So did the German merchants who traveled in convoy to the fairs of
Lyons, and on the river the crews of barges about to embark for a voyage of
several weeks hired women on the shore and took their pleasure with them at
each station along the way.[4]

Nevertheless, prostitution developed fully in an urban milieu, where it
assumed more complex forms and became institutionalized. Most of the cities
of southeastern France had a *prostibulum publicum,* which was built, maintained, and governed by the princely or municipal authorities. Dijon, Beaune,
Mâcon, Villefranche, Bourg-en-Bresse, Lyons, Bourg-les-Valence, Valence,
Romans, Viviers, Bagnols, Pont-Saint-Esprit, Orange, Avignon, Beaucaire,
Tarascon, Arles, Nîmes, Alès, Usès, Cavaillon, Pernes, Bedarrides,
Sisteron—all had their "bawdy house," "good hostel," "good quarry," or
"Château-Gaillard"—houses that were also called the "town-house,"
"communal house," or "house of the little whores," although in popular
parlance they were usually refered to simply as the "brothel." This enumera-
tion only includes those towns that have preserved their archives; the fact that
some towns are not mentioned does not mean that they were different. We
may safely assume that every "good city" had its "good house."[5]

The prostibulum, which had usually been built at common expense—that
is, with public funds—was leased to an "abbess" or to a keeper, who,
theoretically, had the monopoly of the profession. The leasees were responsible for recruiting prostitutes (subject to the approval or veto of an officer of
justice), for enforcing certain rules, sometimes for providing for the upkeep of

the inmates, and always for maintaining order within this little community of women. Whenever it became necessary—if, for instance, the abbess who held the lease died or left town—the consuls did not hesitate to run the house themselves.[6]

The material arrangements varied with the size of the city. The Château-Gaillard of Tarascon was a modest building, comprising a courtyard, a garden, two exits, a kitchen, a common room, and four bedrooms. Dijon, on the other hand—at least after the additions of 1447—boasted an imposing residence, consisting of three separate buildings with interior galleries grouped about a garden. Here the "house of the little whores" included the keeper's quarters, a huge common room, and twenty spacious bedrooms, each with its own stone fireplace. At Lyons, Beaucaire, Arles, and Orange, we find separate neighborhoods; at Avignon, several streets grouped about a small, tree-planted square gave access to individual rooms.[7]

Usually, the brothel was not really a closed house where "cloistered" women were confined. Public prostitutes who lived in the "disreputable" streets or lodged in town were permitted to solicit in taverns and other public places in full daylight, but they had an obligation to take their clients to the "good house," where they were expected to make them feast and carouse before retiring to the rooms. Providing food was almost as profitable to the keepers as providing bedding.[8]

In addition to the public brothel, every big city also had several houses of toleration, namely the *étuves,* or bathhouses. Whenever one is able to determine how these functioned, it is evident that the public baths were either straightforward establishments of prostitution or that they served both honorable and dishonorable purposes. This was so notwithstanding countless regulations designed to keep prostitutes out or to stipulate the days or hours reserved for men or women only. The baths always employed large numbers of young chambermaids, and although most establishments were equipped with hot rooms and tubs, they also had many separate rooms and the finest bedding. G. Bayle, who published the inventory of a bathhouse in Avignon, found a great many beds, but not a single bathing installation. We know that around 1470 Avignon had six such establishments, and Lyons and Dijon had seven. At Lyons, the most famous baths, the Etuves Tresmonnoye, were located in the heart of the judicial quarter, a stone's throw from the seat of royal justice; and in the parish of Saint-Nizier, where the merchants lived, the Etuves de la Pêcherie were said to be of immemorial antiquity. They were so extensive that they could accomodate several dozen men, as could the Etuves Saint-Philibert at Langres, those of Vertbois at Dijon, and those of la Servellière or Pont Trocat at Avignon.[9]

Who owned these establishments? Frequently the owners were the authorities or persons of high rank who had no illusions as to the activities of the bath-keepers to whom they rented. Owners like the Villeneuve or the Baronnat families at Lyons, the Falentans family, the bishop of Langres or the abbot of Saint-Etienne at Dijon, or the Buzzaffi family at Avignon had no qualms about collecting the profitable rents to which they felt entitled in view of the crowds of clients of every description who flocked to their establishments.[10] The bathhouses, I repeat, were notorious and permanent centers of prostitution, but in addition they also served as trysting places and as headquarters for procuring operations. From 1470 to 1480 at Lyons, the expression "to go to the bathhouse" had a very specific meaning when used in popular parlance, a meaning that was understood by everyone.

Nor should these bathhouses make us overlook the existence of yet a third level of prostitution, which was practiced as an individual craft, as it were. It involved small, private establishments known as *bordelages,* kept by a procuress who, in her own house, provided the services of two or three prostitutes, chambermaids, or women called in for the occasion. These procuresses used their own homes to receive clients, served as intermediaries and sometimes also availed themselves of the services of so-called "loose" prostitutes, who represented the fourth and lowest level of prostitution. These women worked on their own, went from house to house, and were concubines or prostitutes "common to many" as the circumstances demanded. They solicited in taverns or fairs and markets, but only if they could find effective protection, whether official or private, for this was a dangerous activity, and competition was fierce. Periodically, moreover, on the occasion of a public festival, at the peak of the harvest season, or when a fair was held, women from out of town came to swell the ranks of the local prostitutes in order to profit from the temporary crush of workmen, draymen, and tradesmen.[11]

The vocabulary clearly differentiated among these different levels in the amorous trade—proof that this was a permanent situation. Every regulation, as well as public proclamations and judicial proceedings, distinguished between the inmates of the prostibulum and the prostitutes who plied their trade in the bathhouse or in a private room. Thus, a distinction was made between communal public prostitutes and clandestine ones, and among roaming *(cántonnières)* and resident *(clostières)*, clandestine, loose, and vagrant prostitutes.[12]

The authorities endeavored to enforce certain rules. As a sanitary measure, the prostibulum and the bathhouses were closed down in times of pestilence, just as commercial gatherings and public dances were canceled. As a religious measure, efforts were made to enforce the interdicts, which applied, however, only during Holy Week and Christmas. Public decency demanded that scandalous scenes not take place in the vicinity of churches or in patrician streets, while certain vestimentary regulations were designed to enable the public to distinguish respectable women from the others and also to prevent the overly elaborate finery of the latter from inciting poor and innocent girls to go astray.

Finally, fiscal regulations attempted to prevent the "private sector" from ruining the municipal monopoly.[13]

But the efforts of the consulates were lukewarm. Only in exceptional cases—as in Bourg-en-Bresse in 1439—was the construction of the prostibulum publicum motivated by the desire to improve the moral tone of urban life. In this case, the authorities hoped to put an end to the reprehensible acts that were committed daily in the market square. More often, the town councils decided to make prostitution official "for the common good" or "in the public interest." But even after the house had been built, the aldermen and notables were never able to contain fornication within the municipally supervised ghetto or to enforce their interdicts, however often these were promulgated. Until the beginning of the sixteenth century, efforts to enforce regulations were rare, unsustained, and generally ineffective. As a result, public and clandestine prostitutes were smuggled into all parts of the city, making their way to the smartest parishes as well as the poorest suburbs.[14]

Emmanuel Le Roy Ladurie, following Felix Platter, the sixteenth-century student from Basel, recalls an adage commonly cited in the Comtat and in Provence: "One cannot cross Avignon Bridge without meeting two monks, two donkeys, and two whores." But we know that by about 1550, Avignon still preserved a situation that had existed in all the towns of southeastern France fifty to a hundred years earlier. From a public proclamation of the municipal authorities of Lyons we learn that it was no longer possible to distinguish communal prostitutes from respectable women, and the municipal "little whores" of Tarascon or Dijon periodically complained about too much competition, demanding that steps be taken to curb—"debauchery."[15]

Did contemporary commentators exaggerate? Did they feel that the situation was scandalous and therefore purposely inflate the evidence? But what of the tiny towns like Viviers, Pernes, or Bedarrides, which had their own prostibulum, and of Tarascon, which in about 1435 had some ten communal public prostitutes (for five to six hundred households)? Or the existence of at least seventy to eighty of them at Lyons before 1480, and far in excess of one hundred at Dijon, a town of fewer than 10,000 inhabitants? And these, it should be added, were only the public prostitutes, for it is quite impossible to gauge the extent of clandestine or occasional prostitution. Generally speaking, one has the distinct impression that public prostitution everywhere was at least as extensive as the well-policed prostitution at the end of the nineteenth and the beginning of the twentieth century.[16]

Can this situation be associated with the ports, the major intersections of trade routes, and the centers of commercial, ecclesiastic, and legal affairs? This would mean that prostitution was practiced, perhaps not exactly outside, but at least on the fringes of, the urban community, as one of the commercial services provided to visitors. On the other hand, one may also ask whether prostitution was spawned by the collectivity for its own purposes. It would be futile to answer this question without having first analyzed the sexual behavior of the townspeople.

Sexual Order, Juvenile Subversion, and Mediating Institutions

It is possible to outline the contours of the "sexual economy" of Dijon, thanks to the investigations and the criminal procedures instigated by the public prosecutors of the municipality. This series of judicial documents, a great chronicle of the lives of humble people and a record of truculence and sordidness, immediately conveys an overwhelming impression of sexual violence.[17]

SEXUAL VIOLENCE

For the period 1436–86, we know of 125 cases of rape from investigations, decisions in civil cases, and judgments handed down by the mayor in proceedings brought before the town council. This figure does not include rapes committed against prostitutes dragged more or less against their will into a den of prostitution, nor does it by any means represent the real number of aggressive acts. Studies of victimization by experts in the sociology of crime have shown that even in societies where primary security is greater than it was in the fifteenth century, and where sexual tabus are attenuated or disappearing, the *numerus obscurus* in this type of offense amounts to 75 or 80 percent in both middle-sized towns and metropolitan areas.[18] This means that no more than between one-fifth and one-fourth of the sexual crimes committed emerge from the judicial archives. Even then, our series is not complete, since it is composed of bundles rather than registers; and eighteen of the fifty years have left practically no trace at all. Moreover, most of the victims of aggression did not lodge a formal complaint (and without a "plaintiff" there was no case), either because they were ashamed, or from fear of reprisals, or because their family sought to obtain a monetary settlement from the aggressors and was not interested in involving the law.[19] It is therefore reasonable to assume that at the very least twenty "public" rapes were committed each year at Dijon.

Actually, 80 percent of these rapes were collective attacks, perpetrated by groups of two to fifteen individuals who, having planned their undertaking for a specific evening, would force the doors of a woman's house and, without concealing their identity and mixing brutality with blandishments, threats, and insults, would rape their prey on the spot, often in the presence of two or three terrified witnesses. Sometimes they would drag the victim through the streets, eventually pulling her into a house whose keepers were accessories to the plot, where they would do as they pleased, all night long. In four out of five cases, the neighbors did not interfere because they were afraid.[20]

Were the perpetrators marginal individuals or outsiders? The extraordinarily stern reports of the municipal prosecutor J. Rabustel give us the names of more than four hundred perpetrators and accessories for the ninety cases he investigated. Only about thirty outsiders participated in these assaults; the others were townsmen, the sons or servants of resident families, and most of them were identified. They came from all walks of life, but the overwhelming majority were artisans or laborers and not pimps. Only one-tenth of the assaults can be imputed to hired ruffians carrying out the orders of a chief. Eighty-five percent of the assailants were "young townsmen" or "marriageable bachelors," half of them between the ages of eighteen and twenty-four. There is no correlation between this aggressivity and such things as public festivities, heavy drinking during the summer months, or the peak season of the agricultural year; the incidence of rape is spaced evenly throughout the year.[21]

All this does not mean that every young female of Dijon lived in terror as soon as night fell. There were many women and girls who had little reason to fear rape. It was only among certain segments of the female population that one or two rapes per month sustained a climate of insecurity. Dijon was, in fact, a medium-size town where security was no worse than elsewhere. Brief episodes of turmoil such as the Ecorcherie, the Coquillards, and the occupation by royal troops did not result in an upsurge in the incidence of rape. The town was relatively prosperous; the presence of ducal officers, jurists, and churchmen provided stimulation and outlets for commerce and the trades, and the period under consideration was the heyday of Burgundian influence. On the other hand, Dijon was not the capital of a prince, so that soldiers and bands of young pages did not enter into the picture at all, much less set the tone of social relations.

Significantly, the minutes of the debates in the council of aldermen—which are preserved in their entirety and very carefully recorded—provide no inkling of such rowdy behavior. To be sure, the viscount-mayor handed down decisions punishing crimes and abductions in some council-sessions, but the aldermen never discussed or protested the activities of the town's aggressive bands. Once or twice in fifty years, there are some vague allusions to "nocturnal disturbances," which the aldermen were quick to impute to vagrants from the outside, rather than to the local *galants,* who were criticized only by J. Rabustel.[22] Let us not be deceived, therefore, by the apparent lack of concern in the deliberations of town councils, especially in cases where the consulate did not hold judicial power and thus did not concern itself with matters over which it had no control. In documents of this kind, whether pertaining to Lyons, Valence, or Avignon, any slight allusion to "insolences'' committed *campana pulsata* and some very rare remarks about scandals and armed *galants* most certainly refer to occurrences analogous to those I have just described.[23] Under these circumstances, one can confidently assert that sexual violence was a normal and permanent aspect of urban life. No doubt this violence was—relatively speaking—somewhat less pronounced in smaller towns, and even greater in very large cities. In this connection one immediately thinks of the obsessive fear of urban insurrection that haunted the chroniclers of Languedoc, whose fantasies have been evoked by Le Roy Ladurie: the poor would carry off and enjoy the wives of the rich, and all women would be shared by everyone. Both Georges Duby and Jacques Le Goff have rightly stressed that control over women was one of the issues at stake both in social conflicts and in the competition between age groups.[24] An analysis of demographic and matrimonial structures is a first step toward finding the causes of such behavior.

THE MATRIMONIAL ORDER

Following the crime and the lodging of a complaint, the public prosecutor and his recording clerks would betake themselves to the scene and question the neighbors of the victim. We thus have at our disposal an impressive series of depositions that, unlike investigations involving matters of customary law, were not made by the more prestigious citizens. In these depositions men and women, old people and adolescents, whether married or unmarried, made a sworn statement as to their civil status and their age. After the year 1500, the many investigations of suspects, most of whom were ''youths,'' give us the date of marriage [of the witnesses], among other information. This enables us to reach an approximate figure for age at marriage and to state the age differential between the spouses. On the whole, this group shows a rather poor perception of time, much like the people of Reims who were questioned for the census of 1422. Almost identical in men and women, the perception of time is relatively good for the age group involved in a first marriage.[25] However, since I cannot hope to develop precise data for age at marriage, owing to the gaps in the documentary material, I shall limit myself to outlining its long-range trends.

Age at marriage. For the period 1500–1550, age at marriage is known to us for only 84 individuals belonging to the lower classes, namely, 52 men and 32 women. In this group the average age at first marriage is 24.5 for the men and 21.9 years for the women.[26] This sample may look entirely too small, but its findings are confirmed by two other, numerically more important series. Here too, the average age difference between husbands under 30 and their wives (150 couples) is less than 3 years; furthermore, the population of marriageable girls between 16 and 25 years shows a very sharp decline—almost 75 percent—after age 22.[27]

For the fifteenth century, there are no data with which to approach this problem directly. But it is legitimate to compare the average age of married men between 20 and 30 (the ten years during which the overwhelming majority of men married) with the average age of married women between the ages of 15 and 25 (same observation). In the 350 cases for which we have data between 1500 and 1550, the average age of the men is 26.8 years, that of the women, 22.5. To be sure, these figures must not be taken as absolute values. But if we make the same calculations for the two identical series of married couples appearing between 1440 and 1500 (300 cases), it turns out that here, too, the average age of the men is 26.8, while that of the women is only 21.5. This is corroborated by the average age differential between husband and wife in "young couples," which is now four, rather than three years (even though this is a different series, which lists husbands under thirty and their wives, whatever their age).

With all due caution, and because the subjects themselves did not know their age to the exact year (the perception of time among the lower strata did not change between 1450 and 1550), we may reasonably conclude from these figures that the age at marriage for men remained unchanged during this century of demographic growth, 1450–1550, that is, it was still between 24 and 25 years. This was a fairly high age (and is probably even somewhat underestimated, since I excluded men over 30 from the calculations concerning my control group). During the same period, age at marriage for women rose from 20/21 years to 21/22 years. I must therefore try to explain why the age at marriage for men remained stable even though the economic and demographic situation underwent significant change.

The "matrimonial custom." The age differential between husbands and wives can be analyzed precisely and directly here. For the period 1440–90, I have assembled a population of 241 couples in which both spouses officially stated their age *on the same day*. (This sample approximately equals the number of couples in one parish of Reims in 1422). The data very clearly exhibit three structural features:

1. Age-inversions are rare: in 14.5 percent of the cases, the husband is younger than his wife (this is within 1 percent of the situation at Reims in 1422); but the age differential is "visible," that is, greater than 2 years, in only 11.7 percent of the cases. Age-inversion is unusual in first marriages and among couples in which the husband is elderly. Quite naturally, it is most frequent among husbands in their thirties; and I am therefore inclined to believe that the union with an "older woman" (usually a widow) implies belated marriage for the man. The infrequency of age-inversion no doubt indicates that in fifteenth-century Dijon, as in other French towns of the

Ancien Régime, the collective mentality of the young people disapproved of social advancement by means of marriage with an "old woman."[28]

2. In 85.5 percent of the couples, the husband is older than the wife, the average difference in age being 7.9 years. But while the husbands under thirty are 4.2 years older than their wives (maximum difference: 8 years), husbands in their thirties are on the average 6 years older than their wives (maximum difference: 16 years), and husbands in their forties and fifties are ahead of their young spouses by almost 11 years (maximum difference: 34 years). Nor are these findings in any way surprising, since they reflect the effects of second or third marriages, which always accentuate the age differential. This situation had not changed very much by the beginning of the sixteenth century, the period when a slight tendency toward equalization of age among young couples can be observed.[29]

These age differentials are more or less comparable to those found at Reims, but smaller than those of Tuscany.[30] Nonetheless, Florence, Reims, and Dijon, despite some variations, all exhibit identical matrimonial structures: relatively belated marriage for men, few age-inversions, and pronounced difference in age, always in favor of the husband. There is reason to believe that this was true in other towns as well, for the matrimonial order of the fifteenth century was predicated on the mature husband and the young wife. Marriage represented a negotiated transaction, and although the terms of the exchange included a number of considerations—ethnic origin, occupation, social standing, patrimony—it stands to reason that the "freshness" of the wife was an essential factor in the marriage of an established man, even among modest craftsmen.[31]

3. All of this enables us to take a closer look at the realities of the marriage market. Thirty percent of the men between 30 and 39 years of age had a wife 8 to 16 years younger than themselves (10 to 16 years in 20 percent of the cases), and 15 percent of the men in their forties and fifties lived with a wife 20 to 34 years their junior. This means that these men had chosen their wives from an age group for which young men were also competing. I am not so naive as to conclude that this situation resulted in a real shortage of women for the young man in search of a wife; nonetheless, the point must be made that almost a third of the marriageable girls and "remarriageable" women under thirty were removed from circulation by established or elderly men. Such a reduction of the pool was sufficiently drastic to be perceived by the young city dwellers, both in the sixteenth and in the fifteenth centuries.[32] Even if we disregard the consequence of this disparity in age for family life or the affective ties within marriage, it seems to me that this situation was bound to lead to social tensions between the young men who had neither money nor wives, and the old men who had both, and particularly to rivalry between the young men in search of wives and the married men and widowers over thirty. It may well be that this competition created solidarity among age groups and gave rise to the specific collective behavior of the young.

AGE GROUPS, COLLECTIVE RITUALS, AND
MEDIATING INSTITUTIONS

Anyone who applies these notions to our traditional societies of the past is liable to encounter some resistance on the part of certain historians who feel that this is tantamount to the unwarranted use of an "ethnographic model" that is too far removed in time and space, or of a "sociological model" that will lead to anachronism. Paul Veyne, following Philippe Ariès, even goes so far as to write that the people who arranged a charivari performed a ritual they virtually no longer understood.[33]

I believe, on the contrary, that the urban societies of the waning Middle Ages, like those of the Renaissance, tended to preserve, indeed to develop, age groups; and the arguments to the contrary advanced by Philippe Ariès do not strike me as convincing. Apprenticeship, for instance, far from integrating the young boy into the adult world, frequently had an alienating effect—at least temporarily—certain aspects of which have been pointed out by B. Geremek and Natalie Z. Davis. Apprenticeship could, to be sure, transmit physical skills, but not social skills. Immigration, which, as N. S. Eisenstadt has stressed, played a fundamental role in the formation of juvenile solidarity, prompted the sons of newcomers, young déracinés, to band together in homogeneous groups. (My own research, to be completed soon, shows that a majority of the populations of the Rhône Valley consisted of recent immigrants). The conditions of family life, finally, also led adolescents to seek the company of their peers. Many of them did not live with a father who could provide them with an adult role model, since fathers were often crossing the threshold of old age just as the sons reached the age of twenty; but above all, it was the quality of collective life in the city that compelled young men to seek that model outside the household.[34]

It is possible, as David Herlihy has suggested, that in more advanced cultural areas, and in well-to-do milieus, where women occupied an enviable position, maternal upbringing exerted a profound influence on the sensibility and the social attitudes of the young. But it was a far cry from Florence to most French cities, where a thoroughly masculine morality induced the "fellows"—unless they were born into a patrician family—to band together in aggressive and disruptive youth groups.[35]

These groups of young males who disturbed the nightly peace of Dijon showed some very clearly defined characteristics, the first of which is a relative homogeneity in age. In eleven of the fifteen groups that lend themselves to this analysis, more than half of the members were of the same age, and the presence of two or three older bachelors who played the part of experienced ringleaders does not detract from this basic coherence. Two-thirds of these groups had marked socio-occupational affinities, since they consisted of bachelors and young lads who were connected with a specific trade or related occupations or else were lads of the same social standing. An equal proportion of groups was formed "on the street corner" and brought together no more than three to five individuals who knew each other well. In more than 80 percent of the cases—and this is the essential point—these groups had no previous record of group delinquency. In other words, the *juvenes* of closed cities, from sheer boredom, spontaneously set out in search of nightly adventure and fighting, defying the patrols, chasing girls, and engaging in rape.[36]

Collective rape? This, sociologists of crime will tell us, and rightly so, is a "welter of ambiguities." Such things as group motivation, a girl's careless-ness, private or collective revenge, fortuitous opportunity, and clan rivalry all provide a partial explanation.[37] But in this society, where images of violence pervaded everyday life and where the sexual impulses of adults were subject to few constraints, the aggressive instincts of these nocturnal groups found a natural outlet in sexual violence. Under these circumstances it seems to me that this behavior was motivated by two main aspirations.

First, there was the desire to acquire the privileges of manhood; for man-hood was a social role, an acquired form of behavior. One common image for man and woman conveys the idea of their respective places in the fifteenth-century city: the cock, who must dominate and overpower the hen. In addi-tion, this society subscribed to a strictly Manichaean view of the female, who could only be one of two things, either pure or "common to all." It was this view that helped the young cocks to legitimize their venture, for their assaults always involved degrading insults, humiliation and beating. It was a matter of clearing the conscience of the offenders even before proceeding to the act, which is why the woman to be raped was presented from the outset as guilty, stripped of her humanity, and obligated to submit.[38]

Every year some one hundred individuals were involved in such cases of rape. Even if we subtract from this total men from out of town, repeat offenders, and adult ringleaders, we still have a minimum of fifty to sixty young men between the ages of eighteen and twenty-four. This means that one out of two young city dwellers participated at least once in such an assault. It seems to me that this type of aggression must have constituted a veritable rite of initiation or virilization for the neighborhood bands.[39]

Second, if on these occasions the participants satisfied their sexual desires (for the women were raped over and over again), collective rape was for many—poor bachelors, domestic servants, penniless lads—the expression of even deeper impulses and aspirations; it was a denial of the established order. Rape was a way of ruining the chances of a young widow or a marriageable girl by making her lose her good name. Aggression was also directed against the servant girl who was reputed to be "kept" by her master, the servant-sweetheart of the bachelor in more affluent circumstances, the concubine of the priest, or the temporarily "deserted" wife, who, it was said, should "give pleasure to the young fellows."[40]

The leading townspeople and the heads of established households were therefore vitally interested in curbing such disruptive behavior. This is why they provided their sons and servants with ample opportunities for fornication under the aegis of the municipality—opportunities, incidentally, from which they themselves also stood to profit. Thus, it may have been by way of compromise with the unmarried men that the established community accepted certain aspects of their solidarity and the noisy manifestations of their joyous confraternities.

MEDIATING FUNCTIONS

These complementary realities—the matrimonial order and its subversion—may shed new light on the issue of the place and the significance of the youth abbeys in urban society.*

We know that such fraternities of young men existed under a wide variety of names, both in towns and in the countryside. Natalie Z. Davis has recently given us an excellent interpretation of these groups, in which she emphasized their role in the life of the rural community, particularly with respect to the socialization of the young, the control of their impulses, and the defense of the community and its traditions.[41] However, by basing her conclusions on the example of Lyons (which, in fact, was an atypical metropolis), Davis was led to make too sharp a distinction between rural and urban abbeys and to contrast the *maugouverts,* or "misrules," of the sixteenth century with the *bachelleries,* or societies of bachelors, of an earlier period. Davis feels that living conditions in the large cities of the Renaissance, expanded forms of apprenticeship, and the diffusion of a new culture reduced the social pool from which these fraternities were recruited. She argues that these groups, henceforth composed of both married men and bachelors, became friendly neighborhood associations which, in addition to their traditional role as guardians of the matrimonial mores of the community, now acted as social, political, or religious critics. Without addressing myself to all the problems raised by Davis's analysis, I shall limit myself here to showing the continuity I observe in the structure and the objectives of these groupings within the urban milieu between the end of the fourteenth and the middle of the sixteenth century.

In all the towns of southeastern France, the abbeys of *jovens,* or joyous confraternities, were recognized institutions that constituted an integral part of municipal life. Very often the abbot, his treasurer, and his priors were elected in the presence of the town's magistrates; any internal conflicts within the group were arbitrated by the town council, which also controlled its finances,

*For a discussion of the Youth Abbey and its function, see also Lucienne Roubin, "Male Space and Female Space within the Provençal Community," in *Rural Society in France; Selections from the Annales, Economies, Sociétés, Civilisations,"* ed. Robert Forster and Orest Ranum, trans. Elborg Forster and Patricia M. Ranum, (Baltimore, 1977).

granted or denied permission for its various activities, and controlled the exercise of its mock jurisdiction. This was true everywhere from Arles to Dijon in the sixteenth as well as the fifteenth century. The few traces of conflict between the abbeys and the urban authorities should not overly concern us; the fact is that the abbey was never a spontaneous formation; it was either created or controlled by the urban collectivity.[42]

These youth groups exercised certain rights over bachelors and newlyweds. These rights continued to be fundamental in the sixteenth century. Yet it should be noted that the rights of the abbey amounted to very little in cases of a first marriage between young people (a few small coins or a share of the banquet), although they could be quite onerous whenever a union was harmful to the group as a whole or when it violated the matrimonial custom. In such cases the abbey levied actual fines, which filled its coffers and helped defray the cost of its banquets. The abbey used its rights coercively only when the newly married couple refused to submit to the usages. If this happened, charivaris or parades on the ass *(chevauchées)*—which did not involve physical violence but always ended in drinking bouts—made the participants feel better about an order which, deep down, they felt to be intolerable.[43]

For the kings, the prince-abbots, and their retinues, these activities were a way of reaching a compromise with the matrimonial order, of coming to terms with its basic principles. As for the married men, they had good reasons to pay the dues imposed by the abbey, for their contributions erased their transgression and protected them against possible aggression. Moreover, the married men controlled these youthful revels, both through their representatives in the town council and because some of them were members of the youth groups.[44]

The solidarity of the youths was clearly restricted to males, and the orderly troups who lined up behind their chiefs and danced a wild and noisy saraband around the house of the "guilty" or followed the parade on the ass with their raillery did not protect the girls as they protected the boys. For although a man was sometimes the victim of these rituals, the responsibility for the scandal censured in this manner was almost always attributed to the woman, whether she was domineering, unfaithful, or perfidious to the point of having caught a young man in her snares. A woman married to a dotard was blamed either for the stupidity inherent in her very nature or for her acquiescence, which amounted to treason against the group of eligible bachelors. To be sure, sanctions were levied against the husband who beat his wife—in May; but even he would have to make quite a "nuisance" of himself or be an outsider in the community. And it was precisely those young men who were known and respected as notorious fornicators who made it their business to cast public aspersions—for this was the custom in May—upon girls whose virtue they questioned; and since girls were not protected by solidarity of any kind, their notoriety might well be the prelude to future collective assaults.

In this connection, the vocabulary of the time is highly significant. Anyone who lived in the city and was young and not too poor no doubt owed it to himself to band together with the *gars* [fellows] who chased the *garce* [trol-lop]. Such a young man qualified as *homme joyeux* [joyful fellow], while a *fille joyeuse* was nothing but a whore. The *abbé* [abbot] was an influential and prestigious figure (while the *reinagières* [queens] were only ephemeral extras) and the *abbesse* was simply the keeper of the brothel.[45] I therefore believe that until the sixteenth century, and probably until much later, the youth abbeys—except for the so-called bourgeois ones—were hotbeds and per-petuators of the most traditional anti-feminism and that they contributed to keeping women in their subservient condition, at least in the middle and lower strata of the population.

The young men who prowled about at night looking for victims, these *ephebes of the night*[46] of the medieval city, served their apprenticeship of adulthood in darkness and among their peers; their inarticulate and violent ways attested to the existence of a veritable counterforce to the matrimonial order. But when these prowlers and other (richer) young men lined up behind their chiefs in the very center of the civic space, applauding a parade on the ass or jeering a remarried couple, they were not performing a ritual they did not understand, nor were they acting out a collective psychodrama whose roles and situations were fixed since time immemorial. The "kings," "ab-bots," and Mother Follys who governed the youth in the light of day ex-pressed the frustrations of youth only rarely, and then in a tempered form. The Youth Abbey was nothing more than the counterpart of His Lordship, Married State; above all, it was, rather like the municipal brothel, an institution de-signed to promote peace between different age groups, different social groups, newcomers and established residents—in short, an institution de-signed to integrate, socialize, and entertain its members. Yet in the final analysis, in their acts of aggression as in their noisy jeering, the young also revealed their basic faith in an order to which each one of them aspired to belong some day.[47]

Literature, legend, and popular myths record only the pleasant aspects of this juvenile solidarity; but those who like to believe that popular culture was primarily a matter of laughter and the so-called gaulois tradition should take care, lest the groups of grotesque masks and the comic figures of farce and *sotie* make them forget the victims, most of whom were "abandoned" to vagrancy and prostitution.[48]

The Fate of the Victims—Procuresses and Prostitutes

THE CONSEQUENCES OF RAPE

The population of the town included a large number of unattached females, namely, widows, wives whose husbands were temporarily absent, and younger spinsters. They alone were fully exposed to the hazards of being a woman and were the favorite target of all kinds of rowdy behavior on the part of young males. The victims of collective rape were usually between fifteen and thirty-three years old; in other words, they were women and girls of marriageable or remarriageable age. Rape of little girls was unusual. It may be, of course, that many such cases went unreported, but I am more inclined to believe that the rape of a little girl under fourteen or fifteen was considered a serious crime by everyone. This attitude can be inferred from the questioning of the victim, for the investigators tried to elucidate every last detail of an act which they—and the witnesses—perceived as an abomination.[49] This is also why cases of pimping involving girls between twelve and fourteen were prosecuted with exceptional dispatch and severity. Marriage for girls under fifteen in the urban milieu must therefore be considered unusual and contrary to custom and to social consensus—a conclusion that leads, incidentally, to another observation: this society did indeed make a distinction between childhood and adolescence; not only for girls, but also for boys, who for identical transgressions were punished with greater or lesser severity, depending on their age.

Sixty percent of those who lodged a complaint about rape were unmarried. Half of the others were in a perfectly normal marital situation (their husbands were absent for a few days or weeks). Thus, it is clear that both the girls and their assailants were members of the community and that this was not just a game involving people living on the fringe of society. Socially, however, these women belonged to the poorest segments, for they tended to be servant girls and the daughters or wives of common laborers or textile workers. Only seven of them were wives of master-artisans, and only one came from a well-to-do milieu.[50] Nor is this surprising. The rape of a humble woman was easier to commit, liable to lesser punishments and fines, and less likely to expose the perpetrators to dire vengeance or severe social disapproval, for collective solidarity was not well developed among the members of these laboring classes, most of whom had only recently arrived from a variety of places. Moreover, the leading townspeople considered the "virtue" (honnê-teté) of a woman to be directly related to her "estate," so that the wife of a common laborer simply did not have the virtue of the wife of a bourgeois. In any case, the first targets of the aggressors were always the weak and the isolated, and aside from servant girls and chambermaids, this meant confirmed spinsters or women who had remained widows for too long. In a society whose dominant morality was based on marriage, their way of life was automatically viewed with suspicion or contempt.

In this manner, a woman's fate was shaped by the *fama publica,* that confused welter of malicious gossip and idle talk.[51] Heading the list of victims were the "priests' good ladies," who were hunted down with great gusto; also girls engaged to be married, who were sometimes assaulted on the very eve of their wedding; women separated from their husbands (even with his consent and that of their parents); and all girls accused of "less than virtuous" conduct—a slanderous assertion that was all the easier to make as many young immigrants had to earn their livelihood by going from household to household, working for a few days in one, a week in another, thus lending credence to all manner of founded or trumped-up suspicions that the young sons of the town were only too eager to seize upon.[52]

In the end, the consequences of rape were exactly the same as those of questionable or shameful conduct. The victim was almost always disgraced, and reintegration into society—or even into the family—proved extremely difficult. If she was unmarried, her value in the marriage market dropped sharply; if she was married, her husband was apt to abandon her. Her neighbors—even those who testified in her favor—always considered her defiled by what had happened to her.[53] She herself felt ashamed, guilty, and disgraced. In this respect her youthful assailants had attained their objective, for the raped woman realized that in the eyes of those around her, and indeed in her own mind, the distance separating her from the public prostitute had greatly diminished. Reduced to a state of psychological and physical weakness, she had little hope of regaining her honor as long as she stayed in town.[54]

Thus, violence often preceded the involvement of pimps and procuresses, so that the conflicts arising from the matrimonial order became a natural source of supply for prostitution.

PANDERING AND PROCURING

The example of pandering was set in high places. In every city, officials of the municipality or the prince had the responsibility of enforcing the regulations regarding prostitution, registering the prostitutes, and keeping them out or admitting them upon payment of a special levy. From Arles to Dijon, these men were notorious panders. The subviguier of Tarascon, noble Ferrand de Castille, was just an ordinary pimp, and there are occasional references to the activities of the provost of Dijon, J. de Marnay, who together with his henchmen impressed girls into the communal house of prostitution or into bathhouses kept by some of his lady-friends in the procuring business.[55] Procuring was a specifically female activity: of the eighty-five charges of "private brothel-keeping" I have found at Dijon, seventy-five were brought against women. But literature has too often dwelt on the figure of the bigoted old go-between, whose wasted body it describes in great detail as the very image of a depraved soul that must be exposed in all its ugliness.[56] While it is true that we find a few "antique" widows among the procuresses of Dijon, forty-one of the sixty-seven women for whom there is information were

married and engaged in this lucrative trade, which nicely rounded out the
family income, with the consent of their husbands, usually artisans, carters, or
innkeepers.[57] Moreover, there was a wide variety of gradations in this trade.
Some women simply acted as go-betweens for lovers' trysts; some furnished
regular service to the young men of the town; others openly kept private
brothels in their houses; while an elite worked for a high-class clientele,
supplying Monsieur le Gouverneur de Bourgogne, Monseigneur le Bailli, or
the Dean of Blois with more or less innocent young girls who had fallen for
their voluble promises. These women were trusted or highly persuasive con-
fidantes, and it was easy for them to renew contact with other women. They
would receive the victim of an assault, unless the aggressors kept her in their
service for a period of time; they solicited women "oppressed by marriage,"
those who were kept in want or were beaten; and they also took in poor
"abandoned" girls, and indeed often went to look for them at the gates of the
hospitals.[58]

The pinnacle of this hierarchy was occupied by the keepers of the baths.
Take the example of Jeanne Saignant, who in about 1460 was known as "the
shrewdest procuress in Dijon" and who reigned over the bathhouse of Saint-
Philibert for twenty years. Attended by a clownish husband, a brother who
was a priest, a protector with connections in high places, and several lovers,
she enjoyed watching the "graceful frolicking taking place in the rooms." In
the town square she freely talked to churchmen and to the young fellows,
vaunting the "luscious flesh" she was offering at her baths and promising that
a fresh supply would be available every day. She was also something of a
"sorceress," and loyal enough to keep the secret of two women of good
family who came to her establishment to "get laid." Clever enough to feign
indignation when she had caused a new servant girl to prostitute herself and to
attach her girls to herself by making them her debtors, she was able for twenty
years to outmanoeuver those aldermen who were not among her clients.[59]

Pimps, by comparison, were rather colorless figures. This is not true,
however, of vagabonding rogues, who belonged to the world of beggary but
in addition occasionally acted as protectors of bawds. But their protegées were
women who also lived "by rip-off" *(sur le bonhomme)* as much as by the sale
of their bodies. Most of the clandestine or public prostitutes undoubtedly had
a lover; but although these "fiancés" pocketed a part of the earnings, they do
not seem to have worked in organized bands or to have made their living from
pandering alone. Most of these men were stocking-makers, tailors, shoemak-
ers, barbers, or clerks; in other words, men engaged in occupations that lent
themselves to such dealings, since they brought both men and women into
their shops. Sometimes small groups of fullers, butchers' assistants, or archers also protected and exploited some of the prostitutes of the outlying
neighborhoods or the public brothels. But these men were not of the criminal
world (so that, in this respect, the case of François Villon is not typical). It

seems most revealing to me that the secret lingo of the Coquillards (who for a time had taken over the municipal brothel of Dijon and fleeced its inmates) did not include a single term concerning prostitution and pandering, for both these activities were so public that there was no need to hide them behind a screen of secret language or a front organization.[60]

CLANDESTINE VERSUS PUBLIC PROSTITUTES

Contrary to what is so often imagined, the world of prostitutes was not one of tramps and outsiders. The repentant Magdalens of Avignon at the end of the fourteenth century came from the Rhône regions: two-thirds of the prostitutes of Dijon were born in the city itself or in the surrounding countryside; and most of them had been residents of the city for more than a year. Only 15 percent of them were just passing through or moving about with a chance acquaintance. Most prostitutes were the daughters of artisans or common laborers, or the wives of master-artisans or craftsmen; only one out of five came from a well-to-do background. Separation from their family or the death of a father or mother had made them vulnerable at an early age. Almost all of them had become prostitutes by the age of seventeen, although one-third of them had been forced to sell themselves before they were fifteen. Half of them had been forced into prostitution by violence (27 percent were the acknowledged victims of rape), and almost one-fourth had been prostituted by their families or had come to grief because of the sordid circumstances of their family life. Only 15 percent of these prostitutes appear to have made the decision to make use of their body by choice, without constraint of any kind, even that of poverty.[61]

Only rarely was a woman thrown directly into public prostitution, as was a certain Catherine, who, after two years of marriage to a riverman of Beaucaire, had "in her folly" run away with a lover, a man of the river and a pimp, and soon found herself reduced to servitude in the prostibulum of Avignon; or that noble widow from Ile-de-France who became separated from her attendants on a pilgrimage, was kidnapped by a chance acquaintance, and spent a few days in the Grande Maison of Dijon.[62] The average age of the various kinds of prostitutes actually gives us a clear indication of the normal "career-pattern" of the profession: clandestine prostitute at seventeen, chambermaid in a bathhouse three years later, inmate of the prostibulum by twenty-eight. Almost all of these women began their careers by engaging in occasional prostitution, combining day-labor and "favors" to one or several men, with whom they lived as temporary concubines or endebted servants. Bought or recruited by a procuress soon thereafter, they became chambermaids in a public bathhouse, where they had to submit to a demanding mistress and large numbers of clients. Sooner or later they were bound to end up in the Grande Maison, either because they no longer brought in enough money at the bathhouse, or because they were conveyed to the brothel by their pimp, by the public authorities, or by the communal prostitutes.[63]

It is in this "public haunt" that we find the greatest proportion of outsiders. These most frequently came from certain areas of the Northeast that were traditionally hard on women, especially in times of crisis or war. Flanders, Artois, Picardy, Hainault, or Barrois supplied the brothels of all the cities along the Rhône Valley with women who, setting out from Arras, Liège, Amiens, or Tournai, had already plied their trade in three or four towns. At times the manner in which they traveled from place to place, alone or in groups, makes them look like members of a veritable female *compagnonnage,* or trade guild; and this resemblance did not go unnoticed in popular parlance, which often referred to the abbess of the brothel as "the housemother of the whores."[64]

Once they were admitted by the town, the communal prostitutes were sworn in by the authorities. They had to pay a weekly rent for their room to the keeper of the house, a fee of a few blancs to the night patrol who protected them, and their share of the heating bill. Sporting a *nom de guerre,* dressed up and bejeweled, Margot la Courtoise, La Petite Normande, or Marion la Liégeoise could now earn "their adventure" at the gates of churches, in the market square, or in the tavern and could sing in the streets at night in order to attract the young men or to bring them into the Grande Maison. They were supposed to refuse very young lads and married men, and two girls were not to lie with one man, although they were permitted to take on several men at a time, provided they were not kin. The price of a "turn" was one blanc, a sum equivalent to a woman's pay for a half-day's work in the vineyard; but a prostitute could charge three to six times as much if she agreed to spend a whole night with a young lad.[65]

Sometimes beaten, or kidnapped by a group of individuals who meant to take advantage of them without paying, they nonetheless enjoyed special safeguards and effective protection; in this respect the "emblem" they were made to wear was not only a badge of infamy, but also a defense against possible violence. Moreover, aside from their pimps, they had other friends who came to talk to them in their room or in the common hall.[66] Before 1490, there is very little evidence about prostitutes as delinquents; they were careful not to become involved in stealing or procuring. Decked out with rosaries and medals of saints, they attended mass at Jacobin or Cordelier chapels; they made a retreat at Easter and Christmas in order not to sin (and sometimes this action was required by the town authorities, in which case all expenses were paid). While they sometimes did lapse into blasphemy and drinking, they always gave generous alms and had their own confessor. Sometimes they posed as victims, shed tears about their past, and moralized freely; sometimes they felt that they were no more sinful than others; and when all is said and done, they do not seem to have worried much about their salvation.[67]

Having arrived at the public brothel rather late—never before the age of twenty in the fifteenth century—the prostitutes were unlikely to stay there very long. Once they had passed the age of thirty, they became the senior members of the group and had to give thought to their later years.[68] This was a time of uncertainty for them. A few might be able to advance in the "profession," become an abbess or the keeper of a bathhouse, and thus provide for their old age. Others chose to enter a cloistered retreat in a charitable foundation for repentant Magdalens. But there were not many of these institutions, and each had room for only a few former prostitutes, and in addition, the rules for admission imposed criteria of age and sometimes beauty. (At Avignon, applicants had to be under twenty-five and beautiful in order to be admitted.) Moreover, these foundations were not always looked upon with favor by the authorities, for they were apt to cause poor girls to prostitute themselves solely for the purpose of qualifying for help. Charitable foundations, then, took in only an "elite" based on poverty or repentance.[69]

A certain number of prostitutes took to wandering and foundered in utter destitution. Reduced to the daily begging of alms, their path led from rags, to the hospital, to death. But by the age of thirty, most prostitutes had a real chance of becoming reintegrated into society. They no longer had much to fear from the violence of the young townsmen, yet they were still of a marriageable age. Since public opinion did not view them with disgust, and since they were on good terms with priests and men of the law, it was not too difficult for them to find a position as servant or wife. To many city people, public prostitution represented a partial atonement for past misconduct. Many bachelors had compassion and sympathy for prostitutes, and finally, the local charitable foundations of the municipal authorities felt a charitable impulse to give special help to these repentant Magdalens and to open their way to marriage by dowering them. Marriage was definitely the most frequent end to the career of communal prostitutes who had roots in the town where they had publicly offered their bodies.[70] To show that they had such roots, they had their wills drawn up in their towns and asked to be buried there. All of this goes to show that, far from being marginal to the life of the city, prostitutes served a real function in it.

Prostitution and Society

THE CLIENTS: YOUNG AND NOT SO YOUNG

As I have pointed out repeatedly along the way, the brothel and the bathhouses were frequented by the young; and these were young townsmen, rather than only transients. But is this true for a minority or for the bulk of the population? For just a few lonely individuals or for the ordinary sons of the town? Was it the exception or the rule? How did these young men feel about their conduct, and how did the rest of the community feel about it?

The fact that some contracts drawn up by notaries of Tarascon or Beaucaire are dated from the prostibulum is a first indication that these establishments had a stable, local clientele. The witnesses were townsmen and came from every walk of life. We know that at Lyons between 1471 and 1478, men of every age and every status—weavers, cutlers, fishermen, clerks—from twenty-two to forty years old—frequented the baths of La Pêcherie. At Dijon, certain incidents in the brothel in which the public prosecutor had to intervene give us a first-hand account of the presence of a wide variety of common laborers, artisans, and shopkeepers, most of whom are identified. They were between eighteen and forty years old, and three-fourths of them were residents of the city.[71]

During the trial that took place at Lyons in 1478, some witnesses for the prosecution stated in a perfectly matter-of-fact manner that they had frequented the establishment in order to bathe and to "frolic." At Dijon in 1461, a twenty-year-old notary's assistant, Didier Maire, declared in the same context that "for the last two years he had gone several times to frolic (in Jeanne Saignant's bathhouse) as young bachelors are wont to do, both by day and by night." Many others also disclosed that they "took their pleasure there." Indeed, in 1457 the prosecutor himself noted that "two young men had gone to frolic there (in the prostibulum) as young servants of marriageable age are wont to do," adding elsewhere, "went to frolic, as young people will do." Other, later statements of an equally normative character confirm this "custom" of bachelors and young lads.[72]

It should be pointed out that the notables and men of the law were by no means critical of these young fornicators. The only individuals to arouse suspicion and concern were those who noisily carried on in these houses for several nights in a row. The authorities felt that the others were "good young lads who behave themselves and lead a goodly life."[73] As for the clients themselves, they did not feel they were doing anything wrong; quite the contrary. Here, for instance, are two servants at the Abbey of Clairvaux who had witnessed a fight: "Nature had moved them to go and frolic." A schoolmaster disclosed that "on Monday last, between two and three o'clock in the afternoon, Nature moved me to go and frolic in the house of the prostitutes."[74] So, whenever "Nature moved them" or "Nature urged them," they went there to "take their pleasure." When one bachelor, lying with a prostitute, heard another who desired her and was knocking at her door, he called out, "we are married for the night."

From all these testimonies it is evident that one did not go to the Grande Maison furtively. The texts are numerous, clear, and unambiguous: for the young men, fornication was a customary activity, and very likely one that was imposed not only by "Nature" but also by the group of elders, namely, the married men and the leading townsmen. And indeed, the "good young lads" and the peaceful bachelors owed it to themselves to go and "frolic"; this may well have been one of the rituals of adolescent groups, whether organized into abbeys or not. In addition, it also was proof of social and physiological normality. One can go even further: those who, for one reason or another, did not occasionally frequent an establishment of fornication were apt to be suspect. Their companions might wonder whether they had a servant-concubine or a bawd of their own; older people might fear that they were seriously threatening social morality, seducing their daughters or their wives.

Thus, almost all married men, even if they abided by the rules of marriage, had previously had dealings with *meretrices* for as long as five to ten years, which was the duration of their "youth." Their behavior as husbands was apt to show the effects of this experience. In 1457, one of the more outstanding notables of Dijon, the honorable Etienne Chambellan, a man of forty who was the financial agent of the Duke of Burgundy, protested to the archers who were about to throw a clerk whom they had mistaken for a priest out of the window of the prostibulum that "this was not right, because this house was common to all, where all manner of people could go and be secure under the protection of the town and the duke."[75] Does this mean that "youthful" habits were tolerated in others as well?

Public places of prostitution were theoretically off limits to married men and the clergy, even more strictly at night than in the daytime for the married men. The abbess was made to swear at the beginning of her tenure that she would not admit them; when she broke the rules and if an official complaint was lodged, so that the offense came to the attention of the authorities, she was liable to be fined in the same manner as the man who had committed the adultery.[76] This rule was never enforced. For one thing, it could not be applied to strangers. For the local clients, the matter was more delicate; but as long as the prohibitions were not flouted too openly, it was always possible to come to an agreement with the abbess or with the officials who supervised prostitution but also made their living from it. In this respect, the greatest possible tolerance seems to have reigned at Dijon. We know that it was not customary for the patrols to search the premises of the house or to have the rooms opened; the constables had to rely on what the prostitutes told them.[77] I do not know what proportion of the married men frequented the prostibulum of their own town, but what should we make of the following accusation: "Matthieu Beauprestre, mason, and J. Desgranges, also mason, even though they are married *and have their wives in this town,* are in the habit of going publicly, both by day and by night, to the brothel, where they commit mortal sins (blasphemy), show contempt for God, the Holy Church, and the Married State, and set a bad example for others." But then, what were the charges against them? They had gone to the brothel and stabbed a client, all of this on 25 May 1466, Whitsunday![78]

The fact is that even if the matter could be taken care of by giving a few extra coins to the abbess or the head of the police, a married man was never quite safe from arbitrary prosecution. The solution, though more costly, was to frequent the bathhouses; they were not subject to search, the girls were younger, and one had nothing to worry about, for all the bathhouses were equipped with hiding places and several exits. We do know that married men frequented the baths of La Pêcherie at Lyons and those of Saint-Philibert at Dijon.[79] Jeanne Saignant actually preferred them as clients, for they paid better. And indeed, her clients were on the average older than those of the prostibulum and were often respectable men of some social standing.[80]

In all cases involving procuring or fights in brothels and bathhouses, we hear about the presence of ecclesiastics, complete with names and addresses in the city. Some of this, to be sure, must be attributed to the virulent anticlericalism of the time, to gossip and stories spread about in performances of farces. Nonetheless, ecclesiastics furnished 20 percent of the clientele of the bathhouses and private brothels. Secular and regular clergy, monks of the old established and the new begging orders, canons, priests, and dignitaries, all were compromised. Some even appear as members of nocturnal bands; others were involved in brawls in the brothel. On the other hand, the constant harping on the guilt of ecclesiastics in this sort of offense also testifies to strong feelings of disapproval among the common people, feelings that not only gave rise to condemnation but also implied a certain concern for the dignity of the clergy. I do not believe that the priests' frequenting of prostitutes was considered truly scandalous, at least by most of the faithful. The real object of scandal—for everyone—was the priest who lived with a concubine or who availed himself of the services of a procuress to get in touch with young girls or married women.[81] There were three reasons for this attitude: in this society, fornication was an accepted form of behavior for all unmarried men; the reverence for the secular clergy and the monks of the old established orders was not such that anyone imagined them to be endowed with heroic virtue; and husbands and fathers preferred seeing all the youthful, vigorous clerics of the urban churches frequenting a brothel or a house of toleration to having them make advances to their own wives and daughters. They might make fun of them, but they did not condemn them.

Furthermore, the laxity of certain theologians in matters of sexuality had led many clerics to adopt a rather casual attitude toward the old prohibitions. Out of this more lenient sexual morality had come an image of the prostitute that was in many ways similar to that held in the municipal council chambers. Many alderman and many clerics felt that the communal prostitute fulfilled a two-fold function.

PROSTITUTION AND COLLECTIVE
MENTALITIES

Images of a golden age hovering in the deepest recesses of the consciousness of the poor; the desire for the return to a primitive communality incoher-
ently expressed in every revolt—the notables who reveal to us their haunting
fear of having to share their women were well aware of these fantasies. Under
these circumstances, the construction of the brothel not only met the need for
collective security, it also afforded at least partial satisfaction to the most
hidden aspirations of the bachelors. The Communal Great House welcomed
them, and they were able to share the communal prostitutes under the benevolent protection of the authorities. Here the prostitutes practiced their *minis-
terium,* their *"métier"*—and it is no coincidence that this is the term that was
constantly used. In other words, they fulfilled a function.[82]

They not only had a social responsibility, but indeed a moral charge, for to
some extent the protection of public order was incumbent upon them. The
arguments presented by public prosecutors and lawyers again and again
stressed a point that was never questioned: the communal prostitutes contributed to protecting respectable women from rowdyism. They also helped combat adultery, and that in a two-fold manner: being theoretically obliged—
under oath—to report those who disregarded the commands of marriage, their
occasional failings were but the lesser evil for the community and prevented
more scandalous occurrences; and since they also had charge of the youths
and bachelors from other places, they were in a position to temper their
aggressivity and to divert them from more serious crimes.[83] Finally, the
communal prostitutes were more interested than anyone in hunting down
clandestine prostitutes and debauched wives, whom they threatened to convey
to the brothel.[84]

Of all this the citizens in responsible positions were well aware. This is
why, in trials of procuresses and keepers of private brothels who had become
careless, the witnesses for the prosecution always included a number of public
prostitutes or their abbesses, who testified at the behest of the authorities. This
also explains why the brothel was calmly referred to as "the house of the
town," why the owners of bathhouses-cum-brothels were so often great personages whose honor was not jeopardized by such ventures, and why the
keepers were respectable people. Staid notaries went *"in prostibulo"* to draft
their documents and were willing to collect some of the revenues of the house.
The consuls administered the oath to the prostitutes, discussed fees and revenues with them, exempted them from the *taille,* and tolerated their presence at
certain public events. The consuls annually accepted a gift presented *coram
publico* by the abbess and also admonished the keeper of the brothel to recruit

"comely and enticing partners in wantonness," whom they then invited to participate in urban festivities and in the games of the young people. Public prostitutes were also used in ceremonial entries of princes and were sometimes entrusted with public tasks.[85]

There were times, of course, when sudden flare-ups of purifying morality stirred the cities of southeastern France. An abrupt increase in mortality, a catastrophic crop failure, or a "flamboyant" itinerant preacher might temporarily influence the collective consciousness and summon the people to penitence. At such times, concubines and clandestine prostitutes were given notice to leave town, and the public suddenly seemed to discover the crimes of procuresses and the moral squalor of the keepers of bathhouses. Such flare-ups were as short-lived as they were vehement, and chroniclers and diary-keeping bourgeois took notice of them precisely because they considered such sudden outbursts to be miraculous.[86]

While it is true that we know about clandestine prostitution only from the legal proceedings that sought to curb it, we should not let ourselves be deceived by such trials, for when the charges were brought, the procuring had been going on for several years; nor did the trial put an end to it.[87] In 1478, for example, some of the residents of the rue de la Pêcherie at Lyons wanted to put an end to the activities of the keeper of the bathhouse, Casotte Cristal. The city backed them, though not too energetically. Casotte won her case and her bathhouse continued to flourish. As for Jeanne Saignant, she had been practicing her trade for fifteen years when the town decided to bring a whole set of serious charges against her. Nonetheless, four years passed before her activities were put to an end, and that was because she had dared to blackmail two young women belonging to the best families of Dijon.

In these trials, the accusers and their arguments sometimes strike us as rather odd. To us, it seems a mockery to find competitors, jealous of the business success of the accused woman, among the accusers; and although the preamble of the indictment always decried "scandals and dishonorable activities," the accusers or their counsel did not dwell on this point. Having no illusions about the effectiveness of such arguments, they were careful to include charges of a more disquieting nature. Those who wanted to get rid of Casotte Cristal accused her of being—like most of the women she took in—Flemish-speaking, and of maintaining constant contact with Burgundy. Her establishment thus represented a threat to the city's security. These charges were brought at a time when it was not certain that Burgundy could be conquered and when war was about to break out to the north of the kingdom. Clearly, the charge that seemed most likely to result in a condemnation was spying for the enemies of the king, rather than procuring. The arguments used by the aldermen of Dijon against Jeanne Saignant were similar. They involved not so much the "debaucheries" she had arranged as the threats of death she had uttered and the potions she was said to have poured into the goblets of some of the clients she wanted to ensnare. Potions, charms, and sorcery were the things that were sure to bring about the conviction of a high-class procuress. As for the others, their accusers had to make them admit to the abduction of married women or the seduction of little girls, that is, to crimes against the family, in order to to get rid of them, since prostitution or procuring in themselves were not enough to arouse a public outcry. Nor could it have been otherwise. In this sphere, public opinion was very largely derived from two cultural currents, one secular and one religious, both permeated with contradictions.

The tone of the social life of the city seems to have been set to a large extent by the jurists. Many of the consuls and aldermen were men of the law who had attended the universities, and it was the young *robins,* or clerks of the court, who were the leaders of the joyous societies. (The only two Kings of Youth known for fifteenth-century Burgundy were law clerks, and one of them was also the King of the *Basoche* [association of law clerks].) It was they who arranged the rides on the ass and wrote or performed farces and *soties.* They were heirs to a libertinism that they personally kept alive by propagating its fundamental values at every urban festivity.[88] One of the Kings of Love, elected at Dijon ca. 1440, has left us an astonishing drawing of his carnival parade, where we see him marching as the king of the cocks amidst masked figures and impersonations of visibly male animals, blowing on a rose clutched in his fist. There is nothing mysterious about this allegory, and the prevailing spirit of the commentaries surrounding the drawing—made up of antistrophes and equivocations—further reinforces the already obvious meaning of the grotesque and phallic figures. It is the spirit of the *Roman de la Rose,* preaching the exaltation of Nature and the search for Pleasure. Such a morality was all the more acceptable to the notables as many of them had themselves frequented the circles of the *Basoche.* But the influence of these fun-loving clerks was also welcomed by the rest of the bachelors, who felt that these assistants to notaries and court recorders were indispensable sources of good stories and secrets suitable for use in farces, purveyors of clever jokes, scandals, and family shenanigans to be unearthed from the secrecy of bathhouse and courtroom.[89] Acting as accomplices of the *jeunesse dorée,* but also playing an essential role in the bands of "joyous bachelors," these groups of law clerks constituted what we would call the "trendsetters" of urban society. No wonder, then, that the upper-class youth adopted a libertine attitude, which expressed itself not only in their licentious demeanor but also in their vocabulary: "Nature moved them," "Nature urged them," they went to "take their pleasure," to "play and disport themselves" in "graceful frolicking" with prostitutes who submitted to the commands of Venus but who, for that very reason, and in keeping with the teaching of Jean de Meung, were seen as both indispensable partners and objects of contempt.

The doctrine of the Catholic Church was not without ambiguity, even in this sphere. We know that sexual morality had become less rigid during the thirteenth century under the influence of the canonists and the great theologians. Saint Thomas Aquinas, P. de la Palud, and J. Bromyard had contributed to softening some of the old tabus, excused contraceptive practices under certain circumstances, and made some timid attempts to rehabilitate sexual pleasure. In short, they had modified the hierarchy of the sins of the flesh and at the same time mitigated their gravity, at least within the confines of marriage. But such a doctrine—and the Cordelier and Jacobin friars had read their theologians—was bound to have wider consequences as well. In a vague way, it made it easier to excuse certain forms of behavior even outside marriage.[90]

If, by the end of the Middle Ages, fornication was no longer among the cases reserved for absolution by the bishop but implicitly sanctioned by the parish priest, the reason may well have been that the religious orders that were closest to the people had to recognize, whether they liked it or not, the plight of the poor who were unable to marry.[91] Parish priests, the shepherds of their flocks, came to view the prostitute as both an auxiliary and a witness. Poor and humiliated though she was, she contributed in her own way to the struggle against the very vices whose victim she had become. She thus bore witness to human misery. When certain inhabitants of Dijon expressed some of their anticlericalism by calling the bawds "Jacobines" and claimed that no one but the whores followed the processions of the mendicant friars,[92] the insult had a double meaning. Above all, however, it indicates that the mendicant orders cared about the salvation of their Mary Magdalens, regarded them as future repentant sinners, accepted their alms, and permitted them to follow their crosses and be buried in their churchyards.

As for the artisans and the poor bachelors of the outlying areas, the contempt for prostitutes they sometimes liked to exhibit was greatly tempered by their social proximity. They too were acquainted with uncertainty about the morrow; they too knew that calamities always left in their wake a long line of victims who had to live out their miserable lives as best they could. This explains the twofold set of names by which the prostitutes were called. Some of these were perjorative (bawd, old shoe, etc.), but others convey a certain sense of sympathy, understanding, and friendliness: the good ladies, the little whores, the joyous girls were not rejected by a social community which, though ever ready to swell their ranks by adding more and more victims, was also ready to redeem them, once they had served their term of penance. The hell of the prostitutes was only a purgatory that lasted as long as their "youth."

Thus, it appears that in the fifteenth century, from Burgundy to Provence, prostitution—whether official or tolerated by the powers that be—was a natural consequence of a specific demographic structure and morality. Prostitution served a mediating function, and the brothel, like the joyous confraternities, must be seen as an institution designed to keep the peace between age groups and social groups. All young men, and many others, too, went to the brothel to fornicate. Prostitution, whether under the aegis of the municipality or not, was a means of curbing, though not of conquering, adolescent aggressivity. Every son of the town and every servant had at least once in his youth chased wenches and raped a poor girl without being ostracized by the community. Only persistent aggressive behavior of this kind was apt to mark an individual as a delinquent; and even this was a matter of social standing. Such behavior did not jeopardize the future of the young bourgeois in any way; people of middling condition could pay or be pardoned, while the others were banished. But it was less disgraceful to be a pimp than a gambler, less disgraceful to violate a chambermaid than to steal a penny. A dangerous and troubled period, male adolescence was not only a time of resentment and frustration but also one of adventure, of nocturnal mascarading and uninhibited fornication. Literature has paid scant attention to this stage of life, but the poets, whenever they wept about their past and foreswore the ways of their youth, never failed to recall that it had been "mad."

Women, on the other hand, had little reason to regret the passing of their youth. Married early, hemmed in by prohibitions, mere extras at public festivities, confined to a civic space and time much smaller than that of the young males, they did not belong to confraternities or peer groups. On the rare occasions when girls assembled of a winter's evening for an *escreigne* [comparable to an American sewing bee] it was under the eyes of their mothers and the old women who closely watched their demeanor and their every word. It is true, of course, that some widows took full charge of their family's affairs and that some well-born girls were able, to some extent, to do as they pleased. The minority status of such women was related to age and wealth. All the others had to submit to their fathers, their husbands, or their masters; for them, youth was a time of insecurity and uncertainty. It is not surprising that at the very time when young men led a freewheeling life and yet aspired to set the rules of decency, the example offered to all wives was the edifying story of Griselidis.[93] Liberty was not for them, who were exhorted to "fear God, their husbands, and dishonor."[94] To them, the Church offered consolation; but clerical pronouncements, whether tendered in a spirit of tolerant complicity or, at times, with severity, meant little to the husbands and the young men who might or might not listen to such pronouncements, who adapted them to their own ends, or who altogether changed them.

On one point only—and it is a capital point indeed—was the fundamental attitude of the youth groups compatible with the morality preached by the men of the Church, and here the exaltation of Nature by the young implicitly complemented the condemnation of Anti-Nature by the Church. It therefore seems likely to me that husbands conducted their conjugal intercourse according to nature, just as most of them had earlier conducted their intercourse with prostitutes, so that the uninhibited fornication of the youths with professionals probably had no consequences as far as demography is concerned.

Such freewheeling mores for males did not survive the "crisis of the Renaissance," and it is easy to discern between 1520 and 1570 various signs of a progressive rejection of prostitution on the part of the urban community; but this trend can be shown here only in its bare outline. In the late Middle Ages, the very scope of prostitution had revealed the precariousness of the female condition, but that condition tended to improve in the first decades of the sixteenth century. Very slowly, women began to conquer a part of civic space,[95] to acquire an identity of their own, and to become less vulnerable— all of which is undoubtedly related to a greater emphasis on the value of the couple, which has been evoked by Natalie Z. Davis and André Burguière.[96] Religious polemics had greatly contributed to modifying the existing relationship between husband and wife. The Church now felt obliged to pay greater attention to daughters and wives. The uncompromising austerity of spokesmen of Protestantism was echoed in the new and rigorous attitude of the reform movements within Catholicism. These circles severely criticized priests living in concubinage, protectors of prostitutes, and procuresses. In a parallel development, the social reaction to prostitution also underwent a slow change.

Nor was this new attitude a result of the onslaught of syphilis. The corps of aldermen never held deliberations on the problem of the "Neapolitan disease"; at most, they occasionally removed disease-carrying prostitutes. Moreover, the closing of brothels preceded the great epidemic outbreaks by at least thirty years; and we know that contemporaries did not believe that sexual intercourse was the only cause of contagion. If public places of prostitution became more dangerous, it was not because they were the haunts of "Lady Pox," but because they were so often the scene of mayhem and murder, as quartered troops and idlers fought the pimps and scuffled with the local lads. For the first time, prostitution and delinquency appeared to be linked.[97] Also, poverty was becoming more acute, and the wages paid to women on the labor market fell to a dangerously low level.[98] The municipal authorities, with the support of the Church and the monarchy, eventually took severe measures against an institution that was henceforth seen as a social scourge, necessarily leading to unrest and divine punishment.[99] Consequently, the bathhouses were either closed down or strictly policed, while the concubines of priests and the clandestine prostitutes were periodically run out of town. The municipal brothels disappeared one after the other, and shortly after 1580 the Edict of Amboise finally did away with the most venerable of these houses. Prostitution did not die with them; it only became more costly, more dangerous, and more entangled in ignominious relationships; and despite the respite of this time of troubles the late sixteenth century already foreshadowed the situation

PROSTITUTION, YOUTH, AND SOCIETY

of the seventeenth century, when branding and whipping were in store for prostitutes, and scorn and opprobrium for their clients.[100]

Must we attribute the "scandalous indulgence" of the municipal governments at the end of the Middle Ages to the misfortunes of their time, to a desperate lust for life in the face of death? In short, was the sexual freedom I have described here part of a "moral crisis"? Once again, the emphatic answer is no. Prostitution flourished alike in areas untouched by war and in those that were devastated; it was more developed in expanding population centers than in declining cities, and it was no less tolerated in the strongholds of the Church than in areas where religious practice was declining. Prostitution was thriving as part of a social system that had existed long before the calamities of the fourteenth century, and may indeed have had its first beginning in the Gregorian reform movement. It was only the doubly distorting mirror of monarchical absolutism and the Counter-Reformation that reflected an image of scandalous decadence where there was nothing more than a fundamental aspect of medieval society.

NOTES

1. This is the character of the studies by G. Bayle, "Note pour servir à l'histoire de la prostitution dans les provinces méridionales de la France," *Mémoires de l'Académie du Vaucluse* 5 (1886); J. Chalande, "La maison publique municipale aux XVᵉ et XVIᵉ siècles à Toulouse," *La France Médicale* (1912); J. C. Delannoy, *Pécheresses repenties, notes pour servir à l'histoire de la prostitution à Amiens du XIVᵉ au XIXᵉ siècle* (Amiens, 1943); J. Garnier, *Les étuves dijonnaises* (Dijon, 1867); Dr. J. Lacassagne and A. Picornot, "Vieilles étuves de Lyon et d'ailleurs," *Albums du Crocodile* (Lyons, 1943); P. Pansier, *L'oeuvre des repenties à Avignon du XIIIᵉ au XVIIIᵉ siécle* (Paris, 1910).
   As for actual histories of prostitution, almost all of them treat this phenomenon from the most remote times to our own day. Among these works, I remind the reader of P. Lacroix-Dufour's *Histoire de la prostitution chez tous les peuples du monde* (Brussels, 1861), and Dr. Le Pileur's *La prostitution du XIIIᵉ au XVᵉ siècle* (Paris, 1908). A bibliography of the subject can be found in J.-J. Servais et J.-P. Laurent, *Histoire et dossier de la prostitution* (Paris, 1965).
   2. The first examplar of this attitude is L. Ménard who, in his *Histoire civile, ecclésiastique, et littéraire de la ville de Nîmes* (Paris, 1754), bk. 12, p. 23, attributes the existence of public prostitution in a fifteenth-century city to "scandalous indulgence" on the part of the consuls. This attitude is often expressed by nineteenth-century historians and can sometimes be discerned even in contemporary studies.
   3. I would like to express my particular appreciation to Professor Georges Duby, who allowed me to present this research to his seminars at Aix-en-Provence and the Collège de France in Paris in November 1974 and February 1975. I also wish to thank all those at Paris or Aix who have shared their suggestions with me, among them G. Bois, A. Burguière, N. Coulet, R. Fossier, C. Klapisch, E. Patlagean, J.-M. Pesez, F. Piponnier, K. Werner, P. Toubert, as well as N. Z. Davis, M. Morineau, and J.-L. Flandrin, with whom I have often discussed these problems.
   Having chosen to present this subject in its entirety here, I cannot hope to treat every one of its aspects in detail. Consequently, I have not fully developed all of the demonstrations; I have shortened some of the notes and almost completely omitted the evidence from the judicial archives. However, the problems relating to urban youth are the subject of an article to appear in

Cahiers d'Histoire in 1976. My next project will be to complete a sociological study of prostitutes.

4. R. Vaultier, *Le folklore pendant la guerre de Cent Ans* (Paris, 1965), pp. 121–281, gives examples of vagrant prostitutes. At Dijon, the judicial archives (Archives départementales [hereafter A.D.], Côte-d'Or, *Justice criminelle*, B 11 360–16, 1498 and B 11 360–33, 1542) contain the cross-examinations of prostitutes who went to the countryside at the time of the grain or wine harvest. In Dauphiné, certain agreements between the seigneur and the village community stipulated that the inhabitants were not permitted to receive traveling prostitutes for more than one night (cf. Lacroix-Dufour, *Histoire de la prostitution*, 4: 151). For prostitutes kept by mowers, see "Chroniques d'un notaire d'Orange," ed. L. Duhamel, *Annuaire du Vaucluse*, 1881, p. 41: "The plague began with a whore whom Malhet's field hands were keeping at their grange" (1545). See also A. D., Bouches-du-Rhône, B 2043, f⁰ 5, 1471 for similar statements. For merchants, see Archives municipales [hereafter A.M.] Lyons, FF inv. Chappe, XIII, 62/67, referring to the proceedings against the bathhouse of La Pêcherie (1478). According to the witnesses, the German merchants who came to the fairs made a practice of bringing whores they had picked up along the way. For the rivermen, cf. A.D., Bouches-du-Rhône, Notaires de Tarascon, 407 E 64, f⁰ 322 v⁰, July 1452. This document refers to a brawl between the archers of the garrison and the boatmen in the service of a carrier from Lyons who were disporting themselves on their barge with a woman. The rectors of the Charité [hospice] of Lyon repeatedly lodged complaints against rivermen who brought women from Savoy on their barges (Archives Charité, E 4, f⁰ 101 v⁰, 1534 and E 5, f⁰ 304 v⁰, 1543).

5. Proof of the existence of a "good house" can be found over and over in municipal deliberations and accounts. When no brothel is mentioned in a series of municipal documents, it simply means that it was neither owned nor managed by the urban authorities, who consequently were not legally responsible for it and thus had no call to attend to it, except in unusual circumstances. The best example of this situation is found in Beaucaire. While the deliberations allude to the house only twice, the records of the notaries frequently refer to leases, statements of indebtedness, or wills of public prostitutes who practiced there. The situation was comparable at Valence and Lyons.

6. We know that the term *abbess* was already used in this sense by William of Malmesbury (*Gesta regum anglorum*, *Patrologia Latina* 179, 1384–85) in connection with the *lupanar* founded by G. de Poitiers. This comparison was bound to have a great success. It should be noted that the title "abbess" was used above all in the regions where the youth groups were referred to as "abbeys." The abbess was either one of the communal prostitutes or a former prostitute who might even be married. By the turn of the fifteenth century, male managers had often replaced the abbesses. Officials of the judiciary, such as the assistant *viguier* at Arles or Tarascon, the chatelain at Beaucaire, the head of the police [*prévôt*] at Dijon, or the King of Ribaldry at Lyons, were in charge of hiring or rejecting the prostitutes. The abbess—who was, among other things, a source of information for the authorities—was also supposed to enforce the rules of the "profession" in her establishment (and we shall see presently what this meant in terms of behavior), to make sure that the brothel did not become a gambling den, to watch out for blasphemy, and not to let any client stay for more than one night, so that the brothel could not become a hideout for tramps. When the abbess of the municipal house of Tarascon died in 1467, two municipal officers [*syndics*] took charge (A.M., Tarascon, BB 9, f⁰ 276) until a replacement was found. In similar circumstances, two aldermen of Dijon "administered the oath to the prostitutes" (A.M., Dijon, K 84, 1517).

7. For Tarascon, see A.M., Tarascon, BB 16, f⁰ 16, 1449 and BB 13, f⁰ 92, 1527. The archives of Dijon contain a fair number of accounts relating to the reconstruction or the upkeep of the best-known brothel of the kingdom in the Middle Ages (A.M., Dijon, K 83, and I 142). The "hot" neighborhood of Avignon has been described by P. Pansier, *Dictionnaire des anciennes rues d'Avignon* (Avignon, 1930), p. 206. At Beaucaire, the brothel was made up of two or three houses located in the middle of a street where the prostitutes lived. At Orange, a house was built rather late in the "good quarry" (A.M., Orange, BB 10, f⁰ 91 v⁰, 1511); this was also done at Arles (A.M., Arles, BB 6, f⁰ 171, 1497).

8. Many examples of such "nonresidence" can be found at Arles, Tarascon, and Dijon (A.M., Dijon, B 151, f⁰ 64, 1426; B 168, f⁰ 151, 1508; B 169, f⁰ 93 v⁰, 1517; and A.D., Côte-d'Or, B 11 360–17, 1501).

9. For such "sexual segregation," see A.M., Dijon, B 148, f° 15, 1410, which stipulates that men were to use one set of baths, women another; ibid. f° 112, 1412, a regulation in which two days were reserved for men, two other days for women. Except during these "reserved" hours or days, it does seem that all bathhouses were open to both sexes. For Dijon, see Garnier, *Les étuves dijonnaises,* describing the bathhouses of Vertbois, Langres, Le Palais, Saint-Michel, Sainte-Seine, La Rochelle, and Saint-Philibert. At Besançon, the bathhouses were such notorious places of prostitution that the keepers paid a special tax assessed on the number of prostitutes they sheltered (Lacassagne and Picornot, "Vieilles étuves.") At Lyons, the bathhouse of La Tresmonnoye included twenty rooms, that of La Pêcherie probably many more. In addition, Lyons had the bathhouse of Le Sabliz (located in the vicinity of one of the public brothels), those of Bourgneuf, La Chèvre (near the Rhône bridge), Les Augustins, and Combremont. Such establishments were not only found in large cities. Cavaillon also had a public bathhouse.

10. In 1388, the bathhouse of La Pêcherie belonged to G. Marchis, a prominent merchant; in 1446 it was owned by the illustrious Baronnat family. By the end of the fifteenth century, this establishment paid a high rent to the archbishopric, while the Tresmonnoye building was owned by Aynard de Villeneuve. At Dijon, the bathhouse of Saint-Michel belonged to the abbey of Saint-Etienne, that of Langres to the bishop, and that located on the rue des Chanoines to the Faletan family. At Avignon, prostitutes rented the rooms to which they took their clients from the Buzzaffi family. At Valence, Francis de Genas, a trusted adviser to Louis XI and General of Languedoc, rented a building to a brothel-keeper on an annual basis (A.D., Drôme, Notaires de Valence, E 2541, f° 240, 1466, and E 2490, f° 4 v°, 1453).

11. At Lyons in 1478, it was said that prostitutes came in large numbers at the time of the fairs and moved on when the fairs were over (A.M., Lyons, FF, Chappe inventory, XIII, 62). At Dijon, there was a place where women would assemble to apply for work in the vineyards; some of them seized this opportunity to prostitute themselves (A.D., Côte-d'Or, B 11 360-7, p. 914, 1459; ibid., p. 968, 1468; B 11 360-8, pp. 2-20, 1462, etc.).

On the influx of poor women: In August 1502, there was a public outcry against the great number of "disreputable" women at Valence, but it turns out that they had been forced to leave Crest, Romans, and other places because of food shortages there (A.M., Valence, BB 3, f° 36 v°, 69, 115). The same thing happened at Bourg-lez-Valence in 1504, during one of the century's worst droughts (A.M., Bourg-lez-Valence, CC 31, f° 825 v°), and at Montélimar in 1511 (A.M., Montélimar, BB 25, f° 20). There is no question, of course, that periods of calamity were most unfavorable to venal love; prostitutes or keepers of houses of prostitution always asked for a reduction in rent in times of dearth or high mortality, when the clients "deserted" the brothel (A.M., Dijon, K 83 for 1476, 1484, 1495, 1502, and K 84 for 1519 and 1520). During better times, on the other hand, such as the year 1454, the town of Villefranche-sur-Saône enlarged its brothel (A. Besançon and E. Longin, eds., *Registres consulaires de la ville de Villefranche* [Villefranche, 1905], 1: 309); so did Dijon in 1446-47 (A.M., Dijon, B 157, f° 126). The number of bathhouses at Dijon almost doubled between 1410 (four) and 1470 (seven). New bathhouses were opened at Lyons in 1471 and 1473. In other words, the construction of a brothel and the opening of a new bathhouse are good indicators of demographic and commercial recovery.

12 At Avignon, there were public, clandestine, and "in-between" [*destrales*] prostitutes (statutes of 1441, *Annales d'Avignon et du Comtat* [1914], p. 178); in case of doubt, one referred to a *"ruffiana publica vel privata"* (J. Girard and P. Pansier, *La cour temporelle d'Avignon aux XIVe et XVe siècles* [Paris, 1909], p. 128). At Lyons, the public proclamations of the *Officialité* distinguished between the prostitutes who plied their trade in the brothel, those who worked in the bathhouse, and those who practiced in a private room (A.D., Rhône, 1 G 184, f° 29 v°, 1468). At Dijon, these last were called "resident" [*claustrières*] (A.M., Dijon, B 151, f° 64 v°, 1426) or sometimes "loose girls, lovers, or trollops," all terms that could also be applied to occasional prostitutes or to women whose conduct left something to be desired.

13. On sanitation: At Beaucaire, the patients of the Saint-Lazare hospital used to frequent the neighboring brothel, a practice the authorities found so disturbing that they decided to move the house to another location (A.M., Beaucaire, BB 2, f° 29 v°, 1492). At Avignon, public prostitutes were automatically obliged to purchase any meat they might touch in the market, but every year at Nîmes the *meretrices* would knead with their own hands a cake for the poor, which they presented to the consuls!

Restricted times: It is significant that certain leases for houses of prostitution took effect at the beginning of Lent. This proves that in the distant past, Lent was observed. Once the old tenant had gone, the new one had time to settle in and could then reopen the house after Easter. In most towns, the house remained open on Saturday and Sunday, its busiest days. But the keeper was enjoined to see to it that no "frolicking" took place during the hours of Mass.

On off-limit places: Most of the time, this was a matter of confining public prostitution within its traditional streets or of removing it from the vicinity of a church upon the request of the inhabitants of a "respectable" street or of the Church authorities. For an example at Lyons in 1470 see A.D., Rhône, 1 G 184, f⁰ 29 v⁰; for Tarascon, cf. BB 11, f⁰ 39; for Arles, cf. A.M. Arles, BB 2, f⁰ 59 v⁰, BB 6, f⁰ 166, etc.

On regulation of clothing and the compulsory wearing of an "emblem" by prostitutes: Ordinances to this effect were promulgated frequently and everywhere (in 1441 and 1458 at Avignon; in 1468 and 1475 at Lyons, etc.), but it should be noted that with the exception of the wearing of the special mark (the shoulder-knot), clothing restrictions for prostitutes were included in more general sumptuary regulations, applying to all social categories, none of which could ever be enforced.

On fiscal concerns: At Tarascon in 1451, a certain J. Denis was condemned by the *viguier* to a fine of 12 s.cor. for "keeping a loose woman without permission of the court." The court, then, granted (or denied) permission to take charge of a newly arrived "professional" (A.D., Bouches-du-Rhône, Viguerie de Tarascon, B 2041/3). At Tarascon in 1473, the consuls protested the activities of the *sous-viguier* who invited public prostitutes for luncheons and dinners "to the detriment of the abbot and the profits of the *prostibulum*" (A.M., Tarascon, BB 10, f⁰134 v⁰).

14. On the lukewarm efforts of the consulates: At Dijon in 1426, it was discovered, following a series of Lenten sermons, that the brothel was located right next to the school; and since the schoolboys "took notions of folly" there, it was decided to move it elsewhere. This was to remain a pious wish; the brothel stayed where it was, and so did the schoolboys (A.M., Dijon, B 151, f⁰ 64 v⁰). At Tarascon, no heed was paid to the neighbors of a house of prostitution who had demanded no more than that one of its exits opening onto their street be closed, the reason given being that this was a "very small inconvenience" (A.M., Tarascon, BB 11, f⁰ 162 and 181 v⁰, 1486).

At Romans, the brothel was called *"pro servicio reipublicae eiusdem villae"* in 1487; see U. Chevalier, *Oeuvres historiques*, vol. 1, *Annales de Romans* (Valence, 1897), p. 69. Resistance to any curbing of prostitution sometimes came from very high places. In 1447 at Dijon, the attorney of the bishop of Langres in effect spoke on behalf of the town's clandestine prostitutes (A.M., Dijon, B 157, f⁰ 161 v⁰). In 1486 the sergeants who had imprisoned a number of notoriously dissolute women—they were the concubines of priests—were excommunicated by the bishop and had to implore his forgiveness. Indeed, the bishop had stated publicly that "the mayor himself had taken his carnal pleasure with some of these very women" (A.M., Dijon, B 166, f⁰ 35, 1486). In a more general sense, certain aldermen profited indirectly from prostitution, and houses of toleration usually enjoyed protection in high places.

15. Emmanuel Le Roy Ladurie, *Les paysans de Languedoc* (Paris, 1966) p. 278; See abbreviated English translation by John Day (Urbana, Ill., 1974). See also A.D., Rhône 1G 84, 1468; A.M., Dijon, K 83, 1492, 1498; K 84, 1511; I 142, 1505, etc.

16. For Tarascon, the list of prostitutes is based on the notarial archives and is, therefore, necessarily very incomplete. For Lyons, we know of 20 public and clandestine communal prostitutes in the two public houses of prostitution, 30 in the two main bathhouses, and at least as many in the other public baths. At Dijon, 20 to 30 were counted "in prostibulo" and at least as many in the bathhouses, while the 18 private brothel-keeping operations listed for 1486 account for some 60 more. Dijon had 2,614 households in 1470. These figures conform to what we know of other places. Amiens had at least 50 public prostitutes in 1453 (see J.-C. Delannoy, *Pécheresses repenties*). At Reims in 1422, twelve "courtesans" were counted in the parish of Saint-Pierre alone, an indication that seems to imply a figure five times as high for the town as a whole (cf. P. Desportes, "La population de Reims au XVᵉ siècle," *Le Moyen Age* 21 (1966): 463–509. Compare these figures with the census of 1872, which listed 144 public prostitutes for Dijon— although it should be noted that by that time the town numbered more than 40,000 inhabitants. In other words, there were at least three times as many prostitutes in the fifteenth as in the nineteenth century.

17. On the judicial system of Dijon, see C. Bertucat, *La jurisdiction municipale de Dijon, son étendue* (Dijon, 1911). The viscount-mayor and the aldermen had full jurisdiction over the town and its suburbs, and even such cases as were formerly reserved for the ducal courts (abduction, repeated theft, arson, and murder) were now brought before the mayor. The mayor exercised this complete jurisdiction by the fifteenth century.

The departmental archives of Côte-d'Or preserve a large series of investigations and procedures in criminal cases: Forty thick bundles—each composed of several hundred items ranging from a single sheet to thick notebooks—are the vestiges of the daily work of public prosecutors up to 1550. The records of these proceedings are the main source for the demographic and sociological analyses of the present study (series B 11 36Q). The rather spotty series B 11 336 and B 11 337 contain the records of judicial proceedings involving the granting of pardons, civil and criminal matters; they occasionally also mention a sentence. Many of the fines imposed in civil cases can be found in series M of the municipal archives. Finally, the sentences in criminal cases were often recorded in the deliberations of the council of aldermen, though usually without the grounds for the judgment. J. Garnier availed himself of this series of records of criminal procedures for his articles on the Coquillards and the bathhouses, as did A. Voisin for "La nuit à Dijon au XVe siècle," *Annales de Bourgogne* 9 (1937): 265–79, an article that treats two or three nocturnal incidents in an anecdotal manner.

18. Concerning the relation between real and visible criminality (the *numerus obscurus*), studies conducted in England, the United States, Germany, and France, both for rural communities and big cities, come to relatively uniform conclusions. A résumé of these conclusions can be found in R. Hood and R. Sparks, *La délinquance* (Paris, 1970).

19. Far from being exceptional, reprisals were levied even against women who enjoyed the most thorough protection of the town or the duke. See B 11 360-5, p. 538, 1453 or B 11 360-7, p. 830, 1458. Families had good reasons—which they might or might not state—to settle such a matter out of court, for the involvement of the law could well turn to the disadvantage of the victim or the plaintiffs or lead to an unfavorable "social reaction." Examples of settlements with damages of 18 gros paid to the victims, one of whom was only a servant girl, are found in B 11 360-9, 1464, and in ibid., 1465. The public prosecutor himself would push for a private settlement when the aggressors were sons of the town or when the raped girl was not a virgin and did not belong to a good family (B 11 360-12, 1475).

20. This was the usual course of events in such assaults; there were, however, some variations. Sometimes the attack took place in the street, and the victim was dragged to the dry moat surrounding the cities. Making the rounds with the night-watch was a good opportunity and an excellent cover for the *galants*, who either left the group or demanded entry to a house in their official capacity. Almost all these rapes were carried out with unbelievable brutality (pregnant women dragged through the snow, etc.), but the aggressors never attempted to maim or kill their victims.

21. The aggressors were of all occupations—vineyard workers, weavers, fullers, butchers, barbers, goldsmiths; law clerks also were well represented. For the period 1436-86, we can identify 398 participants (out of a total of between 430 and 450 aggressors). Eighteen of these were unquestionably married; 99 were definitely unmarried (young lads, marriageable bachelors), and 166 were most probably unmarried (young fellows [*compagnons*] and youngsters [*varlets*]). The marital status of 115 others is unknown. Of a total of 125 rapes during this period, 98 were collective rapes (between 1492 and 1520, there were 82 rapes, 65 of them collective). In the 73 court cases of the fifteenth century for which we have records of the investigation, the groups consisted on the average of 6 individuals. Only 20 percent of the rapes were perpetrated by bands of 10 or more.

For the fifteenth century the age of the aggressors is known in only 9 cases (20-29 years, mean age 25). But for the first half of the sixteenth century, we know the ages of 72 of these individuals: ranging from 16 to 36 years, the mean age was 24 years, 10 months—despite the fact that the age at marriage had remained unchanged from the period 1450-1500.

The distribution by months of the 207 rapes committed between 1436 and 1542 (the monthly average is slightly higher than 17) shows a slight falling off in March (14), May (11), September (12), and October (14). For the last two months this is not surprising, since this was a difficult period and also the time of the wine harvest. But the minimum observed in May may have a social significance. Many youth festivals and dances for the whole community took place in May; this may confirm the observation of certain moralists, the earliest of whom was Gerson, who felt that collective festivals had a "socializing" and tempering effect upon violent behavior.

22. A.M., Dijon, B 161, f⁰ 50, 1458, and f⁰ 138, 1454. J. Rabustel was public prosecutor for thirty-six years (1436–72) and exercised his functions with the utmost conscientiousness. Despite the uncompromising severity of the law with respect to the poor, he always applied its rules in the most humane fashion.

23. Du Clerc's *Chronique* (J. A. Buchon, ed., *Choix de chroniques* [Paris, 1838], pp. 1–318) evokes this climate of violence for Arras. J. Deniau in *La Commune de Lyon et la guerre bourguignonne* (Lyons, 1934), p. 159, sensed a similar atmosphere for Lyons. Mention is made of "nocturnal scandals" at Valence (A.M., Valence, BB 3, f⁰ 89 v⁰, 1503), Tarascon (A.M., Tarascon, BB 12, f⁰ 355, 1516); Beaucaire (A.M., Beaucaire, BB 5, f⁰ 102, 1525). Generally speaking, the dearth of such allusions should not surprise us too much, for the members of the town councils were not worried about a crime that was unlikely to affect the women of their own milieu.

24. See Le Roy Ladurie, *Les paysans de Languedoc,* p. 398; J. Le Goff, *La civilisation de l'Occident médiéval* (Paris, 1964), p. 376; G. Duby, "Au XIIᵉ siècle, les 'jeunes' dans la société aristocratique," *Annales, E.S.C.* 19 (September-October 1964): 835–46.

25. Applying the method used by P. Desportes for "La population de Reims" (cited in n. 16) to a population of married couples in order to compare the perception of time in men and women, I find that 50 percent of the men and 50 percent of the women gave round multiples of ten; 40 and 37.5 percent respectively gave even numbers; 10 and 12.5 percent gave odd numbers. Nor are these findings appreciably different for the first half of the sixteenth century. It is noteworthy that here, as in the Reims sample, people progressively forgot their age as they grew old. Generally speaking, no tendency to make themselves appear younger can be observed among the women. One only sees that the ages as given tend to stick, as it were, to clear-cut milestones; people alternately made themselves appear older or younger than they were. But these discrepancies involve only one or two years; furthermore, they cancel each other out in statistical calculations.

26. For men, we can only observe four cases (out of fifty-two) of marriage before the age of twenty, and four after the age of thirty. For women, marriage before the age of 16/17 was extremely rare in the fifteenth century, and before 17/18 years in the sixteenth century.

27. Note that on the basis of these testimonies, it is possible to separate married women from marriageable girls without running a serious risk of error, for the former were always identified as N——, wife of——, while the latter were identified as N——, daughter of——. In my analysis of unmarried girls, I have examined 216 cases of girls between the ages of 18 and 25 (even younger witnesses were extremely rare), indicating their ages in two-year blocks (in order to compensate for their imprecise perception of time). In this group of unmarried girls, 87 were 18/19 years old, 82 were 20/21, 24 were 22/23, and 24 were 24/25 years old. Clearly, the major break in this series occurs at about age 21/22 (and it should be noted that neither this sample nor that of Reims indicates any clear-cut preference for the figure 20 over that of 25 among this age group).

28. Among the "young couples" (husbands younger than thirty), the proportion of age "inversions" is 14.5 percent. Amounting to 20 percent among men in their thirties, it drops to 10 percent for men in their forties and fifties. Indeed, those men who, at the time of their first and belated marriage—that is, at about the age of thirty—had married an "old woman," usually married very young girls upon the death of their first wife. Nonetheless, in eighteenth-century Lyons, charivaris were still made against couples who disregarded the matrimonial custom, despite the relatively high incidence of "inverted" marriages (see Maurice Garden, *Lyon et les Lyonnais au XVIIIᵉ siècle* (Paris, 1970).

29. An analysis involving 204 couples shows that in the first half of the sixteenth century, "age-inverted" couples represented only 15 percent of the total number of marriages, which is a very small increase over the fifteenth century. However, in this group 31 percent of the husbands under thirty were married to a woman older than themselves. The one noticeable change in matrimonial customs thus concerns first marriages only.

30. Desportes, "La population de Reims," p. 501, gives an approximate average of 10 years, which would mean that age differentials were even more pronounced at Reims than at

Dijon. For Florence, see David Herlihy, "Vieillir à Florence au Quattrocento," *Annales, E.S.C.* 24 (October–November 1969): 1341.

31. In this respect, there was no difference between the customs of the rich and those of the poor. A number of reasons for this situation can be advanced: To the attraction of a youthful woman was added a concern for security, not only for the husband, who thus "insured" his old age, but also for the young woman who—provided she had a choice—may have opted for a mature man, not because he was likely to offer her a better "position" than a young man, but because he was a safer prospect, being further removed from the "follies" of youth. Indeed, this behavior may have had its roots in even deeper considerations, for at that time the ages of life were perceived differently for men and women. Eustache Deschamps in his *Miroir de Mariage* points out that old age in women begins at thirty, but at fifty in men (cited in Johann Huizinga, *The Waning of the Middle Ages* [New York, 1954], p. 35).

32. A word of caution against contrasting the village too sharply with the city when dealing with the behavior of youth groups: There is no question that in the village the "pool" of women was small, while it was large in the city. Nonetheless, the young city dwellers were bound to feel the effect of the tapping of that pool by their elders; after all, at least one girl in four was taken away from those who were her legitimate suitors in terms of age.

33. See Philippe Ariès, *L'enfant et la vie familiale sous l'Ancien Régime,* 2d ed. (Paris, 1972), p. vii [English translation by Robert Baldick, *Centuries of Childhood,* New York, 1962], and, also by Ariès, *La France et les Français* (Paris, 1972), p. 872. See also Paul Veyne, *Comment on écrit l'histoire* (Paris, 1971), p. 236.

34. B. Geremek, *Le salariat dans l'artisanat parisien aux XIIIe-XVe siècles* (Paris, 1968), p. 32–25. Natalie Zemon Davis, "City Women and Religious Change in Sixteenth-Century France," in *A Sampler of Women's Studies,* ed. Dorothy McGuignan, (Ann Arbor, 1973), reedited as chap. 3 in N. Z. Davis, *Society and Culture in Early Modern France* (Stanford, 1975); N. S. Eisenstadt, *From Generation to Generation; Age Groups and Social Structure* (Glencoe, Ill., 1956).

35. Herlihy, "Vieillir à Florence," p. 1345.

36. Structure of these groups:

1. *Homogeneity in age.* The fifteen groups that lend themselves to an analysis date from the first half of the sixteenth century; but we know that there was no change in the age at marriage between 1450 and 1500. I define a group as homogeneous when more than half of the individuals composing it show only age differentials of less than five years.

2. *Socio-occupational structure.* Among the thirty-four groups of the fifteenth century we find pronounced homogeneity in twenty-five (sons of workers in the same occupation or sons of men of the same social standing), some homogeneity in eight (clerks and sons of shopkeepers, together with a majority of sons of artisans), and little or no homogeneity in one group (domestic servants, soldiers, artisans, workers, etc.). In the first half of the sixteenth century, the respective figures for a total of thirty-three groups studied are twenty-three, eight, and two.

3. *Size.* In the fifteenth century, fifty-four (of a total of ninety-eight) consisted of three to five participants.

37. Publication no. 15 in the series *Déviance et contrôle social* is entitled *Image du viol collectif et reconstruction d'objet* (Paris, 1974). Written by a team of researchers of the chancellery and the University of Bordeaux, this is a socio-criminological analysis of rape, its meaning in contemporary societies, and a survey of the current literature on adolescent gangs.

38. The figure of the cock, which dominates every carnival parade (see below, n.88) is also found in literature. In about 1460 even so amiable and placid a man as the Lyons shopkeeper F. Garin could include this statement in the instructions to his son: "When a woman lords it over a man, the man is not worth much; a good cock is master of the hen." (see R. Fédou, "Le legs du moyen âge à l'humanisme lyonnais," in *L'humanisme lyonnais au XVIe siècle* [Grenoble, 1974], p. 12.)

39. I base the following statement on the number of young men between the ages of eighteen and twenty-four in a city comparable to Dijon, namely, Reims. In 1422, out of a total population of almost ten thousand, that category included seven hundred and fifty individuals. At Dijon, at least seven hundred were involved in such affairs over a seven-year period. Subtracting the categories mentioned earlier, this leaves us with three hundred fifty to four hundred unmarried

men. But this still does not explain such unlawful forms of collective behavior. Was the law really unable to prevent these occurrences in all cases? The enforcement of sexual morality within the urban community was incumbent upon the authorities. Whenever the conduct of a woman was considered particularly scandalous (blatant adultery or outrageous concubinage), it was perfectly legal for the aldermen, accompanied by a police patrol, to surprise the guilty parties in their bedroom and to fine them (examples in A.M., Dijon, B 157, f⁰ 161 v⁰, 1447; or A.D., Côte-d'Or, B 11 360-8, p. 22, 1461; or A.M., Dijon, series M, *Amendes de nuit*). Indeed, women who refused to heed official warnings and who lacked effective protection might be publicly conveyed to the brothel by the authorities (A.D., Côte-d'Or, B 11 336-63, f⁰ 98; and A.M., Dijon, B 161, f⁰ 110 v⁰). Nor should we forget that the perfectly "legal" charivaris and parades on the ass, though free of physical violence, nonetheless bore the stamp of an extraordinary moral violence. Many of these "vice-squad" types of activity were delegated to the confraternities of youths by the judicial authorities, and sometimes even to informal bands of youths who asked the mayor's permission to catch a specific individual living in concubinage—usually a priest—and his mistress "in the act" in order to collect a fine or to go after the girl (A.D., Côte-d'Or, B 11 360-2 item 150, 1450). Such delegated authority often ended in violence pure and simple. But above all—and without prompting, let alone permission of the authorities—these youthful bands made it their business to ransom lovers caught in amorous pursuit, to lie in wait for the priest's concubine, and to "knock at the door" of "engaged couples." It was therefore easy for them to put a "legitimate" face on any plot to lay hands on a girl who had aroused their desire. Thus, one may conclude that the phenomenon of collective rape was located in the border area between culture and subculture.

All these acts of violence committed without delegated authority were prosecuted; but unless such an act was perpetrated against a married lady of Dijon or a little girl, rape did not entail severe punishment. The steps taken to curb such behavior could hardly qualify as deterrents. Once the guilty parties were identified (and this was not always possible), they were taken to prison. If the victim withdrew the charges (and for the obvious reasons I have already set forth, this was not rare), the aggressors were set free at once. If the charges were pressed, the aggressors were usually set free on bail, to be fined later in keeping with their ability to pay and in proportion to the victim's reputation and social standing. Those who were too poor to pay were given a "long prison term" (usually amounting to several weeks rather than several months) or a whipping; and sometimes—if they were outsiders—they were banished.

Lastly, the competition between various jurisdictions and the appeal proceedings before a higher court also tended to temper the efforts of the public prosecutor and the mayor. For it was in the interest of the urban authorities to stretch the judicial privileges of the inhabitants as far as possible—even if this meant toning down a criminal case to a civil offense—in order to avoid handing over the accused or his property to ducal justice. On the other hand, a sizable number of offenders was pardoned by the Duke. Many townspeople claimed to be subject to the jurisdiction of Monseigneur [the bishop] of Langres, and in a strange way the privileges of clerical status seem to have been extended to hosiers, butchers, and yarn bundlers. Moreover, it was customary to free prisoners whenever a prince of the royal house made his first formal entry (all criminals were pardoned, except those imprisoned for debt). This happened seven times between 1450 and 1475.

Since the social reaction to rape was rarely favorable to the victim, a young citizen of Dijon could rape a girl without being cast in the role of delinquent or even being considered a "bad lot." The son of an artisan might commit several rapes and armed assaults and become involved in innumerable brawls before the mayor finally decided to banish him for a time. As for the sons of notables, the cruel games of their youth did not jeopardize their "careers" in the slightest, and they lived out their lives in the city as honored members of the community.

40. The testimonies of both victims and offenders provide a glimpse of this resentment against the "haves." The bachelors knew very well that young and pretty servant girls were often "kept" by their master or his sons. We often hear of chambermaids, made pregnant by their master, who received a compensation and were married to another man. G. Robelin, a butcher's assistant, told a girl that "her master was keeping her" and that he, too, would "have his pleasure with her" (A.D., Côte-d'Or, B 11, 360-4, item 364, 1449). A weaver's son, speaking to a certain Jacquette, age twenty-two, servant in the household of a bachelor of law, told her: "I must work you over, just as the others work you over" (A.D., Côte-d'Or, B 11 360-31, 1533). Two

journeymen-masons accosted the niece of the viscount-mayor in the street (she was sixteen and her conduct was above reproach): "We will f—— you; we can f—— you as well as anybody" (ibid., B 11 360-18, 1505). Bitterness is also expressed against young men of sufficient means to keep a servant-girl. Mongin, an unmarried carpenter, had one, and six of his fellows tried to take her by force (ibid., B 11 360-5, p. 619, 1454). Of one pregnant woman, widowed and working for a priest, they said: "We are going to get our share of her, just like those priests" (ibid., B 11 360-7, p. 817, 1458). A woman whose husband, working out of town, had left her for a few days, was told that she had to "give pleasure to the fellows, to them too, and that they would pay" (ibid., B 11 360-11, 1471). Widows were solicited in the same manner (ibid., B 11 360-13, 1479).

41. Natalie Z. Davis, "The Reasons of Misrule, Youth Groups, and Charivaries in Sixteenth-Century France," *Past and Present* 50 (1971): 41–75. My own conclusions concerning the youth groups will be further developed in *Cahiers d'Histoire* 1 (1976).

42. Nor could it be otherwise in a city where "congresses" of any kind were looked upon with suspicion. Why, a group of men could be fined for holding a bowling contest without the proper authorization! (A.M., Dijon, B 157, f° 99 v°, Oct. 1445).

43. Gerson, for instance, was in favor of the "Fool's Day," which "gave the people a chance to let off steam, just as we open up the new wine to prevent the cask from bursting" (cited in C. Gaignebet and C. M. Florentin, *Le Carnaval* [Paris, 1974], p. 44). Many notables were aware of the "therapeutic" value of popular festivities, and my own observation of the pattern of distribution of rape throughout the year seems to corroborate their views. However, it is obvious that participation in a charivari could not possibly constitute a "rite of passage" for a young man, as C. Gauvard and A. Gokalb claim ("Le charivari en France au Moyen Age," *Annales, E.S.C.* 29 [May–June 1974]:704), since people of all ages participated in these noisy gatherings along with the young and since no real test was involved for any of the participants.

44. The youth abbot was assisted by four priors at Beaucaire (two for the bachelors, two for the married men), see A.M., Beaucaire, BB 4, f° 63 v°, 1515, etc. Thus, only a fraction of the married men—very probably the youngest—was represented. This was already the case at the end of the fourteenth and the beginning of the fifteenth century (see Vaultier, *Folklore*, pp. xvii, xviii, 55).

45. The same thing is true for the "boon companions" and the "goodly dames", etc.

46. All of this is reminiscent of the situation described by P. Vidal-Nacquet in "Le Philoctète de Sophocle et l'éphébie," *Annales, E.S.C.* 26 (May–June 1971): 623–38.

47. Natalie Z. Davis has rightly pointed out that the bachelors' association of the village acted as a vehicle for the transmission of a whole set of traditions. Veyne (*Comment on écrit l'histoire*, p. 236) is partially correct. These young people were indeed acting as faithful guardians, though not of a ritual but of a moral code. Acts of aggression were almost always committed in the name of "matrimonial morality," and charivaris and parades on the ass castigated unfit brides-to-be or wayward wives. But then, the bachelors realized that their youth would not last forever, and all of them knew that some day they would benefit from such customs.

48. This cultural image is implied in M. Bakhtin, *L'oeuvre de Rabelais et la culture populaire au Moyen Age et sous la Renaissance* (Paris, 1970) and, to a lesser extent, in Gaignebet and Florentin, *Le Carnaval*.

49. For example, A.D., Côte-d'Or, B 11 360-3, p. 242, 1444; B 11 360-12, 1473; B 11 360-18, 1504.

50. For the fifteenth century we know the ages of 40 victims. For the servant girls among them, the average age was 17; for unmarried girls it was 20; for women living alone due to widowhood or separation it was 25. There is only one aberrant case, where the victim was 47 years old. (For the first half of the sixteenth century we have 47 examples, the average age being 22.5 years.)

Civil status: In the 101 cases known to us, 18 are servant girls, 14 unmarried girls, 14 widows, 13 temporarily "deserted," 3 separated from their husbands, 8 living with their husbands, 9 temporary visitors, 6 of unknown status. Twelve of the victims had led truly "disreputable" lives before the rape.

Family ties: In 95 cases providing sufficient information, 50 women have either a husband, an uncle, their parents, or their brothers living in town; the rest are working away from their families. Information for occupational background of the family exists in 64 cases. Eighteen were daughters of domestic servants; 31 daughters or wives of laborers in the fulling, weaving, or vinedressing trade; 3 were daughters or wives of master artisans, 3 of municipal watchmen or messengers, 4 of archers or garrisoned soldiers, and one was the widow of a shopkeeper.

51. The following judgment made by one woman about another is revealing indeed: "The said Jacote is a woman who was never married and whose conduct is not good" (A.D., Côte-d'Or, B 11 360-16, 1494). Equally revealing, because it shows how pervasive and internalized the dominant morality could become, is the deposition of a tailor's wife, who was attacked in the street by three bachelors and would have been raped had it not been for her resistance and the help of her maid-servant: "even though she was *as respectable as she could be in her estate*" (A.D., Côte-d'Or, B 11 360-20, 1509). The notables were always ready to see a natural connection between "modest estate" and "bad conduct" (ibid., B 11 360-2, p. 153, 1432).

52. For an example of a woman separated from her husband by mutual consent, see B 11 360-5, p. 627, 1454; for a woman who had left her husband, B 11 360-8, p. 35, 1461. For wives who, even when their husbands were present, visited too often with other couples, see B 11 360-3, 1442. One woman, the wife of a carpenter, was raped "because she was ribald, laughed a lot," and called out to people in the street, even by name (B 11 360-3, p. 317, 1447). There was trouble for women who left the house at night, even in the company of a kinsman, for this was no time "for women to be out in the town" (B 11 360-14, 1485 or B 11 360-5, 1453, or B 11 360-5, p. 607, 1453, or B 11 360-9, 1464). There is no better way to illustrate the vulnerable position of young female newcomers than to tell the sad story of Jeanne, age fifteen. She had left the employ of her masters, who ran a cookshop, where she had been raped by one of the servants. Boarding with a local woman, she earned her living by day labor, either in the fields or in town, and this life pleased her, because it was easier than domestic service. But there were days when she could not find work, and "when it became known that she went back and forth and had nothing to do, *the young men of the town began to chase her, and they harried her so much that she gave up and let them use her body for their pleasure*" (B 11 360-17, 1492).

53. This is why families were reluctant to lodge a complaint. Here are two telling cases: In July 1425, a domestic servant committed a sexual misdemeanor involving Regnaulde, a girl of ten; it was not a rape but a most offensive gesture. He was sentenced to a public whipping on market day. The parents of the victim asked (and obtained) that the sentence not be executed, "in order not to dishonor the said Regnaulde" (A.M., Dijon, B 151, f⁰ 54 v⁰). In 1455, when a certain young woman was suborned to prostitution by her mother-in-law, the older woman was banished, but not whipped, for the judges feared that "in that case the son would have abandoned his wife" (B 11 360-6, item 676).

54. There are many examples of this attitude. One woman, pregnant as a result of rape by a group of archers from Picardy against whom the city instituted legal proceedings, did not admit that she had been raped; but she revoked her original deposition after the delivery, saying that she had not told the truth "out of shame" (B 11 360-12, 1473). Another woman settled her case out of court, "fearing that legal proceedings would ruin her good name" (B 11 360-9, 1464). Catherine, a young woman of twenty-six, knew that the duke's archers, who had been on a wild rampage for several days, were planning to take her to the brothel. So she went there of her own accord "so that she would not be dragged there in a more disgraceful manner and in order not to scandalize the neighbors" (B 11 360-6, p. 772, 1457).

And here are some reactions of the neighborhood: in December 1483, Jeannette, who for two years had been a good servant in a locksmith's household, was raped by a youthful band; "everyone was so afraid that none dared take in the said Jeannette, not even her former masters" (B 11 360-14). In 1527, the mother of one of the victims wanted to take the girl away from Dijon for, as she said, "she would never regain her honor in this town" (B 11 360-29). In the same year, a servant girl was attacked and insulted by three bachelors; when she complained about it to her mistress, she was given notice, for "if she was accused of such bad things, she [the employer] was not about to keep her, unless she was given convincing proof indicating whether the girl was a respectable person or a nasty hussy" (B 11 360-29).

Saint Thomas had suggested the possible consequences of illicit sexual acts, and of course his interpretation reflected the views of female sexuality current in his day. He felt that if the seducer did not make amends by marrying the person he had seduced, such a woman's chances of marriage would be greatly reduced. Once her natural modesty had been broken down, it would be easier to induce her into debauchery.

55. Complaints concerning his activities were lodged in 1444 (A.M., Tarascon, BB 7, f⁰ 183 v⁰), in 1470 (BB 10, f⁰ 63), in 1473 (ibid., f⁰ 134 v⁰), etc. At Beaucaire, the subviguier was "unlettered, leading a disreputable life, spending his time with ruffians and pimps" (A.M., Beaucaire, BB 2, f⁰ 112 v⁰, 1495). At Avignon, Lyons, and Dijon, we hear of "sergeants" keeping rooms for the purpose of prostitution and running bathhouses.

56. Cf. J. Bailbé, "Le thème de la vieille femme dans la poésie satirique du XVIᵉ et du début du XVIIᵉ siècle," *Bibliothèque Humanisme et Renaissance, Travaux et documents* vol. 26 (1964): 98–119. The same image is found in Villon's poetry and in the *soties*.

57. Of the seventy-five procuresses, eight are presented by name only, forty-one are identified as married, fourteen as living with a man or engaged to be married, and twelve as widows.

58. Examples to be found in A.D., Côte-d'Or, B 11 360–5, p. 584; B 11 360–8; B 11 360–14, etc.

59. For Jeanne Saignant as protégée over many years of J. Coustain, first valet to Duke Philip the Good, see Garnier, *Les étuves dijonnaises,* and A.D., Côte-d'Or, B 11 360–8, item 986.

60. To be sure, protests against the activities of pimps are sometimes found in the deliberations of the town councils, but these individuals are usually identified as vagrants from the outside and idlers (see for example A.M., Valence, CC, 31 June 1483; A.M., Arles, BB 2, f⁰ 93 v⁰, 1435; A.M. Tarascon, BB 12, f⁰ 226 v⁰, 1507). For the "Coquille," see J. Garnier, *Les compagnons de la Coquille* (Dijon, 1842).

61. The figures concerning the public and clandestine prostitutes of Dijon between 1440 and 1540 that I am using here necessarily reflect the manner in which prostitutes presented themselves and such information as was given by the officers of justice. My conclusions are based on the brief autobiographical statements that were part of every interrogation and on the testimony given by other citizens of Dijon.

Place of origin. Sample, 146 cases. Thirty-eight were from Dijon, 45 from the Burgundian countryside, 63 from farther away. On the basis of the 123 cases containing information on this point, it appears vhat 21 prostitutes came from a big city, 23 from a village, and the vast majority from middle-sized towns or small market towns.

Stability [of residence]. Sample, 130 cases. Sixty-nine living permanently in Dijon, 42 fairly stable (chambermaids or domestic servants, employed in the same place for more than six months), 19 vagrants or temporary visitors.

Marital status. Sample, 136 cases. Sixty percent unmarried, 32 percent married, 8 percent widowed. However, only 20 percent of the inmates of the public brothels admitted to having been married.

Family circumstances. Sample, 96 cases. The father was living in two-thirds of the cases, the mother in almost one-half. Less than one-third of the prostitutes had lost both mother and father by death.

Social standing. Sample, 61 cases. Less than one-fourth were daughters of wholesale merchants or well-to-do people. The others were in equal proportion daughters of artisans and peasants. However, among those who were married, two out of three were wives of journeymen-artisans and common laborers.

Reasons for prostitution. Sample, 77 cases. Twelve were pushed into prostitution by their mother-in-law, stepfather, mother, or close relative (uncle, aunt); 8 had come to it as a result of conflict with their family, 8 because of poverty, 17 following a case of procuring compounded by violence, 21 as a result of rape. Only 11 stated that they had freely chosen this profession.

Age at entry into prostitution. Sample, 48 cases. The average age was 17 years.

62. Cf. Pansier and Girard, *La cour temporelle,* p. 196; also A.D., Côte-d'Or, B 11 360–12, 1475.

63. The averages were arrived at on the basis of thirty-nine cases for public prostitutes, ten cases for prostitutes serving in bathhouses, and nineteen cases for clandestine prostitutes. For the sixteenth century, a sample of thirty-seven cases in which the average age is twenty-four years, ten months, indicates a definite decline in the age of public prostitutes. A number of individual examples corroborate the trend of these age averages. Jeanne la Rousse, for instance, had left her parental home at sixteen, first lived with some priests, then exercised her profession in a room of her own, and finally became an inmate of the brothel of Troyes (B 11 360–26). One of the sentences handed down by the mayor of Dijon mentions Simone Plateau, who began as a concubine, then became a clandestine prostitute, and finally ended up in the Grande Maison.

64. This was clearly the case also at Villefranche-sur-Saône, Avignon, Beaucaire, and Taras-con. At Dijon, fifty-five of the public brothel's sixty-six inmates came from distant regions, with twenty-six among them originating in a rural or urban milieu of northeastern France. This vagabond existence is well depicted in the confession of Jeanne d'Arras (A.D., B 11 360–18), who in four years went from Arras to Amiens, then to Lille, Douai, Thérouanne, Mex, Pont-à-Mousson, Neufchâtel, and Nancy; she was only twenty-two years old when she settled down at Dijon in 1504. Instances of *"compagnonnage"*: five common prostitutes left the brothel of Verdun together to "do" the harvest season in Burgundy before going into another town (B 11 360-33, 1542). At Dijon in 1433 a common prostitute was punished for having told a woman that, since she was "of the profession," she was expected to give the prostitutes "their wine." This was an equivalent of the "welcome," which the journeymen of Dijon exacted from traveling journeymen who came to work in their town (B 11 336–45, f° 219). The expression "house-mother of the whores" was used by a journeyman from Lille (B 11 360–19, 1528).

65. They paid rent and a fee for police protection (A.M., Dijon, I 142, 1434) and were exempt from the *taille* (ibid.) at Dijon as at Besançon (see Lacassagne, *Vieilles étuves*). They took their meals either at the grande Maison or at the tavern (A. M., Dijon, K 83 and A.D., Côte-d'Or, B 11 360-7, item 964). On singing in the streets at night, see Vaultier, *Folklore,* p. 218, and A. Eyssette, *Histoire administrative de Beaucaire depuis le XIIIᵉ siècle* (Beaucaire, 1884, 1889), 2: 284. Felix Platter describes the prostitutes' rich accoutrements and the tricks they used to entice the boys into the prostibulum.

A girl usually stayed with a client for half an hour. This was the length of time prostitutes or brothel keepers always advanced as proof that the "contract" had been honored whenever they appealed to the authorities for help in getting a young man to vacate the premises (A.D., Côte-d'Or, B 11 360–4, 1450, and B 11 360–8, 1462; also A.M., Lyons, FF Chappe inv., XIII 62/67). It is known that candles were used to measure the time and that in Italy, prostitutes were called "candle dames."

As far as the prices charged are concerned, it is obviously rash to name figures that would apply to all cases. But it seems that in the fifteenth century the sum of one blanc was customary for the most summary service (A.D., Côte-d'Or, B 11 360-2, p. 115, 1433; B 11 360-5, 1454; B 11 360-10, 1467). In June 1462, women were paid 2 blancs for a day's work in the vineyards, while clandestine prostitutes of fifteen to seventeen years were paid 2 to 6 blancs (B 11 360-11, 1469 and B 11 360-14, 1480). At the bathhouse of Saint-Philibert, a group of boon companions—who had also feasted there—gave Jeanne Saignant 3 or 4 gros for a "big evening" (B 11 360-8, p. 986). Sometimes the prostitutes agreed to be paid in kind, with a dinner, for example (B 11 360-17, 1500).

66. The prostitutes' rooms were heated, and some of the young fellows would come in to warm themselves and to chat (B 11 360-10, 1467 and B 11 360-23, 1515).

67. Except in ports, such as Arles, we rarely hear of provocative behavior. In May 1501 at Valence, a group of *meretrices* made an indecent spectacle of themselves in the presence of innocent girls on the way to the washhouse (A.M., Valence, BB 3, f° 21). As for their own feelings about their profession, one of them said about the woman who had "got her into it" that she would "curse her as long as she lived" (A.D., Côte-d'Or, B 11 360-5, p. 533, 1452); another said that she had been "dragged into evil" (B 11 360-18), and a third, a woman of thirty, called out to a "little wench of thirteen" that "if she knew that she was already a bawd, she would wring her neck right now" (B 11 360-31, 1532). On the other hand, one common prostitute who was dressed down as a "lewd harlot" by a patrician lady answered back that she was "no worse than she" (B 11 360-18, 1505). In only one of the five extant testaments of the prostitutes of Beaucaire-Tarascon do I find any expression of concern about the suffering in hell that might be in store for those who had led a life of debauchery (A.D., Gard, Notaires de Beaucaire, 2 E 18–31).

68. In the fifteenth century, seven of the forty-seven inmates of the brothel of Dijon whose age is known to us were 30 years old, the youngest being 27 and the average age being 27.9 years. For the sixteenth century (until 1542), we have data for forty-one cases. Here three of the inmates gave their age as over 30, and the youngest as 16. The average age is 24 years, 10 months. The appreciable decrease in the age of the public prostitutes may be the result of a more effective enforcement of the rules against clandestine prostitution and perhaps also of the deterioration in working conditions for women.

69. In their late-fifteenth-century version, the statutes governing admission to the home for repentant Magdalens of Avignon make spicy reading indeed: "Under no circumstances shall admission be granted to anyone but young women of twenty-five who in their youth had taken pleasure in lewdness and who, by dint of their comeliness and pulchritude might still, owing to the weakness that pervades this world, be ready and willing to partake of such sensual delights as will attract and utterly ensnare men" (see Pansier, *Oeuvres des repenties,* p. 40). At Lyons, the Great Hospice had room for only twenty-five repentant Magdalens (A.M., Lyons, BB 25, f° 206 v°, Dec. 1507, which cites older regulations).

70. Many examples of prostitutes whose marriages were sponsored by the consulate or the neighborhood charities can be found in Pansier, *Oeuvres des repenties,* 3: 18, 19, and 4: 19; in one of these cases, the document cited expressly states that the prostitute will become a respectable woman. At Beaucaire, a plowman married a prostitute from the brothel; here too, the notarized marriage contract specified her status (A.D., Gard, Notaires de Beaucaire, 2 E 18–82, Nov. 1480). At Dijon, one of the inmates of the Grande Maison was betrothed before Easter, and "we hope that she will be married within a week and thus become a respectable woman." Lacroix-Dufour, *Histoire de la prostitution,* 4: 38, cites a reaffirmation of the statutes of the main meat market (Grande Boucherie) of Paris (1381), a statute forbidding apprentices of that trade to marry a woman who had been, or still was, a public prostitute. However, if one of them did marry such a woman, he would be barred from the main meat market but permitted to cut meat in one of the little stalls of the Petit Pont. Clearly, such cases were by no means unusual.

71. A.M., Lyons, FF, Chappe inv. XIII, 62/67, 1478. Who were the clients of the prostibulum of Dijon? For the period 1442–92, 107 individuals can be identified with respect to their occupations, and 28 occupations are represented. Outsiders—and this category also includes domestic servants, soldiers, and paupers—account for only slightly over one-fourth of this population (by the beginning of the sixteenth century, 19 out of a total of 63 clients fall into this category). As for their social standing, 47 were artisans or common laborers, 11 were merchants or practiced one of the "better" professions, 9 were clerks in the Church or in the courts, 10 were domestic servants, 5 were soldiers, and 5 were paupers. From this we may conclude that the municipal brothel was neither the haunt of tramps and paupers, nor a haven for the well-to-do clientele, which accounted for less than 30 percent of the total.

72. A.M. Lyons, FF, Chappe inv. XIII, 62/67. Also A.D., Côte-d'Or, B 11 360–8, pp. 37 and 986; hearings in the proceedings against Jeanne Saignant in 1461 and 1464; and B 11 360–6, item 772, 1457; B 11 360–19, 1508, etc.

73. Character evaluation by the public prosecutor who made this statement when investigating a young man who had witnessed a brawl in the Grande Maison (A.D., Côte-d'Or, B 11 360–15, 1490).

74. B 11 360–6, item 772, April 1457, and B 11 360–15, 1490.

75. B 11 360–6, item 772.

76. At Tarascon, the abbess was fined 48 s.cor., and a certain E. Gras, a married man, was fined 75 s.cor. (A.D., Bouches-du-Rhône, B 2043, 1477). Since we do not know the details of this offense, however, it would be premature to conclude that such severity was customary.

77. The mayor's office of Dijon accused the police chief, Richard Faultrey, of overstepping his responsibilities under the customary law when he inspected the rooms of the prostibulum and made the prostitutes pay "one a gros and the other three gros, on the grounds that they were harboring married men, priests, or clerics; a matter over which the said police chief of the said place has no jurisdiction unless there is a plaintiff" (A.D., Côte-d'Or, B 11 360–8, Nov. 1463).

78. A.D., Côte-d'Or, B 11 360–10. They were in the company of other married men who were not prosecuted.

79. The rare occasions when the patrol inspected the bathhouse had no untoward consequences for the clients. Thus, according to his own testimony, O. Fremyot, the alderman who was in charge of the patrol, had gone into the bathhouse of Saint-Philibert on several occasions "without, however, inconveniencing anyone, even though he had noted the presence of priests and married men and women at times when they were not supposed to be there" (B 11 360–8, f 2, 1463). In 1467, charges were brought against the deputy police chief on the grounds of brutal conduct in the bathhouse kept by Marion La Liégeoise (B11 360–10, Nov. 1467).

80. The average age of the clients of the bathhouse (27 cases) was thirty years, three months; that of the clients of the prostibulum was only twenty-seven. Among the 104 clients of the

bathhouse (between 1440 and 1550), there were 24 clerks of the court and men of the law, 21 ecclesiastics, 18 artisans, 17 journeymen, 11 merchants and "bourgeois," 5 high officials of the ducal or royal government, 5 domestic servants in noble houses, and 3 soldiers. In other words, two-thirds of these clients belonged to a well-to-do milieu; which is the exact reverse of the clientele of the prostibulum. As for the private brothel-keeping operations, the public prosecutor had to admit that they "afford an opportunity to highly placed personages, who are not anxious to become involved in wrongdoing" (B 11 36–15, 1486).

81. The situation seems to have been the same at Lyons. For Dijon, I shall cite only a few of the more revealing examples. Priests were unconcerned about the scandal of their presence in the brothel (B 11 360–4, item 359, 1449); the chaplain of Mgr. le Maréchal was found at the brothel (B 11 360–6, p. 783, 1457); priests as perpetrators of nocturnal rapes (B 11 360–12, 1475, etc.); in June 1502, the aldermen claimed that the abbot of Saint-Etienne had been involved in several nightly "insolences," armed and in disguise (A.M., Dijon, B 168, f⁰ 51); the attorney of Monsieur [the bishop] of Langres defended the fornicators of his jurisdiction against the mayor of Dijon (A.M., Dijon, B 157, f⁰ 161 v⁰, 1447), while the assistant to the vicar-general lived in concubinage at the residence of the Cathedral Chapter (B 11 360–11, 1469) and Messire le Promoteur kept whores in his house (B 11 360–18, 1506), etc. Public opinion was particularly exercised about ecclesiastics who summoned married women to their houses (B 11 360–8, 1463, B 11 360–13, 1476, etc.).

82. This term was used by the prostitutes themselves, by the townspeople, and by the authorities.

83. I do not mean to play the devil's advocate here, nor am I particularly fond of paradoxes. Nonetheless, I have to record a number of interrelated facts. First, given the brutal behavior and the moral standards of the time, the brothel served to prevent even greater insecurity. For example, on the eve of Saint Catherine's Day, 1439, three boon companions "were looking for a priest's woman to have some fun with" (and we know what that meant). However, one of them had been caught in such an act once before, so they decided to betake themselves to the rue des Grands Champs (to the prostibulum) instead. They later engaged in some horseplay that did not hurt anyone but still led to an investigation (B 11 360–2, item 149, 1439).

Second, during the proceedings against the bathhouse of La Pêcherie at Lyons, the defense made it a point to explain that bathhouses were permitted both by the ordinances of the kings of France and by the good cities of the realm "ad evitandum majus malum" and that their existence was the reason why "no attempts were made to corrupt good girls and respectable women." And in 1535, that is, at a time when the authorities and public opinion were beginning to judge prostitution more severely, the governors of Besançon promulgated an ordinance concerning houses of prostitution and bathhouses that expressly stated that "as a precaution against the depredations of youth and in order to prevent greater evil, houses of ill-repute are tolerated by the Church" (Le Pileur, La prostitution, p. 109). It seems to me that in all these justifications the idea that prostitution limits the number of adulterous women weighed most heavily. Indeed, in terms of social morality, adultery committed by a woman was one of the most serious crimes. That is why I do believe that a married man's dealings with a prostitute constituted a lesser evil for the community.

84. Concerning "raids" by public prostitutes on clandestine prostitutes, see A.D., Côte-d'Or, B 11 360–5, p. 633, 1454; B 11 360–8, p. 986, 1460; B 11 360–9, 1465; B 11 360–15, 1489, etc. Needless to say, the number of "raids" depended on the prosperity of the "profession-als." Always more frequent in bad years, such actions became more prevalent in the sixteenth century, as clandestine prostitution was increasingly frowned upon.

85. Cassotte Cristal's husband was provost of the workers of the mint at Dijon; Jeanne Saignant's brother was a priest. The notaries of Tarascon and Beaucaire were often called into the prostibulum to draw up a contract; some of them even derived an income from that institution (A.D., Bouches-du-Rhône, Notaires Tarascon, Muratoris 395 E 14, f⁰ 616, 1436). Every year on Charity Day, the inmates of the house of prostitution of Nîmes officially betook themselves to the consuls in order to present them with a sweet bread for the poor. The first consul would kiss the abbess and give her a return gift of some wine or a sum of money (A.M., Nîmes, RR 5, inv. ms). At Alès, the lease of the brothel specified that the leasee was to engage "comely and pleasant whore-girls" or else "comely and enticing partners in wantonness" (A.M., Alais, inv. ms. Bardon, vol. 2, pp. 553 and 683). On Saint Bartholomew's Day the town of Pernes arranged

prize-games featuring, between the archery contest and the children's running match, the race of the public prostitutes (A.M., Pernes, inv. ms. CC 27). As for the ceremonial entries of the princes, we know that they included living tableaus, in which nude girls represented allegories of Truth, the Graces, and so forth. Obviously, those who displayed their charms in this manner were not young patricians, or even the daughters of artisans. Other public responsibilities were similar in most places. At Toulouse, Besançon, and Amiens, for example, public prostitutes were supposed to be on the lookout for fire (just as they were helping to prevent the fire of lewdness from spreading).

86. Aside from the measures taken in truly calamitous years—when tramps, debauchers, and prostitutes were thrown out indiscriminately—and not counting the half-hearted attention given to various prohibitions during Lent, serious attempts at "cleaning up" a town were made only after major religious events—which, incidentally, by no means affected sexual behavior only. Thus, at Dijon, the Lenten preaching of 1426 by the "notable preacher and excellent good man J. Foucauld of the Cordeliers" really aroused the aldermen. Brother Foucauld wanted to keep the *meretrices* away from the youths and "confine" the common prostitutes; but he also wanted to prohibit blasphemy and swearing, drive the hucksters out of the cemeteries, abolish the holding of markets on holy days, and so forth (A.M., Dijon, B 151, f° 64 v°, 19 March 1426). The first proceedings against Jeanne Saignant (B 11 360-8, p. 986) were launched shortly after a general meeting of the preaching orders was held at Dijon.

87. "Marguerite, keeper of la Muraille," stayed in the procuring business for ten years (B 11 360-5, p. 533), J. de Bouchaud continued for eleven years (B 11 360-4 and B 11 360-9), Marie du Château continued for more than thirteen years (A.M., Dijon, B 166, f° 81 v°, and B 167 f° 16 v°). P. Bouju (implicated in several cases of rape) and his wife stayed in business for a dozen years (A.M., Dijon, B 166, f° 141). Let us not miss the implications of the statement that in 1488 one procuress was banished for five years "because this time she has taken advantage of her niece and [because] moreover she was wont to do this despite repeated warnings" (B 11 337-4). At Tarascon, a "drunken old woman" accused of the same iniquities was reported to the consulate in 1467 (A.M., Tarascon, BB 9, f° 283), but she turns up in the documents again in 1472-73 (A.D., Bouches-du-Rhône, B 2043, f° 7 v°), etc.

88. L. Petit de Juleville, *Les comédiens en France au Moyen Age* (Paris, 1885), p. 141. I shall comment on the drawing of the carnival parade of the King of Love of Dijon in *Cahiers d'Histoire,* 1976 (1. issue).

89. In 1497, a group of law clerks and other young men of Dijon performed *L'hystoire du roy Assuaire et la royne Ester;* in 1509, they performed the *Jeu de la Ste. Suzanne* in the place Saint-Michel (A.M., Dijon, B 131). Such plays lent themselves to racy allusions about old men carrying off young virgins.

90. Cf. J.-L. Flandrin, *L'Eglise et le contrôle des naissances* (Paris, 1970), pp. 55-68, and John T. Noonan, *Contraception: A History of Its Treatment by the Catholic Theologians and Canonists* (Cambridge, Mass., 1966).

91. Fornication, to be sure, was never condoned by the Church, but we do know that this question was discussed by the Councils of Vienna and Basel.

92. A.D., Côte-d'Or, B 11 360-9, 1465. The assertion was made by a master carpenter. As for the epithet "jacobine," it was in current use at the time.

93. Cited in E. Sullerot, *Histoire et mythologie de l'amour* (Paris, 1974), p. 78.

94. These words of Guillemette, a vineyard worker's wife (B 11 360-11, 1471) show that the social image of the wife was very well internalized by those who had to play that role. For further examples of female submission to the model, see B 11 360-11, 1469.

95. The first evidence that women—with or without their husbands—took part in nocturnal masquerades is found for Dijon in 1515 (B 11 360-23)—and these were "respectable" women. In 1508, a group of "worthy ladies" living in the rue Saint-Pierre had sent a petition to the mayor, protesting the invasion of their neighborhood by concubines and procuresses (A.M., Dijon, I 142). At Orange—but this was in 1567—women had offered to make gunpowder to help with the defense of the city (A.M., Orange, BB 16, f° 115). It does seem (a first example dates from 1533) that as early as the 1530s certain women played a leading role in the organization of charivaris. On the other hand, especially in the identification of a married woman, the model hitherto reserved for the daughters of patricians (daughter of N, wife of Y) was beginning to spread throughout all strata of society.

96. André Burguière, "De Malthus à Max Weber, mariage tardif et esprit d'entreprise," *Annales, E.S.C.* 27 (November–December 1972): 1134. English translation in *Family and Society, Selections from the Annales, Economies, Sociétés, Civilisations,"* ed. Robert Forster and Orest Ranum, trans. Elborg Forster and Patricia M. Ranum (Baltimore, 1976), pp. 237–50. See also Davis, "City Women."

97. At Orange, the brothel was wrecked by the pages of Monseigneur de Bayard in 1523 (A.M. Orange, CC 417, f⁰ 40), by a group of men-at-arms in 1525–26 (CC 419, f⁰ 10), by lansquenets in 1536 (CC 428, f⁰ 50) and in 1537 (CC 429, f⁰ 12 v⁰). The brothel of Dijon was sacked repeatedly: 1495 (A.M., Dijon, K 83), 1499 (ibid.), 1514, 1525 (K84), 1527 (I 142), 1536 (K 85), 1542 (ibid).

98. Le Roy Ladurie, *Les paysans de Languedoc*, p. 276.

99. A general police ordinance of Dijon (mid-sixteenth century) describes the situation as follows: "For this reason, most of these male children [of poor families] engage in begging, and since they have not learned a craft, they take to stealing and fall into bad ways and some of the girls of the said kind go in for whoring, take to the brothel, and live in idleness." From about 1520 onward, public opinion often ascribed outbreaks of pestilence, famine, and upheaval of all kinds to lewdness, blasphemy, and debauchery (A.M., Dijon, I 142).

100. After about 1520 at Dijon, the concubines of priests and the clandestine prostitutes were driven out of town or taken to the public brothel every four or five years. At Lyons, the bathhouses of Tresmonnoye, La Pêcherie, La Chèvre, and Le Sabliz were torn down or abandoned. At Dijon all the baths were closed before 1560. At Le Puy, the brothel was "shifted" to a suburb. The brothels of Tarascon and Cavaillon were made into hospitals (1527–28), that of Alès disappeared in 1553, and that of Dijon was permanently closed in 1563.

2
Abandoned Children in Eighteenth-Century Paris

Claude Delasselle

The judicial, institutional, and administrative history of the Foundling Hospital* of Paris from its creation in 1670 until the Revolution has already been written, so I shall not summarize here the basic studies on this subject.[1] However, although we now are very familiar with the inexhaustible devotion shown by the Ladies of Charity and the administrators of the hospital, and with the enormous financial problems created by a steadily increasing tide of children needing help, we still know little about the abandoned children themselves. We know what happened to them once they were taken in by the hospital. We know everything about the attempts to keep them alive, feed, and educate them, and we know all about the terrible mortality rate that transformed the Foundling Hospital into an abyss that swallowed up the greater part of the children sheltered within its walls. But in the eighteenth century no one knew—and we still do not know—the exact geographical and social origins of these children, nor even why so many of them were rejected by their parents.

This chapter will attempt to bridge part of that gap. By means of a statistical study of available information concerning the identity of these children for two years (1772 and 1778) of the period in this study, I shall try to explain

Annales, E.S.C. 30 (January-February 1975): 187–218. Translated by Patricia M. Ranum.
*The Foundling Hospital [Hôpital des Enfants Trouvés] was one of the ten so-called "hospitals" making up the General Hospital of Paris. It had two units: the main house, the Couche, in the center of the city, and a house in the Faubourg Saint-Antoine, just east of the city gates. Other hospitals included such workhouses as La Pitié, La Salpêtrière, and Bicêtre. Created as part of what Michel Foucault has called the *Grand Renfermement,* the "Great Confinement," these institutions were established to rid the capital of the many poor people, beggars, prostitutes, and foundlings who roamed its streets. Specifying a regime of hard work, a Spartan diet, and sermons, the founders and directors of the General Hospital hoped to rehabilitate what were deemed undesirable elements of the population; should that attempt fail, these quasi-prisons would at least keep such individuals off the streets.—Trans.

why the number of abandoned children increased during the final century of the Ancien Régime.

First, however, I would like to summarize a few points that are indispensable to an understanding of the problem. The term *enfants trouvés* ["foundlings"] was used throughout the eighteenth century, although the actual manner in which the children were abandoned was completely transformed as the years passed. Indeed, at the end of the seventeenth and during the first years of the eighteenth century, virtually all children admitted to the Foundling Hospital had actually been "found"; they had been "exposed," that is, left in the street (under the portals of churches or on the thresholds of shopkeepers or surgeon-accoucheurs), in most cases by night, and had been collected in the morning. Exposure was the only form of child abandonment employed at that time.

During the course of the eighteenth century, this type of abandonment gradually became less frequent and was replaced by new forms; and all the while abandonment as a whole increased. By the 1770s, although the Foundling Hospital still occasionally took in an infant exposed in the streets of Paris, the majority of the children admitted had been born either in the Hôtel-Dieu [the hospital adjoining the Cathedral of Notre-Dame] or somewhere else in the city of Paris and carried directly to the shelter by a midwife, nursemaid, or the parents themselves; or else they had been born in the provinces, from where they had been brought by agents specializing in such shipments. In order to avoid any possible misunderstanding, I therefore prefer to use the more general term *abandoned children* to designate this population as a whole.[2]

What happened to these children once received? Infants not yet weaned (by far the most numerous) were sent to the Couche, located on the rue Neuve Notre-Dame, adjoining the Hôtel-Dieu and facing the cathedral. There they were nursed by resident wet nurses until a wet nurse from the provinces could take over, to return home promptly with the nursling who had been entrusted to her care. Older children, those over one year old, either were sent to the home in the Faubourg Saint-Antoine, an affiliate of the central Foundling Hospital, or to the hospitals of La Pitié or La Salpêtrière, or else they were boarded in the countryside.[3]

Next I would like to point out some changes that occurred in the pattern of admissions to the Foundling Hospital over the period 1670–1791.[4] The curve of admissions (fig. 2.1) reveals a steady increase between 1670 and 1772, followed by an irregular decrease between 1773 and 1791. Looking at this graph more closely, we see that the increase was far from perfectly regular between 1670 and 1772. We find a rapid increase in abandonments between 1670 and 1700, with an extraordinary jump in 1693–94, a reflection of one of the worst economic crises of the Ancien Régime. Then we note a certain degree of stagnation in the number of admissions between 1700 and 1721, with an average of 1,700 admissions per year. This near plateau was tem-

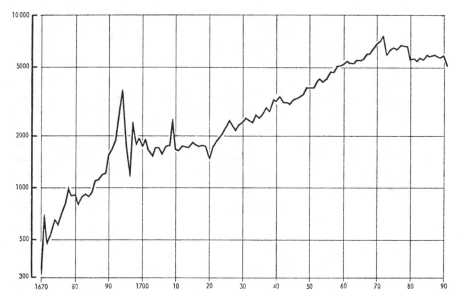

Figure 2.1 Number of Children Admitted to the Couche of Paris between 1670 and 1790

porarily broken by another brief upsurge, representing the economic crisis of 1709. After 1721 this lull was followed by a steady increase that continued until 1772, when the eighteenth-century maximum of 7,676 admissions in a single year was reached. Two sharp drops, in 1773 and 1779, broke this rise; then, between 1780 and 1790, the incidence of abandonment stabilized somewhat at approximately 5,800 children per year, before again dropping in 1791.

This was an extraordinary overall increase, for the number of children admitted went from 312 in 1670 to 7,676 in 1772—in other words, an almost 25-fold increase! For the entire period under study, the exact increase was 563 percent, between the average for the period 1670–89 and the average for that of 1780–90. This meant a sizable increase in the costs of running the Foundling Hospital and was a major cause of all the serious difficulties experienced by the administrators during the eighteenth century. Although the burden lightened somewhat after 1772, it still was three or four times greater than it had been during the first two decades of the century.

On the basis of this graph, therefore, one might conclude that abandonment increased considerably in Paris during the period 1670-1791, and one might immediately look for the causes of this surprising phenomenon. Yet it would be imprudent to assume a priori that the number of children admitted to the Foundling Hospital of Paris coincided exactly with the number of abandoned children, and hence to trust the admissions graph when evaluating the extent of abandonment in eighteenth-century Paris. The truth is much more complex, in view of the extremely varied origins of these children and the manner in which they were abandoned, which also varied greatly as the century progressed.

I have already pointed out that, after the mid-eighteenth century at least, some of the children received in Paris had not been born there but instead were brought in from the provinces or even from abroad.[5] The number of such children varied considerably between 1772 and 1778.[6] Having reached the maximum of 3,071 in 1772, the number fell to 1,753 the following year, then increased slowly and remained at between 2,000 and 2,500 admissions annually. Calculated in percentages, the number of children coming from the provinces or from abroad fluctuated between 30 and 40 percent for the same period.[7]

I have already pointed out the sharp drop in the number of admissions in 1773 and again in 1779. This can be explained by the promulgation of two royal decrees forbidding the transport of abandoned children to Paris. However, according vo Desbois de Rochefort, the number of children coming from the provinces and from abroad never dropped below 1,200 per year after 1779.[8] This permits me to assume that the children from Paris rather consistently accounted for approximately 4,500 admissions per year during the period 1780–90. This estimate meshes with my computations for the period 1772–78 (between 4,000 and 4,600 per year). I therefore propose that the number of children abandoned in Paris proper remained virtually stable between 1770 and 1790, with a yearly average of approximately 4,500.

A study of the written admission reports for 1778 enabled me to map the geographic origins of provincial and foreign children (maps 2.1 and 2.2 and table 2.1). These documents reveal that abandoned children were being brought to Paris from far-distant regions. Excluding[9] children from such foreign cities as Brussels, The Hague, London, and especially Liège,[10] and from such distant French cities as Lyons and Périgueux, the area from which abandoned children sent to Paris were "recruited" was extensive. It encompassed the entire Paris basin and at times even spread farther afield to Alsace, Lorraine, the Franche-Comté, and Brittany. The region providing the greatest number of abandoned children was, naturally, the diocese of Paris; then came Picardy, Champagne, Burgundy, Normandy, and the lands along the northern frontier. But almost every region in the Paris basin sent abandoned children to the capital.

Yet we must not let ourselves be deluded, for the geographic origins shown on this list may be deceptive. Indeed, the records do not provide information about abandonment in the provinces, only about the conveying to Paris of a certain number of children abandoned in the provinces, and that is not the same thing at all. Prior to 1779 certain provincial hospitals refused to accept

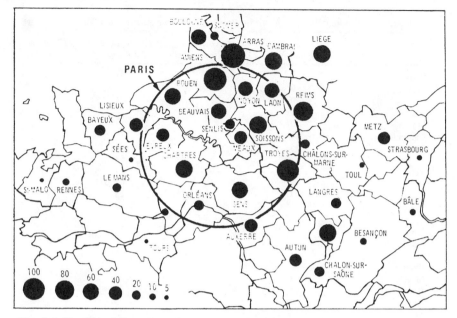

Map 2.1 Number of Foundlings Sent to Paris in 1778, by Diocese

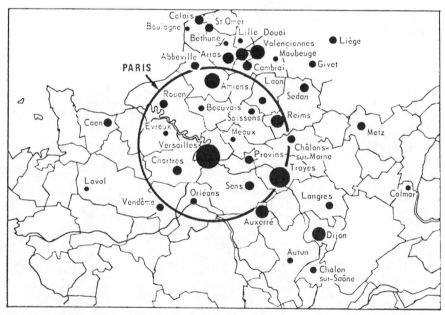

Map 2.2 Number of Foundlings sent to Paris in 1778, by City (Cities sending fewer than five children are not indicated.)

Table 2.1—Foundlings Brought from the Provinces or from Abroad in 1778

	From the City Proper	From the Hôtel-Dieu of that City	From the Diocese at Large	From the Généralité
Paris			207	30
Troyes	9	84	10	
Amiens	40		61	
Chartres	19		58	
Soissons	10		53	
Cambrai	19		43	
Rouen	15		46	
Liège	13		47	
Reims	26	10	23	
Beauvais	8		42	
Arras	27		22	
Noyon			47	
Sens	6	13	27	
Laon	12		32	
Lisieux	2		39	
Auxerre	5	30	1	
Evreux	6		30	
Meaux	3	3	29	
Boulogne	5		29	
Autun	8		25	
Metz	16		14	
Langres	12		13	
Chalon-sur-Saône	10		12	
Orléans	10		12	
Senlis	4		17	
Châlons-sur-Marne	14		4	
Saint-Omer	15			
Le Mans			13	
Rennes	1		10	
Besançon				10
Bayeux			9	
Strasbourg	4		2	
Sées			5	
Saint-Malo	.1		3	
Toul			4	
Basel (Bâle)			3	
Nancy	1		1	
Tours	1		1	
Versailles	120			
Dijon	40			36
Valenciennes	45			
Douai	30			
Calais	18			
Sedan	18			
Caen	15			
Provins	15			
Abbeville	14			
Vendôme	13			
Givet-Saint-Hilaire	11			
Colmar	6			
Maubeuge	6			
Lille	6			
Béthune	6			
Laval	5			

NOTE: Fewer than 5 children were sent to Paris from Blois, Brussels, Lyons, The Hague, London, Belfort, Vesoul, Amboise, Lens, La Flèche, Périgueux, etc.

abandoned children and systematically had them sent on to Paris; or else they collected a group of exposed children before finally shipping them to the capital. For example, in 1772 huge shipments of children were sent out from the hospitals of Troyes, Thiers, Auxerre, Caen, and Metz; and in 1778 the hospitals of Troyes, Auxerre, Vendôme, Orléans, Rouen, and Sens were the principal departure points for convoys of children, many of them already quite grown (from one to ten years of age, and sometimes older).

In addition, those seigneurs whose courts judged in *haute justice* [that is, heard all civil cases and all criminal cases with the exception of high treason and counterfeiting] were theoretically required to care for the foundlings discovered in their seigneuries.[11] They generally used any means to be rid of these children and whenever possible had them taken to a neighboring seigneury or to the closest hospital,[12] or more frequently, entrusted them to transport agents who would take them to Paris.

Thus, the arrival of abandoned provincial children in Paris was related to the attitudes of provincial hospital administrators and the local seigneurs dispensing haute justice; above all it was related to the activities of the *meneurs*[13] and transport agents, their itineraries, and the frequency of their trips. The fact that during the two years studied not a single child came from the region of Nevers does not mean that prosperity and virtue reigned in that region but, probably, that no meneur provided a regular delivery service or that the hospitals of that region were fulfilling their obligations in a satisfactory manner.

Above all, the high mortality rate for these children during their journey to the capital undoubtedly varied according to the length of the trip. For any two equal groups of children reaching Paris alive—one group from a region close to the capital (around Beauvais, for example) and the other from Burgundy or Alsace—one might hypothesize that the number of children leaving the more distant province must have been greater than the number coming from near at hand. But one would also have to know the precise means of transportation used, the actual duration of the trip (and not merely the distance covered), the season (the role played by such factors as bad weather and heat), and the care given to his load by each meneur—factors it is impossible to evaluate completely. It nevertheless remains highly probable that abandoned children from those regions that were farthest from Paris are underrepresented in comparison with those from the regions closest to the capital.

It is, therefore, impossible to use the total number of provincial children as an index of the poverty or depravity of any given province. The phenomenon merely proves that abandonment was also prevalent in the provinces and indicates both the saturation, inefficiency, or negligence of provincial hospitals and the attractiveness of the Parisian establishment for provincials, who wanted either to entrust their children to a highly reputed institution or, on the contrary, to send them as far away as possible, to be swallowed up in an anonymous mass of unwanted offspring.

The most intriguing question is how these shipments of children to Paris were organized. Evidence is rather scarce. The most famous comment is that of Louis-Sébastien Mercier: "There is a man who carries on his back newborn infants, in a padded box that can hold three of them. They are upright in their swaddling clothes, breathing the air from the top. The man stops only to eat and to let them suck a little milk. When he opens his box, he often finds one dead; he finishes his journey with the two others, impatient to be rid of his load. When he has left them at the hospital, he starts back at once, in order to resume the same job, by which he earns his daily bread."[14] Obviously, the mortality rate of infants carried for more than 400 kilometers [about 250 miles] on a man's back must have been extremely high. According to Desbois de Rochefort, "almost nine-tenths perish before the age of three months."[15] This figure does not appear an exaggeration, considering the distances covered,[16] the inadequate protection from the elements, and the ages of the children, as well as the fact that these agents were unable to give the proper food to the infants entrusted to their care and showed little personal concern for the infants' survival. Indeed, parents probably paid them at departure,[17] and "the price is the same for the shipper, regardless of whether the child reaches its destination alive or dies along the way."[18]

The person transporting the child undoubtedly did not care whether he reached Paris with live children. Indeed, he probably hoped the children would not live, since the survival of his initial passengers would prevent him from picking up new infants along the road to Paris. Mercier asserted that "almost all of children brought from Lorraine via Vitry[-le-François] perish in that city."[19] It seems plausible that the shipper, disinclined to travel with an empty load or to carry only one or two survivors, attempted to complete his load for the trip between Vitry and Paris. His profits rose with the prompt deaths of the infants, and no one could check up on him. Without going so far as to suspect these agents of trying to kill the children entrusted to them,[20] we may conclude that they offered only minimal care. Mercier mentioned "lack of nourishment," and Desbois de Rochefort confirmed that people transporting infants were negligent and failed to feed the babies or else gave them wine. I should also like to point out that they would have been hard-pressed to feed infants adequately, for in those days artifical nursing was rudimentary (the baby sucked a milk-soaked sponge), and even the greatest care on the meneur's part would not have adequately protected the children from cold, rain, or heat, nor from the length and discomfort of the journey.

Is it possible to make even an approximate estimate of the mortality rate among provincial children being carried to Paris? If we accept the estimate that nine-tenths of them died during the trip or during the initial three months at the Foundling Hospital, and if we use Tenon's figure for the number of provincial children dying during the initial three months at the Couche, it is possible to venture a hypothesis that for the period 1773–77 the number of children accepted in the provinces by meneurs averaged approximately 8,000 per year (although the number of children from the provinces actually admitted varied between 1,750 and 2,500 per year during the same period). The practice of sending abandoned children from the provinces to Paris was, therefore, much more prevalent than the figures gleaned from the hospital records would lead us to suspect.

Despite the decrees of 1773 and 1779, which threatened these shippers with stiff penalties,[21] this traffic did not completely disappear, for the meneurs modified their itineraries to escape being checked. Nevertheless, the practice decreased noticeably after 1779, in part because surveillance was undoubtedly quite efficient. But above all, provincial hospitals seem to have received instructions to keep their shipments to Paris below a certain limit;[22] at the same time they were given government subsidies to help meet the expenses involved in caring for the children they took in.

Let us return to the children who were born and abandoned in Paris. I have already observed that, for the second half of the eighteenth century at least, they fell into three distinct categories: children brought from the Hôtel-Dieu, those who had been exposed in the streets and picked up by the commissioner of that quarter, and those who were taken directly to the Couche.

A study of the admission records for 1772 and 1778 and of the statistics supplied by Tenon yields the following percentages. For the period 1772–78 the children from the Hôtel-Dieu accounted for about 20 percent of all children admitted to the Foundling Hospital and 30 percent of the children abandoned in Paris. Exposed children were not very numerous at that time, composing between 4 and 5 percent of all children abandoned in Paris. The rest (about 65 percent) belonged to the third category.

The children from the Hôtel-Dieu constitute an indistinct mass that is a source of great discouragement to the researcher, for the admission records and the notes attached to the children included only the sex, approximate age, mother's name, and the child's first name. Such information as the mother's address or the legitimacy of the child is completely lacking. There were many reasons for abandoning a child. A child would be brought to the Couche if its mother had died at the Hôtel-Dieu after delivery; or perhaps it had been abandoned during its mother's stay at the Hôtel-Dieu for childbirth or illness. Some children had been patients at the Hôtel-Dieu and were subsequently transferred to the Foundling Hospital.[23] One curious observation is that 87 percent of the children born at the Hôtel-Dieu each year were sent to the Foundling Hospital.[24] How do we explain this percentage? True, the death rate was frightfully high for both newborns and women in childbed.[25] But perhaps we should also view the Hôtel-Dieu as a sort of haven for "bad" girls, since its proximity to the Couche made it easier to abandon the infant. The Jôtel-Dieu probably took in a number of unwed mothers who had come from the provinces for the specific purpose of giving birth and then abandoning their child. In addition, I hasten to point out that the children from the Hôtel-Dieu showed the highest mortality rate (83 percent died within a month of their birth and a bare 7 percent survived until the age of five, compared with 17 percent from the other categories of abandoned children). Only a very few of them can have reached adulthood.

Fortunately, I had better luck with the rest of the ''Parisian'' children. The records frequently include many more details and permit a more complete study. For the moment I shall limit myself to a discussion of the geography of abandonment in Paris. For a certain number of the children the copy of their record is included in the admission papers and indicates the parents' names and addresses.[26] I have, therefore, been able to show in maps 2.3 and 2.4 and in table 2.2 the number of abandoned children from each parish for the year 1778.

This map reveals that the largest parishes supplied the greatest number of abandoned children. I am referring to the very extensive parishes of Saint-Eustache (no. 8), Saint-Sulpice (no. 30), Sainte-Marguerite (no. 32), Saint-Laurent (no. 16), and Saint-Nicolas-des-Champs (no. 22). The latter was the smallest but accounted for the most children. Most of these parishes were on

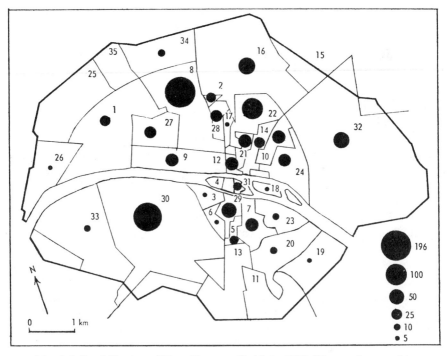

Map 2.3 Total Number of Foundlings per Parish in 1778 (The numbers on this map refer to the numbers of the parishes listed in table 2.2.)

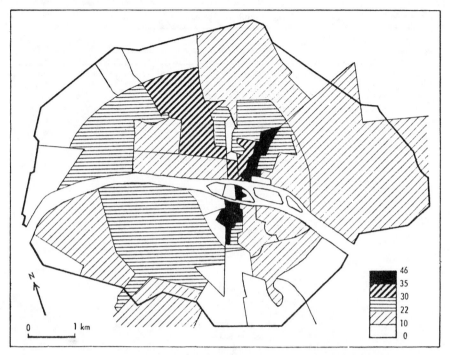

Map 2.4 Number of Foundlings per 100 Inhabitants per Parish in Paris, 1778

the periphery of the city. The small parishes in the old center of Paris, on the Ile de la Cité and around the Halles [central market], supplied a smaller number of abandoned children, the exception being the parish of Saint-Séverin (no. 29).

This is, however, only a very makeshift approach, at the most permitting a comparison of the number of abandoned children with the population of each parish. This gives us map 2.4, which is quite different from map 2.3 and table 2.2.[27] The parishes in the old heart of Paris show a high percentage of abandoned children compared to their population, especially the parishes of Saint-Jean-en-Grève (no. 14), Sainte-Marie-Madeleine-en-la-Cité (no. 31), Saint-Séverin (no. 29), Saint-Jean-de-la-Boucherie (no. 12), and Saint-Merry (no. 21), which form a dark band running north-south through the city. The fact that all these parishes were relatively near the Couche may be considered an indication that their proximity to that institution prompted abandonment. But a high percentage was also found in the large parish of Saint-Eustache, some distance away. The percentage decreases as we move out from the Ile de la Cité. A slightly greater percentage is encountered in the western quarters of the city than in the eastern ones, while the parishes along the western and

58   CLAUDE DELASSELLE

Table 2.2—Number of Children Found per Parish, in Paris, in 1778

Parish Number on Map 2.3	Parishes	Foundlings
8	Saint-Eustache	196
30	Saint-Sulpice	188
22	Saint-Nicolas-des-Champs	100
16	Saint-Laurent	72
32	Sainte-Marguerite	69
29	Saint-Séverin	55
12	Saint-Jacques-de-la-Boucherie	42
7	Saint-Etienne-du-Mont	40
10	Saint-Gervais	39
21	Saint-Merry	38
24	Saint-Paul	37
9	Saint-Germain-l'Auxerrois	35
27	Saint-Roch	33
28	Saint-Sauveur	33
14	Saint-Jean-en-Grève	26
1	Sainte-Marie-Madeleine-de-la-Ville-l'Evêque	26
2	Bonne-Nouvelle	23
5	Saint-Benoît	18
31	Sainte-Marie-Madeleine-en-la-Cité	17
34	Saint-Pierre-de-Montmartre	12
20	Saint-Médard	12
23	Saint-Nicolas-du-Chardonnet	11
33	Notre-Dame-de-Bonne-Délivrance	10

NOTE: Between 5 and 10 foundlings came from Saint-André-des-Arts, Saint-Côme, Saint-Hilaire, Saint-Jacques-de-la-Villette, Saint-Leu-Saint-Gilles, Saint-Pierre-des-Arcis, Saint-Pierre-de-Chaillot, Saint-Martin, Saint-Louis-en-L'Isle.

southern limits of the capital are remarkably light on both maps, for the number of children abandoned there was virtually nil.

This leads to several observations. First of all, interesting though they are, these indications only assume their full meaning if they can be compared with the socio-occupational structure of the inhabitants of each of these parishes. It is not enough to know that the parish of Saint-Eustache produced a great number of abandoned children during the eighteenth century, but if we could discover that the predominance of one Parisian social category corresponds to a high or low percentage of abandoned children, we would be well on the way in our search for the causes of abandonment and an understanding of the social attitudes of the period.

But at this point a second observation may totally destroy such hopes. The admission records give the addresses for only about 27 percent of the parents. From what parishes did mothers come who died in childbed or abandoned their children at the Hôtel-Dieu?[28] From what quarters of the city did the 2,054 children born and abandoned in Paris, outside the Hôtel-Dieu, come?

No address is available for any of them. We cannot even cling to the hope that the 27 percent constitute a "random," and therefore a representative, sample, for most of these children had been baptized and it is through the copy of the baptismal record pinned to their clothing that we know the addresses and social categories of their parents. Now, if they had been baptized, it is highly probable that a majority of these children were unwillingly abandoned by their "devoted" parents, owing to the "extenuating circumstances" of poverty. We would therefore be dealing with a selected group from a similar social level, not a heterogeneous group of unscreened individuals. Whenever we attempt to pin down the problem of legitimacy and approach the question of the parents' social origins, we continually encounter the same contraditions and uncertainties. I have been forced to conclude that here the admission records are no more valid than they were for children from the provinces. They do not permit us to know the exact geographic origin of the abandoned children of Paris and can provide no more than the foundation of some cautious hypotheses.

Are we even sure that we know the exact number of children born and abandoned in Paris during the eighteenth century? Yes, we can come rather close for the period already discussed, that is, 1772–90, for by that time exposing a child had become a rarity in Paris.[29] That does not mean, of course, that every child born and abandoned in Paris was the offspring of a truly Parisian mother, since Paris is known to have served as a rather safe haven from scandal and censure. Thus, a certain number of girls from the provinces and even from abroad came to Paris to give birth and abandon the newborn infant.[30]

But the degree of uncertainty about the exact number of children abandoned in Paris is much greater for the late seventeenth and early eighteenth century. At that time almost all abandoned children were infants who had been exposed in the streets of Paris and about whom the admission records provide very little information. So we must ask how many of these children died before being picked up by the commissioner of that quarter. These children had usually not been baptized. Were those who died before being collected still included in the parish records, or were they part of a mass of beings who never legally existed, who were never recorded and are untraceable in any archives? The mortality rate must have been very high for newborns wrapped in a few wretched rags and placed in doorways or under church portals at night, winter and summer—and slightly more were exposed in winter than in summer—in a city swarming with stray dogs and rats. But how does one go about making even a rough estimate of such a mortality rate? Even if we refuse to be influenced by the famous film *Monsieur Vincent* [a biography of Saint Vincent de Paul]—after all, it did not snow every night in Paris—the mortality rate of infants during their exposure could not possibly have been less than 10 percent. I shall cautiously say that, for the early years of the period under study, the number of children admitted to the Foundling Hospital was certainly always less than the actual number of abandoned children.

This leads me to the following conclusions. The number of admissions to the Foundling Hospital of Paris does not correspond exactly to the actual number of abandoned children in Paris during the first half of the eighteenth century; nor does it correspond to the actual number of abandoned children brought to Paris from the provinces during the second half of that century. Admissions were always much lower. We must therefore conclude that abandonment both in Paris and in the provinces was much greater than the records of the Foundling Hospital would lead us to believe. On the other hand, if we look at the increased incidence of abandonment for Paris alone during that century, we will note that it is lower than one might assume on the basis of the admission records. I have already estimated that the number of truly Parisian abandoned children remained virtually constant between 1770 and 1790, at about 4,500 per year. Using a mortality rate of 10 percent for infants exposed before being admitted to the Couche, we would arrive at an increase of about 125 percent between 1700–1720 and 1770–90, instead of the 250 percent indicated by the gross admission totals. In Paris, therefore, abandonment— which increased to such a point that contemporaries were horrified—probably only doubled. What did increase considerably was the transport of children to Paris; but we know that the number brought in was far less than it would have been had all the children survived at least until they reached Paris. Instead of between 2,000 and 3,000, the hospital would have been receiving at least 8,000 a year by 1770. This would have thrown the Parisian institutions into total confusion; mortality would have soared apace with the quantity of children admitted, and the disastrous surplus would have rapidly been eliminated.

Despite the major limitations discussed above, a systematic search of the admissions records has permitted me to learn more about the geographic origins of abandoned children. It also enabled me to pin down the phenomenon of abandonment through a study of the sex, age at abandonment, and legitimacy of these children, and even the social status of a certain number of parents.

My analysis of the sexes of these children was disappointing, since it revealed no noticeable difference between males and females. Girls constituted 49.8 percent of the total compared with 50.2 percent for boys. This insignificant difference does create one problem, however, for it is below the normal discrepancy at birth.[31] But we must remember that all abandoned children were not newborns and that in a normal population the difference in number between the two sexes at the time of birth gradually decreases as a result of a greater number of male deaths. Here, however—keeping in mind that 94 percent of the children were under one year of age when they entered the Couche—this decrease seems overly rapid. Were parents more apt to abandon girls than boys? I am not sure about that, since the discrepancy is too slight to draw any firm conclusions and since other factors may be clouding the issue. For example, some of the exposed children—and a majority of them would be boys—may have been eliminated before they could be admitted to an institution. Indeed, the number of boys exposed was twice that for girls, both in Paris and in the provinces. Were parents more hesitant to expose a girl than a boy?

My study of the ages of these children at the time of abandonment was rather more satisfactory, for it revealed some of the causes of that phenomenon. Once again using the years 1772–78, I observed that 98 percent of the Parisian children were under one year of age when they entered the Couche, while this was true for only 87 percent of the provincial children. This difference is easy to explain, for we know that a portion of these provincial children came from hospitals that grouped their shipments and got rid of sick children (especially those suffering from venereal diseases) by sending them to Paris, even though many of them were ten years old or over.[32] When I analyzed the age at abandonment in terms of legitimacy and the method of abandonment, I obtained the results displayed in table 2.3.[33]

The meaning of this table is very clear: markedly fewer legitimate children were abandoned during the first months of their life; and the incidence of their abandonment decreased much less rapidly with age than that among the other two groups, so that an appreciable number of legitimate children were still being abandoned after seven years of age. In contrast, exposed and illegitimate children were usually abandoned during the first month, and after the first year their number was quite low.[34] Parents generally seem, therefore, to have kept their legitimate children longer: and when they were finally forced to abandon them, when the children were already quite grown, it was probably owing to poverty and to the inability of the parents (or the widow or widower) to provide for their offspring. In contrast, the decision to abandon the illegitimate child was usually made shortly after its birth, if not before. Poverty was not the only reason; it was compounded by the desire to be rid of its embarrassing presence.

Table 2.3—Age at Time of Abandonment Related to Legitimacy and Method of Abandonment

Age	Exposed (%)	Illegitimate (%)	Legitimate (%)
0 to 1 month	80	76	59
1 to 6 months	3	13	8
6 months to 1 year	2	2	4
1 to 3 years	8	3	8
3 to 7 years	6	5	10
Over 7 years	1	1	11

One of the questions most frequently discussed at that time was the legitimacy of some of the abandoned children. Montlinot proposed that at least one-seventh of the abandoned children were legitimate, but this percentage applied only to the *généralité* of Soissons. The eighteenth-century figures for Paris were much less sure: one-third, said the Committee on Mendicity; half, said the directors of the Couche, who were seconded by the compilers of the *Encyclopédie méthodique*.

The results of my computations, based on the admission records of 1778, were noticeably lower: 16.7 percent of the children were legitimate.[35] Does this mean that Montlinot, a perspicacious observer, was correct, while the administrators of the Foundling Hospital were grossly mistaken? Here again I would hesitate to make a categorical statement, for many factors are involved in underestimating the number of legitimate children, as Montlinot himself was the first to point out. In order to be consistent, I could use as evidence of legitimacy only those admission records that included a copy of the baptismal record, a sure sign that the parents were married. But a certain number of legitimate children must have been included among those for whom no information is available (especially the large group from the Hôtel-Dieu) or for whom the parents' names were given with no indication of a marriage.[36] How can this surplus be computed? The Committee on Mendicity indicated that, according to the members of the Society of Maternal Charity,[37] "'1,200 to 1,400 legitimate Parisian children are exposed yearly at the Foundling Hospital.'"[38] In this case—and accepting my previous figure of approximately 4,500 Parisian abandoned children per year for the period 1788–90—legitimate children would account for 30 percent of the total. But how did these charitable ladies arrive at such a figure? Can we accept it as valid? To be on the safe side, I would propose that legitimate children accounted for between 20 and 30 percent of the total number of Parisian abandoned children, and that is already quite a high proportion.

Despite large blank areas, we are beginning to perceive more clearly the physiognomy of this crowd, which until recently has been quite anonymous. Through the baptismal papers included in the admission records, we are also able to lift a corner of the veil concealing the social origins of abandoned children. These copies of church records usually specified the occupation or social position of the parents—the father when the parents were married, the mother when the father was unknown, and now and then both parents of an illegitimate child.

For the year 1778 the occupations or social position of 1,531 parents were given; this represents 22.5 percent of the children for that year, if we include the rare cases in which both the father's and the mother's occupations are stated. Most parents with occupations recorded were men (91 percent), and 86 percent of them were Parisians. The other 9 percent was made up of those women whose occupation was given; 59 percent were from the provinces and 41 percent were Parisians. Lastly, although the majority of the men were married (70 percent), those women whose occupations are known were rarely married (only 7 percent); most of them were unwed mothers, but there were some widows.

These data have enabled me to pin down the largest female group: the unwed mothers from the provinces. They were servant girls or textile workers (ranging from the cotton-spinner from Picardy to the suit-cutter from Cambrai). We also learn something about unmarried Parisian girls. These unwed mothers had worked in domestic service or in the garment industry or were middle-class widows or widows who worked as street vendors. These were virtually the only two female categories, with the exception of a few noble young ladies who revealed their names to the baptizing priest despite their social position.

Among men the socio-occupational range was much more varied (table 2.4). Turning first to Parisians, we note that four groups clearly predominate: the "bourgeois of Paris" are far in the lead with 33.1 percent of all known parents. Next comes the group made up of master-artisans and shopkeepers (24.5 percent); then the markedly smaller group of wage earners, journeymen, and hand-workers (13.5 percent), and the group composed of "fashioners" and peddlers (12.3 percent). Between 5 and 10 percent were in domestic service. Then comes a smattering of diverse categories, each accounting for less than 2.5 percent, or under 30 cases: liberal professions (29 cases), employees (23), and soldiers (22). Present, but at the very bottom, is a small group from the upper classes: one wholesaler, twelve commoners serving as civil officials or military officers, and four noblemen.[39]

In the provinces the more modest social categories were better represented than in Paris. Leading the list is the group composed of journeymen and hand-workers (30 percent of the cases), followed by the group of master-artisans and shopkeepers (22 percent), and the group of poor peasants and day workers (16 percent). Other groups of some size are fashioners and peddlers (7 percent), domestics (6 percent), laboureurs ["independent farmers"] (5 percent), and soldiers (4 percent). The remainder belong to various miscellaneous categories (a few employees, commoners holding civil or military office, but no nobles).

The proportion of illegitimate fathers for the various social levels is of considerable interest. Almost half the bourgeois (48 percent to be precise) and domestic servants (42 percent) were not married to the mother of the child. Among the journeymen, hand-workers, and gagne-deniers the proportion drops to just over one-fourth (28 percent) and falls to 19 percent among master-artisans and shopkeepers, and to 12 percent among fashioners. In the very smallest socio-occupational categories the number of illegitimate fathers

Table 2.4—Socio-occupational Distribution for the Year 1778

	Paris	*Provinces*
Journeymen, hand-workers, *gagne-deniers,* day workers	162	59
Fashioners, peddlers, minor street trades	148	14
Master artisans and shopkeepers	294	44
Domestic servants, accountants, secretaries	85	12
Bourgeois of Paris	397	
Soldiers, subordinate officers	22	8
Tradesmen of undetermined status	16	4
Employees	23	6
Wholesalers	1	1
Liberal professions	29	2
Commoners holding civil office	6	2
Commoners holding military office	6	2
Nobles	4	
Miscellaneous	6	3

NOTE: Though I made some changes for provincials, I used the categories in the socio-occupational distribution established by Adéline Daumard and François Furet, *Structures et relations sociales à Paris au XVIIIe siècle* (Paris, 1961), pp. 18–19. [These categories are divided into those activities that were directly involved in the economy and those that were carried on outside the economy. Starting at the bottom of the ladder, the groups involved in the economy were the following:

1. The eighteenth-century equivalent of today's "commercial and industrial wage-earners." This group includes skilled journeymen working for a master; *gagne-deniers,* who ranged from persons performing such menial tasks as carrying water in order to "earn a few *deniers,*" or pennies, to persons buying or selling on a commission basis for another individual; and day workers (*journaliers*)—that is, workers hired by the day—and hand workers (*ouvriers*)—chiefly employed in the stocking or lace trades—provided their possessions were limited to their tools and perhaps a small amount of money and did not include a shop or stock of merchandise.

2. The lowest level of artisans, including those who plied the minor street trades such as vegetable vendors or peddlers; "fashioners" (*façonniers*) who worked at home for one or more masters or dealers on a piece-work basis, frequently in the fabric or garment trades; and artisans working at home in order to circumvent guild regulations. Since these individuals carried on their work independently and owned their tools and their raw materials, they formed an intermediate group between wage-earners and true artisans.

3. Master-artisans and shopkeepers who owned their workshop or business; some both produced and sold their wares.

4. Wholesalers and manufacturers, the highest economic category and one with relatively few members.

The category "tradesmen of undetermined status" was applied to those individuals for whom precise information about property was lacking, beyond their description as "mason," "carpenter," etc.

Groups carrying on activities outside the economy included:

1. Individuals receiving wages for service to private parties. In addition to domestic servants, this category included secretaries, accountants (*commis*), and financial directors (*intendants*) who saw to the proper functioning of private households.

2. The "bourgeois of Paris," who lived, without working, on the income from state bonds or private investments. (Any "bourgeois" who also carried on a trade or profession was removed from this category.)

3. "Employees in the service of private parties," a small group whose salaries were considerably higher than those of mere domestics. This diversified category ranged from an employee

(continued)

ranged from 55 percent among soldiers to 16 percent among employees and remained low—or nil, in the case of nobles—in those categories at the top of the social scale.

This statistical approach has permitted me to inventory and describe the different types of parents included in the admission records.

In Paris the most frequent category is the "bourgeois of Paris," half of whom were not married to the mother of the child; about 50 percent of these men came from the three parishes of Saint-Sulpice, Saint-Eustache, and Saint-Nicolas-des-Champs, although they can be found in every parish of the city. Next come the master-artisans and shopkeepers, found all over Paris; they were usually married men. Then come journeymen, *gagne-deniers*, and hand-workers, about 75 percent of whom were the legal father of the abandoned child. Almost all these men resided in a mere six parishes: Saint-Eustache, Saint-Sulpice, Saint-Nicolas-des-Champs, Saint-Laurent, Sainte-Marguerite, and Saint-Etienne-du-Mont. Also numerous were fashioners (in the clothing and trimming trades), peddlers, water carriers; these were usually married men and were scattered about Paris like the master-artisans. The final group of any great size is the domestic servants, numerous in the parish of Saint-Sulpice but also scattered about the city; a high percentage of them were not married to the mother of the child. After that, the various known social groups become so dispersed throughout Paris that clear-cut categories can scarcely be discerned. Soldiers—chiefly members of the French or Swiss guards—do stand out, however, but they are spread throughout the city. In contrast, the few nobles identified resided in the quarters adjoining the Tuileries: Saint-Germain-l'Auxerrois, Saint-Roch, and Saint-Eustache.

For the provinces it is easier to delineate rather homogeneous groups. First come laborers doing heavy chores, day workers, journeymen, and hand-workers in the countryside and villages, who make up 45 percent of the total. The abandoned child was legitimate for three-fourths of these men, who ranged from the weaver of Picardy, to the hired plower of the Beauce, to the journeyman tailor of Flanders, and on to the vineyard worker of the Paris

---

at the leather market, to a Swiss guard, to a business agent for a nobleman, and on to a gentleman-in-waiting to a duchess.

"Employees in the service of the king" included those members of the royal bureaucracy who served by appointment rather than through purchase of an office.

4. Members of the "liberal professions," ranging from the physician, lawyer, and professor, to the dancing master.

5. Commoners serving as officials—both civil and military—who owned the office, which formed part of their patrimony.

6. Nobles, at the top of the pyramid. Furet and Daumard determined nobility by the presence of a title or by the use of the words "squire" (*écuyer*) or "knight" (*chevalier*). Sons of squires and knights were classified as nobles. The nobility can be subdivided into three categories: those who lived nobly, without working, on the income of their family fortune; those who were civil officials; and those who were military officers.

See Daumard and Furet, *Structures et relations sociales*, pp. 25–38.—Trans.]

region. We also find many master-artisans and dealers in wood and horses; these men were also legal fathers and were mainly city dwellers. After these two very distinct groups comes a scattering of the various categories, from which we can barely pick out urban domestic servants, soldiers from the region of Paris or from the northern frontiers, and *laboureurs*. Lastly, the higher social categories are represented by approximately the same percentages as in Paris, the exception being the nobility, which is absent.

It would be tempting to consider these results as representative of the social origin of abandoned children as a whole and to use them as the foundation for conclusions about the basic motivation behind abandonment. But that is impossible, at least until some attempt has been made to evaluate the degree to which the information I have used actually reflects the questions under study. In other words, how much have I overestimated or underestimated the various social categories as a result of these very incomplete data? For we must not forget that the data involve only 22.5 percent of the children admitted to the Foundling Hospital in 1778.

The first source of error is inherent in the documentation itself, for the indications of occupations or social status in the copies of baptismal records are often rather vague and make it difficult to fit the indicated occupations into the socio-occupational hierarchy with any degree of certainty. This is not too serious when it is a matter of numerically well-represented categories, for the small number of possible errors cannot perceptibly modify the percentages obtained. But the risk of error is much more serious in the case of such underrepresented categories as the nobility.[40] Equally serious is the potential distortion resulting from the absence of information about more than three-quarters of the parents of abandoned children. Here we run into the same problem encountered for the geographic origins of Parisian children.[41] It would be extremely imprudent to assume that the identified parents constitute a representative sample of the parents of abandoned children and to employ a simple coefficient in order to extrapolate reliable percentages for all abandoned children. On the contrary, there is reason to fear that the bulk of those parents whose name, address, and social position are available would fall into certain social categories and not into others. Should the baptismal copies available for Parisian children be viewed as proof of the parents' desire to take the child back one day? If this were true, it would mean that abandonment resulted from poverty, or at least from straitened circumstances. But if the data involve only those abandonments triggered by poverty, we might incur the risk of overestimating their frequency and of underestimating the role of immorality and dissolute living.

To this already fundamental objection another equally disconcerting one can be added. The percentages I obtained for the social origin of abandoned children can only have meaning if they are compared with statistics concerning the socio-occupational distribution of the Parisian population. Only percentages obtained through this comparison can give any reliable indications of the part each Parisian social group played in abandonment and can in the end allow us to understand the motives behind such an act. Unfortunately, although research has made it possible to establish a precise hierarchy of social categories for mid-eighteenth-century Paris and to determine the characteristics of the various social levels, we still do not have reliable quantitative data about the size of each category compared with the Parisian population as a whole.[42]

Serious though these arguments may be, they should not be allowed to prevent us from using these data, as long as we take certain precautions. For in the end they may not be distorting the truth too much, after all. Indeed, if Daumard and Furet's findings about Parisian social topography are compared with the percentages for the various socio-occupational categories of the parents of abandoned children, computed by parish or by quarter, some rather strong correlations can be noted. The first correlation concerns the Faubourg Saint-Antoine (that is, the parish of Sainte-Marguerite) and the working-class sections of the Marais (parishes of Saint-Jean-en-Grève, Saint-Merry, Saint-Nicolas-des-Champs, and Saint-Gervais). These were all working-class neighborhoods that included a high percentage of people of low social status, while the number of domestic servants (considered to be roughly proportional to wealth for eighteenth-century Paris) was very low. And these very parishes, especially Sainte-Marguerite, show by far the highest proportion of parents of inferior social rank, while the superior categories (nobles, those in liberal professions, officials) were not represented at all and domestics and the bourgeois of Paris were quite scarce. The second correlation involves the "attractive neighborhoods" of the day, where domestic help was plentiful and "economic" occupations were less evident (Saint-Sulpice, Saint-Roch, Saint-Germain-l'Auxerrois, Saint-Eustache, and Saint-Paul) and the quarters inhabited by the nobility (the aristocratic section of the Marais [Saint-Paul and part of Saint-Gervais], the Faubourg Saint-Germain, and the quarter of Saint-Honoré). Parents from these areas who chose to abandon their children included a great number of the bourgeois of Paris and numerous domestic servants (especially in the parish of Saint-Sulpice). Most of these parents came from the superior social categories, while the lower categories were scarcely evident. Here again the agreement between the two series of data is remarkable.

Therefore, it seems safe to conclude that the incomplete information about parents available to us does not seriously distort reality. The same analysis also helps confirm the impression already created by the raw figures—the impression that abandonment cannot be attributed solely to the most unfortunate social classes—the "dangerous" classes—but that instead it involved every Parisian social group.

At this point in my analysis an important question arises. How does one explain the increased incidence of abandonment in Paris during the period

1670–1790? In order to answer this question I shall have to describe that fraction of the parents for which data are available, tally the causes of abandonment, and attempt an evaluation of the importance of each cause.

I have already noted that the increase in the number of abandoned children admitted to the Foundling Hospital during the eighteenth century to a large extent reflected the increasing practice of bringing children from the countryside to the capital. This was a related, almost parasitic, phenomenon that must be dealt with separately before a valid study of events in Paris can be made.

Earlier in this article I concluded that the actual number of Parisian abandoned children doubled between the period 1700–1720 and 1770–90, increasing from between 1,800 and 2,000 abandonments per year in 1700 to 4,500 per year during the final two decades of the Ancien Régime.

It has often been hypothesized that the increase in the population of Paris during the eighteenth century partially explains the increased number of abandoned children. Unfortunately, although the Parisian population undeniably increased throughout the century, we still do not know exactly how much. As a result, it is difficult to compare this increase with the increased abandonment of children. The most I could do was attempt a comparison with the Parisian birth rate. The number of abandoned children constituted 10 percent of the total number of children baptized in Paris between 1711 and 1721 and increased to 22 percent between 1773 and 1777. During this period, 1711 to 1777, the number of Parisian abandoned children increased by more than 100 percent, while the number of baptisms in Paris rose by a mere 11 percent. It is therefore clear that the increase in the number of abandoned children was not caused solely by the increase in the number of Parisians, although the expanding population probably played a part.

The difference between the two curves showing the Parisian birth rate and the number of abandoned children is very clear in figure 2.2. Although the curve designating abandoned children begins to climb after 1721 and continues to rise until reaching its peak in 1770–80, the birth curve reaches a plateau (showing only minor increases or decreases every few years) by the 1720s and remains virtually stable for about fifty years, only starting to rise once more after 1770–80. Although there seems to be a slight correlation between these two curves, it is not clear enough to permit any sure conclusions, especially since a factor having nothing to do with the Parisian birth rate appears after the mid-eighteenth century. I am referring to the shipments of provincial foundlings to Paris. Figure 2.3—covering the period 1772–78, the only period for which the exact number of Parisian abandoned children is known—does not reveal any clear relationships between births and abandonments in Paris. Thus, we remain in doubt, and our uncertainty can only be removed by a precise knowledge of the evolution of purely Parisian abandonments throughout the entire eighteenth century.

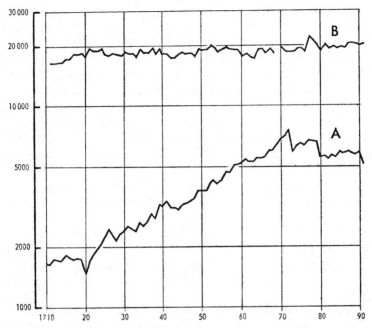

Figure 2.2 (A) Children Admitted to the Couche of Paris (B) Baptisms in Paris

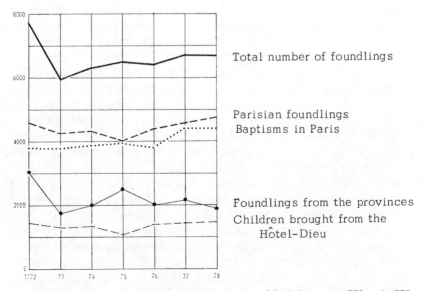

Total number of foundlings

Parisian foundlings
Baptisms in Paris

Foundlings from the provinces
Children brought from the
Hôtel-Dieu

Figure 2.3 Breakdown of Admissions to the Couche of Paris between 1772 and 1778

In addition, people of the time generally placed little emphasis upon the possible relationships between the expanding population of Paris and the increase in abandonments, but instead stressed a cause that many of them considered primordial: poverty. Mercier asserted that "this cruel abandonment . . . bespeaks a host of needy people; and indigence has always caused most of the disorders that all too frequently are attributed to man's ignorance and barbarity." Then he added that "in an ordinary year, six thousand to seven thousand children are abandoned by their parents and left at the Foundling Hospital, while the rest of the population does not go beyond fourteen thousand to fifteen thousand [births]. What a terrible and striking picture of the poverty of the people and the degradation of the species."[43] Desbois de Rochefort exclaimed in a similar vein: "The most widespread and exact cause of this increase in poverty, which has weighed upon the common people for many a year."[44]

Is poverty, therefore, the main culprit? Ernest Labrousse has shown the influence of grain price fluctuations upon the cost of living and the income of the common people.[45] If poverty was indeed the cause of these abandonments, the curve of abandoned children ought to reflect the curve of the price of wheat.

And, indeed, it is clear that the two curves vary in a similar though unequal fashion throughout the period under study. From 1726–41 to 1771–89 the average nationwide price of wheat increased by 56 percent, while abandonments more than doubled. Even more convincing is the detailed comparison of the curve of wheat prices with that of the number of admissions to the Foundling Hospital in figure 2.4. Indeed, there is a striking correlation between low prices and a deceleration in the abandonment rate, and high prices and an acceleration in abandonments. The period of low prices between 1715 and 1722 saw virtually no increase in abandonments; then, when wheat prices began to climb in 1723, the number of abandonments broke all restraints, jumped sharply, and continued to rise until the paroxysm of 1766–72. Whenever the price of wheat dropped, the number of children admitted to the Foundling Hospital decreased slightly and then slowly resumed its climb, as in 1726–36, 1741–45, 1749–51, 1753–55, and 1759–65. As soon as the price of wheat began to rise once more, the number of abandonments would also shoot up in an ever-sharper curve, as in 1721–26, 1736–41, 1745–49, 1751–55, and 1756–59. The rise in wheat prices during the period 1764–70, the greatest increase since 1720, was reflected in the extraordinary upsurge in the number of abandonments between 1765 and 1772.

It is clear that the pattern of the abandonment curve between 1720 and 1772 is partly due to the constantly increasing non-Parisian contingent. These provincial children are also evident from 1773 to 1779, though to a lesser degree; after 1780 they cease to distort the curve by filling in hollows or accentuating peaks. In fact, after 1785 the total number of abandoned children, both Pari-

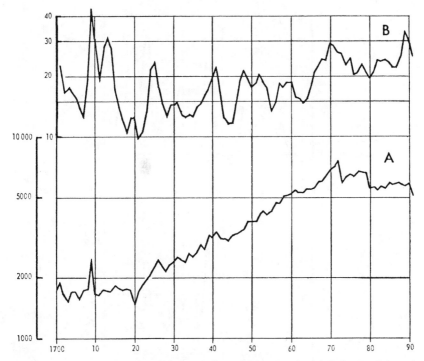

Figure 2.4 (A) Number of Children Admitted to the Couche of Paris (B) Price of Wheat in France (based on Labrousse, *Esquisses* . . .)

sian and provincial, lost momentum and then declined; it was not even affected by the unusually high prices of 1788–89.[46] The overall correlation between the two curves for the period 1720–72 is so close that it must provide an explanation and so constant that it cannot be a coincidence. Price fluctuations directly influenced the number of abandonments.

Before 1720 the link between price fluctuations and abandonments is even more evident. In fact, figure 2.5 shows a spectacular cause-and-effect relationship during the great crises of 1693–94 and 1709. The high point in the incidence of abandonment—the greatest peak of all—came during 1693–94. This involved an increase of 150 percent between 1690 and 1694, with 3,788 abandoned children during 1694, a record that would not be beaten until 1750. Figure 2.5 shows that this sharp increase was accompanied by an unusually large price increase in Paris: 190 percent for that same period, 1690–94.[47] The same perfect correlation is also found in 1709, although on that occasion the sudden spurt in the number of abandoned children was less acute.

These analyses all lead me to conclude that fluctuations in grain prices definitely influenced the incidence of abandonment. But this influence is

72 CLAUDE DELASSELLE

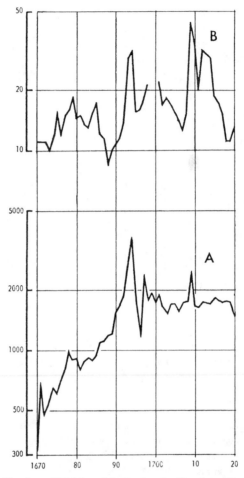

Figure 2.5 (A) Number of Children Admitted to the Couche of Paris (B) Price of One *Setier* [156 liters] of Wheat in the Central Market of Paris (based on Baulant and Meuvret, *Prix des céréales . . .*)

much more evident during the major crises marking the end of the reign of Louis XIV than during the latent crises of the eighteenth century. This is partially explained by a difference in the magnitude of the two types of crisis. The earlier ones were veritable catastrophes that brought death to the poorest segment of the population and profound poverty to a large part of the lower classes. This sent a flood of orphans and children from poverty-stricken homes to the Couche of Paris. The later type of crisis resulted less in death than in indigence. Non-Parisian children constituted another important factor after the 1720s; they undoubtedly tend to mask to some degree the role played by price fluctuations. The extraordinary increase in abandonments between 1694 and 1709 is also explained by the influx of a part of the nearby rural population into Paris during periods of high prices. These people would flee their poverty and seek bread and work, or at least succor and charity, in Paris. This large, floating population of men, women, and children must have contributed greatly to the increased incidence of abandonment; and the presence of a special institution for abandoned children must have encouraged these "loving" parents to protect their children from hunger by placing them where they would receive shelter and care.

Now let us move from prices to people, from graphs to specific evidence of poverty. Attached to the admission records of the Foundling Hospital I found twenty-five letters written by parish priests during 1778, attesting that the parents were unable to provide for their children. I also found a few notes from parents pleading indigence.[48] True, this evidence is scanty; but it is supplemented by promises to fetch the child one day and by numerous tokens—such as ribbons, figurines, or medals—placed in the infant's clothes. These tokens can be interpreted both as a means of future identification and as proof of the parents' desire to retrieve the child when they were able to provide for it. In these notes from parents the same expressions constantly recur: "We pray these laidees to take grate care." "His father and mother whose hearts is broken at being forced to abandon him for a little while." "We greatly recommend this child, who will be in a situation to be taken away when circumstances permit." Together, these letters, tokens, and notes have permitted me to credit indigence as the indisputable motive behind one hundred of these abandonments. True, that is not many; and we cannot conclude that all parents felt the same love and sorrow. But the fact that a baptism was performed before the child was abandoned and that the parents did not conceal their identity or their address can be interpreted as a strong indication of their intention to take the child back one day, and therefore of their temporary inability to provide for it.

Desbois de Rochefort did not hesitate to consider all abandoned, legitimate children as victims of poverty. Montlinot was more cautious: "Poverty is not the only reason why legitimate children are abandoned; loose living, laziness, private misfortune, and—must I say it—fathers' and mothers' dishonesty and lack of morals result in the desertion of a progeny that is no longer protected by paternal honesty. Here the offspring of persons who have been imprisoned or branded mingle with the offspring of homeless peddlers, deserters, beggars, etc."[49] He then advised that the throng of wandering peddlers and beggars be kept moving about and that they be forbidden to drag their wives and children along. He also cited orphans whose close relatives refused to provide care and who went to swell the population of the hospitals for abandoned children. But he, too, considered poverty the basic cause for abandoning legitimate children, especially in the countryside. "The poverty of rural

day laborers is extreme when they are burdened by too many young children. . . . Total indigence is a destructive force. When he reaches this final
stage of distress, the poor man leaves his home and exposes his children."[50]
    Information about provincial parents gleaned from the admission records
for 1778 seems to confirm Montlinot's observations. The majority of these
parents were day laborers, common laborers doing heavy tasks, and low-
income peasants. But close behind come master-artisans and shopkeepers; and
some distance behind them come fashioners, domestics, and *laboureurs*. This
reservation is even more valid for Parisian parents. The bourgeois of Paris,
master-artisans, and shopkeepers—rather than journeymen, workers, *gagne-
deniers*, or fashioners—appear most frequently in the archives I have been
consulting. Should I therefore conclude that the greatest number of children in
the Foundling Hospital of Paris were not there as a result of poverty? Not
necessarily, for the category "bourgeois of Paris" is heterogeneous and included, in addition to comfortably wealthy people, a large number of individuals with very modest means, and even some paupers, such as widows and
domestic servants, living on small annuities that kept them on the brink of
indigence.[51] In like manner, the low incomes of a sizable number of the
master-artisans and shopkeepers were very close to those of the lower
categories of Parisian society, that is, wage earners and domestics. These are
the so-called *pauvres honteux* ["shamefaced paupers"] who were aided by
the class-conscious Great Bureau of the Poor.[52]
    Now let us compare two maps. Map 2.4 shows the relationship between
abandoned children and the populations of the various Parisian parishes; map
2.5 shows the percentage of indigents compared with the total population per
section of Paris during Year II [1793–94].[53] Note that certain parishes—which
correspond to sections having high numbers of indigents (Sainte-Marguerite,
Saint-Médard, Saint-Etienne-du-Mont, Saint-Nicolas-du-Chardonnet, Saint-
Gervais)—show a very low percentage of abandoned children. Similar low
abandonment rates are likewise found in certain low-indigence parishes
(Saint-Roch, Saint-Germain-l'Auxerrois, Saint-Paul). If at this point we compare the percentage of abandoned children and the number of domestic servants (which may be considered a rather reliable criterion of wealth and high
social position),[54] we observe the same phenomenon. The richest quarters of
Paris—quarters chiefly inhabited by nobles and the "solid bourgeois" who
had abundant domestic help—produced only a relatively small number of
abandoned children in terms of the population of the quarter; the same is true
for the poorest quarters, where none but workers, day laborers, journeymen,
and master-artisans resided. In contrast, those parishes with a high percentage
of abandoned children (Saint-Jean-en-Grève, Saint-Séverin, Sainte-Marie-
Madeleine-en-la-Cité, Saint-Jacques-de-la-Boucherie, Saint-Merry) were quarters with a moderate amount of indigence and few domestic servants.

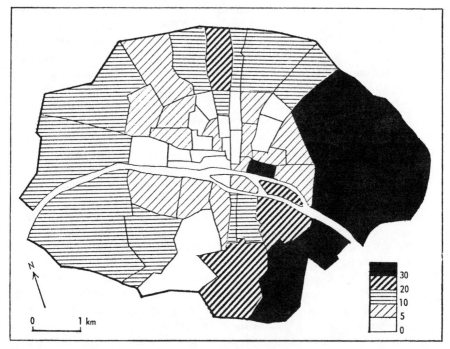

Map 2.5 Number of Indigent Individuals per 100 Inhabitants, by Quarter (based on Soboul, *Les sans-culottes parisiens . . .*)

After studying these two subdivided maps, one is justified in wondering whether abandonment in Paris did not involve the groups that appear most frequently in the admission records (master-artisans and shopkeepers and small bond-holders living in the heart of the city, members of social strata that just barely can be termed "middle class") more than it involved the poorest and most scorned classes living in the faubourgs. In that case, it is tempting to discern two distinct ways in which people viewed abandonment. The first attitude, and the one easiest to understand, would be born of the direst poverty and would involve the least fortunate social classes. "How can she think of feeding children when the woman in labor is herself poverty-stricken and sees only bare walls from her childbed? A quarter of Paris is not sure at nightfall whether the morrow will bring enough work to provide that day's bread."[55] The only solution for this wretched population of wage earners, *gagne-deniers,* and beggars was to abandon the superfluous child, a step frequently decided upon before the infant's birth. In this case the child was abandoned once and for all; there was no desire to take it back and therefore no concern over being able to identify it at a later date.

The second and contrasting attitude would, at least in part, be that of the bourgeois and artisans, who did everything they could to make the eventual recovery of their children possible. The reasons behind their decision are complex. First of all, they were in financial straits and could not raise the child as they would have liked. Second, the excellent reputation of the Foundling Hospital of Paris weighed heavily in their decision. The public sincerely believed that the care given children admitted to the hospital was quite acceptable—indeed almost enviable—and that no obstacles could prevent any parents from withdrawing their children after a few years. A parental note of 1778 reads: ''. . . being in addition persuaded that she will be well off there and that they can take her back as has been said above.'' This note expresses the thoughts of Jean-Jacques Rousseau, who asserted that, ''having weighed everything, I chose the best for my children, or what I believed to be the best. I wished, and I still wish, that I had been raised and fed as they were.''[56] Such was the widespread ignorance of the true fate of abandoned children. Many parents were convinced that by leaving their child at the Foundling Hospital for a few years, they were making sure it would receive care and an education that they themselves were unable to provide, all at no cost to them.[57]

Such blindness pains us, for these parents seemed unaware that their child had one chance in ten of surviving until the age of ten, and that in some years his chances were even less.[58] Even if he survived, it would be difficult for the family to get him back. Indeed, very few parents were able to recover their child, for the administration of the Foundling Hospital demanded a high fee for searching the records, plus 100 livres per year to repay expenditures for the child's upkeep. This measure was not so much an attempt to improve the institution's financial situation as a move to do everything possible to discourage the practice of temporary abandonment. Under some circumstances, however, the directors were entitled to reduce the sum required for recovery (this was especially frequent during the Revolution). But compared with the many requests from parents (between six hundred and seven hundred per year at the end of the Ancien Régime), the yearly average of between 3 and 5 recovered children was pathetically small. What a contrast to the hopes and illusions of hundreds of parents who each year carefully placed in their infant's swaddling clothes some indispensable means of identification.

Whether they took the form of profound poverty or only temporary financial troubles, the material difficulties of life were always a factor when a child was abandoned. Yet all the men of the day who pondered this problem saw another basic cause: debauchery. And some even viewed the increased incidence of abandonment as an indication of the breakdown of morality triggered by the ideas of the philosophes.

Libertinage among the upper levels of eighteenth-century society is so frequent a theme in the literature of the period that there must be some truth in it. Once again Rousseau is the most interesting witness. In the Parisian social milieu in which he circulated in the 1740s, a milieu that included only "officers of the guard and musketeers," nobles, or "businessmen, financiers, and food suppliers for the army," all of them from the best circles, the main topics of conversation revolved about amorous adventures: "Respectable persons brought low, cuckolded husbands, seduced wives, and concealed pregnancies were the most usual topics there, and the person who sent the most offspring to the Foundling Hospital was always the most loudly acclaimed."[59] The archives support this statement, for they reveal that quite a number of children came from those at the upper levels of Parisian society: physicians, artists, lawyers, civil officials, military officers, and nobles. Yet most of these children were legitimate. How do we explain their abandonment? Some parents may have been in financially straitened circumstances. In some cases a cuckolded husband may have rejected a child born of an adulterous liaison.

In any event, children born of "debauchery" were numerous among both the upper and the lower classes, for debauchery was not limited to the noble and the rich. First of all, its main victims were lower-class girls. "It is cruel to see the common people continually devoured by the rich man in a thousand different ways. . . . Servant girls, working among unmarried men of an age prone to passion, are exposed to temptations that are very difficult to avoid: in large households they become the playthings of valets, sometimes after having first been the toy of the master, and finally they are dismissed by the mistress of the house; . . . it is, therefore, among the lowest classes of the common people, for whom pure morals are not lucrative, that one must seek the main source of corruption."[60] There is no point in citing further examples, for the romantic literature of the eighteenth century offers proof of the debauchery of those in high society and the depravity of the poor; and traps set by debauched Parisians for innocent provincials are a recurrent theme of the day.

The archives of the Foundling Hospital give almost no direct evidence concerning the part that corrupt morals played in abandonment. Few letters from priests or copies of baptismal records assert that the abandoned child was the "fruit of libertinage." It is to be expected that children born of debauchery would be the very ones whose origin was the most mysterious. People of the day were well aware of this and were concerned about the effect of keeping admission records confidential. Montlinot noted that secrecy about abandoned children promoted "the loosening of the marriage bond, the protection of low morals," and Mercier admitted that because the authorities made a practice of accepting "without question" every child presented to them, "they have put libertinage a little more at ease."

Yet it would be hazardous to draw too sharp a dividing line between poverty and debauchery as causes of abandonment and omit all nuances in contrasting these two motives. If the illegitimate child was the most frequent type of abandoned child and was part of "a population born of libertinage and weakness," this was not solely because his parents were immoral or indifferent. Social pressure, prejudice against unwed mothers, and a ruined reputation were equally powerful motives. Yet in many cases poverty was also a motive for abandoning illegitimate children. Debauchees, working girls of easy virtue, and prostitutes were not the ones who flooded the hospitals with the fruits of their libertinage; instead, these infants were born of young servant girls whose subordinate position and youth had made them yield to their master. In like manner, the number of abandoned children was not much greater in cities with military posts than elsewhere,[61] and soldiers did not constitute a very large category in the admission records of the Foundling Hospital. "Debauchery does not increase the population,"[62] for prostitutes had long been familiar with ways of avoiding pregnancy, while the lower classes were still generally quite uniformed about contraception. The French Revolution offers proof that illegitimate children were not always abandoned willingly, but usually through necessity. When the old prejudices against unwed mothers and bastards were replaced by understanding and broad tolerance, many unwed mothers kept, nursed, and raised their children themselves. Therefore, poverty, shame, and moral pressures exerted by society were in most instances inextricably mingled with "depravity."[63] An attempt to study each of these motives separately at any cost would result in our misunderstanding the generally complex nature of the act of abandonment. Even when it was a matter of "saving her honor," Thérèse Lavasseur was not easily convinced by Rousseau's simplistic reasoning ("Since it is the custom in the region, when you live there you can do likewise") or by her mother's petty concerns ("too many brats"); in the end she "obeyed, but she wailed." We can assume that the majority of unwed mothers only allowed themselves to be parted from their child under the weight of the combined pressures of their associates, their social milieu, and the material and moral distress into which they were sinking—and that they did not conform to Debois de Rochefort's assertion and do so "without violent heartbreak."

The sources I used in this study turn the spotlight upon abandonment resulting from poverty and leave "libertinage" in the shadows. On the basis of the above evidence, must we consider the archival sources I have consulted as faulty? And is it even reasonable to draw such distinctions? The depravity of the common people was linked to their poverty. What options remained for the servant girl, impregnated by her master, when she was expelled from the household and found herself alone, without money, the object of scandal in her village or town? She went to Paris to give birth in secret and to abandon the child, for she could not keep it. She lacked the means to support it, and its presence would provoke additional scandal that would prevent her from obtaining lodging and work. Poverty and despair might push her into prostitution. And even though the moral code relaxed during the eighteenth century, the increasing poverty of the common people surely cannot be ignored.

Still, "merrily and without scruples," Rousseau was imitating the "custom of the region." Each year hundreds of legally married Parisian couples—respectable though rather poor—joined him in temporarily depositing their progeny in an institution. Are we dealing with a still misunderstood problem involving a *mentalité*, a new attitude toward children shown by certain levels of society? If so, how can we make this attitude jibe with the new interest in children that was developing during the same period and in which Rousseau himself was one of the leading forces? These are the most disturbing questions to be answered by those of us who are attempting to break down the wall of secrecy that has surrounded "foundlings" to this very day.

NOTES

1. I refer the reader to the following works: Léon Lallemand, *Histoire des enfants abandonnés et délaissés* (Paris, 1885); Louis Parturier, *L'assistance à Paris sous l'Ancien Régime et pendant la Révolution* (Paris, 1897); Jacques Dehaussy, *L'assistance publique à l'enfance. Les enfants abandonnés* (Paris, 1951); Albert Dupoux, *Sur les pas de Monsieur Vincent, 300 ans d'histoire parisienne de l'enfance abandonnée* (Paris, 1958).

2. Cf. Dehaussy, *L'assistance publique*, intro., p. 4.

3. Official regulations concerning the placing of children varied during the course of the period under study. Cf. Lallemand, *Histoire des enfants abandonnés*, chap. 2.

4. Several series of statistics exist concerning the number of children admitted to the Foundling Hospital. These various series disagree with one another in many respects, yet this disagreement is generally of minor importance. For this study I used the statistics of the Foundling Hospital (today the Hospice of Saint Vincent de Paul of Paris); for years when records are missing, I have used the figures in the *Annuaire statistique de la Ville de Paris* of 1880.

5. A precise study of the geographical and social origins of abandoned children is only possible through a tally of the written information included in the admission records drawn up by the commissioners for the quarters of Paris where the children were abandoned (regardless of the form the abandonment took). These records indicate the child's sex and approximate age and the place of abandonment. Then comes a description of his clothing; if pertinent, the text of a note or the description of the various tokens attached to clothing—a frequent practice of parents—was included. In addition, if a copy of the child's baptismal record had been placed in his clothing, the admission records would indicate the parents' names, residence, and occupation. These various tokens, notes, and certificates were preserved with the admission records.

6. These data came from Jacques-René Tenon's *Mémoires sur les hôpitaux de Paris* (Paris, 1788), p. 272, and also from my tallies of the admission records for two years, 1772 and 1778.

7. See figure 2.3, which shows a detailed admissions curve for the period 1772–78.

8. Eléonore-Marie Desbois de Rochefort, *Encyclopédie méthodique* (Paris, 1788), s.v. "Enfant-Trouvé," p. 281. In passing I would like to point out that Desbois de Rochefort, curate of the parish of Saint-André-des-Arts, seems to have been one of the best informed men of his day on problems involving abandoned children.

9. Because there were not many of them; we would need additional detailed studies for different years in order to see whether this fluctuation was normal or unusual.

10. Abbé C.-A.-J. Leclerc de Montlinot, *Observations sur les Enfants-Trouvés de la généralité de Soissons* (Paris, 1790), p. 10, points out that a large number of children born at Liège were brought to the hospitals of the *généralité* of Soissons and abandoned.

11. On this point see Dehaussy, *L'assistance publique*, chap. 1, sec. 1, p. 12.

12. With (theoretically) a financial contribution to assist that hospital in providing for abandoned children.

13. *Meneurs*—and their female counterparts, *meneuses*—were individuals paid by the Foundling Hospital of Paris to recruit wet nurses in the provinces and accompany them back to Paris;

there the nurse would take an abandoned child and return with it to her province. Sometimes these meneurs would also transport abandoned children to Paris.

14. Louis-Sébastien Mercier, *Le tableau de Paris* (Amsterdam, 1782–88), 3, chap. 271, p. 234.

15. Desbois de Rochefort, *Encyclopédie méthodique*, p. 283. He was merely repeating the proportion cited in the decree of the Council of State of 10 January 1779—as did the Committee on Mendicity of the Constituent Assembly (see Camille Bloch and Alexandre Tuetey, *Procès-verbauz et rapport du Comité de Mendicité* (Paris, 1911).

16. Remember that survivors reaching Paris were sent back to the provinces a few days later, either with a wet nurse or "on commission," that is, with a transport agent, who would search for a wet nurse.

17. By contrast, hospitals giving the children to a shipper only paid the man's wages after he had presented an arrival certificate from the commissioner who received the children in Paris.

18. Naturally we should try to verify this assertion. It is probably possible to find evidence concerning the routes taken by these shippers and then to determine the percentage of deaths occurring during these journeys by examining parish registers for the localities through which they passed (although one wonders whether these children, objects of scorn and outsiders to the parish, were always listed).

19. Mercier, *Le Tableau de Paris*, 3, chap. 271, p. 234.

20. Yet Montlinot denounced "the infanticide of the meneurs" and cited a meneuse accused of having killed and secretly buried several children entrusted to her by hospitals.

21. The decree of 10 January 1779 forbade all shippers to accept abandoned children, except to convey them to the closest foundling hospital or to a wet nurse, under penalty of a fine of 1,000 livres.

22. This was the case at the hospital of Auxerre, from which only sick or infirm abandoned children were sent on to Paris after 1779. For the entire period 1779–96, only thirty-one children were sent to Paris, while that institution had sent thirty during 1778 alone.

23. Some children, abandoned by persons detained in La Salpêtrière, were also taken from that workhouse to the Foundling Hospital.

24. Based on information found in Tenon, *Mémoires sur les hôpitaux*.

25. Ibid.

26. Not to be confused with the place of birth, which usually was not the mother's residence but that of the midwife or surgeon-accoucheur, quite possibly located in a different parish.

27. The population per parish is found in Abbé Jean-Joseph Expilly, *Dictionnaire historique, géographique, et politique des Gaules et de la France* (Paris, 1762–70); the figures are no more reliable than the rest of Expilly, but nothing else is available.

28. Some of these mothers had certainly come from the provinces. But how many?

29. But not in the provinces, where it was still widespread at the end of the Ancien Régime.

30. To this add the women who had been forced by unusually severe famine to leave their province with their family during the major crises at the end of Louis XIV's reign and who had come to seek help in Paris; they gave birth there and abandoned the infant they could not feed. See below my analysis of the graphs for the years 1693–94 and 1709.

31. Remember that the male birth rate usually varies between 1.04 and 1.06, in other words, that 4 to 6 percent more males than females are usually born. These percentages are not evident here.

32. Although most children abandoned in Paris were admitted to the Couche within a few hours after having been abandoned, this was not the case with children from the provinces. The length of the journey and above all the delayed departures in groups from hospitals led to an age at admission that did not reflect the age at abandonment. The two percentages are, therefore, meaningless.

33. I am making a distinction here between exposed children (legitimate or not), legitimate children, and illegitimate children, that is, those whose legitimacy is not proved by a copy of a baptismal entry. (See below the problems involved in defining legitimacy.)

34. Yet a conspicuous number of children over one year of age were abanfoned by exposure. These must have been orphans admitted to the Foundling Hospital or (intentionally?) lost children.

35. This figure corresponds rather closely with the figure—14.6 percent of legitimate children

in 1760—given in the section on public assistance in *Annuaire statistique de la Ville de Paris* (1880), later used by Lallemand.

36. We may assume that a legally married couple abandoning its child because of poverty would first want to have the infant baptized and would then place in its swaddling clothes specific information that would facilitate a search when they later came to reclaim the child. This was probably true in the great majority of cases. But some parents were afraid of being prosecuted for having exposed or merely abandoned their children and intentionally neglected to place identification in the child's clothing. In addition, the commissioners drawing up the records may not always have transcribed every bit of information attached to the child.

37. A benevolent women's group created in 1788 to help the poor women of Paris and enable them to keep their children; Bloch and Tuetey, *Procès-verbaux . . . du Comité de Mendicité*, p. 693.

38. Ibid., p. 700.

39. For details concerning these results, see table 2.3.

40. Hence I have been especially cautious for this specific group. I used a title as the only valid indication of nobility and did not include names with a *de* or any other indication of presumed nobility.

41. Naturally there were just as many variables for provincial children—and perhaps even more—since the arrival of these children in Paris was affected by all manner of factors that totally distort our view of abandonment in the provinces.

42. Especially Daumard and Furet, *Structures et relations sociales*. In particular it is very difficult to grasp and establish figures for the lowest levels of the Parisian population.

43. Mercier, *Le tableau de Paris*, 3, chap. 271.

44. Desbois de Rochefort, *Encyclopédie méthodique*, s.v. "Enfants-Trouvés."

45. Camille-Ernest Labrousse, *Esquisse du mouvement des prix et des revenus en France au XVIII*e *siècle* (Paris, 1932), the source of the figures and graphs used here; and *La crise de l'économie française à la fin de l'Ancien Régime et au début de la Révolution* (Paris, 1943).

46. As I indicated in note 37, this decrease can be explained by the creation of the Society of Maternal Charity, created to help needy mothers and thus prevent abandonment. According to the Committee on Mendicity, after 1789 this society was responsible for a great decrease in the incidence of abandonment in Paris (three hundred to four hundred cases per year). During the same period the legislation forbidding transport of provincial children to Paris was more strictly enforced.

47. The price of wheat in Paris is found in Micheline Baulant and Jean Meuvret, *Prix des céréales extraits de la Mercuriale de Paris, 1520-1698* (Paris, 1960-62).

48. Here is one example: "The father and mother of this child are poor wretches overwhelmed by misfortune and incapable of feeding her at present. Their hope that fortune will be more favorable to them in the near future leads them to request the unusual favor that, at the time she is admitted to the Foundling Hospital, they be sent a letter entitling them to withdraw her when they are able to feed her and show her their paternal and maternal tenderness."

49. Montlinot, *Observations sur les Enfants-Trouvés*, p. 46.

50. I found one case of a child who was sent to the Foundling Hospital in 1772 because his father had been shot as a deserter.

51. Cf. the analyses in Daumard and Furet, *Structures et relations sociales*, pp. 22–25.

52. Cf. Léon Cahen, *Le Grand Bureau des Pauvres à Paris au milieu du XVIII*e*siècle* (Paris, 1904). [The Grand Bureau des Pauvres, a committee composed of parlementary and judicial officials, clergy, and bourgeois, collected fees from all nonindigent inhabitants of Paris, rich or poor, noble or clergy. These sums were used to succor master craftsmen who had fallen upon hard times, and children, old people, and the infirm, providing they were Catholics and had resided in Paris for three years. The Bureau also administered two hospitals not included in the General Hospital.—Trans.]

53. Map reprinted from Albert Soboul, *Les sans-culottes parisiens en l'an II* (La Roche-sur-Yonne, 1958).

54. These statistics for domestic servants were found in Expilly, *Dictionnaire historique,* and transferred to a map showing the quarters of eighteenth-century Paris. This comparison was not always easy to make, for the limits of quarters are often quite different from those of parishes.

55. Mercier, *Le tableau de Paris,* 3, chap. 271.

56. Jean-Jacques Rousseau, *Les confessions*, book 8.

57. Cf. Desbois de Rochefort, *Encyclopédie méthodique*, p. 283. "Mothers currently believe that their child will be at least as well treated at the Hospital as in their gloomy hovel; they are sure they will be able to take the child back whenever they wish and they expect to do so, even if their luck does not change, for when it is older the child will not cost them as much." In a similar vein, Jacques Necker, *De l'administration des finances de la France* (Paris?, 1784), denounced the inconveniences of admitting children to foundling hospitals for short periods.

58. I cannot go into detail here about the death rate among abandoned children, which is touched upon in the previously cited works of Tenon, Lallemand, and Dupoux. I shall limit myself to using as landmarks a few figures published by Tenon in his *Mémoires sur les hôpitaux de Paris*. By 1 September 1778, 85 percent of the children admitted to the Couche after 1 January 1773 had died. The same figures show that 73 percent of the children under one year of age had died during the first month of residence at the Couche. These data are confirmed by Lallemand's studies. In short, using the rates in Duvillard's table of children still alive after five years, I estimate that no more than 5 percent could have survived until adulthood.

59. Rousseau, *Les confessions*, book 7.

60. Montlinot, *Observations sur les Enfants-Trouvés*, p. 14.

61. As Montlinot shows, using the garrison city of La Fère as an example.

62. Montlinot, *Observations sur les Enfants-Trouvés*, p. 15.

63. To this, add the pressures and entreaties of midwives and accoucheurs. According to Desbois de Rochefort, it was in the accoucheurs' interest that mothers be shown "the inconveniences caused by feeding this child, the exaggerated advantages of the Foundling Hospital, the ease with which the child can eventually be recovered, and the widespread practice of hiding the fruits of love for a few years," because mothers planning to abandon the infant would give the accoucheur money and clothes for the child. In addition, midwives often prodded unwed mothers to take up prostitution.

3
Galley Rowers in the Mid-Eighteenth Century

André Zysberg

The naval archives of Toulon, Brest, and Rochefort contain the enrollment records of galley oarsmen and convicts for pre- and post-revolutionary France.

FROM THE GALLEYS TO THE BAGNE

The city of Marseilles remained the chief French galley port until the mid-eighteenth century, when the ordinance of 27 September 1748 made the Galley Corps part of the French Navy. This official decision tolled the knell of a fleet that had by then become merely a "glorious ruin." Vessels that were still seaworthy were moved to Toulon to serve as temporary prison hulks. Toulon became the site of the first land-based bagne,[1] and the crews of galley oarsmen were converted into forced laborers. Three more prison compounds were created: Brest (1749), Rochefort (1767), and Lorient (1795), providing the navy with a cheap source of labor for its major war ports.[2]

THE DOCUMENTS

Although the oldest convict registers go back to the years 1670–74, a systematic study of the entire series of available documents is impossible for the years prior to 1685, because the oldest seventeenth-century enrollment records were copied and recopied at later dates and the outdated record books were discarded.[3] This practice of destroying obsolete records was discontinued toward the end of the century, and all lists were preserved from then on.

Annales, E.S.C. 30 (January–February 1975): 43–65. Translated by Patricia M. Ranum.

These registers provide information about each convict's civil and socio-occupational status, his physical appearance, the circumstances leading to his conviction, and his subsequent fate. Even the earliest registers provide enough data for us to answer the basic questions to be asked about galley rowers. The quality of the data improves as we move on into the eighteenth century, increasing the reliability of a statistical study of these documents.

Enrollment Lists: Documentary Evidence of Crime. These convicts registers provide rich source material—''a fascinating mass''[4]—for all of France.

The eighteenth century produced no judicial studies like the demographic ones conducted by Messance and Deparcieux.[5] Making observations about delinquency long remained a prerogative of moralists and philosophers, while statistical studies of unlawful behavior did not appear until the period 1825–35.[6] Therefore, as a part of my study of crime in France between 1685 and 1825, I decided to analyze these enrollment records.

Methodological problems. Having decided to carry out a computerized study of the records concerning galleys and bagnes, I determinedly began a thorough analysis of the registers, at least for the years 1685–1791, roughly a century.[7] I used the FORCOD system originated by Michel Couturier and his coworkers.[8]

FORCOD offers one major advantage: its language, which closely resembles normal speech, permits complete fidelity to the document. Eventually I hope to have the data recorded on magnetic computer tape so that the information will be easily and quickly available.

Galley Oarsmen in 1748

In 1971 I conducted a test run using one particular enrollment list that shows the composition of the bagne in 1748,[9] for in that year the navy requested a complete list of oar crews as of the date it assumed control over the galleys. This article presents the most significant results of the analysis.[10]

The register of 1748 lists nearly four thousand convicts sentenced between 1700 and 1748 (table 3.1).[11] The oldest generations of prisoners are very poorly represented, for two-thirds of the convicts in 1748 had arrived in Marseilles less than ten years before.

The prison population seems to show a rapid turnover, indicative of a high mortality rate among convicts rather than routine freeing of prisoners. Of the gamut of possible sanctions included in the judges' repressive arsenal, a sentence to the galleys constituted a harsh personal punishment [as contrasted with a sentence involving payment of a fine]. Being sentenced to ''life''

Table 3.1—Length of Stay in Bagne

Date Sentenced	Convicts (%)
1700–09	0.5
1710–19	5.1
1720–29	11.8
1730–39	18.8
1740–48*	63.8

*The register ends with the entry of 31 December 1748.

meant being sentenced to premature death. Being sentenced to "a term" left a chance of survival, but only the toughest and luckiest could win.

All categories of offenses were represented in the bagne, which (along with the general hospitals) was early-modern France's great overflow pipe. Despite the persistent legend, few serious offenders were to be found among those sentenced to the royal galleys; petty thieves, tramps, smugglers, and deserters constituted most of the "big criminals" in the bagne in 1748.

Offenses Leading to Prison Sentences

Although the grounds for conviction are stated for 93 percent of the convicts listed, the terseness of the document concerning the reason behind each conviction (table 3.2) makes a classification of offenses difficult.[12]

CRIMES INVOLVING BLOODSHED

Violent offenses.[13]   The principal reason behind 3.5 percent of all sentences was an offense involving violent behavior. This percentage is notewor-

Table 3.2—Offenses Leading to Prison Sentences

Nature of Offense	Sentences (%)
Crimes involving bloodshed and arson	8.0
Disturbing family and religious peace; sexual offenses	1.6
Disturbing the public peace	10.0
Crimes against property (theft, swindling, and fraud)	41.2
Smuggling and offenses related to forests	26.4
Military offenses (including forms of bloodshed punishable as a military offense)	12.8
Total	100.0

thy in a society where harsh and even brutal attitudes were the norm. Indeed, these sentences always involved aggravating circumstances, such as the perpetrator's being a habitual repeat offender, being armed, or having inflicted an injury; the severity of this injury and, above all, the social status of the victim, were determining factors. The "violent" individual was sentenced to the galleys for outrageous behavior; he was a "disturber" of the peace, a "disreputable" individual, a troublemaker who (literally) went beyond the limit. The involvement of the military in this sort of crime is significant, for 32 percent of those sentenced for assault and battery were soldiers.

Homicide. A brawl or rowdyism carried to extremes might end in someone's death. The guilty party rarely paid for such unpremeditated murder with his liberty (less than 1 percent of all sentences). A much greater proportion (3.5 percent) of the convicts was accused of attempted murder, assault, or ambush. A letter of pardon or the victim's survival permitted these condemned men to avoid capital punishment in return for a life sentence to the galleys. Both robbery and vengeance were clear motives for this category of crime. Every social group accepted, and felt justified in, resorting to violence in order to repair wrongs and the harm resulting from such wrongs. Yet, people involved in a vendetta were not well represented among galley rowers, for a vendetta implied a whole network of solidarity on the part of the village community or the noble clan, and this group protection frequently permitted the guilty party to escape all "regular justice."

DISTURBING FAMILY AND RELIGIOUS
PEACE. SEXUAL OFFENSES

I was interested to note that criminologists usually place the "crimes" in this category under quite different headings. This type of offense appeared only here and there in the registers. Accounting for one conviction out of a hundred on the list of prisoners in the bagne in 1748, it indicates a "silent criminality" that rarely appears in these documents. Sometimes the judges pronouncing the sentence were silent,[14] but at other times their sentence was explained more fully, even when the facts spoke for themselves and served as accusation enough. Sometimes the victims, powerless and resigned, remained silent. And sometimes the silence came from the condemned man himself, who might well be a poor devil whose social status did not warrant a *lettre de cachet** but instead sent him to the bagne or to a general hospital.[15]

---

*A royal letter ordering immediate imprisonment or banishment, often for the purpose of avoiding a scandal that might harm a family's honor.—Trans.

Table 3.3—Family, Religious, and Sexual Offenses

Nature of Offense	Number of Sentences
Disturbing the family peace	
Infanticide	2
Exposing a child	1
Incest	4
Kidnapping	1
Polygamy	1
Libertinism	6
Disturbing the religious peace	
Blasphemy	10
Sacrilege	7
Sexual offenses	
Rape	15
Sodomy	2
Bestiality	2
Total	51

DISTURBING THE PUBLIC PEACE

Offenses involving the Religion Prétendue Réformée.   In 1748 about forty Protestant galley rowers were still listed among those sentenced to the bagne. I do not plan to study the Protestants in the bagne, but I wanted to make my data available here for other historians.

Table 3.4—Disturbing the Public Peace

Nature of Offense	Number of Sentences
Disregard of royal edicts and declarations concerning the Religion Prétendue Réformée [Huguenots]	43
Seditious speeches	3
Participation in a popular riot	5
Illegal begging (exclusively)	30
Vagrancy	230
Breaking the *ban**	53
Total	364

*Banishment from the kingdom or from a jurisdiction for a specified period or for life was a personal punishment. Breaking the *ban* was an offense that could lead to the galleys, but it often went unpunished for lack of means of verification.—Trans.

VAGRANCY AND ILLEGAL BEGGING

In 1748 the bagne included only a very few seditious individuals; those provoking riots must be sought among the vagrants. The dividing line between tramp and beggar is a rather imprecise one. I made a distinction between convicts sentenced to the bagne solely for illegal begging and those condemned for vagrancy, although the latter were often part-time beggars.[16]

Vagrancy. Tramps were setenced for being *faynéants* ["loafers"], *oisifs* ["idlers"], or *sans métiers* ["having no trade"]. No trade? In most cases, no permanent work would be more accurate. A number of such vagrants were seasonally employed and practiced various minor trades as their peregrinations dictated. Traveling alone or in a group, they frequently triggered reflexes of "social fear." During difficult times these tramps did not hesitate to extort charity. In 1738 the *prévôté* of Bourges sentenced a man from the diocese of Nevers to the galleys for life. This man, who "had no trade," was a "tramp and beggar, and he exacted money and clothing forcibly, under threat of arson."[17]

The practice of sentencing vagrants to the bagne was hardest on men who were *sans aveu** and *sans domicile* ["homeless"], for they could not call upon the basic solidarity of the village or neighborhood community. Tried summarily, these outsiders were "cut out for the galleys," in the cruel words of one prison warden.

Illegal begging. Royal and municipal charity went hand in hand with the suppression of unjustified begging. Any beggar sent to the galleys was a "sound" beggar who had pretended to be crippled or blind. Only rarely was this type of offender sentenced to the bagne, for most beggars were interned in the general hospitals. Besides, the number of men that town patrols or the mounted police of the *maréchaussée* could send out to "hunt" beggars was pitifully inadequate.

CRIMES AGAINST PROPERTY

Theft. More than one-third (35 percent) of all convicts had been sentenced for theft. Whenever the stolen object is mentioned in their sentences, we encounter thr same list of items we already know from other studies.[18] The preferred finished goods were those with handwork: linens, clothes, and

---

**Gens sans aveu* were "people without a voucher," that is, people without anyone to vouch for their honesty or confirm their identity. Lacking a voucher was tantamount to lacking a good reputation, hence the modern definition, "disreputable."—Trans.

trimmings (such as hats, kerchiefs, and laces). Serious larceny—especially the theft of jewels, watches, and money—meant a life sentence to the galleys. A sizable number of thefts involved edible goods, both "the cooked and the raw,"—in other words, bread and roasts, as well as grains, fruits, vegetables, and poultry. In a category all of their own are the cattle and horse thefts that were frequently committed by individuals in the business—for example, Pierre Bruand, horse dealer, born in the bishopric of Saint-Omer and sentenced to the galleys for life by the Parlement of Douai in 1726 for stealing horses.

Criminologists make a distinction between petty theft (54 percent of those sentenced) and more serious theft (46 percent) accompanied by aggravating circumstances (table 3.5).

The fierce prosecution of thefts violating "public trust" indicates strong social disapproval of pilfering, for such thefts involved objects that in theory were not watched over by anyone but were entrusted to everyone's good faith. Offenses of this sort occurred in fields and gardens as well as in places where linen was stretched out to dry. On 5 May 1735 the Parlement of Aix decreed life in the galleys for a peasant from Fayence, in the diocese of Fréjus, who had "stolen by night some laundry that was still wet."

Thieves in the bagne in 1748 were one of two sorts: the "professional" thief, a category that included few if any large-scale thieves but rather a mass of small fry—such as pickpockets and cloak snatchers (who would grab the garment and run)—who had to employ a variety of expedients in order to survive; and thieves "by opportunity," whose number doubtlessly varied with the ups and downs of the economy. Theft stemming from need was a fact of life that starkly illustrates that this was a society of scarcity.

Table 3.5—Types of Theft

	Frequency of Sentences* (%)	
Nature of Theft	*As a 1st Reason*	*As a 2nd Reason*
Repeated thefts	10.4	6.8
Burglary	28.6	48.5
Theft by night	22.8	8.8
Highway robbery	9.9	15.6
Theft within the household	5.4	3.6
Theft in church	4.6	2.1
Theft that violated public trust	18.3	14.6
Total	100.0	100.0

*One and the same sentence can reveal the juxtaposition of several reasons for sentencing. I have carried the analysis as far as the second reason.

Table 3.6—Swindling, Fraud, Counterfeiting

Nature of Offense	Number Sentenced	
I. Swindling	6	
Breach of trust	2	
Fraudulent bankruptcy	1	
Peculation and malversation	4	
Total		13
II. Crimes involving fraud		
False witness	5	
Forgery	34	
Total		39
III. Counterfeiting		
"Making" counterfeit money	11	
Tampering with coinage	13	
Distributing counterfeit money	35	
Total		59
Grand total		111

Swindling, fraud, counterfeiting. Although judges in pre-revolutionary France used harsh measures to stop the most blatant attacks upon property, they seem to have been indulgent toward the more intelligent sorts of crime, counterfeiting excepted. This attitude can be partly explained by the relative rarity of such offenses. The case of Joseph Blanc, a wholesaler at Marseilles, is unique. In 1734 the Parlement of Aix gave him a life term in the galleys for fraudulent bankruptcy. The guilty party's social status was a major considera-- tion. Even if a government official was guilty of fraud, lying, or peculation, the magistrates hesitated to condemn one of their own kind to such a degrading punishment as the galleys. Yet, this was not the case for counterfeiters, for the judges fiercely and zealously prosecuted such threats to the royal prerogative.

SMUGGLING

Smugglers[19] formed the largest group in the galleys after those condemned for theft (table 3.7). One out of four convicts had been consigned to the oar for

Table 3.7—Smuggling

Nature of Offense	Offenders Sentenced (%)
Illegal salt trade	49.4
Illegal tobacco selling	46.5
Smuggling unspecified items	3.3
Violent treatment of excise officials	0.8

illegal salt or tobacco sales. I shall not go into the complex and varied legislation aimed at curtailing smuggling. After 1721 sellers of contraband salt or tobacco were subject to one and the same law, part of a particularly odious effort to stop the activities of these two groups[20] in order to protect the interests of the farmers-general. This policy met with total failure. The amount being smuggled continued to increase throughout the eighteenth century. Neither regular nor special legal measures were adequate to the task. The evil should have been attacked at the roots; but that is another story.

Illegal salt sellers. Until the 1720s smugglers sent to the bagne were almost exclusively individuals convicted of selling salt illegally; in most cases they earned a mere pittance by carrying a pack of salt to regions where that commodity was expensive and offering their wares there. Although the illegal salt trade attained a sizable volume, it continued to operate like any artisanal craft, despite the existence of well-organized bands.

Illegal sale of tobacco. Smuggling tobacco was a markedly different procedure from smuggling salt. The salt smuggler needed little capital; he carried about with him a commodity that was heavy but cheap; it also represented a basic human need. The tobacco smuggler had to invest considerable funds, but he handled a luxury item that could be compressed into a small packet. Indeed, from its very beginning tobacco smuggling was organized in a quasi-capitalistic manner.[21] Tobacco smugglers were organized into teams with a wide network of accomplices, and the illegal tobacco trade was masterminded by businessmen who invested their capital with a view to making a good profit.

Salt and tobacco smugglers seem almost never to have been delinquents by opportunity. They could not afford to quit their "business," despite the risks involved.

Offenses in rural areas and in the forests. This sort of crime is rarely found on the list for 1748. I tallied eight sentences for poaching, two for "pulling out trees," and one for "poisoning livestock." This category of offense bespeaks the tensions, hatreds, and jealousies at work in the village community. It would seem that the list of galley oarsmen is not a place where we can find valid evidence about offenses committed in the countryside and forests.[22]

MILITARY OFFENSES

In 1748 the bagne also served as a military prison (see table 3.8). More than one out of five prisoners was a soldier and, in almost every case, an "enlisted

Table 3.8—Military Offenses

Nature of Offense	Offenders Sentenced (%)	
I. Infractions pertaining to enlistments		
Enlisting soldiers by force	0.6	
Enlistment in another regiment before the		
end of a previous enlistment	2.0	
Declaration of a false identity	12.8	
Sale of equipment	0.2	
Total		15.6
II. Insubordination		
Disobedience and failure to obey orders	3.5	
Revolt and mutiny	2.0	
Total		5.5
III. Crimes involving bloodshed		
Violence toward a soldier or subordinate		
officer	14.6	
Murder of a soldier	1.3	
Total		15.9
IV. Desertion		62.8
V. Treason		0.2

man.'' For 44 percent of these soldiers, the sentence to the galleys resulted from common-law offenses such as violence, murder, theft, or smuggling; 56 percent were condemned for having committed a variety of infractions against military discipline.

There were four main categories of military offenses. Insubordination, in the strictest sense of the term, was rarely punished by the galleys, either at its lowest level (simple disobedience) or at its highest (mutiny). A soldier's declaration of a false identity was a rather frequent offense. His reason for making such a declaration is clear: to conceal his whereabouts in the regiment in order to make it difficult to locate him in the future. His motive is less certain; he may have been trying to move from one military unit to another in order to collect several enlistment bonuses. Violence seems to have been punished if the victim was a subordinate officer.[23] But the soldier sent to man the oar was above all else a deserter. During wartime desertion was punishable by death; in peacetime it meant a life sentence to the bagne. In actual practice the need for oarsmen resulted in the commutation of a number of death sentences to life in the galleys.[24]

Length of Sentence and the Jurisdiction Passing Sentence

With one exception—smuggling—the length of the sentence (table 3.9) was decided by the judge. Four-fifths of the salt and tobacco smugglers

Table 3.9—Relationship between Length of Sentence and Offense

Length of Sentence	% of All Offenses	Offenses					
		Crimes Involving Bloodshed, Arson	Disturbing Family or Religious Peace, Sexual Offenses	Disturbing Public Peace	Theft, Fraud, Swindling	Smuggling, Offenses in Rural Areas and Forests	Military Offenses
Under 5 years	13.3	6.1	3.6	6.3	4.5	39.5	2.0
5 to 9 years	22.7	9.8	16.1	28.5	17.4	43.4	5.9
Over 10 years	7.0	9.0	10.7	5.5	11.5	0.5	2.5
Life	57.0	75.1	69.6	59.7	66.5	16.6	89.6
Total	100.0	100.0	100.0	100.0	100.0[sic]	100.0	100.0

received short- and middle-term sentences, in accordance with a carefully determined scale fixed by royal order. All other offenses almost exclusively received long-term sentences, for punishment was meant to serve as an example to intimidate potential criminals. Those individuals condemned for specified periods, and who survived, did not always leave the galleys at the end of their sentence, at least not before the 1750s. "The galleys do not function like the chimerical purgatory of the Catholic Church. . . . No matter what the length of the sentence, the term is always forever, especially if the man has the bad luck to possess a strong body."[25] Officers in the galleys, ignoring royal decrees and parlementary protests, simply did not let their strongest rowers go. Thus, convicts sentenced to three or five years might spend thirty or forty years in the bagne! This practice was definitively ended after 1748–50, when the Royal Navy took charge of the crews of oarsmen. Although this change was of little help to the oldest convicts in the bagne, recently arrived men condemned for specific periods were from then on freed at the end of their sentences.

The enrollment list of 1748 enables us to perceive the gamut of jurisdictions sending prisoners to the galleys (table 3.10). The judicial system of prerevo-

Table 3.10—Jurisdictions Passing Sentences

Jurisdiction	Sentences (%)
I. Ordinary jurisdictions*	27.6
Prévôtés	
Bailliages and *sénéchaussées*	
Présidiaux	
Tribunals of the *maréchaussées*	
II. Sovereign courts†	29.6
Parlements and *conseils souverains*#	
Cours des aides	
Cours des monnaies	
Chambre des eaux et forêts	
III. Special jurisdictions‡	27.3
Justice of the *élus* and *intendants*	
Tribunals of the *greniers à sel* and *traites*	
Commissions du Conseil§	
IV. Military jurisdictions	13.7
Military *prévôté*	
War council	
V. Foreign jurisdictions‖	1.8
Legation and vice-legation of Avignon	
Town council of Soleure	
Council of the canton of Fribourg	
Aulic Council of the Grand Duchy of Baden	
Council of Regents of Zweibrücken	

*The ordinary jurisdictions (*juridictions ordinaires*)—an approximate equivalent of our lower courts—included the lesser courts of royal justice, which tried both civil and criminal cases.

(continued)

lutionary France was made up of a complex network of tribunals, often competing for authority, whose jurisdictions intersected and overlapped with-

---

Appeals could be made to a sovereign court (*cour souveraine*) for any major sentence, especially a sentence to death, the galleys, or banishment.

The *prévôté* could, however, judge summarily and without appeal crimes and offenses involving tramps, soldiers, deserters, beggars, and habitual offenders; such crimes were termed *cas prévôtaux* (see below, note 26). Nobles, clergy, royal secretaries, and judicial officials could not be tried before these courts.

The courts of the *bailliages* (the term generally used in the North) and the *sénéchaussées* (their southern equivalent) were regional courts that heard appeals from local seigneurial courts and cases involving nobles, minors, and livings in the church. They could also choose to try any *cas prévôtal*. The financial claims involved in a criminal case being heard by these courts could not exceed a given sum, thus restricting their influence on many matters.

The *présidiaux* were virtually superimposed upon the bailliages and sénéchaussées. A *présidial* could choose to try any cas prévôtal but could judge in last resort only for sentences to a term in the galleys, banishment, flogging, or the iron collar; a death sentence or a sentence to life in the galleys could be appealed before the appropriate parlement.

The *maréchaussées* were the royal mounted police assigned to supervise rural France and keep tramps, thieves, and beggars under control.—Trans.

†The *cours souveraines*—the "sovereign" or supreme courts—included the courts composing the various *parlements* and *conseils souverains*. The parlements served legislative functions and at the same time were among the highest permanent tribunals. The Parlement of Paris was by far the most important parlement, with jurisdiction over about one-half of the realm; various provincial parlements had corresponding powers.

Other sovereign courts included (1) the various *cours des aides,* supreme courts for cases involving taxes (*taille, aides, octroi*), which also heard appeals from the courts of the *greniers à sel,* the judges of the *traites,* and the *élus* (see ‡ below); (2) the *cours des monnaies,* supreme judges of cases involving coinage—especially counterfeiting—which could, however, choose to hear cases normally tried by an ordinary jurisdiction; and (3) the *chambre des eaux et forêts,* which heard cases brought before the *Table de marbre* ["Marble Table"], cases that involved such illegal activities in forests or waters of the royal domain as cutting immature wood or breaking the laws concerning hunting, fishing, or river navigation.—Trans.

#The provinces that had recently been annexed to the French Crown (Roussillon, Artois, and Alsace) had no parlements in 1748, but the functions of a parlement were performed by a superior jurisdiction. The situation of Lorraine was similar. The duchy was not officially annexed until 1766, and a *conseil souverain* sitting at Nancy was transformed into a parlement in 1775.

‡The ordinary and sovereign courts were supplemented by a number of special courts created to try cases involving various branches of the royal administration, further complicating overlapping jurisdictions.

The *élus* supervised the apportionment of tax assessments throughout the parishes included in their administrative district, or *élection*. In addition, they were members of a court empowered to pass judgment upon cases involving such taxes as the tailles or the *aides.*

The *intendants* represented the king in a province. Being outside the network of established courts, they could intervene to see that justice was done should ordinary courts prove ineffectual; sometimes they judged specific matters by order of the king. In short, they could deal with almost any question.

The *greniers à sel* (literally, "salt storehouses") were courts dealing with infractions concerning the gabelle, or salt tax. Major cases of fraud could be appealed to a *cour des aides.* Special judges dealt with cases involving the *traites,* that is, fees levied upon merchandise leaving or entering the kingdom or crossing certain provincial frontiers.—Trans.

§That is, the special boards of inquiry composed of magistrates that were created after 1730 to judge, with no appeal possible, offenses involving illegal tobacco sales.

‖In other words, the criminal courts of small, independent states encapsulated within the kingdom of France or immediately adjacent to it.

out reason. Organizing such stubborn data for any rational analysis was, therefore, a very difficult task.

The percentage of sentences passed by ordinary jurisdictions was about equal to the percentage for sovereign courts. Appeal to a higher court was the rule for a sentence to the galleys, although this rule did not apply to the numerous *cas prévôtaux*.[26] Whenever an offense was considered to be a cas prévôtal, judges of the first and second instance were able to hand down a summary conviction to the galleys, as occurred with a sizable proportion of the convicts listed in 1748. These magistrates frequently showed the greater severity, since ordinary justice handed down 70 percent of all life sentences, while the sovereign courts condemned only 60 percent for life.

Four out of ten galley rowers were not sentenced by a traditional jurisdiction (ordinary justice and the sovereign courts), but by tribunals specifically created to judge smuggling or military offenses. This ratio led me to probe further into the correlation between the type of offense and the sentencing jurisdiction (table 3.11).

Bailliages, présidiaux, and maréchaussées generally heard cases involving theft, vagrancy, and relatively minor violence (assault and battery, beatings, and stabbings). The sovereign courts heard cases involving more serious crimes, such as homicide, disturbing the family or religious peace, and sexual offenses; they participated at least as much as the ordinary courts in prosecuting offenses against property. Smuggling was judged almost exclusively by special tribunals, although here the courts of the *élus* were of minor importance, because most cases went before the judges of the *greniers à sel* or the commissions du Conseil. The *intendants* showed a more eclectic taste, for the "crimes" they judged included smuggling, disturbing the peace (that is, belonging to the Religion Prétendue Reformée), and theft.

Three-quarters of the soldiers sentenced for military offenses were sent to the bagne by a war council during the War of Spanish Succession and the War of Austrian Succession. In peacetime the military prévôtés and *intendants* prosecuted military offenses.

I also studied the relationships between offenses and jurisdictions in terms of the date of the sentence, in order to separate the convicts condemned prior to 1740 from those sentenced after that date. This resulted in a more complex chart in which new factors appear (table 3.12).

For all categories of offense, the percentage of convicts sentenced by ordinary justice decreased sharply after 1740. The powers of the bailliages, the présidiaux, and the maréchaussée seem to have been seriously weakened, to the advantage of the sovereign courts and the special tribunals. The document of 1748 has its limitations, and my hypotheses should be confirmed (or invalidated) by a complete study of the enrollment records. During the course of the eighteenth century the courts of the bailliages, présidiaux, and the

Table 3.11—Relationship between Offenses and Jurisdictions

		Offenses				
Jurisdiction	*Crimes Involving Bloodshed, Arson*	*Disturbing Family or Religious Peace, Sexual Offenses*	*Disturbing Public Peace*	*Theft, Fraud, Swindling*	*Smuggling, Offenses in Rural Areas and Forests*	*Military Offenses*
Ordinary justice	25.3	24.1	69.9	41.0	2.0	0.5
Sovereign courts	45.3	70.4	12.8	47.4	4.9	0.5
Special jurisdictions	8.8	3.7	14.3	2.9	86.7	23.0
Military jurisdictions*	19.3	0.0	0.2	6.0	5.5	75.8
Foreign jurisdictions	1.3	1.8	2.8	2.7	0.9	0.2
Total	100.0	100.0	100.0	100.0	100.0	100.0

*This pertains not to delinquency among soldiers, but to all infractions of discipline committed by men in the military.

Table 3.12—Relationship between Offenses and Jurisdictions according to Date of Conviction

| | Offenses and Date of Sentencing | | | | | | | | | | | |
| | Crimes Involving Bloodshed, Arson | | Disturbing Family or Religious Peace, Sexual Offenses | | Disturbing Public Peace | | Theft, Fraud, Swindling | | Smuggling, Offenses in Rural Areas and Forests | | Military Offenses | |
Jurisdiction	Before 1740	After 1740	Before 1740	After 1740	Before 1740	After 1740	Before 1740	After 1740	Before 1740	After 1740	Before 1740	After 1740
Ordinary justice	36.5	14.6	42.9	3.8	88.7	57.0	51.4	33.5	5.1	1.9	0.9	0.0
Sovereign courts	37.6	52.4	57.1	84.7	6.9	16.8	39.8	52.8	5.1	4.9	0.0	1.1
Special jurisdictions	1.7	15.7	0.0	0.0	3.1	21.9	0.8	4.4	42.4	89.6	0.0	50.3
Military jurisdictions	22.5	16.2	0.0	0.0	0.0	0.4	5.6	6.3	44.1	2.8	98.6	48.6
Foreign jurisdictions	1.7	1.1	0.0	3.8	1.3	3.9	2.4	3.0	3.3	0.8	0.5	0.0
Total	100.0	100.0	100.0	100.0 [sic]	100.0	100.0	100.0	100.0	100.0	100.0	100.0	100.0

maréchaussée came under increasing attack. Judges in these ordinary courts were labeled incompetent, even ignorant; they were criticized for being unduly severe on some occasions and unduly lenient on others. At that point the monarchy created parallel courts with commissioned magistrates who were subject to recall. The *intendants* and the commissions du Conseil pursued their efforts at curbing crime despite marked hostility from the traditional legal corps. Here we encounter one of the constants of the administrative and judicial system of early-modern France; when the monarchy created new mechanisms, it did not abolish outmoded institutions, for it would have been obliged to reimburse the purchasers of the offices being eliminated.

A Socio-demographic Profile of Oarsmen

Age groups. The enrollment list gives the convict's age at the time of sentencing.[27] Royal decrees specified that magistrates should send to the galleys only sound men possessed of great stamina. Little attention was paid to these orders, for weak, ill, crippled, and elderly men, as well as adolescents, were marched off to man the oar. There was no "sorting" of convicts according to age or physical strength.[28]

Table 3.13, which groups convicts by age, reveals an apparently young convict population. Men under thirty years of age predominated; beyond that threshold the pyramid tapers off rapidly. But this picture must not be taken literally. This "youthfulness" of the penal population is partly explained by the high proportion of military prisoners, since soldiers abounded in the youngest age groups. The manner in which the document was drawn up also explains the high proportion of younger men, since only the youngest of all

Table 3.13—Age Distribution of Oarsmen

Age Group	Frequency	Cumulative Frequency	Percentage of Soldiers in Each Age Group
15–19 years	10.3	10.3	21.4
20–24 years	24.1	34.4	38.0
25–29 years	20.6	55.0	29.6
30–34 years	15.9	70.9	18.1
35–39 years	10.0	80.9	14.7
40–44 years	7.7	88.6	7.3
45–49 years	5.0	93.6	5.2
50–54 years	2.8	96.4	2.8
55–59 years	1.6	88.0	3.2
60–64 years	1.3	99.3	2.0
65–69 years	0.7	100.0	0.0

the convicts condemned to the oar between 1700 and 1740 managed to survive and be listed in 1748.

I therefore studied the age pattern for all convicts sentenced in 1747–48. This cross section permitted me to tally the age groups and yet remain free of the intrusive factor of mortality in the bagne, a factor that, in the document in question, tends to show an excessive number of very young men. The results are significant. While the document shows that 55 percent of the total number of convicts were under thirty years of age, my analysis of the men condemned in 1747–48 reveals that only 38.6 percent of the 550 convicts were under thirty. Moreover, the arithmetic mean of their ages shifted from thirty to thirty-five years. We are, therefore, not dealing exclusively with a group of young criminals, since mature men—and, indeed, men of every age group—were also well represented in the bagne in 1748.

Age Groups and Type of Offense.   Each age group has a specific type of crime (table 3.14). This is a known fact, now as in the past, even if the various "ages of man" were not perceived in exactly the same fashion in the eighteenth century and in the world today. Young criminals were either *lazzoroni* who haunted the streets and countryside or, as their age would suggest, military delinquents; to a lesser degree they were also tramps and smugglers. Crime among grown men and men on the brink of middle age is less clear-cut. Men between the ages of thirty and forty seem to have been emotional and intemperate, committing crimes involving violence, violation of moral and religious interdicts, and sexual misbehavior. This was also a greedy and dissatisfied age, exacerbated by the fact that life's die had already been cast. Not only did these men steal, they also committed the whole panoply of offenses involving deviousness, such as swindling, embezzling, and fraud. Another sort of criminality appears in the spotlight among men over forty. Indeed, the majority of offenders in the older age group seems to have been involved in smuggling. Illegal traffic in salt and tobacco provided a livelihood for those who could no longer earn a living as hired laborers. The oldest criminals were vagrants and beggars, senile tramps who were often carried away by a spurt of rebelliousness and violence toward a society that ignored the needs of its "senior citizens."

Marriage and Celibacy Rates.   I also used the sample of convicts sentenced in 1747–48 to analyze the respective percentages of married and single men within each age group. The youngest groups presented hardly any surprises, for very few (one out of ten) of the men under twenty-five had been married before entering the bagne. The behavior of those under thirty seems very revealing, for in that age group more than 70 percent were still bachelors. Although the amount of celibacy among prisoners decreased markedly after age thirty, it still remained "abnormally" high; 40 percent of the convicts

Table 3.14—Relationship between Offense and Age Group

Offense	Age Group										
	15–19	20–24	25–29	30–34	35–39	40–44	45–49	50–54	55–59	60–64	65–69
Crimes involving bloodshed	3.8	10.6	10.1	14.1	10.8	13.8	7.8	5.8	0.0	8.5	8.7
Disturbing family and religious peace; sexual offenses	1.1	1.1	2.2	1.7	1.7	1.8	1.1	1.9	3.6	0.0	0.0
Disturbing public peace	11.9	8.8	10.9	8.6	10.2	9.1	11.7	8.6	16.4	14.9	8.7
Theft and swindling	51.2	41.6	36.7	39.4	34.9	31.7	32.4	24.0	29.1	19.1	17.4
Fraud	1.0	2.1	3.3	2.9	5.4	5.4	3.9	4.8	1.8	0.0	4.4
Smuggling and offenses in rural areas and forests	20.5	16.5	22.6	25.7	31.4	35.7	42.0	52.0	49.1	57.5	60.8
Military offenses	10.5	19.3	14.2	7.6	5.8	2.5	1.1	2.9	0.0	0.0	0.0
Total	100.0	100.0	100.0	100.0	100.0	100.0	100.0	100.0	100.0	100.0	100.0

Table 3.15—Percentage of Married and Single Men among Convicts Sentenced, 1747–48

| | Age Group | | | | | | | | |
Status	15–19	20–24	25–29	30–34	35–39	40–44	45–49	50–54	55–59
Single	100.0	90.4	72.0	46.4	38.2	24.5	15.4	14.8	18.7
Married	0.0	9.6	28.0	53.6	61.8	75.5	84.6	85.2	81.3
Total	100.0	100.0	100.0	100.0	100.0	100.0	100.0	100.0	100.0

between thirty-five and thirty-nine years of age were unmarried. After forty-five, this continually decreasing proportion of unmarried men stabilized at about 15 percent.

Various demographic studies of early-modern France indicate that during the eighteenth century the average male age at marriage oscillated between twenty-five and twenty-seven years. "The largest group of married men were between twenty and thirty years of age, and by age thirty, four-fifths of all men were married."[29] Clearly, this tendency to remain single[30] that I noted among convicts in the twenty-five- to thirty-five-year-old group is a characteristic peculiar to the penal population and undoubtedly reveals an inability or a refusal to strike roots by creating a family (table 3.15).

GEOGRAPHIC ORIGINS OF CONVICTS

An analysis of the entire series of enrollment lists will make it possible to draw a map of crime in early-modern France, but the document of 1748 forced me to set more modest goals. A study of the geographic distribution of convicts on the parish or even the city level was impossible, since the list of names in the document is too short. I therefore chose to do a breakdown by bishoprics, which roughly correspond to the old provinces of the realm.[31]

Geographic Origins and Type of Offense. I was able to compare the place of birth and the reason for the conviction, using a double-entry table that included only the most frequent offenses—crimes involving bloodshed, illegal begging and vagrancy, theft, and smuggling.

The eastern half of the kingdom, from the province of Artois to the province of Provence, shows the greatest number of violent crimes. Individuals convicted of theft are more widely scattered, although certain provinces—Normandy, Guyenne, and Provence—stand out clearly from the others. The geographic origin of tramps follows a distinct pattern; the region around Orléans, the southwest, the region around Lyons, and the duchy of Lorraine were the hotbeds of vagrancy. A majority of those dealing in illegal salt were born in the western or central regions along the Loire and Allier rivers. The frontier provinces—the Artois-Boulonnais-Picardy triangle to the north,

Navarre and Béarn to the southwest, and Franche-Comté and Dauphiné to the east—were, as they are today, active centers of smuggling.

Distribution of the Military Population.[32]   The areas along the northern, eastern, and southwestern frontiers of the kingdom supplied a large contingent of military prisoners. Here my findings mesh with the maps of military recruitment drawn up by André Corvisier.[33] On the other hand, few delinquent soldiers came from the maritime provinces, known for supplying men for the military. The central region of the kingdom, a region that traditionally supplied few soldiers, also shows a low percentage of military convicts. The Ile-de-France is an unusual case, because 40 percent of the oarsmen from that region were soldiers, although the province was not an area of heavy military recruitment.

AN ATTEMPT AT SOCIO-OCCUPATIONAL
DISTRIBUTION

The list of 1748 gives the occupation of four out of five convicts (81 percent). Here I ran into the by-now classic stumbling block encountered by most researchers in social history: socio-occupational classification. The register in question does not list the men of one specific town or region so that, by crosschecking several documents, the historian can determine the importance and the socio-economic implications of his list of crafts and occupations. Nothing of the sort was possible for these galley rowers, all of whom were deportees, uprooted individuals from all the provinces of the realm who constituted a veritable Tower of Babel [as a result of the great variety of regional dialects found in the bagne].

The document confronts us with a whole set of uncertainties. I was unable to separate masters from journeymen, urban artisans from rural ones, and shopkeepers "established" behind their counters from mere peddlers. Classifying the peasantry was less difficult, although certain ambiguities could not be avoided, since the *laboureur* ["independent farmer"] from Champagne had little in common with the *laboureur* from those southern provinces speaking the langue d'oc. I decided to make a distinction between those who worked a farm, regardless of whether they owned it (*laboureurs*, vineyard workers, tenant farmers, or sharecroppers) and those men who were obliged to hire themselves out as laborers (that is, such groups as unskilled laborers, field hands, or *brassiers* ["men whose work was done by arm-power"]). Although this classification is rather makeshift, it nevertheless takes into account a major dividing line in the rural world.

Less than 30 percent of the convict oarsmen in 1748 were peasants, in a kingdom where 75 to 80 percent of the population tilled the soil. I specify "peasants," not people living in the countryside, for an undetermined per-

104 ANDRE ZYSBERG

centage of artisans undoubtedly lived in symbiosis with a village community (table 3.16).

Many convicts stated that they had no specific job; they were the *sans métiers,* handymen who did any odd jobs they could find. There was almost no difference between them and the convicts who said they had a "minor trade," that is, *gagne-deniers* ["working for pennies"], porters, water-carriers, basketweavers, fiddlers, or peddlers. These two categories—the unemployed and those in minor trades—account for 27 percent of the total number of convicts, a percentage' almost equal to that of the peasantry.

More than four out of ten convicts came from the world of artisans and commerce, a world that stretched from the tiny shop to the manufactory. A striking number of prisoners had worked in the cloth, clothing, and trimming trades; almost a quarter belonged to that group. Cloth workers appear most frequently, along with numerous spinners, carders, combers, weavers, and shearers. At times the terminology is explicit, and a convict is designated as a "handworker" in silk, wool, linen, or velvet. Those operating machines,

Table 3.16—Socio-occupational Distribution of Oarsmen

Socio-occupational Categories	Number Sentenced	
I. *Laboureurs,* vineyard workers, *ménagers* ["householders"],* tenant farmers, sharecroppers	18.9	
Wage-earning agricultural workers	9.6	
Total		28.5
II. Minor trades in fields and streets; domestic service	5.1	
Shopkeepers (of all sorts); peddlers	2.6	
Sans métier ["with no trade"]	17.7	
Gypsies	1.4	
Total		26.8
III. Transportation trades	2.0	
Building trades	3.6	
Wood, metal, and leather trades	7.5	
Cloth, trimming, and clothing trades	23.5	
Miscellaneous crafts	1.0	
Trades involving food; cattle and horse dealers	4.8	
Total		42.4
Superior group†	1.9	
Miscellaneous unclassified	0.4	
Grand total		100.0

*A *ménager* was a well-to-do peasant who either owned his own land, rented relatively large plots from someone else, or cultivated a combination of his own and rented fields. Better yet, he might even make his living from farming the land of another individual without doing any of the actual physical work himself.—Trans.

†This category includes officials (notaries, *procureurs,* marshals, registrars), "bourgeois," and physicians and surgeons.

whether brought together in urban workshops or spread throughout the open country, already foreshadow the nineteenth-century equation, *classes laborieuses, classes dangereuses* [laboring classes, dangerous classes] described by Louis Chevalier [in his book by that name, published in 1958].

Social Factors of Delinquency. I drew up a double-entry table to show the frequency of the various offenses represented in the bagne in 1748 for each socio-occupational category (table 3.17).[34]

Smuggling consigned four out of ten peasant offenders to the oar—chiefly for illegal traffic in salt, since illegal tobacco sales involved a much wider socio-occupational spectrum. This high percentage of smugglers gives crime among the peasantry its own individual stamp. Although other sorts of offenses were well represented among the two agricultural groups, they were less frequent compared with the numerous convictions for salt smuggling, a social rather than a criminal act. Following upon the great antitaxation revolts of the seventeenth century, government prosecution of the illegal salt trade is evidence of the silent but stubborn struggle of one segment of the rural world against the unfair system of the gabelle.

The group carrying on minor trades in the fields and streets also committed its own very distinct sort of crime. Half the *gagne-deniers* had been sentenced for theft. Here we are again dealing with *lazzoroni* who had been forced into crime by poverty and had to resort to petty thefts for their daily subsistence.

Military offenses are underrepresented in these first three categories, for a good share of the soldiers sent to the galleys are listed under "occupation unknown." These military delinquents had rarely been apprenticed to a trade, either on a farm or in a workshop; free of all social constraint, they were prepared to try "the soldier's life" and were also ready, whenever the opportunity presented itself, to join bands of smugglers and bandits. Thus, the army unwittingly served as a training ground for delinquents.

The *sans métiers* show a rather similar pattern of criminal behavior; indeed, these two categories—"occupation unknown" and "with no trade"—could well have been combined. Violence was the most common offense among men with "no trade"; they were also frequently sentenced for sexual offenses and for disturbing the family or religious peace. Murder was less common, for the homicide rate among this group was noticeably lower than that among artisans or men running a farm. Crime among the *sans métiers* was of the rowdy and aggressive kind, committed by young, unstable men who upset the daily life of village and urban communities. They rarely went much farther and did not threaten the established order; on the contrary, they profited from the disorders and contradictions that permeated the society of early-modern France.

Delinquency in the world of artisans and shopkeepers was chiefly oriented around "crimes" against property—theft, but also swindling, fraud, and

Table 3.17—Relationship between Socio-occupational Category and Offense

	Socio-occupational Category					
Offense	Laboureurs, Vineyard Workers, Tenant Farmers	Wage-earning Agricultural Workers	Minor Trades, Shopkeepers of All Sorts, Peddlers	"Sans Métier"	Occupation Unknown	Trades in Transport or Commerce, Artisans
Violence	4.5	3.1	3.3	5.8	6.1	5.6
Homicide	5.5	3.8	5.9	2.8	3.9	5.5
Disturbing family or religious peace, sexual offenses	1.0	0.3	1.4	1.9	1.4	1.5
Vagrancy, begging, disregarding decree of banishment	5.5	8.2	9.2	14.6	6.7	8.0
Theft	37.8	41.0	50.1	34.5	34.3	43.1
Swindling, fraud	0.6	0.6	0.7	0.5	1.4	1.8
Counterfeiting	2.0	1.2	0.7	0.7	1.1	2.3
Smuggling	36.7	41.3	20.2	22.7	24.5	22.6
Military offenses	6.4	0.5	8.5	16.5	20.6	9.6
Total	100.0	100.0	100.0	100.0	100.0	100.0

counterfeiting. The most intelligent criminals (with the exception of those in the superior group) almost always came from this socio-occupational category. The group carrying on specific trades had one other marked characteristic: a maximum rate of offenses involving bloodshed. This was undoubtedly a more specifically urban sort of violence, characteristic of the often turbulent world of journeymen.

The superior group does not appear in the table because it included too few individuals. Yet I shall hazard—with the usual reservations—an analysis of the criminal tendencies pertaining to that category. Clerics, bourgeois, officials, and physicians were only rarely sentenced for theft, vagrancy, or smuggling; among these groups we find a high proportion of crimes involving bloodshed, disturbances of the family or of religious peace, and sexual offenses. This was true for the ecclesiastic sent to man the oar as a "corrupter of the young" or the violent and sacrilegious bourgeois youth who scandalized his small town. In this superior group we also find (long before the term was coined) "white-collar crime," as in the case of the *procureur* convicted of fraud or the marshal who confiscated another's possessions and then claimed them for himself.

Thus, three levels of crime can be found among the mid-eighteenth century galley rowers:

1. Crime committed by peasants. The average age of convicts from the peasantry was higher than that of the penal population as a whole. Many of these men were "established" and had a wife and children. The "peasant crime" among oarsmen was smuggling, a collective and daily offense in rural communities along frontier regions, whether the frontiers were internal customs barriers or external, national boundaries.

2. Crime committed by men engaged in minor trades and by men with "no trade." This sort of crime was typical of adolescents and young adults, migrants who had been separated from their families. Military offenses, theft, and vagrancy constituted the offenses characteristic of these young outlaws.

3. Crime committed by artisans and shopkeepers. This group shows characteristics more typical of the urban setting, for a sizable number of bachelors were included in the twenty-five to forty-year-old group, and a much greater than average number of their offenses were of the devious kind.

The qualitative and quantitative relationship between crime in the city and crime in the countryside is an essential issue that must be raised. The document under study deals with only a small proportion of all officially recognized crimes, that is, the crimes actually heard and punished by the courts; judges found it easier to prosecute offenses committed in urban settings, where the meshes of the "police dragnet" were tighter than in the countryside. This reservation notwithstanding, compared to its numerical weight in French society during the 1750s, the socio-cultural milieu formed by the peasantry seems to have produced relatively few criminals.

For people of the eighteenth century, the world of the galley oarsmen constituted an "anti-France," a hell that engulfed both criminals and the poor, the big and the little "game" hunted by the tribunals of the kingdom. A chain gang of convicts passing through a town triggered disgust and fear, on occasion charity, but only rarely a questioning and a critical attitude toward the judicial system. Although the enrollment lists permit analytical computations of recorded crimes, they also show something of the fears, the refusal to see, and the tensions present in the world of "honest folk."

NOTES

1. The most complete history of the galleys is still Paul Masson's *Les galères de France,* Annales de la Faculté d'Aix, 1937. The most recent work is that of Paul W. Bamford, *Fighting Ships and Prisons: The Mediterranean Galleys of France in the Age of Louis XIV* (Minneapolis, 1973). [Bamford's glossary defines the word *bagne* as follows: "prison or prison compound; many Mediterranean port cities had one, particularly if their inhabitants engaged in slaving. At Marseilles after 1700, and at other ports later, the workhouse manufactory where workable invalids and many able-bodied forçats [convicts] were housed, fed, and worked in conditions resembling those in some early modern factories" (p. 321).—Trans.]

2. The bagne at Lorient was closed in 1823, that at Rochefort in 1852, and that at Brest in 1858. Toulon's bagne remained functional until 1873, by which date most convicts were being interned in the colonial penal colonies. The enrollment lists remained at the locations of the closed bagnes and can be found in the local archives of Rochefort, Brest, and Toulon, in series 10, "Institutions de répression." The archives at Lorient were the only ones destroyed during the bombings of 1943.

3. The enrollment registers were recopied whenever the names contained in them were almost gxclusively those of the dead or missing. At that point the names of the survivors were transferred to a new book and a new series of enrollments was begun.

4. Bamford's comment in a letter to me. Bamford also used these registers while preparing his *Fighting Ships,* which deals with the history of the galleys. The group volume, *Crimes et criminalité en France (17ᵉ-18ᵉ siècles),* Cahiers des Annales, no. 33 (Paris: Colin, 1971), refers to a project of the Law Faculty at the University of Aix about "the galley oarsmen and convicts of Toulon and Marseilles in the eighteenth century." I checked this out, only to find that the project has been dropped. As far as I know, the only work now under way on these registers is that of Loffreda, "Les galériens de Marseille, 1686–90," master's thesis, Faculty of Aix.

The records of the crews of oarsmen have, however, served as sources for other studies, including François Vaux de Foletier's *Les Tsiganes dans l'ancienne France* (Paris, 1961) and Gaston Tournier's *Les galères de France et les galériens protestants* (Cévennes: Musée du Désert, 1943).

5. There is one exception: the Montyon file discovered in the National Archives by Jean Lecuir; cf. his "Criminalité et moralité: Montyon, statisticien du Parlement de Paris," *Revue d'Histoire moderne et contemporaine* 21 (July–September, 1974): 445–93.

6. The research of A.-L.-J. Quételet (*Physique sociale* [Brussels, 1835]), and of André-Michel Guerry *(Essai sur la statistique morale de la France* [Paris, 1833]) marked a decisive step forward. The "cartographic school" also prompted the general statistical accounting by the office of criminal justice that began in 1825. [For a discussion of these statistical studies, see Chapter 7 of this volume.—Trans.]

7. There is no doubt that more than 100,000 convicts were sent to the bagne during this period. Despite the cost of the undertaking, this population deserves a computerized study.

8. Centre de Recherches Historiques, Ecole Pratique des Hautes Etudes, VIᵉ Section.

9. Archives nationales, Fonds marine, series D 5, *chiourmes* [crews of galley rowers]. The register contains data of a quality equal to that of the enrollment registers of Toulon, but the two documents were drawn up in a different fashion. The document in the Archives nationales is a sort

of "still photo" of the bagne at a given moment, while the more typical series of registers resembles a "moving picture" of the successive entrances of oarsmen after 1685.

10. I would like to thank Mme Karp and MM. Abehassera, Béaur, and Coulier for their patient help, especially during the crucial moments of the computer run.

11. To be specific, 3,997 convicts. Actually, only 3,934 of them showed up in the results of the computerized analysis. My inexperience was one of the chief reasons for this loss of 1.5 percent of the data.

12. Gérard Aubry, *La jurisprudence criminelle du Châtelet de Paris sous le règne de Louis XVI* (Paris, 1971), proposes a classification of offenses that closely follows that found in seventeenth- and eighteenth-century legal commentaries on crime.

13. In 1748, fourteen men were in the bagne for arson. An exceptional sort of crime, a "monstrous" crime for the norms of the day, arson was regarded as another form of violent crime. I therefore placed it in that category. [See also Chapter 5 of this volume.—Trans.]

14. A twenty-five-year-old carpenter from the bishopric of Rieux was sentenced to life in the galleys by the Parlement of Toulouse on 25 January 1725 for "having done away with a child." The sentence does not specify whether or not it was his own child.

15. The judges were hard on extreme forms of behavior, especially on the part of women, but were more willing to tolerate it among men. Here is one exception: On 22 September 1725 the Parlement of Douai sentenced thirty-two-year-old Charles Minard, a native of the city of Liège and a man with "no trade," to twenty-five years in the galleys for "having abandoned his wife and children and taken up with a woman who was supporting him with stolen money."

16. This type of delinquency has been discussed in the works of Jean-Pierre Gutton: *La société et les pauvres. L'exemple de la Généralité de Lyon, 1534–1789* (Paris, 1971), and *L'Etat et la mendicité dans la première moitié du XVIIIe siècle. Auvergne, Beaujolais, Forez, Lyonnais* (Paris, 1973).

17. André Abbiateci, *Les incendiaires devant le Parlement de Paris,* included in the joint volume of the Cahiers des Annales cited in note 4, discusses "blackmail by fire."

18. For example, Aubry, *La jurisprudence criminelle,* or Annette Farge, *Le vol d'aliments à Paris au 18e siècle* (Paris, 1964), which presents a detailed analysis of one type of theft and its social significance.

19. On smuggling, see J. Bonneau, "Les législations françaises sur les tabacs sous l'Ancien Régime," law thesis, Paris, 1910; and Paul Bequet, *Contrebande et contrebandiers* (Paris, 1959). The most recent work on the subject is that by Marie-Hélène Bourquin and Emmanuel Hepp, *Aspects de la contrebande au XVIIIe siècle* (Paris, 1969), which provides a careful analysis of Mandrin's activities [see translator's note in Chapter 4 of this volume] and includes in its second half an interesting synthesis about tobacco smuggling in the eighteenth century.

20. Smugglers working alone were sentenced to pay large fines, fines far beyond their ability to pay. Flogged and branded with the letters GAL [for *galérien,* 'galley rower'], they would be sent to the galleys for a period ranging from three to five years. When the offense involved aggravating circumstances (such as smuggling as a member of a band, or on horseback, or while carrying a weapon), the sentence was for life. If violence was done to employees of the tax "farms," the law required a death sentence. If a solitary smuggler was a recidivist, he was sentenced to the bagne for life.

21. According to Hepp's analysis in Bourquin and Hepp, *Aspects de la contrebande.*

22. To give but one example: In 1707 the Parlement of Rouen handed down a life sentence to the galleys for Jacques Moulin, a twenty-year-old shepherd from Longru, in the archbishopric of Rouen, for having poisoned livestock. This shepherd died at Toulon forty-six years later.

23. The victims consisted of fifty sergeants, seven cavalry or artillery sergeants, four corporals, and five enlisted men.

24. During the seventeenth century the punishment for desertion involved mutilation by cutting off the ears and nose of the offender. In the following century a simulated amputation sufficed.

25. Jean Bion, *Relation des tourments qu'on fait subir aux protestants qui sont sur les galères de France* (reprint ed., Paris, 1883). Bion, in 1703 a chaplain on the galley *La Superbe,* provides priceless evidence about daily life in the galleys. Revolted by the treatment of Protestant rowers, the chaplain made his way to Geneva and then, in 1707, to London, where he wrote his account and dedicated it to Queen Anne. During his exile he became a convert to Protestantism.

26. The criminal ordinace of 1670, expanded in 1730, listed the various *cas prévôtaux*. The list is long and detailed, so I shall not reproduce it here. In reality, almost all cases represented in the bagne in 1748 were cas prévôtaux, even though they had not been judged as such. [See Chapter 4 of this volume for a discussion of these cases.]

27. The information is available for 98.9 percent of the convict oarsmen, although to be accurate, in most cases the stated age was approximate, rather than exact. Convicts between thirty-eight and forty-two years of age might well state that they were forty years old. The older the convict, the more pronounced this tendency.

28. The actual "selection" occurred on the galleys themselves. Convicts with little physical stamina disappeared very rapidly from the lists of oarsmen.

29. Marcel Lachiver, *La population de Meulan du XVIIIᵉ siècle au XIXᵉ siècle* (Paris, 1969).

30. It should come as no surprise that an undetermined percentage of the unmarried men probably lived with women to whom they were not wed.

31. This was easy for such provinces as Brittany and Provence, where the diocese had remained an administrative unit; in the other cases, the task was more complicated. This geographic division by groups of dioceses is not altogether satisfactory, for it does not permit comparisons with demographic and economic data, which are usually organized in terms of *généralités* [a financial subdivision of the realm that in most cases was synonymous with the region administered by an *intendant*].

32. In using the list for 1748, I disregarded such distinctions as branches of the armed services, voluntary enlistees, and militia men. Since a large number of soldiers are to be found in the galleys in the late seventeenth century, a more detailed study of crime among soldiers during that period would be possible.

33. André Corvisier, *L'armée française de la fin du XVIIᵉ siècle au ministère de Choiseul* (Paris, 1964).

34. Socio-occupational information is unavailable for one-fifth of the convicts listed. I did, however, analyze the distribution of offenses and ages for the group of convicts listed under "occupation unknown." My findings show that omitting a man's trade was no accident resulting from administrative negligence. The convict did not state his occupation because he did not have one and actually was a *sans métier*.

4
Summary Justice

Nicole Castan

The words *summary justice* immediately evoke arbitrariness. Indeed, this same image came to mind for people of the eighteenth century, people moved by a new determination that all should be equal before the law. It is paradoxical that the courts of the *prévôtés*,[*a] created to deal with the uprooted elements of society, relied upon the same military force as the Tribunal of Points of Honor, created to deal with the nobles located at the opposite end of the social scale. Established in the sixteenth century, strengthened in the seventeenth, and reorganized in the eighteenth, this special type of court had been set up by the monarchy to absorb the surplus cases confronting the established legal system.

As a rule, the authorities' constant concern with maintaining order was usually far from inquisitorial in nature. In fact, for a long while the government trusted that such matters would take care of themselves or could be prosecuted within the ordinary legal system that was a part of established society. Whenever peasant revolts or urban riots caused the authorities to wonder whether this equilibrium would continue, the army would immediately be called out, and it always managed to reestablish a satisfactory degree of order. This held true until the eighteenth century; still, threats to public safety were a common occurrence, though less noisy than revolts or riots.

The fact that such disturbances were committed by persons on the fringe of society aroused anxiety, for these individuals had left their customary place in

Annales, E.S.C. 31 (March–April 1976), pp. 331–61. Translated by Patricia M. Ranum. The author wishes to thank the Centre de Recherches Historiques, Ecole des Hautes Etudes en Sciences Sociales, which did the computer work for this article under the supervision of M. Couturier and his coworkers. I would also like to thank M. Higounet, who agreed to incorporate the mapwork for this article into the course of study in the laboratory of historical cartography at Bordeaux. The skillful artwork was done by Mlle Bugat.

*Many of the legal and administrative terms used in this article (indicated by [a]) are explained in author's and translator's notes in Chapter 3 of this volume.—Trans.

the social order and as a result were becoming dangerously aggressive. In addition, the regular courts, lacking the means of taking action against them and bringing them to trial, were unable to neutralize these disruptive elements. For the courts were dealing with "foreigners," that is, outsiders—and one was quickly termed a foreigner in that closed world where contact with the outside was restricted to a radius of a few dozen kilometers. Venturing beyond that radius without having made advance arrangements meant going beyond the network of acquaintances and becoming part of another group in which one could not be sure of one's safety, in which one was *sans aveu*.[a] The role of "foreigner" was difficult to play, for it was an ambiguous role.[1] Even if he meant no harm, a newcomer aroused anxiety if he did not present some time-tested evidence of his place of origin and his identity, and he could well fall victim to the suspicions he aroused. Relieved to discover that an unsolved crime may have been the work of someone from the outside world, the community would hasten to amass its accusations against this ready-made scapegoat, who had no one to vouch for him and no group solidarity to protect him. Many local courts asserted their authority by being extremely tolerant of their own people while rapidly and fiercely prosecuting individuals passing through the area.

The monarchy determined, therefore, to bring this mututal hostility under control by dividing the judicial system into two clearly demarcated spheres. For the sphere dealing with the uprooted, it specified, under the name *cas prévôtaux*,[a] the types of crimes that would be tried by the courts of the prévôtés. It also strengthened these courts with the physical strength of the *maréchaussée*[a] (the only military force policing the rural areas) and gave these mounted troops the specific mission of pursuing and suppressing this fluid and mobile group whose activities involved marginal behavior rather than systematic aggression. Since the people being tried by these courts were illiterate and penniless, they left few written records and usually can be traced only in the records of hospitals, beggars' prisons, or criminal courts.

During the years leading up to 1789, precisely when peasant society seems to have been much calmer than during the previous century, a climate of fear settled over many rural areas. The judicial archives, which reveal a sharp increase in the number of uprooted persons, provide the germ of an explanation. Although this increase in rootlessness was certainly less spectacular than a revolt by Croquants, it was symptomatic of a profound breakdown that insidiously spread to a dependent and indigent segment of the population, a segment that aroused considerable anxiety. For a long time the exemplary punishments meted out by the courts of the prévôtés were enough to hold back the torrent; but, by the last years of the Ancien Régime, it had become well-nigh impossible for any tribunal—even the harshest courts from which there was no appeal—to function with a reasonable degree of efficiency. Indeed, the record of the sentences pronounced by these courts shows how difficult it was to achieve a balance between the deterrent quality of their proceedings and the weight of this world in disorder.

The Concept of Marginal Delinquency

Provincial registers contain the names of individuals accused of crimes and arrested within the boundaries of that particular province; they also reveal the charges brought against these individuals and the judgments of the *présidial*[a] or prévôté[2] between January 1758 and 26 April 1790. In addition, they provide a detailed description—although the amount of detail varies—of the nature and circumstances of the offense and sentence, as well as information about the accused: sex, marital status,[3] socio-occupational category, age, appearance,[4] and occasionally, place of birth. These records of judgments are, therefore, analogous to the *Etats de crimes* [lists of crimes] that the *procureurs-généraux* were instructed to draw up by order of the Keeper of the Seals. They reveal the same concern for statistics shown by the royal administration, which had undertaken to compile the *Fichier judiciaire du Royaume* [legal file for the kingdom]. The limited value of these documents is immediately apparent, for they involved only persons judged in the provinces and subject to the special jurisdiction of the prévôtés and présidiaux; and this jurisdiction was an exceptional one created for unusual people, for delinquents on the fringe of society, delinquents with heterogeneous backgrounds. Yet there is a common denominator: mobility, the refusal to accept the norms of the community, and a lack of roots that prompted them to rove individually or as part of a group.

An offense heard by these courts was termed, in legal parlance, a *cas prévôtal* or a *cas présidial;* these offenses were defined by royal legislation[5] as "crimes and offenses by tramps, people who are *sans aveu* and homeless or who have been sentenced to corporal punishment or banishment, [and by] soldiers; highway robbery, theft aggravated by assault and battery, possession of weapons or violence in public, sedition, rioting, counterfeiting, provided, however, that these crimes were committed outside the towns in which prévôts reside."[6] If the last requirement was not met, the case fell into the jurisdiction of the présidiaux. In short, these special courts "were not intended to punish all crimes or even the most sensational ones, but rather all those directly affecting public safety."[7]

Although it was easy, at least in theory, to recognize a cas prévôtal by the nature of the crime and the place where it was committed, the maréchaussée nevertheless required solid indices that would enable it to distinguish tramps and previous offenders from the floating population; and, strictly speaking, beggars were not a part of this group. As early as the seventeenth century, the monarchy had begun its efforts to purge the cities and countryside of the

114 NICOLE CASTAN

menacing flood of beggars. It began to carry out what Michel Foucault has called the *Grand Renfermement* ["Great Confinement"], starting with the creation of general hospitals and moving on to beggars' prisons.* Actually, this policy of incarcerating all beggars was never more than partially and erratically implemented; and, whenever a beggar made things worse by insolence, repeated offenses, pillage, or riotous assembly, he became potential quarry for the maréchaussée.

This being the case, it is preferable to use these lists of crimes, which by no means include all marginal behavior, as a means of coming a little closer to the actual sociological situation concealed behind two eighteenth-century legal expressions: *crime prévôtal* [that is, a case for the prévôt's court] and *gibier de prévôt* ["the prévôt's wild game," that is, tramps and highwaymen who were sure one day to commit a *crime prévôtal*].[8] Although the documents do not include the words of the accused and, through the points he made in his defense, the reasons for his degradation,[9] they imply a distinction between two types of deviance. The criteria for these distinctions were based upon both mobility and the more elaborate notion of the degree to which an individual had broken his ties with his family or the established community. The extreme example would be a vagrant who had broken with the peasant society from which he had sprung; a lesser example would be a déclassé living on the fringe of his group rather than outside it.

Vagrants—homeless and *sans aveu*—roamed about with little hope of returning to a stable way of life. The vagrant might be a beggar carrying his sack, even though neither his age nor his state of health entitled him to beg. Or he might be a soldier whose furlough had turned into desertion; or a previous offender who had escaped from the galleys or disregarded the *ban*.[a] Without a legitimate source of income, such vagrants were frequently obliged to resort to force, and did so quite readily, whether the offense was a raid on a henhouse or highway robbery. The perimeter of their wanderings depended upon the means of travel available. (A study should be made of the impact of improved travel during the second half of the eighteenth century; to what extent did these improvements prompt additional vagrancy, and to what degree did they serve as an escape valve?) It was not legal restrictions but rather regional barriers that kept the tramp within a rather limited area, where his knowledge of the language and customs gave him the best chance of survival. Thus, more than half the vagrants under surveillance in the *généralité*[a] of Alençon had come from that province.[10] Out of a sample of 3,768 cas prévôtaux heard between 1773 and 1790, 11.33 percent (or 427, including 47 individuals from outside the kingdom) of the accused were judged in a généralité other than that in which they were born. At Orléans—that great crossroads

*For information about these hospitals, see the translator's note in Chapter 2 of this volume.—Trans.

for tramps—out of 51 accused vagrants from other regions, 39 came from different généralités: 14 from Tours, 9 from Bourges, 5 from Poitiers, 5 from Riom, 4 from Rennes, 1 from Alençon, and 1 from Limoges; in other words, at least 76.47 percent came from relatively nearby areas.

One overwhelming imperative governed the behavior of the tramp and his relationships with others: he had to deceive everyone he met, for it was absolutely necessary to reassure them by appearing to conform to accepted norms. Alibis and disguises were employed in an attempt to mollify the maréchaussée[11] and to appease the fears of the resident population. So it was a good idea to explain away one's presence on the highway by claiming to be a member of one of those accepted trades that involved frequent traveling: seasonal workers, peddlers, horse traders, or wagoners.[12] This resulted in an accumulation of false identities, backed up with forged papers—for example, passports, papers testifying to one's release from the galleys or from the army, or certificates from a village priest or perhaps even one from the archbishop of Paris authorizing the victim of a fire to beg. Vagrants would try to cover up their shady past by changing their name, nickname, address, or identity. With settled folk or with companions on the road or in wayside inns, they tried to arouse pity by displaying physical or mental handicaps, the most lucrative of which seem to have been epilepsy and imbecility. A vagrant might even go further toward outright fraud and risk mascarading as a person of superior social status in order to obtain the advantages of hospitality; for example, he might appear at the door of a château in the guise of a naval lieutenant or in the person of John Doe, Knight of Malta.[13]

Fleeting and relative though the tramp's strength might have been, it existed, and lay in his sheer mobility when compared with the man from a rural area whose family and possessions made him vulnerable to threats and aggressive acts. Indeed, the inhabitant of the countryside felt his vulnerability even more keenly as the increase in crime after 1765 gradually exposed him to more and more violence, rather than the simple begging of the past. Vagrancy almost inevitably led to crime, as an analysis of 1,253 tramps for the period 1770–90 reveals. In 52.85 percent of the cases, vagrancy was compounded by aggression; and, even worse, although 39.9 percent of the vagrants studied moved across the countryside alone, 50.28 percent did so as part of a group, and 9.82 percent moved as a family.[14] Although frequent examples of charity and compassion toward real poverty were still to be found, from that time on "God's poor" began to be replaced by the image of the frightening "foreigner" who had taken up a way of life that inevitably led to crime. Although they understood little about the effects of economic and demographic fluctuations, people in rural areas[15] (because they were more directly affected) and the wealthy (because they had been won over to the triumphant ethic that exalted work) denounced idleness, which they deemed the source of all vice. Moral decline, a heritage from past generations, was irrevocable and irreversible; yet Draconian measures were used in an attempt to curb it. Internment with forced labor, rather than Christian charity, was deemed the appropriate means of remedying this scourge.[16]

In contrast to the tramp, the déclassé did not roam about; and although he might skim off some of the cream of the countryside, he did so in carefully selected places near his home. He was not uprooted but instead was a marginal individual, still partially integrated into the community upon which he lived like a parasite. And he made the community respect him and reward him for his conformity, a reward he earned by maintaining a fixed residence, a family, and even a trade (although it is true that this trade provided more of an alibi than a real means of earning a living). A solitary déclassé took the form of a violent individual, a "disturber of the peace," who might speak in a provocative manner and strike insolent poses, always with a chip on his shoulder. Or he might join with others in an armed band and terrorize the countryside like the outlaws of the American West. Still, these déclassés were bound to the village group by a form of solidarity, if only because they knew full well that they would be handed over to the authorities should they exceed a certain level of violence or attack influential individuals.[17] Thus, they preferred to take the opposite course from that chosen by the vagrant, and they prudently descended upon passers-by at propitious times and places—that is, whenever fairs were being held, taxes were being collected by royal officials, or merchandise was being transported through the region.

A veritable epidemic of banditry broke out in the late eighteenth century and spread across the demoralized countryside. Robberies foreshadowing the stagecoach holdups in Westerns increased in such strategically located spots as the edges of forests. Near the cities of Beauvais, Senlis, and Provins and in the region around Orléans and in the Beauce [between Paris and Orléans], bands of *Hullins* or *cocangeurs*[18] would "stop with violence and tenacity" any travelers[19] and would rob them in conveniently located inns that were the scene of much bloodshed. Well-armed troops of poachers controlled the Montboissier Plain near Chartres and the Rhône Valley between Valence and Nîmes. Living along a royal highway such as the one from Paris to Orléans could be quite profitable. The borders of legal or administrative jurisdictions also constituted good bases of activity owing to jurisdictional conflicts that made prosecution unlikely, or at least delayed it. Such was the case at Agen, which was situated at the junction of the provincial governments of Languedoc and Guyenne, and of the parlementary jurisdictions of Bordeaux and Toulouse.

Rebels—whom criminal ordinances meticulously classified as a special group—do not fit into the above schema. Rebels or brigands? It is difficult to say on the basis of legal descriptions, which usually class them among the brigands. Upon closer examination, it is apparent that this sort of collective violence, whether directed against property or against authority, involved an attitude of refusal either to accept things as they were or to accept change. If we go by the number of rebellions, peasant society seems to have calmed down greatly during the eighteenth century. The grain riots of 1765–70, the revolt in the Vivarais region in 1783, and the conflagration of 1789—all of which mobilized large masses of persons who had been transformed into delinquents by poverty and fear—could be viewed as a direct extension of the seventeenth-century revolts. But actually, the typical insurrection against hoarders or against seigneurial agents seems to have expressed an exasperated refusal to accept mutations that had occurred in the traditional order of things.

In other words, using the classification applied by the courts as the sole criterion, it is not always easy to specify the category to which a delinquent belonged. In addition, most delinquents were charged with several offenses.[20] After I had computed frequencies, I established a number of categories upon which to base my tables and maps. I divided the delinquents into three groups: vagrants (that is, beggars and tramps), previous offenders, and first-time offenders who were members of a community.[21] Then I drew up a hierarchy of offenses based upon the list of cas prévôtaux.[22] The records I used are virtually continuous from 1758 to the first half of 1790 and list approximately 12,500 individuals (with a yearly average of 384 cases for the entire kingdom, exclusive of the city of Paris). The data contained in them were used for a statistical study, although the study was based on an unequal sample for the period as a whole and on the total data for the final years, 1786–90.[23] I made this decision to use all data for the period 1786–90 in the hope that exasperations and tensions that might not have been revealed in regular courts would surface in a nationwide study of these special courts.[24] The two adjusted samples of data were then analyzed by the computer. The questions asked of one sample, which included 6,909 individuals tried between 1758 and 1790, were simple ones. More complex questions—questions that were apt to reveal wider connotations, for example, such physical characteristics as smallpox scars or crippled limbs—were asked about the other sample, which included 3,768 persons accused between 1773 and 1790. The map and graphs in the appendix were drawn on the basis of yearly averages.

Although the results I obtained are based upon what I realize to be insufficiently systematized data—that is, data based upon descriptions rather than homogeneous classification—it is tempting to view them as reflecting the factors spawning crime in a traditional society that had firm roots yet at the same time was swept by floods of paupers, floods of a magnitude never seen in our day. But such a conclusion would be erroneous. At the very most we can find a correlation between certain characteristics involving race, social position, or age and the frequency with which those characteristics appeared in criminal records, and then deduce certain preconditions of delinquency from these correlations.

The bands of gypsies who were at regular intervals denounced to the authorities along the Pyrenean and Alsatian frontiers certainly never became integrated into society.[25] To a lesser degree, the Jews were also the object of a

118   NICOLE CASTAN

spontaneous segregation that might at any time burst out into anti-Semitic
violence. Thus, members of these groups were usually to be found among the
tramps, along with fugitives, deserters, or former prisoners. In like manner,
shepherds, wagoners, or peddlers—and in general all those whose trade made
a seminomadic life inevitable—might well become permanent vagrants. It
appears that only the poorer classes were likely to become uprooted or involved in crime, for among the 401 trades listed in the sample of 3,768
individuals, only 2.49 percent of the accused, including *ménagers*[a]
[householders], had once been economically independent.[26] The social
stratum made up of economically dependent rural inhabitants accounted for
18.7 percent of the total, while trades linked to commerce or transportation
represented only 11.97 percent. On the other hand, the group composed of
artisans and hand-workers reached an astonishing 35.9 percent, a percentage
that reflects the number of unemployed salaried workers transformed into
tramps as a result of the economic crisis in the royal manufactures at Lyons
and in the rural textile industry. Although *gens sans aveu* and outcasts rejected
by communities are shown to have reached 25.94 percent, this figure cannot
be considered reliable—a statement that should probably be applied to all
statistics involving tramps. Thus, the courts of the prévôtes were intended for
persons who had gone astray, but only if they had come from the *bas peuple*
[lowest classes], if not the very dregs of society. Others, such as the prodigal
sons of respectable families, could easily be tried by other courts or escape
prosecution altogether.

Youth—that is, those between puberty and marriage—enjoyed a social
status fixed by custom, and the liberty and freedom from family responsibilities conferred by this status were favorable to rebellion and mobility.
There is little significance in finding this group's place in the world of crime
unless we also look at its place in society as a whole (see table 4.1).[27] Given
an average age at marriage of twenty-five years for women and twenty-eight
years for men—and the age would surely be higher in the case of the marginal
individuals under study here, in view of their lack of financial resources—

Table 4.1—Age Distribution of Males and Females

| | Delinquent Population* | | Population as a Whole† | |
	Men (%)	Women (%)	Men (%)	Women (%)
Under 15–20 years	11.1	9.71	10	9.5
20–25	19	14.29	9	9
25–30	20.13	21.14	8	8
30–40	28.77	29.14	13.5	14
Over 40	21	25.72	26	2.6

*1,454 individuals whose age is given, from the sample of 3,768 persons.
†According to Guillaume and Poussou, *Démographie historique*, p. 31.

youth, at least for males, can be said to have lasted until almost thirty years of age. A man could, therefore, potentially spend between ten and fifteen years in temporary vagrancy.[28]

The high percentages for the under-thirty group also show that the marginal life required physical stamina and endurance. Women, therefore, were less attracted to this sort of life, and those who did join the marginal world almost always lacked family ties. Only 1.62 percent were legally married, 91.09 percent were single,[29] and the 7.29 percent who were widows had gone off alone or with their children to beg. The social status of women can explain both this distribution and the discrepancy between the ages of female and male offenders. Women became part of the marginal world later than men (about 30 percent of the men were under 25 compared with 24 percent of the women), but widowhood clearly prolonged their criminal years after age forty (26.7 percent, compared with 21.11 percent of the men).[30]

This degradation, which lay in wait for the weak, contrasts with the sort of marginal behavior found among males, which more closely coincides with their prime years. Yet youth can go hand in hand with a physical condition that negates any chance of fitting into society. Thanks to 1,492 physical descriptions, which represent 39.5 percent of the 3,768 accused individuals,[31] it is possible to outline a preliminary anthropological report.[32] Written by the physician or his surgical assistant at the time of internment, such descriptions of an individual's physical condition have nothing in common with the identifications included in the judicial records. In a world that lacked irrefutable proof of a person's identity, the administration collected for its files any clues that might help them recognize a delinquent.[33] These subjective and rather unsystematic descriptions attempted to capture the overall appearance ("walks with a very nimble step, well-built, shapely"); described the morphology, complexion, and pigmentation of the face, occasionally adding an esthetic judgment ("pretty face," "agreeable appearance," "heavy features," "frightfully ugly"); or commented upon the individual's behavior ("seems tough and wily," "always appears smiling and affable").[34] Indeed, this descriptive style served a purpose, for it captured in a few words the portrait of a violent criminal who was "robust and happy in his corpulence" or a poor wretch who was "extremely emaciated."

The most useful notations for a statistical analysis involve height and any physical infirmities, such as scars resulting from an injury, smallpox scars, and brand marks.[35] Of course it is impossible to establish a causal relationship between criminality and the inadequately described biological and physical traits of these atypical individuals. Physical defects—and it is impossible to discover whether they were accidental or hereditary—are found in a mere 5 percent of the individuals concerned. This percentage does not appear abnormal, especially since all anomalies were not equally serious. Having one little finger longer than the other has less effect than a crippled leg upon an indi-

vidual's ability to fit into a community. And the 19 percent who showed a face
pitted by smallpox were not necessarily excluded from a normal life as a result
of their marred features. In short, this criminal population seems to have had
no more defects than any other segment of the population. Nor can we lay the
blame on physical stature, computed anthropometrically; quite the contrary is
true.

In the 1,492 descriptions available, 1,063 men were measured and only 161
women. The men were of more interest to me than the women, for I could
compare their heights with the results of two studies dealing with a more
representative segment of the French population. In 1780 Abbé Expilly gave
the approximate heights of 3,978,118 males between eighteen and forty years
of age.[36] This would, therefore, be a normal group involving no selection.
Such is not the case for the youth of the period 1819–26, since those exempted
from military service were not included among the young men who were "fit
to serve."[37]

The heights of the 1,063 criminals were distributed as follows: 0.47% were
under 4 feet; 1.13% were 4′ to 4′5″; 13.73% were 4′6″ to 5′; 32.93% were 5′
to 5′1″ (1 meter 651);* 48.16% were 5′1″ to 5′5″; and 3.58% were 5′5″
and over. Thus, 51.74 percent of the marginal population under study were
over 1 meter 65 [that is, five feet five inches in Anglo-American mea-
surements], while only 23 percent of the male population in Expilly's charts
had attained that height.

The French conscript was considered tall if he measured more than five feet
two inches [that is, five feet six inches on today's scale] (1 meter 678). For the
period 1819–26, 30 percent of the soldiers reached that height or exceeded it.
Yet on the eve of the Revolution, only 10.5 percent of the male population as
a whole had attained that height, whereas 51.74 percent of the marginal males
in this study measured at least 1 meter 651. Table 4.2, using the same height
scale for both, shows the results for 1780 compared with those given by
Expilly.

In other words, 44.95 percent of the criminals were at least 1 meter 678 tall,
compared with only 10.54 percent of the French male population as a whole.
These tall men who gradually fell in with the vagrant's way of life were not
physical weaklings. Many of them came from the north and northeast, from
the western regions along the Loire River, or from the eastern foothills of the

*Appearances to the contrary, the author's conversions from "inches" and "feet" to the
metric system are correct. In the Ancien Régime, the *pied* (foot)—composed of twelve *pouces*
(inches)—equaled 0 meter 3248 while today's foot is only 0 meter 3048. Hence the individuals in
Castan's tables are about three inches taller than they appear to be at first glance. This discrepancy
between the two different inch-foot systems becomes greater as the height increases. For example, four eighteenth-century feet equal a bit under four feet three inches today, a discrepancy of
less than three inches. Five feet two inches (1 meter 651) corresponds to five feet five inches in
today's measurements, a discrepancy of three inches. And the maximum Ancien Régime category, five feet seven inches (1 meter 813), is equivalent to five feet eleven inches today, a
difference of four whole inches.—Trans.

Table 4.2—Comparison of Heights of Marginal Males and Expilly's Group

Height	Marginal Males (N = 198) (%)	Expilly's Estimates (N = 3,978,118) (%)
5'1" to 5'2" (1 meter 651)	16.16	12.57
5'2" to 5'3" (1 meter 678)	17.68	6.28
5'3" to 5'4" (1 meter 705)	13.64	2.77
5'4" to 5'5" (1 meter 732)	7.58	1.01
5'5" to 5'6" (1 meter 759)	2.53	0.38
5'6" to 5'7" (1 meter 786)	2.02	0.08
5'7" and over (1 meter 813)	1.52	0.02

central mountains. Most stated that they had once carried on a trade involving great strength—they had been woodcutters, pit sawyers, carters. This corroborates my earlier conclusions about their general appearance. There is no doubt that physical misfits did not become tramps or bandits but instead had to seek refuge in beggars' prisons or the general hospitals.[38]

Although many people during the eighteenth century chose to make rather puritanical moral judgments about this break with the normal way of life—a break resulting from the individual's social and cultural level rather than his physical or mental inferiority—every economically dependent individual was potentially a marginal person, for he was at the mercy of high prices and unemployment. Coexisting along the frontiers of the normal world, which it threatened by its antisocial attitudes, this aberrant world nonetheless was never more than a fluctuating fringe group of peasant society.

Typology of Delinquency

The map and graphs in the appendix show the chronological and geographical distributions of delinquency, but some general discussion of the various categories included in the appendix will be helpful.

The various généralités—in which the royal ordinance of 28 April 1778[39] established the thirty-two brigades of the maréchaussée—form the basis for my division of France into nine regions, which also reflect large geographical or provincial ensembles.

I subdivided the period 1758-90 into five unequal segments in order to measure the impact of changing economic conditions and the resultant legislative measures upon the prévôtés, the courts most sensitive to change.

1. *1758-63.* This was the period before the beginning of the physiocratic offensive, when stability went hand in hand with low grain prices: 15 livres per *setier** in 1762.[40]

*A grain measure equaling 156 liters, or 240 pounds of the period.—Trans.

2. *1764–75*. This decisive period reveals the combined effects of political, economic, and demographic conditions. People were becoming increasingly distressed by a price rise that began in 1764 (although such increases were unjustified until the bad harvest of 1770, when a setier of grain climbed to 29 livres) and continued until 1775. This was also a period that saw many young people reach maturity. At the same time, the state carried out a major reform inspired by physiocratic philosophy. It reorganized the judicial system and promoted individual initiative in agriculture, land consolidation, and "good prices" for grain by authorizing free trade and by promulgating edicts of *triage* [permitting seigneurial landlords to take over one-third of the communal land in their village], enclosure acts, and acts providing for the division of communal lands.

3. *1776–86*. This was the beginning of the reign of Louis XVI, when the return of the parlements relaxed tensions. The stagnant price curve and apathetic market resulted in a low grain price of 20 livres per setier in 1780. However, certain provinces, among them Languedoc, experienced economic crises between 1778 and 1783.

4. *1787–88*. The paralysis of the judicial system subsequent to Lamoignon's reform focused increased attention upon the courts of the prévôtés, which had to assure order in the face of another rapid increase in grain prices (an average price of 25 livres per setier in 1788) and the inability of institutions to function.

5. *1789–July 1790*. Urban riots and revolts in the countryside created an enormous backlog in the courts of ordinary justice.[a] All the while the setier of wheat was climbing to its peak price of 36 livres. Thus, the overall trend of the period involved a marked price increase in conjunction with overpopulation, and general confusion in the face of changing institutions.

With the exception of the hiatus of 1787 and 1788, the pattern of crime over this thirty-two-year period roughly reflects the peaks and plateaus traced by price fluctuations and changes in the political situation:

1. 1758–63: 125 cases (yearly average)
2. 1764–75: 524
3. 1776–86: 370
4. 1787–88: 262
5. 1789–90: 574

During the second period, therefore, the number of cases increased by 319.2 percent, followed by a near plateau of 370 sentences per year, or a 29.8 percent decrease (although the amount varied with the region).

It was to be expected that the economic crisis that began to take shape in 1786 would lead to a sharp increase in crime and that the paralyzed courts would be unable to keep up. This failure of the courts was highly prejudicial to public safety and certainly marks the beginning of the zeal for law enforcement that is evident in 1789, a year that brought a high tide of 624 cases.

Yet the crisis created by the Revolution—a crisis that one would expect to find reflected in crime statistics—should not be allowed to draw attention from the crucial years 1765–75, when the number of crimes committed by marginal individuals increased sharply (the yearly average was 524 cases, but there were 579 in 1770). This increase gains even more significance when it is compared with the rate for the preceding period. These transitional years reveal the profound disarray of peasant society, which was unable to deal with the sudden changes that had disrupted its equilibrium.

The maps do not contradict this hypothesis. On the contrary, they reinforce it by revealing the fluctuations in criminality over the period under study. I could have carried out my analysis on three levels: the prévôté or présidial, the généralité, and the region. But such an approach would merely reveal that eighteenth-century France, where so little standardization is evident, was far from consistent with regard to crime. My expanded framework of nine regions is more suitable than the alternate approach for portraying the circumstances of the period and, hence, for establishing a classification that holds true until the first incidents of the Revolution (table 4.3).

1. A low-crime area existed along the northern, northeastern, and southeastern borders of France. These areas accounted for 11.39 percent of crime for the nation as a whole, although they encompassed 21.1 percent of the French population.[41] The large number of military installations contributed to this low profile in the north and northeast. The southeast was crisscrossed by a network of smugglers—typified by the exploits of Mandrin*—who were trying to outwit the tribunals of the farmers-general. This smuggling activity led to the creation of the awesome commision du Conseil[a] at Valence.

2. Paradoxically, western France and the province of Languedoc, which had been so turbulent during the seventeenth century, were peaceful during the eighteenth.[42] Yet Normandy had to deal with floods of vagrants, and Brittany was the center of rebellion after 1788. But the vagrants were drained off into beggars' prisons, and the rebels were harbingers of an awakening spirit of rebellion that once appeared to have been extinguished. There was, however, one exception in the pacified part of France: Lower Languedoc, which was troubled by an increase in crime and rebellion between 1773 and 1783. In Languedoc there was a three-year time lag between inflation and the increase in the number of uprooted individuals. At the same time one of the few peasant revolts of the eighteenth century was provoked by the increasingly harsh demands of managers of noble estates who, while exercising seigneurial justice in the name of their frequently absent employer, would twist the law to their own advantage.[43] With this single exception, western

*Louis Mandrin (1724–55), a ruined businessman-turned-bandit, became the self-proclaimed "captain-general of smugglers" and led a troop of two-hundred men. A sort of Robin Hood, he won popular affection by respecting private property while killing tax agents and stopping tax collections. Pursued by entire regiments, he was finally caught and broken on the wheel at Valence in 1775.—Trans.

Table 4.3—Geography of Crime in France, 1758-93

Area	Percentage of Delinquency	Percentage of Population
LOW-CRIME REGIONS		
North	2.78	6.6
(Lille, Valenciennes, Amiens)	(and 2.62)*	
Northeast	7.1	8.06
(Metz, Nancy, Strasbourg)	(and 5.27)†	
Southeast	3.54	5.93
(Aix, Grenoble)		
TOTAL	13.42‡	20.59
MODERATE-CRIME REGIONS		
Westcentral	11.2	12.68
(Poitiers, La Rochelle, Bordeaux, Limoges)		
Northwest	11.89	17
(Rouen, Caen, Alençon, Rennes)		
Jurisdiction of Parlement of Toulouse	13.6	13.23
(Languedoc, Upper Guyenne, Armagnac)		
TOTAL	36.69	42.91
HIGH-CRIME REGIONS		
Center	17.65	16.12
(Tours, Orléans, Bourges, Moulins, Rion)		
Center-Paris basin	16.34	9.73
(Soissons, Ile-de-France, Châlons-sur-Marne)		
East	15.9	10.14
(Dijon, Besançon, Lyons)		
TOTAL	49.89	35.99

*Only 2.62% if 1789 is excluded.
†5.27% is 1789 is excluded.
‡11.39% exclusive of 1789.

and southern France had indeed settled down. The good old seventeenth-century revolts of the Croquants and the Nu-pieds would remain dormant until 1789, and even then they would be less extensive than elsewhere.

3. The high crime rate in central France, the Ile-de-France, and eastern France beat all records, with 49.89 percent of the general total, although these areas accounted for only 35.99 percent of the French population. The main highways and navigable rivers of the kingdom converged upon the Paris basin. Along them traveled a tide of poverty-stricken wretches who had been forced to desert the barren lands they had been working. These regions of fertile soil became the battleground of large-scale capitalist agriculture. The tensions and disarray within peasant society have been discussed in detail in a number of studies;[44] here we can see them in action. In the late eighteenth century, therefore, a new geographic distribution of violence and uprooted-ness is revealed, both in western France and in the entire kingdom.[45] Even

distributing the various categories of crime according to généralité or prévôté does not affect the total picture. In addition, the demographic situation highlights both the role of overflow conduit played by the main routes of transportation and the influence of necessary commercial exchanges between two adjoining regions—in short, it enables us to determine the most active centers of crime (table 4.4).

An analysis of the fluctuation in the various categories of crime shows sharp contrasts between peaks and relatively stable plateaus. The years 1758–63 reveal a pattern of delinquency that is not found again until the Revolution: that is, the lowest incidence of female criminality (9.84 percent of the total in 1758), no marked concentration of vagrancy (23.77 percent), and a moderate number of previous offenders (16.39 percent). An overwhelming proportion (80.33 percent) of those on the fringe of society were involved in theft; any violent acts against private individuals or against the authorities that they committed did not pose a serious threat to public safety. More than half of them roamed about alone; fear had not yet spread throughout the countryside.

After 1764 this marginal world began to stir, and the annual increase—an average of 329.51 percent wkthin a few years—eloquently speaks for itself. Women began to roam the highways—30 percent of the women arrested were tramps—a clear sign of a breakdown in the family as an institution. Women

Table 4.4—Centers of Criminal Activity

Généralité*	Criminal percentage	Demographic percentage	Judiciary seats	Criminal percentage
Orléans	9.23	2.89	Lyons	4.37
Montpellier	8.05	7.18	Le Puy	3.17
Châlons-sur-Marne	7.56	4.47	Orléans	3.04
Dijon	7.54	4.47	Montargis	2.71
Ile-de-France	6.31	4.56	Nîmes	2.59
Lyons	5.95	2.54	Agen	2.43
Bordeaux	5.6	5.11	Bourg-en-Bresse	2.29
Tours	4.49			
Rennes	3.92	9.16	Rouen	2.21
Rouen	3.88	2.92	Senlis	2.14
		5.22	Strasbourg	2.14
Nancy	3.27	3.71	Troyes	2.0i
			Beauvais	2
			Nantes	1.99
			Périgueux	1.64
			Nancy	1.56
			Château-Gontier	1.43

*I cannot go into detail here about the results obtained for the 32 généralitiés and the 126 prévôtes and présidiaux. I have given only the most significant results in order of decreasing importance.

accounted for 18.4 percent of all accused, the highest rate for the entire thirty-two-year period. They specialized in robbery; and in those days of high prices and inefficient distribution, it is not surprising that they played a major role in the riots that disturbed markets and halted convoys. Equally significant are three basic changes to be discerned in the pattern of criminality: an increase in vagrants, who swelled from 23.77 percent of all accused persons to 50.84 percent; an increasing tendency for mere tramps to become involved in illegal acts; and an increase in banditry (13.25 percent) or, at least, in the number of organized or spontaneous bands formed for aggressive ends. In addition, the number of recidivists constantly increased, as if poverty and the courts were continually creating a new supply of unemployed déclassés or individuals who had nothing to look forward to after release from the galleys or beggars' prison. Although theft was still common (46.55 percent of all crimes), armed robbery and crimes of violence continued to increase, whether they took the form of a highway robbery or a food riot. These years, which were also troubled by unemployment among young people, brought a con- stantly growing mass of uprooted humanity into contact with a marginal milieu that was developing its own special way of life (table 4.5).

These basic characteristics of the criminal population remained valid until 1786, but they are partially masked by a decrease in delinquency (29.39 percent). The statistical averages confirm that women were compensating for their lack of roots by aggressive group behavior. In like manner, we see a continually decreasing percentage (18.41 percent) of "professional" re- cidivists and a relative aging of the persons accused, since 31.8 percent, compared with an earlier 34.61 percent, were under twenty-five years of age. Rebellion and banditry decreased, but the more ordinary sort of violence increased, a clear indication of social disequilibrium.

There is almost no trace of this crisis in the court records for 1787–88, for resistance by the legal profession to Lamoignon's reforms for all practical purposes blocked access to ordinary justice. Moreover, the case load in the courts of the prévôtés decreased by 35.25 percent during the same period, a sure sign that these tribunals were unable to compensate for the inactivity of the ordinary judges, whose cause they had espoused. This cessation of prose- cution is a major element of the prerevolutionary period. At any rate, this is why we know practically nothing about the phenomenon of crime for these years. It can simply be observed that the prévôtés, pressured by the general consensus of opinion, took care of the most threatening criminals. Neglecting the small fry of tramps and unemployed poor, they hunted down those indi- viduals who specialized in highway robbery and armed assault. Indeed, 22.14 percent of the accused were previous offenders and only 26.57 percent were under twenty-five years of age.

Thus, the records reveal no trace of the disorders occuring during the fall of 1788 and the bad winter that followed. However, the fact that Louis XVI

Table 4.5—Felonious Associations (3,768 individuals charged between 1773 and 1790)

	Individual (%)	Collective (%)	Family (%)
Beggars and tramps	43.9	47.56	8.54
Previous offenders	68.83	26.16	5.00
Rebels	2.16	89.73	8.11
Bandits	0.27	95.88	3.85
Other	27.02	58.4	14.58

finally gave in to the judges in September of 1788[46] set the courts back into motion during the early weeks of 1789; but the lethargy shown by the legal system during the previous months undoubtedly prompted a great deal of aggressive behavior. Riots, violence, and rebellion filled the days that led to the birth of the French Revolution. These fisorders immediately triggered frantic activity by the courts.[47] Prosecution reached its peak in 1789, when the number of cas prévôtaux increased by 163.29 percent. Primarily concerned about crimes involving property and the public peace, the prévôts rarely hunted down run-of-the-mill criminals. In 1790, women accounted for only 7.17 percent of the total, an indication that the courts were no longer arresting mere tramps or minor offenders. The authorities were singling out the most dangerous criminals—recidivists who had formed bands throughout the countryside and who broke into houses and, by ingenious means of torture, forced the occupants to reveal the whereabouts of the stocking stuffed with valuables.[48]

By March 1789, however, the prévôts were unable to keep up with the rural or urban rebellions being carried out by large mobs of poor people against hoarders, local lords, and government agents. Collective violence erupted throughout France, and the popular uprising became the typical crime of 1789–90. It mobilized the victims of the economic crisis of the preceding years,[49] people who were driven to break the law in order to subsist or who had previously severed family ties and had been transformed into outlaws by poverty or the contagious behavior of the marginal world. The majority of those arrested during these years (86.68 percent of those whose ages were given) were over thirty years old. This may reflect the fact that the courts were prosecuting only the "instigators of unlawful assemblies," that is, those who attracted attention by their seditious words and their incitements to riot.[50] Such individuals were accused of stirring up the crowd to the sound of the drum or the tocsin and of leading troops armed with scythes, axes, staves, and occasionally even side arms and guns, "claiming they had orders from the King to burn down the châteaux of the nobility" and even, in the province of Rouergue, to "carry the heads of all nobles to Paris after having pillaged and destroyed their châteaux."[51]

The first manifestations of popular revolt took the form of the traditional food riot sparked by high prices and hoarding; but belligerent phrases quickly began to reverberate. The chain of rebellions, chiefly urban, followed a path that largely circumvented the Paris basin. It cut through Normandy (via Caudebec, Rouen, and Caen), where linen workers pillaged bakeries and imposed a price for bread that was "perforce lower." At Alençon, a volunteer militiaman was shot to death during an incident involving plunder. At Château-Gontier women reenacted the assaults of 1765 upon grain convoys. At Nantes, Angers, and Chinon similar scenes were the prelude to punitive expeditions against nearby sharecropping farms.

South of the Loire River, only a few regions were affected, at least as far as I can ascertain from these court registers. From Fontenay-le-Comte to Saintes, rebellion was also triggered by high grain prices. The Loire River seems to have served as a barrier that shunted the rebellion toward the east and the Saône River, from where it spread to Champagne, the northeast, and the north, all the way to the region around Cambrai, which was the scene of violent riots.[52] The records of the courts of the prévôtes reveal nothing very new—nothing that has not already been said by Georges Lefebvre[53]—but it is no accident that the prévôtés concentrated all their efforts upon the precincts of the great grain-producing regions, where the most violent events in the wheat revolt attempted to block the transport of grain, establish "fair prices," and carry out an equitable distribution.[54]

The geographic distribution of antiseigneurial revolts—as determined on the basis of the cases heard by the prévôtés—does not exactly coincide with the localities where subsistence riots occurred. Although not absent in the west and especially in the center of the realm,[55] this form of rebellion moved toward the eastern portion of the Paris basin and on to northern and northeastern France, as far as the Rhône Valley corridor, where the way had been paved for rebellion and panic by economic and social developments that had demoralized the countryside and created ominous waves of vagrants.[56] An unexpected and basically rural phenomenon, the rebellion hammered away at everything that evoked the seigneurial, noble, bourgeois, or ecclesiastical social orders. Virtually the same scenario was followed almost everywhere; an armed crowd would gather after the ringing of the tocsin and then, becoming more excited and tense as each minute passed, would besiege the château or abbey. Participants in this sort of riot demanded that the victim turn over his deeds and receipts to be burned at once, that he renounce his feudal rights, and that he distribute food and contribute money. At times the riot would end with the pillage of the entire château or abbey. The sentences pronounced by the prévôtés doubtlessly did not include all antiseigneurial rebellions, for not all such riots led to trials, and a sizable number of rebels were never arrested or were granted amnesty before the actual trial.[57] But this is of little consequence, for no matter what document one studies, there is undeniable evi-

dence that those areas witnessing the greatest number of antiseigneurial revolts were those same rural regions in the center and the east-northeast where
the offensive promoting seigneurial rights had been most intense.[58]

Other demonstrations against expanding capitalism can be found in both
city and country. The indebted or ruined clients of bourgeois, notaries, businessmen, or merchants—regardless of whether these men owned seigneuries—
insisted that they, too, destroy promissory notes, statements of indebtedness,
or records of legal proceedings.

This widespread aggressiveness naturally led to a total breakdown of authority. Many administrators abandoned their posts or were reduced to a
defensive role. The *intendants,*[a] the judiciary, and the General Tax Farm
became the focal points for a kind of hatred that was expressed in identical
ways throughout the major cities of the realm: offices were sacked, papers
destroyed, customs barriers burned down, and staff members violently attacked. Throughout France the same rebellious scenes were played out, but
this time the maréchaussée and the National Guard [created in 1789] were the
victims, for the latter quickly compromised themselves by attempting to establish order.[59] Throughout France the humiliated joined together to oppose the
sentences of the courts and threw themselves against the doors of prisons or of
beggars' prisons in order to free the inmates. In the face of such widespread
violence, private and corporate interests lost no time in settling their own
accounts,[60] as is so often the case in such situations. It is, therefore, not
surprising to find anti-Semitism rekindled among the common people of Alsace, where violent attacks were launched against the persons and property of
the Jews.[61] These events brought every conceivable form of sordid behavior
into play; yet the most interesting aspect of these rebellions, with their often
complex motives, lies in the study of those motives, which reflect profound
mutations in the structures of society (table 4.6).

Criminal Prosecution

The methods employed to control crime are familiar.[62] The poor were
terrorized by the excessive strictness of the authorities, who extinguished any
hope by carrying out the sentence without delay. Although the courts of the
prévôtés were civil courts, they resembled military courts in many ways,
beginning with prévôt himself, whose sentence could not be appealed. In
eliminating the appeal, the monarchy intended to provide rapid and definitive
justice for an elusive criminal group. Indeed, any appeal to a parlement
offered considerable hope of adjournment of the case or a lightening of the
sentence, especially if the initial decision had been severe. In such a case, the
parlement was inclined to reduce the sentence or dismiss the case for lack of
sufficient proof of guilt.[63] The appeal generally took the form of prolonged

Table 4.6—A Profile of Delinquents for the Period January 1758–July 1790 (yearly averages)

	Number Charged	Sex (%)		Group (%)		Category (%)			Offense (%)						
		Men	Women	Individ-ually	Collec-tively	Vagrant	Previous Offender	First-time Offender	Vagrancy	Theft	Violence	Sexual	Money	Rebellion	Banditry
1st period: 1758–64	122	90.16	9.84	49.18	50.82	23.77	16.39	59.84	15.58	78.69	1.63	—	1.64	1.64	0.82
2d period: 1765–75	524	81.6	18.4	31.06	68.94	41.3	15.7	43	21.79	46.65	7.5	1.14	3.52	6.15	13.25
3d period: 1776–86	370	85.19	14.81	37.85	62.15	32.4	18.4	49.2	11.62	61.45	9.1	0.6	3.92	5.53	7.78
4th period: 1787–88	262	83.02	16.98	40.84	59.16	29.58	22.14	48.28	9.16	64.31	8.97	0.95	4.2	3.44	8.97
5th period: 1789 to July 1790	574	90.71	9.29	16.03	83.97	10.57	6.74	82.69	2.79	19.67	5.34	0.3	0.35	7.67	63.88

	Ages* (%)			Trades† (%)			Sans Aveu	Punishment (%)							
	Under 25	25–40	Over 40	Rural	Travel	Work		Hanged	Broken on Wheel	Galleys and Life	Hard Labor Time	Banish-ment	Punish-ment II	Freed	Case Not Completed
1st period: 1758–64	—	—	—	—	—	—	—	8.04	—	33.93	32.14	19.64	4.46	1.79	8.2
2d period: 1765–75	34.61	42.65	22.74	27.6	24.4	35.5	12.5	12.94	5.76	18	43.21	7.24	2.72	9.53	5.1
3d period: 1776–86	31.8	48.66	19.54	20.52	24.73	38.2	16.55	18	4.94	22.23	45.8	4.09	1.69	3.05	5.5
4th period: 1787–88	26.57	53.87	19.56	24.14	22.41	48.28	5.17	11.92	1.67	26.57	45.83	4.39	4.81	4.81	8.78
5th period: 1789 to July 1790	18.32	48.02	33.66	25	31.24	34.38	9.38	11.43	2.98	14.66	30.19	10.68	16.27	13.79	6.5

*Ages are given in 32.6% of cases for 2d period; 48.7% for the 3d; 51.72% for the 4th; and 23.46% for the 5th.
†Trades are indicated in 9.87% of cases for 2d period; 13.43% for the 3d; 11.07% for the 4th; and 3.72% for the 5th.

incarceration and transfer to the prisons of the parlement in question. However, although the brief stay in the well-guarded prisons of the prévôtés made
escape difficult, it did considerably reduce one's chances of dying there (only
29 of the 3,768 detainees died);[64] but this advantage was on the whole offset
by the rapid execution of the sentence, which allowed no time for a royal
pardon. In short, unless a prison break could be arranged, it was no easier to
escape the justice meted out by the prévôtés than that handed down by a
council of war.[65]

Judgment was also hastened because the first hearing had been simplified
by sheer necessity; for most delinquents had broken with the community or
else the crime had been committed in an outlying area. Thus, the court could
not begin a detailed inquiry that would involve a great deal of administrative
correspondence and the transport of witnesses. Since it lacked the means to
conduct such an inquiry, the court had to rely on just a few witnesses and
accept suspicions rather than proof. The courts of the prévôtés owed their
reputation for arbitrariness as much to these summary hearings as to the
rapidity of the entire trial.

At the end of the eighteenth century, however, the total time required for
completion of a trial began to decrease in all the courts of the realm, although
none matched the brevity of the trials conducted by the prévôts. How many
chances in a hundred did the accused have to receive his final sentence within
a year's time? At least eighty-six, if he fell under the jurisdiction of a prévôt;
between twelve and fifteen, if the case was heard by the Châtelet;* a little
more than sixty-seven for the présidial of Rennes; and about fifty if the case
was being heard as an appeal before the Parlement of Toulouse. This reputation for excessive slowness was actually more applicable to civil than to
criminal cases. Yet the justice meted out by the prévôts remained particularly
speedy, for it eliminated one entire level of courts and left only 5 to 6 percent
of all cases unfinished, a very low percentage indeed.[66]

Sovereign, rapid, but not arbitrary, the proceedings of the courts of the
prévôtés were defined by the criminal ordinance that specified the composition of the tribunal and established the offenses to be heard and the appropriate
punishments. Neither the prévôt nor the members of the présidial presided
over the proceedings alone. An *assesseur* ["assistant judge"] had to be present, and the decision itself had to be reached by seven judges, who must be
royal officials or at least holders of a law degree. Whether the accused individual appeared before the prévôt or the présidial depended upon where the
crime had been committed.[67] The various présidiaux tried an average of 14
percent of the crimes for the period 1758–90, a percentage that conceals the

*The tribunal of the prévôté and viscounty of Paris, the Châtelet heard both civil and criminal
cases. Subordinate to the Parlement of Paris but its virtual equal, it was one of the main jurisdictions for the entire kingdom, in terms of the number of cases heard and the importance and
diversity of the questions handled.—Trans.

continual decrease in their activity in favor of the courts of the prévôtés (the présidiaux heard 10.83 percent of the cases in 1783, 8.86 percent in 1788, and 2.56 percent in 1789). This gradual effacement confirms the decline of the présidiaux and also indicates that crimes committed by the marginal world predominated in rural areas. This conclusion remains valid, despite the surge of activity by the présidiaux during 1765 (18.76 percent of the cases tried that year), owing to renewed urban food riots.

During the last decade of the Ancien Régime, therefore, the prévôts assumed almost total disciplinary control of the marginal population in the countryside. This can be accounted for by the double nature of the prévôt's office, for he was both a judicial and a military figure. Performing as a judge, while serving as an officer in the rural police, he had the armed men of the maréchaussée at his disposal. The strength of the maréchaussée, however, amounted to very little. How could it possibly maintain order in a kingdom with twenty-five million inhabitants? In addition to 33 prévôts généraux the maréchaussée was made up of 111 lieutenants, 151 *maréchaux des logis* [subordinate cavalry officers assigned to the stables], and 732 brigadiers commanding 2,650 men. Pierre Goubert has estimated that the population of the entire province of Brittany totaled 2,200,000 people at the end of the eighteenth century;[68] yet its safety was in the hands of a mere 46 brigades (made up of 4 men each, including the brigadier).[69] The province of Languedoc, with more than 1,700,000 inhabitants, had 51 brigades, or 204 men. Such numbers were patently inadequate, and order was only maintained through collaboration between the maréchaussée and the communities of the region, which policed themselves and handed over to the royal troops "by public clamor" any "foreigners" or unruly individuals they wished removed from their midst.[70]

Thus, the prévôt had power over only a small fraction of the population— and only a small fraction of the impoverished population. Does this mean that these registers provide a record of everything he did? It would be hazardous to advance any reply beyond a simple comparison with the average activity of a sovereign court[a] judging cases of similar magnitude. Between 1765 and 1775, the Parlement of Toulouse heard an average of 130 appeals a year from persons sentenced for major crimes, and between 140 and 150 a year for the period 1780–90. Thus, a yearly average of 384 cas prévôtaux and cas présidiaux for the entire kingdom, exclusive of Paris, seems plausible. Be that as it may, rather than trying to obtain a specific figure, which would of necessity be hypothetical, we must try to discern any changes in the way in which the authorities attempted to reduce the crime rate and in the punishments themselves. The terror and rebellion aroused by the courts of the prévôtés would make no sense to us if we merely totaled up the number of individuals tried. It is the severity of the sentences that we must stress, remembering all the while that no appeal was possible.

First of all, the percentage of death sentences was extremely high:[71] an average of 19 percent of those accused in 1773 and 1790 were condemned to death. And more than one man out of every four condemned to death was broken on the wheel. This means that, year in and year out, at least fifteen people were publicly executed either in person or in effigy throughout the kingdom as a whole, and that about fifty men and women were hanged (table 4.7). A public execution, which accomplices were forced to witness, added to the pedagogic value of the punishment, but at times it triggered unexpected demonstrations of support for the condemned. In May 1779, two men convicted at Cahors of murder, theft, and profanation of the cross were sentenced first to apologize publicly for their actions and then to be hanged. The execution of the first man went smoothly, but the cord broke for the second man, who fell and dragged the hangman along with him. When the executioner persisted in trying to throttle the criminal, the gleeful populace fell upon him, stoned him, and put the soldiers of the maréchaussée to flight. It then carried off the condemned man, of whom no trace was ever found.

The excessive zeal of these courts outdistanced that of the parlements. Between 1765 and 1780, the Parlement of Paris pronounced an average of 60 death sentences a year; the Parlement of Toulouse, which had a bad reputation after the Calas Affair, handed down about 25. The prévôt was thus the most formidible of judges. True, he was dealing with a clientele that by definition was predisposed to violent crime. And we must take into account escapees sentenced in absentia if we are to judge the real effect upon the population—but that is also true for the parlements. The prévôts were dealing with the most frightening criminals, who were eager to elude justice (between 1758 and 1790 an average of 19 of those sentenced to death each year were executed in effigy, which would bring the number of official executions to 46). During 1773 alone the the prévôts handed down 141 death sentences (61 of which involved breaking on the wheel), that is, 25.18 percent of all sentences; 45 of the accused had fled, but 96 were actually executed. Even in 1789, when the courts were overwhelmed by their case load, the prévôts carried out 90 of the 105 death sentences decreed. This inflexibility shown by the courts of the prévôtés made them closely resemble military tribunals. Indeed, several cases brought before a parlement reveal the desperate efforts of the accused, who had been caught red-handed on the highway, to escape the prévôt's clutches by having the case referred to the local *sénéchal*. [a72]

The eighteenth century was feeling its way, trying to clarify its position on the punishment of criminals. Such men as Beccaria [an Italian philosophe who wrote about crime] were dreaming of new approaches to the problem; but at the practical level of the courts, exemplary punishment was the word of the day. From that time on, little interest was shown in minor sentences, some of which obviously had little impact upon rootless individuals. Among such inappropriate sentences was the *ban,* that is, banishment—which was decreed

Table 4.7—Offense and Punishment, 1758, 1773, 1783, and 1789

	Vagrants					Previous Offenders				First-time Offenders					
	Tramp	Theft 1	Theft 2	Violence	Recid.	Tramp	Theft 1	Theft 2	Violence	Theft 1	Theft 2	Violence	Rebel	Bandit	Total
1758															
Broken on wheel															
Hanged			1								12				13
Galleys or workhouse:															
Life		1	4	1	1	1	3	3		1	18	1		3	37
5–10 years			1	3	1		4	3			10			3	26
0–5 years				2				1		1	3				7
Banishment	7	4	1	2						4	6				24
Punishments II*										1	1				2
Freed										1	1				2
Case not completed					1						10				11
														TOTAL	122
1773															
Broken on wheel			1						3	1		41		2	61
Hanged			16			1		11	1		44	7		1	80
Galleys or workhouse:															
Life	6	11	16	3		10	4	11		2	32	21	2		117
5–10 years	17	30	17	2		1	4	9		3	19	1	1		114
0–5 years	35	23					2				8				70
Banishment		5	1							2	6	8	13	2	34
Punishments II*	2										8	2	8		23
Freed		3	7				1			6	21	3	14	6	61
Case not completed	5	12	4		1					3	20	4			19
														TOTAL	579

	Vagrants				Previous Offenders					First-time Offenders					
	Tramp	Theft 1	Theft 2	Violence	Recid.	Tramp	Theft 1	Theft 2	Violence	Theft 1	Theft 2	Violence	Rebel	Bandit	Total
1783															
Broken on wheel									1		1	2	5	20	29
Hanged			2					4	1		27	18	10	20	82
Galleys or workhouse:															
Life	7	11	17	3	1	7	16	14	5	4	14	2	4	9	97
5–10 years		18	9			7	8	5	2		3		13	3	75
0–5 years	17	17	6		1	4	3	3		1				1	56
Banishment		1	1				1			1				2	7
Punishments II*		1											1		1
Freed			4								3				7
Case not completed			1								30		3		34
														TOTAL	378
1789															
Broken on wheel									3	2	1	5		10	21
Hanged						2		1			8	5		68	84
Galleys or workhouse:															
Life	3	4	5		3	9	2	8		2	15	7		55	102
5–10 years	5	3	7	5	2	10	2	12		12	12	4	5	49	116
0–5 years	9		4	3	3	4		1			1	2		44	73
Banishment		1	1		1					1	8	1		35	41
Punishments II*		1			2								2	87	103
Freed											4	1	3	41	48
Case not completed											2	3		34	36
														TOTAL	624

*That is, second-degree offenses that did not deprive the culprit of his liberty. This category included flogging, branding, reprimand, warning not to become a repeat offender, and the iron collar.

for only 6 percent of the accused—for what was the good of excluding such people from the community? The standard punishment for *real* foreigners— those who had come from outside France—banishment was also a particularly common sentence for women whom the court wanted to send away, even at the risk of turning them into tramps. For minor offenses, the prévôts preferred to pronounce a sentence that would degrade the accused without depriving him of his freedom; physical punishment would be linked with a humiliating public execution of the sentence, a harsh warning for both the delinquent and the crowd of spectators.

Punishment was intended to serve as an example both through frequent sentences to capital punishment and, even more commonly, through sentences involving loss of freedom, namely, the galleys for men and the workhouse for women. For the years 1758–90 as a whole, 17.36 percent of the punishments meted out involved death sentences, 19.07 percent life sentences to the *bagne,*[a] and 39.19 percent imprisonments for terms of three years or more. In other words, society permanently disposed of at least 36 individuals out of every 100 convicted; and it saw to it that the 39 who one day would return suffered an almost identical fate, for the process of becoming a recidivist had been set into motion. But freedom was granted very parsimoniously, at a rate that fluctuated between 6 and 7 percent, although the Parlement of Toulouse freed a minimum of 20 percent of all accused, not including those who had been released after their initial trial. Thus, the delinquent tried by a court of ordinary justice had a four times greater chance of being freed than one tried by a court of the prévôtés, for the latter criminal was doomed to a very harsh sentence. A more detailed analysis would only confirm the implacable nature of such courts (see appendix).

Such an analysis would reveal a desire to eliminate any individual who posed a serious threat to the peace. Indeed, although punishment involving loss of liberty (solely through galley service or the workhouse) on the average increased at approximately the same rate as crime, permanent punishment (death or life sentences) increased much more rapidly in accordance with anticrime measures adapted to the new types of crime. During the period 1758–64, the prévôts removed more than two-thirds of the accused from society; of this rather sizable contingent, only 8 percent were permanently excluded, by death, and 32.14 percent were excluded for a specified period (table 4.8). These are reassuring indices that crime was under control. By contrast, during the succeeding decade, the prévôts had to face up to a crime rate that was 4.3 times greater. From then on, 80.4 percent of those sentenced were permanently or temporarily deprived of their freedom; and the preference ran to the permanent solution, since 18.7 percent were broken on the wheel or hanged and 18.5 percent were sentenced to the bagne for life, their only hope lying in escape. In the early 1770s the rate of 43.21 percent temporary punishments reveals new penal practices that had come into use.

Table 4.8—Sentences Eliminating Culprits from Society (Courts of Prévôtés, 1758–90)

| | Capital Punishment (%) | | | | |
	Broken on Wheel	Hanged	Total	Life in Galleys or Workhouse (%)	Total Permanently Eliminated (%)
1st period: 1758–64	—	8.04	8.04	33.93	41.97
2d period: 1765–75	5.76	12.94	18.70	18.5	37.20
3d period: 1776–86	4.94	18.00	22.94	22.23	45.17
4th period: 1787–88	1.67	11.92	13.59	26.57	40.16
5th period: 1789–July 1790	2.98	11.43	14.41	14.66	29.07

The apparent stabilization in this rate between 1776–86 also reveals these by then well-established procedures, for 90.97 percent of those found guilty were excluded from society. True, 45.8 percent received term sentences, but capital punishment or life sentences were meted out to virtually half of those convicted, because convicts were becoming increasingly dangerous recidivists. We know that the decrease during the period 1787–88 (85.98 percent of the sentences involved loss of freedom, but among them 45.83 percent were for prison terms of specified length, 40.16 percent were life sentences, and 13.59 percent were death sentences) does not reveal a new policy in stopping crime, but rather the paralysis of the means of doing so. This is proven by the fact that during the next period, 72.4 percent of all offenders were eliminated from society for a specific period or for the rest of their lives by a legal system that was functioning once more but was unable to keep up with the heavy case load produced by rebellious activities.

Of 3,768 cases, only 660 sentences were not served, owing to death, escape, pardon, or failure to appear at trial. Of those who did not serve, 8 percent were vagrants, 3.15 percent were recidivists, 46.49 percent were rebels, 23.24 percent were members of a mob, and 19.02 percent were other delinquents.

In sum, although the means of stopping crime were pitifully inadequate, the sentences of the courts were implacable.

Instead of being built, as in England, upon a parish police force that was concerned with apprehending and eliminating idlers and undesirable outsiders and that was empowered to do just that, the French legal system was organized according to the individuals involved in the crime and the type of crime committed. In addition, it used a centralized court system whose machinery was more rapid and summary. But the French system lacked the constantly increasing financial resources that might have enabled it to cope with the threatening tide of rural people who had failed to adapt to the economic changes of the late eighteenth century. As the narrow competences of the courts of ordinary justice gradually weakened, and these courts were no longer able to deal with the deteriorating situation within the courts themselves, the undermanned troops of the maréchaussée had to spread themselves thin and even give up trying to catch minor offenders, although the number of arrests increased and punishments became ever harsher.

When prices fluctuated freely on the open market and when men had to risk looking for work beyond their home base, the state could no longer afford only cursory surveillance of the links of communication between various communities. Efficient, if not charitable, control would have eaten up a large share of tax revenues, as it did in England. In order to consent to such a measure, taxpayers would have had to be accustomed to assuming such responsibilities.

Lacking this, France's only alternative lay in meting out formidible sanctions and proving in the process the worthlessness of exemplary punishment, for public executions were no longer aimed at a small audience that was intimidated by the emphasis placed upon punishment and upon past offenses.

Appendix

The map of France that follows is divided into nine regions, each identified by a Roman numeral. In each of the five charts following the map, this numeral reappears at the head of a column of chronologically arranged graphs. The left-hand portion of each graph shows the number of men (*hommes*) in percent; the right-hand half shows the percentage of women (*femmes*). The numbers running down the center of each graph refer to the numbered categories shown immediately beneath the title of the chart.

In other words, in the first chart, "Provincial Registers: Typology of the Accused," information about northwestern France is to be found in column VIII. This column reveals that, in 1758–63, one hundred percent of the women were arrested as beggars or tramps, compared with only thirty-six percent of the men. Fifty-nine percent of the men were first-time offenders and five percent were recidivists. By 1789–July 1790 the pattern had changed, and almost all men and women arrested in that region were first-time offenders.

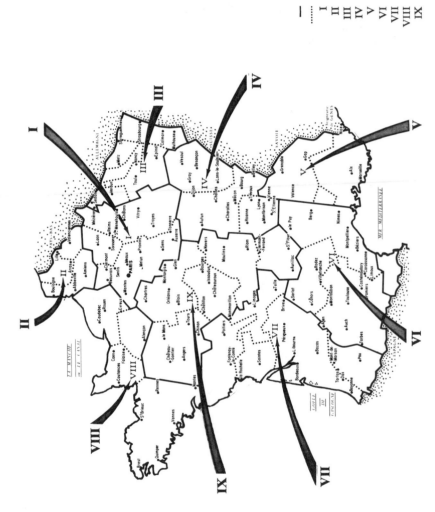

Regional boundary — |
Boundary of a **généralité** ┈┈
Center of Paris Basin I
North II
Northeast III
East IV
Southeast V
Jurisdiction of Parlement of Toulouse VI
Center and Southwest VII
Northwest VIII
Loire Valley IX

140

Provincial Registers: Typology of the Accused

1. Beggars, tramps
2. Recidivists
3. First-time offenders

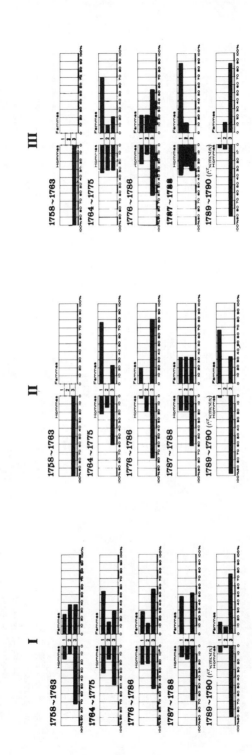

(continued)

141

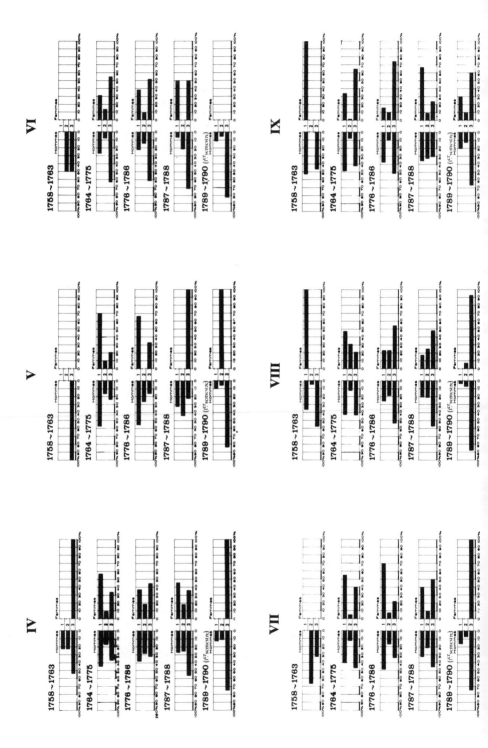

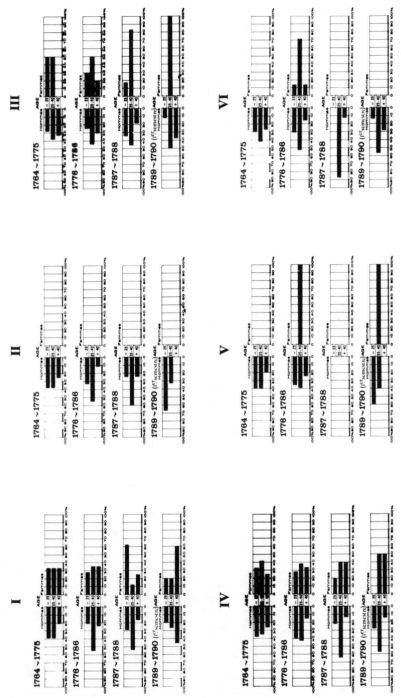

(continued)

143

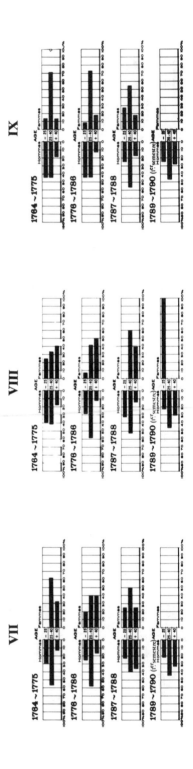

144

Provincial Registers: Offenses

1. Vagrancy
2. Simple theft
3. Theft with aggravating circumstances
4. Counterfeiting

5. Violent acts
6. Sexual offences
7. Rebellion
8. Riotous assembly

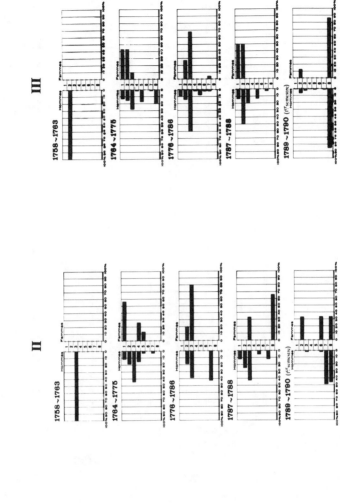

(continued)

145

VI

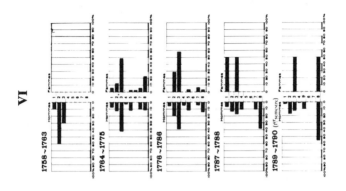

V

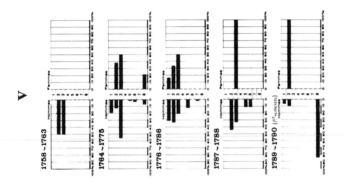

IV

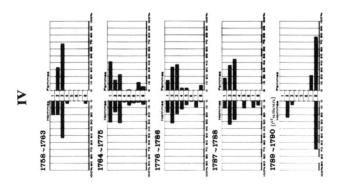

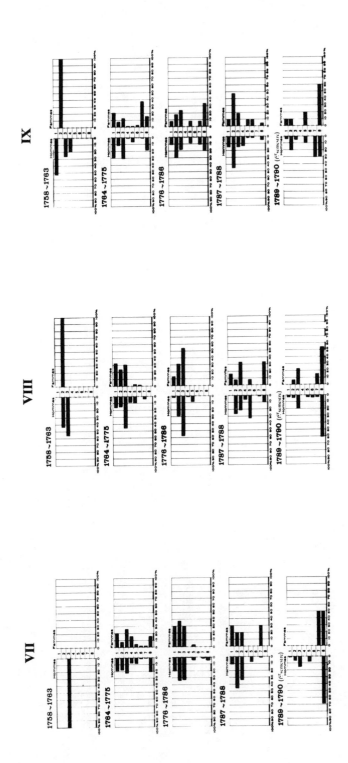

Provincial Registers: Group Activity

1. Individual
2. Collective

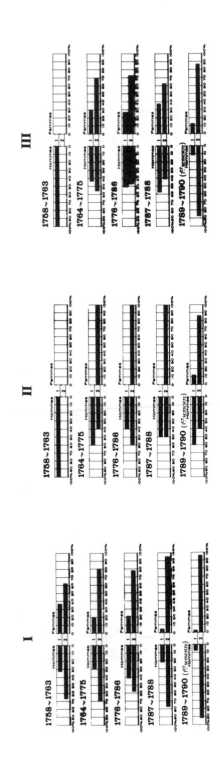

(continued)

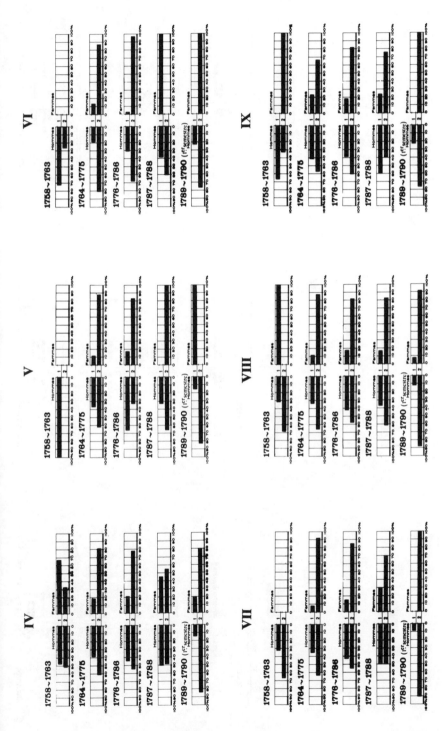

Provincial Registers: Punishments

1. Burned or broken on the wheel
2. Hanged
3. Life sentence
4. Term in galleys or workhouse

5. Banished for specified period
6. Minor punishment
7. Freed
8. Case not completed

I

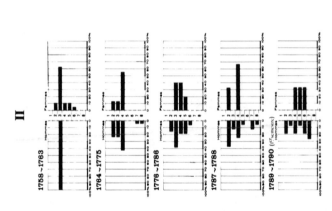

II

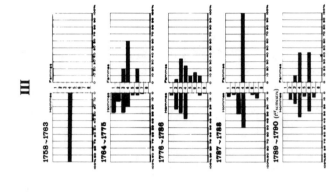

III

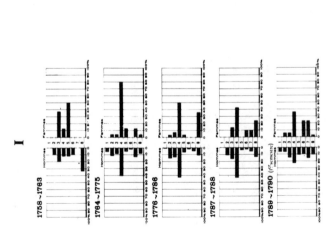

(continued)

150

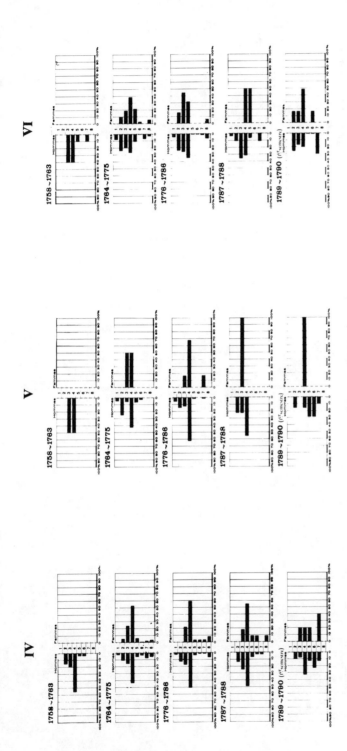

(continued)

151

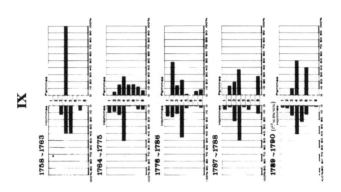

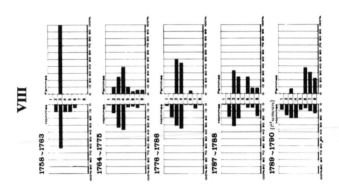

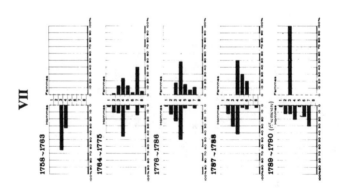

152

NOTES

1. Compare the manner in which certain English communities handled this problem. They were willing to help the "certified" poor, who were identified by a badge, but arrested unknown tramps, whom they expelled, imprisoned, or sent to the galleys. These arrangements are described by George Taylor, *The Problem of Poverty, 1660–1834,* Seminar Studies in History (London: Longmans, 1969), p. 146.

2. Archives nationales, AB 384, 389.

3. Always indicated for women, but rarely for men.

4. Not routinely indicated until about 1772 and, after that date, for between 33 and 58 percent of the cases, depending upon the year.

5. The criminal ordinance of 1670, title 1, article 12, lists these crimes; the list was later revised by the declaration of 1731, which transferred premeditated murder to the courts of ordinary justice.

6. This measure was taken so that the prévôts would not be diverted from their task of assuring safety in rural areas.

7. Henri-François d'Aguesseau, *Oeuvres* (Paris, 1759–89), 8:314, "Matières criminelles."

8. The criteria for recognizing a tramp were set forth in the declaration of 3 August 1764.

9. Only the questioning of the accused and the statements of the witnesses would provide clues on this point; in other words, one would need the records of the entire trial.

10. Véronique Boucheron, "La montée du flot des errants de 1760 à 1789 dans la généralité d'Alençon," *Annales de Normandie* 21 (1971): 55–86.

11. Two horsemen from each brigade of the maréchaussée had to make daily rounds of the "highways and byways, as well as the market town, villages, hamlets, châteaux, farms, and suspicious spots within its district." They would arrest tramps and check up on suspicious people.

12. They would actually carry on these trades from time to time.

13. Other examples of fraud included claiming to be a seer and extracting money from the credulous. In 1780, at Valenciennes, a "man in disguise, dressed as a mounted soldier of the maréchaussée and carrying a sword and false papers" took up a collection that he claimed would go to deserters sentenced to the galleys. In 1784, at Valence, "two tramps were arrested who had just come from Genoa wearing religious garb and carrying false *lettres d'obédience* [a statement from the superior of the order authorizing a religious to move from one convent to another] that had been forged by a person in the locality who was known to supply them to 'foreigners.'"

14. These couples were not always legally married; the statement of their liason is the determining factor here.

15. Cities were better protected as a result of their police forces and the presence of public authorities. Village priests in Lower Languedoc indicated that more than five hundred vagrants per year passed through those parishes situated along the highway. Archives départementales, Hérault, series C 5955.

16. See the *cahiers de doléances,* which generally expressed a desire to limit charity to truly indigent individuals, that is, individuals who were known to be paupers because they came from that parish.

17. When crime went beyond a certain level, townships and the maréchaussée, unable to cope, requested that the provincial *intendant* or commander intervene; then detachments of troops would be sent out and at times veritable pitched battles would ensue.

18. I have been unable to find any explanation for the meaning of these terms.

19. In a letter, Jacques-Pierre Brissot, journalist and future Girondist leader, commented that "people should never be permitted to plant trees in those declivities that have earned their name of *coupe-gorges* ["cut-throats," a pun on "throat" and "gorge," or "valley"]; quoted in Albert Desjardins, *Les cahiers des Etats Généraux en 1789 et la Législation criminelle* (Paris, 1883), p. 357.

20. For example, vagrancy and armed robbery. Certain criminal charges accumulated one after the other are significant, as in the case of a violent young man of twenty-eight, from the region of Autun, who terrorized the community, mistreated his own father, and destroyed some statements of indebtedness. All of this was more or less tolerated until the day he began to steal horses. This sparked a break between him and the villagers, who turned him over to the authorities.

21. It is to be assumed that vagrants were also first-time offenders. I adopted the combined category in order to reduce the number of headings.

22. Yet I made a separate category for sexual offenses and crimes.

23. For the period 1758–73 my sample involved one-third of all cases. After 1773 the records included a greater amount of data, which I analyzed thoroughly in order to have exact information about agrarian revolts, the actual functioning of the courts, and manifestations of the Great Fear of 1789. One case before 1773 therefore equaled three for period 1773–90. I used this ratio to adjust my computations.

24. No thorough counting was done, for I undertook my study of the courts of the prévôtés in order to draw comparisons. Indeed, I wanted to compare these results with those obtained in my study of crime, punishment, and the judicial system in the province of Languedoc, which is based upon an analysis of all the criminal cases extant in the archives of the Parlement of Toulouse.

25. They could be recognized by their swarthy skin, the braids worn by the men, and their distinctive speech.

26. However, the prévôt could handle no cases involving noblemen, clerics, or royal officials.

27. We must, of course, take into account the fact that the under-fifteen group is not included and that the over-fifty group was less common among tramps, whose way of life required a certain amount of physical stamina. In contrast, the latter age group was more commonly found in hospitals and beggars' prisons.

28. For example, bands of young men would go off together to seek work.

29. They often lived in concubinageB

30. The average age of tramps was, however, lower than that noted in beggars' prisons. At Lyons, 80 percent of the beggars interned were over fifty, and the majority were women. See J.-P. Gutton, *La société et les pauvres: l'exemple de la généralité de Lyon, 1534–1789* (Paris: Belles-Lettres, 1971?), Bibliothèque de la Faculté des lettres et sciences humaines de Lyon.

31. Among them, the 15 percent who failed to appear for trial were not described.

32. However, there is no indication of their cultural level, especially as far as education is concerned (as revealed by their signatures, for example). At the very most a reference was made to the unusual garb of certain ethnic groups (gypsies) or social groups ("dressed as a servant girl"). Differences in accent (Provençal or Parisian accents) were always used as proof of identity, especially if the tramp had left the region of his birth. See Roger Chartier, "Les Elites et les Gueux. Quelques représentations (XVIᵉ-XVIIᵉ siècles)," *Revue d'Histoire moderne et contemporaine* 21 (July–September 1974): 376–89.

33. Here, for example, is a description of a female tramp in 1773: "Beaumont, Rosalie, brought up in the Foundling Hospital of Marseilles, has a Parisian accent, is forty-two years old, four feet six inches tall, brown hair, eyebrows, and eyes, dark complexion, large nose, medium-sized mouth, thin lips, oval face, flat-chested, broad forehead, spiteful and proud expression, sturdy beggar, already branded with the letter *V* [for *vagabond*, tramp] on both shoulders."

34. Which did not prevent this particular fifty-year-old tramp from begging, "with threats that he would kill and burn."

35. The surgeon always checked the prisoner's shoulders for any sign that the individual was a previous offender. A brand served as evidence of a criminal past but did not constitute absolute proof.

36. Abbé Jean-Joseph Expilly, *Tableau de la population de la France* (Paris, 1780), p. 29, reprinted by Editions d'Histoire Sociale (Paris, 1973).

37. Jean-Paul Aron, Paul Dumont, and Emmanuel Le Roy Ladurie, *L'anthropologie du conscrit français* (Paris, 1972), pp. 217–30.

38. Of course, women were smaller. A sample of 161 women described between 1773 and 1790 reveals the following heights: 1 under 4'; 11 from 4' to 4'5"; 97 from 4'6" to 5'; 37 from 5' to 5'1''; 13 from 5'1'' to 5'5''; and 2 who were 5'6'' or over.

39. This royal ordinance reorganized the maréchaussée.

40. Cf. Georges Frêche and Geneviève Frêche, *Les prix des grains, des vins, et des légumes à Toulouse (1486–1868)* (Paris: Presses universitaires françaises, 1967), p. 108.

41. Cf. Edmond Esmonin, "Statistiques du mouvement de la population en France de 1770 à 1789," in *Etudes et chronique de démographie historique* (Paris, 1964), pp. 27 ff.

42. Yves-Marie Bercé, *Croquants et Nu-pieds* (Paris: Gallimard-Julliard, 1974), collection "Archives," p. 55.

43. M. Sonenscher, "La révolte des masques armés en 1783," *Vivarais et Languedoc,* 44ᵉ Congrès de la Fédération historique du Languedoc méditerranéen et du Roussillon (Montpellier, 1972), pp. 229 ff; and Nicole Castan, "Emotions populaires en Languedoc au XVIIIᵉ siècle," 96ᵉ Congrès national des Sociétés Savantes (Toulouse, 1971).

44. Cf. Pierre de Saint-Jacob, *Les paysans de la Bourgogne du Nord au dernier siècle de l'Ancien Régime* (Paris, 1960), p. 643.

45. Emmanuel Le Roy Ladurie, "Révoltes et contestations rurales en France de 1675 à 1788," *Annales, E.S.C.* 29 (January–February 1974): 6–22.

46. Lous XVI restored the full prerogatives of the parlements and invalidated the edict of 1788.

47. The parlements also speeded up their preliminary hearings and gave criminal cases precedence. For example, in 1789 the Parlement of Toulouse surpassed all its previous records for the number of cases tried.

48. Elsewhere, and chiefly along the outer limits of the Paris basin, the groups of poachers mentioned earlier became formidible bandits.

49. As early as August 1786 the présidial of Lyons punished a rebellion of hat workers that had occurred within that city; the ringleader was sentenced to be hanged.

50. At Reims a peddler of songs was tried for making seditious statements to the townspeople, whom he had called together with his drum. At Epinal rebels went to people's homes to force them to join up and broke the windows of those who refused. The same thing occurred at Rouen, where, in addition, they employed "the most frightful threats."

51. Storming and burning of the château of Meljac, near Rodez.

52. In the region of Cambrai rioting crowds demanded the sale of wheat at a moderate price by "claiming orders from the King" and made the same claims about grain exports.

53. Georges Lefebvre, *La grande peur de 1789* (Paris: Armand Colin, 1970); English translation by Joan White, *The Great Fear of 1789* (New York, 1973).

54. Muslin workers at Reims acted in the same manner as the linen workers at Rouen.

55. At Caen and Rouen, at Tulle and Limoges, and in the provinces of Rouergue and Périgord. At Alençon a crowd gathered about the seigneurial château, broke in, demanded the records of feudal claims, and burned them while insulting the nobleman personally. Meanwhile, another group of rebels was cutting and carrying off his rye, although it was still green.

56. The areas most affected (the regions to the east and south of the Paris basin, the region along the Saône River, and the Rhône Valley as far as Valence) were also the regions affected by the Great Fear (see Lefebvre, *The Great Fear of 1789,* pp. 169 ff.) as well as those prévôtés with high crime rates. There was, however, one anomaly, namely, the rebellions that occured during the first year of the Revolution in the northeast (Lorraine and Alsace).

57. In addition, the elimination of the jurisdictions of the Ancien Régime in 1790 left a great number of cases pending.

58. The distribution of crimes tried by the prévôts in 1789–90, for a total of 861 cases: north, 4.65%; northwest, 12.6%; Ile-de-France, 20.44%; center, 13.7%; westcentral, 9.18%; northeast, 15.1%; east, 11.96%; southeast, 3.72%; jurisdiction of Parlement of Toulouse, 8.83%.

59. The mayors of Rouen, Lyons, and Nantes were victims of violent riots. At Troyes the mayor was strangled and his body dragged through the streets; at Thann the mayor was imprisoned and placed in leg irons.

60. At Rouen, workers "destroyed several machines."

61. Throughout Alsace the houses of Jews were looted and their papers burned; the synagogue of Colmar was broken into.

62. Although the *cahiers de doléances* demanded additional funds to enable the maréchaussée to carry out its police duties, on the whole they opposed maintaining its jurisdictional powers.

63. Calculations show that for the period 1780–90 the Parlement of Bordeaux judged appeals by 437 individuals from the rural areas of the province of Guyenne who had been accused of major crimes. (These offenses were, therefore, of similar magnitude.) The initial sentences were upheld for 42.79 percent of the individuals, reduced for 39.59 percent, and increased for only 17.62 percent. Cf. Jean Lecuir, "Criminalité et moralité: Moutyon, statisticien du Parlement de Paris," *Revue d'Histoire moderne et contemporaine* 21 (July–September 1974): 445–93, in an issue devoted to crime and marginal groups during the early-modern period.

64. Mortality in prisons was very high during the last years of the Ancien Régime, especially

after 1788, when organized charity to prisoners ended. People detained by a prévôt were sent to the prison of the sénéchal, from which it was more difficult to escape than from local prisons, especially those of seigneurs.

65. Of 3,768 accused, only 11 (0.29 percent) escaped, and 15 percent were judged in absentia. Moreover, an order of 1788 stipulated that no decision involving a death sentence could be carried out for a month, in order to permit royal intervention.

66. For lack of sufficient proof; 1788 was an exception, with 15.19 percent of the cases left pending.

67. In 1764 the kingdom of France included 100 *bailliages*[a] and *sénéchaussées*[a] having the rank of présidial. In other words, these courts handed down the final judgment in certain cases that were analogous to the cas prévôtaux. Unlike the prévôts, however, these legal officials belonged to the world of the *robe* [that is, they were magistrates rather than police officers].

68. In Pierre Goubert, *Histoire économique et sociale de la France* (Paris, 1970), 2:13.

69. Cf. E. Bertin Mourot, "La maréchaussée en Bretagne au XVIIIᵉ siècle," typewritten thesis, Rennes, 1969; and T. Muracciole, "La criminalité de 1758 à 1790, d'après le fonds du présidial de Rennes," master's thesis, Rennes, 1969.

70. In 1974 the *gendarmerie nationale* [national rural police] totaled 73,000 men divided into 3,800 brigades; yet the authorities felt that another 10,000 men should be added.

71. Any act of armed banditry, violence, or premeditated murder would in all probability end in breaking on the wheel. Two beggars from the province of Auvergne were sentenced to be broken on the wheel in 1778 at Lyons after having threatened someone with sword and rifle. Any repeat offense with aggravating circumstances led to hanging. If sacrilege was added to theft from a church, where offering boxes and costly objects were a great temptation, the punishment was even more severe. For example, the leaders of the so-called Blue Child gang, which for a number of years had been robbing churches situated between Bordeaux and Toulouse, were sentenced to be burned alive. (The name of this gang may indicate that one or more members had once been foundlings, for the colors of the uniforms worn by the inmates of some institutions for abandoned children led to the sobriquets "Blue Children," "Red Children," etc.)

72. Judging in last resort, the présidial was even more strict than the prévôt, doubtlessly because urban criminals were easier to apprehend and because such criminals were more dangerous to the public. Thus, the punishment of urban crimes had to provide an even more forceful example. In a sample of 3,768 cases, the présidial judged 14 percent of the accused; yet it accounted for 17.96 percent of the sentences to the wheel, 19.49 percent of hangings, 18.95 percent of life sentences to the galleys or workhouse, but only 11.45 percent of all acquittals.

5
Arsonists in Eighteenth-Century France: An Essay in the Typology of Crime

André Abbiateci

Can a study of crime provide the basis for the study of a society? Can we attempt to do for the Ancien Régime, and for its rural areas in particular, what Louis Chevalier has done for nineteenth-century Paris? In an effort to find an answer to this question, I have studied one crime, arson, as reflected in the cases appealed before the Parlement of Paris between 1730 and 1789.

Arson is a crime that has always been with us and has been interpreted in a number of ways. In the Middle Ages, the firesetter *(boutefeu)* was regarded as one in league with the devil, with the powers of hell. In our own day, the pyromaniac is considered mad; the crime of arson is symptomatic, not so much of social conflicts as of psychic and sexual disorders. What were the motives of eighteenth-century arsonists within the jurisdiction of the Parlement of Paris? When I began my investigation, I intended to study this crime as an expression of social revolt. What immediately came to mind were the peasants of the Great Fear of 1789 banding together to put the torch to the records and even the châteaux of seigneurs; hungry people of the years of scarcity threatening to burn the houses of hoarders; hard-pressed taxpayers setting fire to the residences of the farmers-general. The facts uncovered by this research, however, turn out to be less unusual than expected, more bound up with daily life, though equally important. Because of the fear it aroused, fire could be used to apply social pressure.

Annales, E.S.C. 25 (January–February 1970): 229–48. Translated by Elborg Forster.

My study of a group of 200 lawcases has enabled me to determine how the offenders were distributed along the social scale; it has also revealed their accomplices and their language.

To one nineteenth-century jurist, arson was "the favorite crime of the lower classes."[1] To the historian of the peasants of Languedoc, "the shepherd intent on arson, a torch clenched in his fist, is a familiar figure whom we encounter again and again."[2] The occupational distribution of the arsonists whose cases were judged in appeal proceedings before the Parlement of Paris appears in table 5.1.

This table calls for two remarks. It is true that these arsonists did belong, for the most part, to the "lower class" of rural society; more than half of the offenders were of very modest means or even outright poor people (belonging to categories 1 and 2; also female spinners, wool carders, small-scale dealers in wax, etc.). In addition to these indigent arsonists, however, one is struck by the relatively high number of independent farmers and tenant farmers (46 cases, or approximately one-fifth of the total). Moreover, people of this category were often the instigators of arson, although the actual deed was carried out by their domestic servants.

The offenders acted more often alone (123 cases) than in concert with accomplices (74 cases).[3] In most of the cases complicity was confined to the family (42 of these 74 cases); otherwise, it involved people of the same occupational category or in the same marginal milieu (tramps, beggars) or else a group sharing a common interest.

The attitude of the accomplices during the trial is interesting. Except in very rare cases, the accomplices never incriminated or charged the principal defendant. The family, above all, faced the judges as a unified bloc of silent

Table 5.1—Occupational Distribution of Arsonists Judged in Appeal Procedures between 1750 and 1789

Category	Number of Persons Involved, including Accomplices
Tramps, beggars, unemployed persons, deserters, prostitutes	30
Domestic servants, laborers, field hands	52
Skilled labor	
textiles (weavers and spinners)	27
vineyard workers and gardeners	13
Other	
artisans, persons engaged in the food trades, employees in administration	29
Retail merchants	14
Independent farmers, tenant farmers	46
Parish priests	3
TOTAL	214

solidarity. The judges tried to break this silence and to "obtain the revelation of the accomplices" by inflicting the "question" [i.e., torture] on those condemned to death before their execution—usually to no avail.[4]

In their interrogations the judges attached great importance to the words spoken by the defendant before the commission of the crime, that is, to the threats he had made to his intended victim. This fact provides us with the material for a brief study of the language of the criminals. It is a concrete peasant language, full of images taken from their rural way of life: "I will have you awakened by the red cock";[5] "He threatened people by saying that he would light their pipes";[6] "He was going to send a man dressed in red who would pull everything down";[7] "He would fix him by sowing a seed that he would not soon forget."[8] Using a language characteristic of his occupation, the butcher G. Villain told his intended victim that he "deserved to be roasted like a pig." At times, the language is more enigmatic: "If they took away his land . . . they would see Damson plums."[9] "You don't want to give the wheat . . . alright, alright, alright, [he said], looking angry."[10]

At the trial, such ambiguous threats could be interpreted in two ways. P. Darras, accused of arson, granted that before the fire he had indeed said several times, as some hostile witnesses indicated, that he had "three things to do"; but he explained that these three things were not, as the witnesses claimed, "to kill, to burn, and to do away with himself," but "to give the curé . . . his inheritance . . ., to pay back what he owed . . ., and to make a formal acknowledgement of his debt."[11]

To some extent, of course, the court proceedings of the period attached such great importance to words in order to make up for the scarcity of real proofs. But there is another consideration: in a rural society every utterance is weighed because it has real consequences, because it is the magic key-word that has the power to accomplish things. This characteristic of peasant mentality stands in marked contrast to the more casual volubility of urban speech.

The minutes of the hearings give us the motive of the crime in only about sixty of the cases. There is a great variety of motives: family quarrels over a piece of land or unpaid debts; conflicts with the parish priest or the seigneur over users' rights in the forest or the right to the "last third" of the communal land; divisions within the village community; conflict between servants and masters. Yet we find three major categories of arsonists: madmen; beggars and day laborers who threatened to set fire unless they were given bread; and tenant farmers who refused to vacate their farms.

The Insane

Dancing around the fire on Saint John's Day, still a lively tradition in certain areas of rural France, was a joyful occasion for peasants in the

eighteenth century. To some of our arsonists, flames were a call to celebration
and rejoicing. When Jean Dumont had set a fire, he went home to tell his wife:
"The house is burning, let us rejoice, it is a beautiful fire."[12] Following a
sanity hearing, Jean Dumont was declared insane and confined to the General
Hospital.

Today, every criminal, and especially the pyromaniac, must undergo a
psychiatric, even a psychoanalytical, evaluation. Gaston Bachelard considers
arsonists mentally ill. "Modern psychiatry has elucidated the psychology of
the arsonist and has shown the sexual nature of his tendencies."[13] In the
course of this research project, I found a relatively large group (27 cases) of
defendants for whom the court demanded a sanity hearing. The records relating to such hearings include a deposition by the chaplain, the warden, and the
turnkey of the Conciergerie prison where the accused was kept; the crossexamination of the prisoner; and the report of the "physicians and surgeons of
the court." The presence of these last reports is an a priori indication that
these defendants were indeed suffering from mental disturbances.

The legal texts seem to confirm this first impression, for they always refer
to the current legislation, namely, the Criminal Ordinance of 1670, which
states that "the frenzied or insane person, having no will of his own, must not
be punished, his own madness being sufficient punishment." In Muyart de
Vouglans's treatise madness is included among "the causes that make crime
cease"; the frenzied and the insane are to be placed in the category "either of
children or of defendants tried in absentia."[14] The jurist must establish different degrees of responsibility, and the judge must impose different punishments "according to the nature of the madness" and "the time of its incep-
tion."

One of these defendants, Laurent Dupont, tried to deny his guilt by saying
"that he did not remember having set fire to the Gilson woman's place," but
the judge asked him "whether it was not in order to avoid punishment for his
crimes that he pretended not to be aware of them."[15] Nonetheless, it is true
that several of the accused (five in all) were exempted from capital punishment on the basis of a sanity hearing. Madeleine Chien, for instance, was first
sentenced to wear a tag with the inscription boutefeu [firesetter] and to be
burned alive; upon appeal and a sanity hearing, the magistrate sentenced her
"to be conveyed to the General Hospital, there to be confined for life, and
treated like the other insane."[16]

The only sentence imposed on those of our arsonists who were mad, then,
was confinement for life;* the women were sent to La Salpetrière, the men to
Bicêtre, institutions that were part of the General Hospital of Paris. In this
hospital, "they will be treated, detained, and provided for like all other insane

---

*The French text says "Grand Renfermement," an allusion to one of the chapters in
Michel Foucault's much discussed work, Madness and Civilization, cited in note 28.—Trans.

persons.'' Does this mean that they were to receive medical treatment, having been diagnosed as mentally ill by the "physicians and surgeons of the court"?

Actually, the reports of the physicians and surgeons were very superficial. The physician who had seen Jeanne Rivière admitted as much himself: "She answered in a manner that proves, in short, that she is totally insane."[17] Muyart de Vouglans in his treatise points out that the Parlement of Paris, before mitigating or revoking the punishment, establishes the "reality of the madness by means of a summary hearing."[18] Moreover, almost equal weight was given in these sanity hearings to the medical report and to the depositions of the chaplain, the turnkey, and the warden of the Conciergerie. These depositions bring to light some rather unusual behavior on the part of the prisoners. The turnkey was obliged to scold Laurent Dupont, who "wet and dirtied his bed."[19] Urbaine Richer walked out of the prison infirmary one day because she wanted to set fire to the Conciergerie. Jacques Diom "does all kinds of extravagant things, constantly dresses and undresses, starts singing like a madman, hides when he says his prayers, but for all that is not a bad fellow and actually makes himself very useful in the prison."[20] The conclusions of the jailers generally conform to those of the physicians, but sometimes there is disagreement. Thus, Jacques Person had always spoken to the turnkey "quite normally, without the slightest sign of madness," except that there was "something confused in his physiognomy"; but the physician's verdict was categorical: "All his responses, his gestures . . . and the confused look in his eyes make it plain that his mind is very weakened and that he must be considered a person whose mind is apt to become so deranged that he might commit the most dangerous excesses."[21] The court condemned the defendant to be committed to Bicêtre, thus following the physician's advice, to which it attached greater importance than to the depositions of the jailers. But the very fact that it solicited the opinion of the jailers at all shows that the physician was not alone in deciding the matter of a prisoner's madness; nor would we expect him to be in that position, given the vagueness of the medical statements. The physician who saw Laurent Dupont, for example, simply declared "that after having questioned him [Dupont], he realized from his responses that the mind of the accused prisoner really was deranged."[22]

Some of the medical reports were more precise and noted that the madness had its origin in a brain lesion. Urbaine Richer "has been struck on the head" and has been "trepanned." In other trials we hear about other "facets of madness":* First, there is "imbecility," characterized by a total absence of speech. Marie-Louise Poullet is "absolutely in a state of imbecility and insanity," for she has "not articulated a single intelligible word" and the physician has been unable "to get a single rational word out of her," even though he has

---

*Another chapter title from *Madness and Civilization.*—Trans.

"asked her many questions."[23] François Paradis is "very quiet, as meek as a lamb, and he plays with the little children."[24]

Other accused prisoners, the "vicious" or "frenzied" mad, were considered more dangerous. Urbaine Richer, "because of the illness from which she suffers, falls into dreadful fits of rage."[25] Vehement speech was seen as one sign of a disposition to violence. In the responses of J. Godard, the physicians noted no more than "a kind of vehemence that can lead to violence, especially after drinking."[26] A last category of the insane were the "maniacs." Pierre Peneau "seemed to be in a state of dementia, judging from the answers he gave to the various questions; he has two large and evil-looking ulcers in the area of his left knee . . . and moreover we were told that he is subject to frequent fits that make him fall down and lose consciousness. . . . There are times when he falls down and goes into a kind of fit of raving."[27]

It is thus not easy to appraise the value of the medical reports concerning the presumedly insane arsonists, for their statements are contradictory. Most of the reports testify to the physicians' continued practice at that "first level of elaboration of medicine,"[28] which, as a social measure, simply called for internment; but some specify organic lesions as causes of the insanity and must therefore be based on a more thorough examination of the accused.

On the other hand, if madness was really perceived as a mental illness, it would also have to follow that the condemnation was imposed as a therapeutic measure, that the insane person received medical treatment in the General Hospital. The fact is, however, that in the correctional institutions of the time, where libertines, criminals, and profligate individuals of all descriptions formed a strange amalgam, the mad arsonist confined with them was not given medical treatment.[29]

On the basis of an analysis of the medical reports and the meaning of the sentences imposed, one comes to the conclusion that the late eighteenth century was a "period of transition" and that the "medical perception" of madness was only slowly gaining admission in the world of the interned. For such a perception was contrary to the "time-honored signification of imprisonment," in which madness was perceived as a social phenomenon by a society ever ready to take offense.

The trial of Pierre Louvet offers a fine example for the persistence of the old signification of internment. Louvet was accused of "blaspheming the Holy Name of God" by stating: "There is no God but Pierre Louvet, and the Eucharist contains nothing but the carcass of Jesus Christ." Louvet was also guilty of trying to put an end to his days, for after having failed in an attempt to hang himself, he . . "set fire to his furniture" and started "a great fire in his own house."[30] This arsonist, who used fire against himself, was institutionalized as a madman. His case shows that the crimes of sacrilege, blasphemy, and suicide no longer carried the "prestige of profanation"; those who committed them were locked up because their behavior was indicative of

moral disorder and characteristic of a world of "unreason which was beginning to be measured in terms of its distance from the social norm."[31]

Arsonists from the Lower Strata of Society

The threat of fire aroused fear and could thus be used as a means of
applying economic pressure or for blackmail. It was the weapon par excellence of the poorest categories within rural society—artisans, hucksters, beggars. These people attempted to use it to obtain minimum subsistence or to
improve their daily fare.

THIEVES

Domestic theft was perpetrated for the same purpose, and sometimes the
thief would set fire to the furnishings or even the whole house in order to
obliterate the traces of his larceny. I have found five cases of theft compounded by arson. The offenders were three domestic servants, one carpenter,
and one huckster.

One of the accused, François Gaudron, was found guilty of "theft by
means of breaking into his master's writing desk . . . and of attempting to set
fire to the room or to blow up the house by placing next to the desk a sack of
15 pounds of gunpowder . . . and some starch."[32] Gaudron was sentenced to
be burned at the stake. Punishment of theft with arson was extremely severe;
of the five accused of this crime, three were sentenced to death (two of these
were domestic servants, always considered to be "gallow-birds" to begin
with).

EXTORTIONISTS

The threat of fire alone could be used for blackmail and as a means of
applying pressure. It was freely used by extortionists, who would write
threatening notes demanding money. Jean Bossu, for instance, the son of the
schoolmaster of Talmay, "tossed into the vestibule of the parish house of
Talmay an anonymous letter containing threats that a fire would be set and the
roof be burned unless by nine o'clock that night eight louis were placed in a
plate at the foot of the garden wall next to the apricot tree."[33] These notes,
incidentally, are the only exhibits I found in my entire study of criminal trials.

Nicolas Péreau, an unemployed domestic servant, wrote several such notes
to the vicar general of the Saint-Lazare congregation. I have a photostat of the
first note, dated 24 December 1761. Its pitifully bad spelling testifies to its

author's poor schooling and extremely low social status. Here are the demands put forth by "ten poor couples": "We wil go to yur farm to get a chontribushon we wants hunnert franks eech . . . be gud enuf to put it to the red gait bye Saint Charl ousid nekst to the Wal at fife oclok be shoor to do it orelse . . . we wil set fyr to al yor farm."[34] The authors of these ultimatums were criminals who knew how to write; indeed, some of the accused advanced the argument that they were unable to wield the pen as proof of their innocence. Thus, Eloy Dubois, "picture peddler but presently beggar," pointed out that "he does not know how to write."[35] Most of the defendants, then, had received rudimentary schooling; they were not beggars or tramps (except in three cases), but artisans and hucksters with fixed residence in their village. (The occupations of the authors of these notes were the following: one drayman, one butcher, one cutler, one shop- and innkeeper, one tavern-keeper, one shoemaker, one cooper, the wife of a common laborer, one carter, one herdsman, the son of a schoolmaster, one domestic servant, one picture peddler presently a beggar, one beggar, and one ploughboy.)

This very specific type of criminality, then, was not related to utter destitution; it simply aimed to supplement the extortionist's resources and to provide him with some hard cash. The victims were the richest people of the village, namely, independent plowmen, tenant farmers, and the priest. Verrier Toussaint made a judicious choice when he addressed his demands to "the eight tenant-farmers who paid the highest amount of *taille* in the parish." The sums demanded varied greatly, ranging from 20 écus to 60 écus and even going up to 1,000 livres.

Four out of twelve trials indicate that this kind of blackmail brought results. Antoine Ravault "extracted 24 livres from the curé by threats of fire."[36] The eight louis d'or obtained by Jean Bossu were "taken and confiscated [by the court] for the benefit of the domain and the seigneury of Talmay. . . ." In the other eight trials it is not clear whether the blackmail was successful. We do know, however, that Nicolas Péreau was arrested when he went to pick up the money he had demanded; the circumstances of his arrest are known from the depositions of the brothers of the Saint-Lazare congregation, one of whom testified that he "had been charged with watching for anybody who might come to the red gate of the courtyard where a sack filled with nails and then a written reply had been placed following the first note."[37] Another brother told the court how he had arrested the offender: "While the police were at Mass, one of the brothers came to tell him that he had seen Nicolas Péreau; with two other brothers he jumped over the wall and seized the man, who was walking along very slowly and seemed to be looking for something."[38] This somewhat comical version of the event (what agile monks these were!) differs from the version given by the police constables who, in order to show their valor, claimed that the individual ran away as fast as he could and that it was they who caught him.

Those who wrote threatening notes thus risked being ambushed when they went to gather the fruits of their odious labor of intimidation. If arrested, they were made to pay a heavy price. The penalties for writers of such notes, whether they carried out their threats or not, were extremely severe. Out of a total of eleven defendants known to us, three were condemned to death, five to the galleys, and two to prison for life.

BEGGARS

Beggars rarely wrote threatening notes because they usually could not write. But they did use oral threats of fire; this form of begging compounded by violence and insolence was vigorously prosecuted by the *prévôts* of the mounted police and greatly feared by the rural inhabitants. The country people were afraid that beggars would set fire to their properties. This apprehension found expression in the *cahiers de doléances* of 1789; the *cahier* of Saigneville in Picardy, for instance, deplored the fact "that one has often been saddened to see this type of poor beggar (and stranger) turn into real brigands, thieves, and firesetters."[39]

Background of the arsonist beggars.   Arsonist beggars were not sickly or crippled. In fact, they were often convicted simply because they were able-bodied beggars. Thus, Pierre Valentin was convicted because "on Saturday 14 January 1786 he begged, even though able-bodied, and also with insolence."[40] Léonard Narbon, who threatened to set fire to the house where he wanted to stay, was "a tramp and an able-bodied beggar."[41]

Actually, begging by infirm and crippled persons was permitted under royal legislation. "The law makes a distinction between those whose begging can be laid to idleness, and crippled or aged beggars who only beg because they are forced to do so."[42]

Nor do we find any very old persons among the arsonist beggars. Of the thirty-six accused whose age is known to us, two were under twenty, twelve between twenty and thirty, twelve between thirty and forty, and ten over forty (although only two were over forty-two).

The economic background of these beggars is clearly shown in the list of occupations practiced by them in normal times: four were day laborers or common laborers and farm hands; three were ditch diggers or masons, six were hucksters or peddlers, two were sailors, two were deserters, and four were weavers and spinners.

For ditch diggers and masons, work came to a halt in winter, so they were reduced to begging. Farm hands also could not find work once the busy main agricultural season of the summer had ended. Claude Vernier, for example, was "without fixed abode since the end of August last, when he left the

employ of Sieur Launay, tenant farmer at Mauny, where he had worked for
thirteen or fourteen months as a farm hand. . . . After he had left Launay's, he
was without work for a month, living at Lagny and in the surrounding
area."[43] Once the year's grain harvest had been threshed, the threshers were
dismissed by their masters. Nicolas Péreau was in service as a thresher at
Saint-Lazare for eight months, "until Saint John's Day last"; then he became
a tramp, an "unemployed domestic servant, sleeping sometimes in one place,
sometimes in another."[44]

These remarks on their background confirm Alexander Vexliard's conclusions concerning tramps and *gens sans aveu*:* "From the fourteenth century
on, the massive scope of vagrancy was increasingly stripped of its ideological
aureole, eventually revealing its economic basis in a very stark light. The
precarious condition of the labor force is the salient feature of the history of
vagrancy in the early-modern period."[45]

The proceeds of blackmail by fire.   Arson was one of the violent forms of
begging, defined by Abel Poitrineau as "a marginal occupation that makes
survival possible for those who have become totally destitute owing to the
absence of sufficiently endowed public-relief organizations."[46] Such begging
assumed violent forms because the beggar was no longer accepted as a man of
God, as he had been in certain periods of the Middle Ages. . . . He had to
resort to threats to obtain shelter, food, and sometimes money. And these
were precisely the things the beggar demanded. Tramps asked to be put up in
the villages through which they passed. Léonard Narbon, a native of the
parish of Lusac-les-Eglises, was convicted for "vagrancy, for swearing, and
for threatening to set fire to the house where he wanted to stay in the village of
Levées in the parish of Veillain."[47] Pierre Valentin, "apparently under the
influence of wine at the time," was even particular about the place where he
wanted to spend the night. He "struck Widow Cappée with a stick when she
refused to put him up in one house, even though he had been told about
another house where he could go and where he was offered a place to sleep,
which he did not accept. . . ." Whereupon he "threatened to set fire."[48]

Other beggars asked for food, for their daily bread. Jean Quentin was
accused of "making the rounds of the different farms, noisily carrying on at
the gates and threatening to set fire unless he was given money, bread, and
cheese."[49] And finally, certain criminals tried to extort money from their
victims, preferably of the weaker sex. Pierre Lorson was charged with "entering the courtyard of J. Normand, plowman at Cambercourt, demanding and
receiving from Normand's wife the sum of six livres by threatening to blow
her and her husband's brains out, to set fire to them, and to break down the
door of their house and their bedroom."[50]

*For an explanation of this term, see translator's note in Chapter 3 of this volume.—Trans.

Motivation: a criminality of extreme poverty. The reason for these crimes of arson committed by beggars was poverty, stark need. On this point the statements of the accused are very revealing. Nicolas Péreau justified his conduct by writing to the vicar of the Saint-Lazare congregation: "You are giving sharitee to some pore peeple that doesent need it as much as wee does, begarts that is siting in the pub evri dai, sharitee is veree naice but they doesent need it as mutch as wee does."[51] Jacques Lone told the magistrates that he and two other common laborers were "asking for bread out of need."[52] This criminality of extreme poverty shows a very specific frequency curve. The date of the crime is known for ten of the trials, and it turns out that six of the crimes were committed in winter (between November and February) and four in the period before the new harvest.

This very pronounced seasonal distribution is not difficult to understand. It was during the winter, when the level of employment was low, and during the preharvest season, when grain prices were high, that begging compounded by violence and threats of arson became a means of survival for the poorest members of the lowest social strata. It should also be noted that the frequency curve of all crimes of arson, whether committed by thieves, extortionists, or beggars, is the same as that for beggars alone. The twenty-three trials for which the date of the crime is known reveal that the crime took place during the winter in fifteen cases and during the preharvest season in seven cases.

Moreover, the corollary offenses of the arsonist beggars are also characteristic of people goaded by stark necessity. The trials show that in addition to the threats, these persons were charged with the theft of inexpensive items, such as a cabbage or a pair of stockings. Claude Vernier stole a capon from the courtyard of a farm and traded it at Lagny for bread, wine, and a meat pie.[53] Other corollary offenses were drunkenness, keeping bad company, and swearing.

Roaming beggars: organized groups and individuals acting alone. All these needy people left their home parishes and wandered along the roads. The route taken by Claude Vernier is known to us and shows that all his wanderings took place within the limits of a day's walk. "From Lagny he went to Mitry, and then to the Hôtel-Dieu of Meaux. . . . On the day he was dismissed there, he slept at Carnetin, and then took the ferry from Danard to Chanteloup. . . ."[54] Eloy Dubois' band, which set a fire at Frémicourt (near Bapaume), was a group of beggars whose home parishes were farther away: they came from Mouchy-Lagache (near Péronne), Neuville-sur-Seine and Flavy-le-Martel (near Ham), Trucy-le-Haut (south of Laon), and from as far as Crespy-en-Valois and the Franche-Comté.[55] Jean-Baptiste Nivelon and Antoine Pera, two sailors arraigned before the bailliage court of Chartres, had undoubtedly crossed all of France; Antoine Pera, "of Genoese nationality," was made to "return to his own country as indicated by his passports."[56]

These tramps moved about in groups or by themselves. Eloy Dubois appeared in the docket together with a number of common laborers, peddlers, and deserters; altogether they were thirteen beggars. The band indicted along with Charles Guérin consisted of two hucksters, a female spinner, two individuals without a trade, one common laborer, one notions-peddler, and one hurdy-gurdist.[57] Some of the accused did have a fixed residence but had organized into groups for the purpose of begging. The magistrate asked Jacques Lone whether he had not "gotten together with Louis Haussart and Clément Legrand in order to force money from the whole region."[58] Pierre Piette, Roch Tilloy, and François Quentin had "gotten together in order to demand wheat at various farms of plowmen by producing false fire certificates,* compounded by harassment and other forms of violence."[59]

These various groups were formed with a view to intimidating the victims and thus increasing the effectiveness of the pressure exerted by threats. Nicolas Péreau, a domestic servant who acted on his own, had recourse to a rather simplistic stratagem when he wrote in the threatening notes he sent out that "we are ten poor couples"; under crossexamination he admitted that he had "said we were ten in order to scare people."[60]

Penalties meted out to arsonist beggars.   In the eyes of the "reactionary" jurists, beggars and tramps were simply idlers fit for the galleys or the gallows. Edmé de la Poix de Fréminville asserted in his *Dictionnaire de la Police* that "most beggars, especially the able-bodied ones, are nothing but outright libertines who from sheer shiftlessness would rather ask for a handout than work."[61] De Ferrière defined tramps as "idle, shiftless people who roam about the country without ties *(sans aveu)*, without a home or fixed residence."[62]

Throughout the eighteenth century, these tramps were considered to be delinquents for whom the state had no use and who, moreover, were a menace to public tranquillity, "for such people often bring with them upheaval and sedition."[63] They were punished in accordance with this attitude. The present study is concerned, not with the very severe, but sporadic, prosecution of beggars and tramps by the rural mounted police following the promulgation of royal edicts concerning this problem (especially the Declaration of 3 August 1764),† but with the sentences handed down by normally functioning courts over the span of a half-century (see table 5.2). Note that the most frequent punishment was condemnation to the galleys; one of these sentences was mitigated upon appeal, but on the whole the judges of the appeal courts were just as severe, and more than half of the sentences in every category were upheld.

---

*Certificates indicating that they were authorized to beg as victims of a fire.—Trans.
†This kind of "summary justice" is treated in Chapter 4 of this volume.—Trans.

Table 5.2—Punishment for Arson Committed by Beggars (thirty-one cases)

Sentence	Passed by the Local Court	Upon Appeal
Death	3	1
Condemnation to the galleys	13	12
Confinement		
[in a General Hospital]	2	3
Banishment	1	0
Injunction not to repeat the		
offense	0	1
Admonition	0	1
Deferral	5	0
Additional hearing ordered	4	8
Not guilty	2	4
Case dismissed on procedural		
grounds	0	1

The jurists who charged beggars with shiftlessness and the judges who meted out severe punishments "thus refused to consider the argument of *force majeure*"[64] that was at the root of begging compounded by threats of fire. And yet "the charge of shiftlessness appears to be totally unfounded in light of the economic reality," that is, "the collapse or the shrinking of the demand for labor . . . the high price and the scarcity of grain . . . and the absence of cash reserves among agricultural laborers and artisans who lived from hand to mouth."[65] This opinion of a twentieth-century historian is confirmed by my own research; it also corroborates the assessment of an enlightened jurist of the eighteenth century, Brissot de Warville, who felt that "since larceny and pilfering are usually committed by the poor, and since three-fourths of the thefts are often provoked by indigence, we must begin by doing away with poverty." "No beggars, no thieves," he concluded;[66] and one is tempted to add: "No beggars, no threats of fire."

Tenant Farmers and Landowners: Refusal to Comply with Eviction

A third type of arsonist takes us into a very different social world from that of beggars and the poverty-stricken: the world of well-to-do landowners and farmers.

The criminal trials sometimes (actually only in two cases) bring to light a positive assertion of sovereignty over personal property. Two wealthy Parisian landowners (one a wood dealer, the other the tax receiver for the city of Paris) came into conflict with provincial landowners at Dormans and Coulange-sur-Yonne, respectively. Jean Boucot had recently acquired the

domain of Dormans; a mill owned by Sieur Drouet formed an enclave within
that property and ''inconvenienced him from the very beginning. . . . He was
planning to destroy it and annex it to his domain in order to have the water
whenever he wished.''[67] He had asked Drouet to sell him the mill, but they
were unable to reach an agreement; at which point he ordered his servants to
set fire to it. This, at least, was the charge brought against Boucot, who
asserted his bourgeois desire to have absolute control over his property.

A trial of a similar kind resolved the civil suit brought by the Parisian wood
dealer Nicolas de Montimier against Claude Gagneux, who was convicted of
''having set fire to one of the farms owned by the plaintiff.''[68]

For the most part, however, rural crimes of arson were committed by
landowners and tenant farmers whose land was threatened. Their strong attachment to the land was usually expressed as a negative reaction. It can be
seen in their efforts to protect a property against minor encroachments. P.
Richer, for instance, had a grudge against a cowherd who ''led his herds into
the alfalfa and into the fields before they had been gleaned.''[69]

Attachment to the land also led to violent opposition to eviction. In one
case, the marshals who came to place the seals on personal property were
treated rudely, and threats of fire were made—and carried out—against those
who had sent the marshals.[70] Homeowners also refused to be evicted from
their houses. Jacques Le Roux did not accept the sale of his house ''without
his consent'' and proceeded to burn it down.[71] Seizure always resulted from
unpaid debts, another indication that indebtedness played a major role in the
process by which fortunes changed hands. The effects of seizure do not seem
to have been so severe for the victims (one independent farmer, one real-estate
broker, one cooper, one wax dealer) that they were reduced to indigence. But
the violence of their reaction is not surprising in a still unpolished society.

The most unusual refusals to comply with eviction were those of independent and tenant farmers who were determined to keep their land. I have found
a dozen court files on them, many of which contain a wealth of detail. These
files show that arson was particularly prevalent among the tenant farmers of
Picardy; and despite the limited number of trial-records at my disposal, the
geographic clustering of the courts from which these defendants appealed is
most instructive. Two appeals came from the bailliage court of Saint-Pierre-
le-Moûtier and the jurisdiction of Thouvenay, three from the agricultural
plains around Paris (Meaux, Melun, Bourg-la-Reine), and eight from the
plain of Picardy (the Santerre, Vermandois, and Beauvaisis regions).

Appraising the social standing of these offenders is a more difficult matter.
As far as occupation is concerned, they were a very homogeneous group. All
of them (except one *ménager,* or ''householder,'' and one mull-weaver) were
tenant or independent farmers, a fact that immediately places them at the apex
of the peasant hierarchy, among the *''coqs de village,''* or village big shots.
These men rented land or seigneurial rights (*terrage,* or rather, *champart*

rights that were paid in produce) from a seigneur or from ecclesiastic communities (the abbeys of Saint-Eloy of Noyon and Saint-Victor or the cathedral
chapter of Amiens). In some of the cases the landlord is not identified.

Occupation, however, is insufficient to determine the social standing of
these farmers, so we must apply other criteria as well. The mull-weaver and
the wife of the "householder" must have been very small operators, judging
from the amount of land they leased: ". . . this *journal* of land [about 1/2
acre]."[72] On the other hand, there is no doubt that five other tenant farmers
were well-to-do.

Pierre Richer offered a considerable supplement *(pot de vin)*—namely,
2,496 livres—to the treasurer of the abbey of Saint-Victor in order to obtain
the lease of one of its properties. He also owned enough livestock to employ a
herdsman and he raised alfalfa.[73] Pierre Darras and his wife had several
domestic servants, a horse, and a wagon. A carter stated that "over several
weeks he had hauled some twenty cartloads of personal belongings, furnishings, wheat, wood, logs, squared timber, mattresses, beds, and linens out of
the farm of Saint-Nicolas."[74] Moreover, the defendant himself provided an
inventory of his storehouses: "At the time of the fire, his storehouses held his
stock of wheat as well as the oats for his horses, and 700 *septiers** that had
already been sold and were to be turned over to a brewer on Saint John's
Day . . ., also 340 *septiers* of barley that he owed to another party and of
which he had only delivered 60 *septiers* . . . which total quantity of oats and
barley has been consumed by the fire." François Chauveau owned a horse[75]
and Jean Favard employed a domestic servant.[76] As for Claude Frottier, he
had experienced a remarkable social ascent. Having started as his master's
gardener, he had become first his gatekeeper, then his tenant, and finally his
partner in a number of agricultural and woodcutting enterprises.[77] In addition
to the wealth of these tenant farmers, we should also note their respectable
cultural level. All were able to sign their names, and P. Richer was an
educated man who consulted legal works, such as the treatise on procedure by
François de Couchot. Despite the gaps in the documentary material, which
provides no details about the other five tenant farmers beyond their occupation, one can conclude that this social category of arsonists was relatively
well-to-do.

Most of these offenders were arraigned before royal courts, especially in
Picardy. In this region, the decisions handed down by the court refer to
specific pieces of legislation. Pierre Levert was convicted of proffering threats
"in violation of the Royal Declaration of 20 July 1764."[78] André Larue was
convicted of "violating the Royal Declaration . . . for the *généralité* of Soissons."[79] Penalties imposed by the court of appeal, incidentally, were less
severe than those of lower courts. Thus, judges of the first instance con-

*156 liters or 240 pounds of the period.—Trans.

demned thirteen of the accused to penalties that had to be served (banishment, the galleys), while eight were granted an additional hearing, given deferred sentences, or exonerated. The corresponding figures for the sentences of the Parlement of Paris are seven and fourteen.

Tenant farmers who resorted to arson were more than farmers bent on revenge because their interests were violated. Their violent reaction also owed something to their mentality, to their particular conception of the leasehold, which clashed with the provisions of the bourgeois written law. The study of their criminal trials sheds light on this mentality.

Two tenant farmers of Picardy, Pierre Levert and André Larue, were in the docket for disregarding "the Declaration of 20 July 1764, also known as the Declaration for the *généralité* of Soissons." This particular piece of legislation, which attempted to curb the criminal activities of the tenant farmers of Picardy, was only a restatement of earlier royal measures that undoubtedly had not been enforced. The most important of these was the Royal Ordinance of 25 March 1724, which "expressly forbids all inhabitants, tenants, plowmen, and others . . . to molest landowners and new tenants in their persons and properties . . . and even to hinder or discourage, by threats or otherwise, those who might apply for the leases of the said properties."[80] This ordinance defines the very type of offense for which the tenant farmers of Picardy were condemned in the trials under study here. Thus, Hélène Quenescourt "attempted, by violent means and against the will of the Cathedral Chapter of Amiens, to keep possession of a lease over five *journaux* of land belonging to the chapter . . . of which four *journaux* were leased to Etienne Pichon and one *journal* to Eloy Sénéchal. . . . The accused said that Sénéchal and his wife would not have the use of this *journal* of land and [she] employed threats to discourage Simon Pautre and Henri Faurel . . . from cultivating this *journal* of land for the said Sénéchal."[81]

Gervais Bardin and his sons were convicted of "disturbing the public peace, of endeavoring to keep their position against the will of the owners of their farms, using violent means and assault and battery to keep out those who might wish to apply for the lease; of using these means, in particular, against Jacques Bécret and his sons by way of revenge for their taking or planning to take the lease of the seigneurial produce rents of La Ville-au-Bois, which had been in their [the Bardins'] family for a very long time, and of setting fire to Bécret's barn."[82]

The decisions handed down by the courts show certain presumptions on the part of the tenant farmers; their particular conception of landownership and leaseholding was in total disagreement with the written law. The bourgeois landowner meant to use his property as he saw fit, but the tenants who resorted to arson refused to be evicted and were unwilling to leave, unless it suited them. Moreover, they wanted to leave the leasehold to their heirs, thus ensuring the continuity of their family on that particular piece of land; and this very permanence could only strengthen the presumptions I outlined above. Thus it was that the leasehold of the rents at La Ville-au-Bois had been in Gervais Bardin's family "for a very long time."[83]

In fact, all the tenant farmers of Picardy who became involved in these crimes based their claims on the tradition of the *fermiers de mauvais gré,* or perpetual leaseholders. The legal aspects of this rural tradition, which was particularly well preserved in the Santerre region, have been studied by François Debouvry in a remarkable dissertation written at the end of the nineteenth century.[84] In brief, it concluded that those who rented land subject to the *droit de marché* [right to the lease], otherwise called the *droit de mauvais gré,* laid claim to three rights. First and foremost, they felt that they could not, under any circumstances, be compelled to leave the land they held under their lease; actually, this was the only right claimed by the offenders studied here. But there were two additional claims, namely, the right to a moderate rent and the exclusive right to purchase the land in case of its sale by the owner. Taken together, these rights conferred de facto ownership on the tenant farmer. One of the royal subdelegates was quick to point this out in 1785: "There is no doubt that landownership in the four bailliages of Péronne, Montdidier, Roye, and Saint-Quentin is virtually fictitious. The sitting tenants keep possession of these lands, for which they always pay very moderate rents, against the will of their landlords, by threatening all comers with the dreadful punishment they inflict on those farmers who dare to take over their leases."[85]

Tenant farmers felt that these rights were part of their patrimony and used them accordingly. In 1787, the provincial assembly of Picardy cited some extraordinary abuses in this respect: "The tenant farmers of these cantons—in the Santerre region—place their landlords' property on the market, either by selling the permission to work them to others or by giving them as dotal property to their children or by bequeathing them to their heirs with provisions for later division."[86]

It was under this tradition that the lease of a seigneurial produce rent could be handed down from father to son in Gervais Bardin's family, "for a very long time." If a tenant agreed to leave his farm, he expected the new tenant to pay him an indemnity as the price of his *bon gré* [willingness]. If he was made to leave *de mauvais gré* [unwillingly], terrible vengeance was in store, not so much for the urban absentee and hence inaccessible landlord, but for the new tenant who was prepared to replace him. When Hélène Quenescourt was outbid by Eloy Sénéchal and his wife, she coarsely insulted them, calling them thieves and home wreckers.[87] She clearly shared the rural mentality of the *mauvais gré* tenants [perpetual leaseholders] described in the memorandum of 1785 referred to above. "All those who have dared to take over the leases of lands already held by someone else are regarded as wicked villains and public enemies; they are spitefully designated by the term 'interlopers' and punished with fire and sword."[88] Here we see that at the very time when the royal legislation branded arsonists as "disturbers of the public peace," the tenant farmers of Picardy felt that the "public enemies" were the "home wreckers" and "interlopers." They saw the outbidding of a sitting tenant as an unjust and base action, an attitude that appears to have been shared by the rural population as a whole.

In one minor treatise of the time, a rural woman of Picardy expresses herself as follows: "In this region the sitting tenant farmers have built their farm buildings; they have dug the wells and planted the trees; and that is why those who outbid them are doing an unjust thing."[89] But then, this opinion of "a mother" is not decisive, for we are not told to which social stratum she belongs, and she may well be speaking as the wife of a tenant farmer or a plowman.

The solidarity of the village community with the evicted tenant farmers is shown more clearly in practices brought to light in the trials under study here. On the one hand, it is clear that the peasant who had betrayed his class was ostracized. No one wanted to work for the new tenant, for those who did were apt to be included in the resentment of the former perpetual leaseholder. Thus, Hélène Quenescourt was charged with "employing threats to discourage Simon Pautre and Henri Faurel from cultivating this *journal* of land for the said Sénéchal."[90]

On the other hand, the courts were faced with a wall of silence when investigating these cases of arson. If the royal judges handed down severe sentences, it was because they were special judges who worked under the aegis of the intendant and therefore had to show their zeal—although this was not too much of an imposition, since many of them were themselves landed proprietors. In any case, the high number of court decisions calling for additional hearings or deferred sentences (especially in appeal proceedings) shows that the courts had great difficulty in finding witnesses who were willing to talk.

What is the real meaning of the tradition of mauvais gré? Debouvry has shown that the mauvais gré "tends to emphasize a very special conception of the leasehold contract. The juridical formula it tends to implement," he writes, "is that of the old perpetual ground rent, which amounts to loss of control over property."[91] As far as the peasant was concerned, such a curtailment of ownership rights was founded upon the right to work and the right to a livelihood.[92]

But the social significance of this tradition is less well known, for it is very complex. First and foremost, the mauvais gré was an assertion of solidarity within the rural community vis-à-vis any outsider. This is the meaning of the notices posted in their village by the inhabitants of Hollain: "Any outsiders who might have the audacity to increase the amount of the tithe [to be collected from this village] are warned that their houses will be reduced to ashes and that they themselves will have to fear for their lives. This threat is harsh, but it is just."[93] The *cahier de doléances* of Outrebois condemns the perfidious machinations of the financial agents of the abbey: "They swoop down upon all the tenants . . . they bleed them white, devour them, and despoil them of their farms by shifting these properties from one village to another and putting in a tenant from the outside."[94]

This hostility was directed against urban absentee landlords and large-scale tenant farmers from the city who grabbed all the land that was for rent. The *cahier* of Saint-Quentin-des-Prés deplored the fact that "the merchants of the cities are not satisfied with running their businesses, but take over the leaseholds in our rural areas and deprive us of the work for which we are qualified." "Ambitious tenant farmers take over all the small leaseholds and thereby make it impossible for young people to settle down on their own."[95]

In this manner the rural community, held together by these middling tenants and farmers, was fighting an economic evolution of the capitalist variety that was beginning to invade the countryside and eventually led to the formation of large-scale leaseholding. In its dislike for competition, the mentality of the rural community was still that of the precapitalist age.

Nonetheless, the solidarity of the rural community was undermined by internal tensions; after all, the tradition of the mauvais gré essentially benefited middling and well-to-do tenant farmers, and the other peasants in the rural community did not feel that this monopoloy of the local rural bourgeoisie was justified.[96] As we have seen above, two small-scale tenants (the mull-weaver and the wife of the "householder") also laid claim to the right of mauvais gré. And so did the "servantry," that is, rural hired labor. Moreover, small peasants tried to obtain leases whenever they could, a fact that greatly worried the sitting tenants. The *cahier* of Seux deplores the continuing stagnation of agriculture, "because everyone wants to try his hand at it. . . . All this unfortunate meddling hampers the proper use to be made of a leasehold and creates unwarranted competition. . . . Thus, we see that nowadays most mortmain landlords award the leases of their lands and seigneurial dues to the last and highest bidder."[97]

The same *cahier* also reveals the social ideal of these tenant farmers. They are sorry to see the passing of the social pattern in small villages, where "the first take care of the last, and where everyone peacefully stays in his own class." The "last class," then, was supposed to remain in its place, in other words, to constitute a docile and abundant labor force for the well-to-do farmers. Seen from this angle, the mauvais gré becomes an assertion of class solidarity that was increasingly contested by the poorer peasants at the end of the eighteenth century.

Thus, the detailed study of the criminal trials for arson judged in appeal proceedings before the Parlement of Paris has brought to light a novel type of arsonist, the mauvais gré tenant farmer. To be sure, the documentary material from judicial sources alone is insufficient for a full study of the social significance of this rural tradition, but I hope that additional research in local archives (those of the *bailliage* court of Péronne) will lead to firmer conclusions than those I have presented here.

The present investigation has shed some light on certain features of rural society during the Ancien Régime. The society that emerges into view was an anxious, threatened, and fragile one, living in dread of fire and the firesetter. It was a rural world in which people lived close to the soil; their very speech took its concrete and vivid images from nature and from their labor in the fields. In this society, which was both unpolished and fragile, justice was severe, yet also sensitive to prestige based on social standing. This rural world was rent by a variety of conflicts, such as dissension within families, rebellion against the seigneur or the parish priest, and tensions within the peasant community. The study of the criminal trials of arsonists makes these conflicts stand out clearly. But these are only isolated examples, which can hardly serve as the basis for general interpretation. As the eighteenth century drew to a close, was the rural world really unsettled, in a state of agitation and fermentation? Or do the few examples from these trials make us overlook the quiet somnolescence of daily life in the village? On the basis of judicial sources alone, one can do no more than raise these questions.

And yet the present study does enable us to establish a number of types of arsonist, and these types do indeed define a specific criminality within certain social categories. Fire was used to apply pressure by every stratum of society. But arson committed by the beggars was a very different crime from arson committed by the tenant farmers, the difference being a matter of techniques, objectives, and incidence in the course of the year.[98]

In the absence of precise documentary material, I was unable to establish the numerical distribution of the different types of arsonist. I wish to point out, however, that obtaining this information is of great historical value, for if it could be shown that the percentage of beggars among the arsonists declined, while that among the insane increased, this fact would indicate that important changes were taking place in society and in its image of the arsonist.

At the very least, then, the criminal archives of the Parlement of Paris can make a rich contribution to studies in social history. Nonetheless, I do not mean to sidestep the fundamental problem: Is it possible to use a study of crime as the basis for a study of social history? As far as arsonists are concerned, the gaps in the documentary material make it impossible to answer this question in the affirmative. A definitive answer will be furnished only by future research in the judicial collections of local archives.

NOTES

1. E. Duché, *Le crime d'incendie* (Law thesis, University of Paris, 1913), p. 33.
2. Emmanuel Le Roy Ladurie, *Les paysans de Languedoc* (Paris, 1966), pp. 88–89.

3. In our own time, the arsonist is almost always an isolated, atypical, or asocial individual. This is an assumption that does not necessarily hold in a retrospective analysis, and one cannot totally accept Gaston Bachelard's interpretation: "Like so many torch-bearers, the poverty-stricken transmit the contagion of their *isolated* dreams from generation to generation" (*Psychanalyse du feu* [Paris, 1938], p. 35).

4. Archives Nationales, Paris, Chatelet X 2 b 1028 (hereafter cited by call number only), sentence against Jacques Bellanger and Louis Bréchard, 23 July 1762.

5. Cited from a document of 1657 in F. Debouvry, *Etude juridique sur le mauvais gré* (Lille, 1899), p. 166.

6. X 2 a 1119, interrogation of F. Carré, 18 December 1755.

7. X 2 a 1127, interrogation of F. Riante, 19 July 1764.

8. X 2 b 1070, sentence of 12 September 1782 against J. Baptiste Scellier.

9. X 2 a 1143, interrogation of Surcy Levert, 12 January 1790.

10. X 2 b 1298, interrogation of P. Lefebvre, 21 June 1731.

11. X 2 b 1316, Darras case, confrontation of witnesses with P. Darras.

12. X 2 b 1305, interrogation of Jean Dumont, 10 September 1743.

13. Gaston Bachelard, *Psychanalyse du feu*, p. 35.

14. Muyart de Vouglans, *Les lois criminelles de la France* (Paris, 1780), p. 27.

15. X 2 b 1313, interrogation of Laurent Dupont, 19 June 1771.

16. X 2 b 1008-9, sentences against Madeleine Chien of 9 June and 30 July 1751.

17. X 2 b 1316, physician's report, 16 October 1782.

18. Vouglans, *Les lois criminelles,* p. 28.

19. X 2 b 1313, deposition of the turnkey against Laurent Dupont, 19 July 1771.

20. X 2 b 1316, chaplain's deposition against Jacques Diom, 13 July 1779.

21. X 2 b 1315, deposition and report against Jacques Person, 27 July 1722.

22. X 2 b 1313, physician's report.

23. X 2 b 1315, investigation against M.-L. Poullet, 10 April 1778.

24. X 2 b 1327, investigation against François Paradis, 23 June 1784.

25. X 2 b 1310, interrogation of Urbaine Richer, 27 September 1764.

26. X 2 b 1316, cited above.

27. X 2 b 1210, investigation against Pierre Peneau, 30 August 1766.

28. Michel Foucault, *Histoire de la folie à l'âge classique* (Paris, 1961), pp. 160–61. Abridged English translation by Richard Howard, *Madness and Civilization* (New York, 1965).

29. Foucault found no reference to care (the word is *medicamenté*) given to interned persons until a court order of 1784. Actually, this word appears in a decision of the Parlement of Paris dated 1 February 1779 (X 2 b 1063): The defendant, Marie Ledoux, was to be conveyed to the Salpêtrière, where she was "to be treated and given medication (*medicamentée*) like the other insane."

30. Y 10063, trial of Pierre Louvet, 14 June 1738.

31. Foucault, *Histoire de la folie*, p. 127.

32. Y 10464, will of François Gaudron (3 August 1784) and sentences handed down by the court (30 July 1784); these documents were brought to my attention by Mlle. Nichole Plutarque.

33. X 2 b 1042, sentence against Jean Bossu.

34. Y 10237, trial of Nicolas Péreau, written notes in the court file. [I have attempted to reproduce the crudity of language in the original French.—Trans.]

35. X 2 a 1119, interrogation of Eloy Dubois, 13 December 1754.

36. X 3 b 1016, sentence against Antoine Ravault, 21 May 1756.

37. Y 10237, investigation against Nicolas Péreau, deposition of the second witness for the prosecution.

38. Ibid., deposition of the fourteenth witness for the prosecution.

39. *Cahiers de doléances of the Bailliage of Amiens*, vol. 4, p. 351.

40. X 2 b 1081, sentence against Pierre Valentin, 7 March 1787.

41. X 2 b 1035, sentence against Léonard Narbon, 9 July 1766.

42. Ferrière, *Dictionnaire de droit et de pratique* (Paris, 1740) s.v. "Vagabond."

43. X 10461, interrogation of Claude Vernier, 13 November 1784.

44. X 10237, interrogation of Nicolas Péreau, cited above.

45. Alexandre Vexliard, *Introduction à une sociologie du vagabondage* (Paris, 1956), p. 70.

46. Abel Poitrineau, *La vie rurale en basse Auvergne au XVIIIe siècle* (Paris, 1965), 1: 583.
47. X 2 b 1035, cited above.
48. X 2 b 1081, sentence against Pierre Valentin, 7 March 1787.
49. X 2 a 1115, interrogation of Jean Quentin, 7 October 1752.
50. X 2 b 1039, sentence against Pierre Lorson, 20 May 1768.
51. Y 10237, already cited.
52. X 2 a 1138, interrogation of Jacques Lone, 3 May 1774.
53. Y 10461, interrogation of Claude Vernier, 12 November 1784.
54. Ibid.
55. X 2 a 1119 and X 2 b 1013, sentence against Eloy Dubois, 13 December 1754.
56. X 2 b 1032, sentence against J. B. Nivelon and A. Pera, 4 August 1764.
57. X 2 b 1150, interrogation of Charles Guérin and others, 8 February 1768.
58. X 2 a 1138, interrogation of J. Lone, 30 May 1774.
59. X 2 b 1020, sentence against Pierre Piette, 4 October 1758.
60. Y 10237, already cited.
61. Edmé de la Poix de Fréminville, *Dictionnaire ou traité de la police générale des villes, bourgs, paroisses, et seigneuries de la campagne* (Paris, 1758), p. 302.
62. Ferrière, *Dictionnaire de droit,* s.v. "Vagabond."
63. Ibid.
64. Poitrineau, *La vie rurale en basse Auvergne,* p. 584.
65. Ibid.
66. Brissot de Warville, *Théorie des lois criminelles* (Berlin, 1781), pp. 82–83.
67. X 2 b 1309, Interrogation of J. Boucot, 3 September 1761.
68. X 2 b 1043, suit by Nicolas de Montimier, 1 February 1769.
69. Interrogation of P. Richer.
70. Cf. X 2 b 1309, interrogation of Joseph Forestier, 4 December 1762.
71. X 2 b 1042, sentence against J. Le Roux.
72. X 2 b 1039, sentence against Hélène Quenescourt, 14 December 1767.
73. X 2 b 1310, interrogation of P. Richer.
74. X 2 b 1316, investigation against P. Darras, deposition of the carter, twenty-second witness for the prosecution.
75. X 2 a 1124, interrogation of François Chauveau, 16 July 1763.
76. X 2 a 1126, interrogation of Jean Favard, 20 July 1779.
77. Y 10398, interrogation of Claude Frotier, May 1779.
78. X 2 b 1088, already cited.
79. X 2 b 1049, sentence against A. Larue, 29 October 1773.
80. Ordinance of 25 March 1724. Text cited in Boucher d'Argis, *Code rural* (Paris, 1749), 2: 529–30, 532.
81. X 2 b 1039, sentence against Hélène Quenescourt, 14 December 1767.
82. X 2 b 1036, sentence against Gervais Bardin, 1 October 1766.
83. Ibid.
84. François Debouvry, *Etude juridique sur le mauvais gré* (Lille, 1899).
85. Cited in Lefort, *La condition de la propriété dans le nord de la France: le droit de marché* (Paris, 1829), p. 75.
86. Cited in Debouvry, *Etude juridique,* p. 45.
87. X 2 b 1039, already cited.
88. Cited in Lefort, *La condition de la propriété,* p. 76.
89. *Entretien d'une mère et d'une fille sur le bonheur de la campagne* (Paris and Amsterdam, 1770), p. 4; cited in Lefort, *La condition de la propriété,* p. 75, n. 1.
90. X 2 b 1039, already cited.
91. Debouvry, *Etude juridique,* p. 211.
92. Georges Lefebvre, *Les paysans du Nord pendant la Révolution française* (Lille, 1924), p. 94, n. 2.
93. Cited in Debouvry, *Etude juridique,* p. 164.
94. *Cahier* of Outrebois, already cited.
95. *Cahier* of Saint-Quentin-des-Prés, in *Cahiers des Etats généraux,* 2: 138.
96. Lefebvre, *Les paysans du Nord,* p. 97.

97. *Cahier* of Seux in *Cahiers des Etats généraux,* 2: 134.

98. A calendar showing the frequency of arson committed by beggars and extortionists—based, however, on only twenty-three cases—shows a peak in winter, a secondary peak in · May–June (the period before the new harvest), and an absence of offenses between the grain and the wine harvest.

6
The Creation of
the Insane Asylums
of Auxerre and Paris

Gérard Bleandonu
and Guy Le Gaufey

Michel Foucault's *Madness and Civilization*[1] can be credited with having opened a new field of research about the mannerisms that make up the "portrait of a madman," which various histories of psychiatry have considered to be a normal face. His book on the leprosarium of the General Hospital described a very specific social space, a space in which, during the years following the French Revolution, the psychiatric asylum as it still exists today appeared and took root with relative ease.

Although Foucault describes the vast movement that culminated in the law of 1838, his book does not go beyond the eighteenth century, at which time the particular form the asylum would assume had not yet been determined. We would like to focus upon that period and examine the specific ways in which the law of 1838 was enforced and the social and economic forces that came into play during this process. In short, we will consider information that has been hidden for more than a century and that even today is only beginning to find expression among psychiatric personnel who are questioning the direction that insane asylums are taking.

Although for decades asylum staffs have been doing psychiatric work within the institutional walls, we know little about the individuals who organized these asylums, the principles that guided them, and the social and economic conditions under which the task was carried out. The asylums established in Paris were relative late-comers, but they became permanent fixtures. However, although the Parisian institutions served as a model for subsequent asylums, they in turn had been modeled after the asylum at

Annales, E.S.C. 30 (January–February 1975): 93–121. Translated by Patricia M. Ranum.

Auxerre. This relationship between the two asylums should not surprise us, since both reflect the ideas of the renowned alienist Dr. Henri Girard de Cailleux and the famous administrator Baron Georges-Eugène Haussmann.

In filling in the blanks of a birth certificate for the asylum, we shall proceed chronologically, beginning with Girard de Cailleux's efforts at Auxerre (1840–60) and Haussmann's brief but decisive stay in that city (1851). Then we shall move on to the psychiatric institutions that Haussmann established in Paris, where he was aided by Girard de Cailleux.

Auxerre, 1840–60

"Two hundred and fifty meters north of the city gate of Auxerre, formerly called Saint Simeon's Gate, to the right of imperial highway number 6, in that day called 'the high road from Paris to Lyons' the insane asylum occupies the spot on which the General Hospital* was built at the end of the seventeenth century. Some distance from this hospital, beyond Saint Simeon's hill, charitable groups of Auxerre built the leprosarium five centuries earlier.'' These are the opening sentences of an anonymous description of the insane asylum of Auxerre in 1865.[2] This text provides the classic pattern, which shows the asylum as the product of a sort of continuum and which we shall rapidly summarize here.

Auxerre before the Law of 1838

By the thirteenth and fourteenth centuries, leprosy, a contagious disease, forced society to make extremely rigorous decisions that resulted in a sort of "internal exclusion" of lepers. Excluded from cities and towns, the leper was a living corpse who wandered about within a strictly determined territory. At that time social space suddenly became polarized. Wherever death revealed its face, certain zones and paths were forbidden.

How tempting it is to view this "cemetery" of the living [i.e., the lepers' colony] as a symbol of a purgatory in which society was purged of its vices, a fascinating mirror held up by God himself so that the sinner might see his own reflection and the reflection of his sins. But this "cemetery" also resulted from what Foucault has called a "heterotopy"—where a holy presence transforms a neutral space into a sharply differentiated geography: sacred/profane, health/illness, life/death. These pairs of opposites, which we shall encounter toward the end of this chapter, were already functioning in the leprosarium.

---

*For an explanation of the General Hospitals, see translator's footnote in Chapter 2 of this volume.—Trans.

The anonymous author of 1865 who described the leprosarium of Auxerre was thinking in this vein when he wrote: "Separatgd from the world by law, the leper could not transfer his possessions to another individual or give them away. Lepers were permitted the usufruct of their possessions, but they could neither make wills nor inherit. These details make it difficult for us to imagine any more horrible fate. In the valley between Saint Simeon's hill and the hill of Les Chesnez, a lepers' hospital was built toward the end of the fourteenth century. . . . A special cemetery was also created to receive the remains of these pitiful lepers, pursued by woeful prejudice even beyond the grave."

However, at the end of the fifteenth century leprosy began to disappear and the void was filled by what were then called "plagues," that is, a variety of infectious illnesses. Toward the mid-seventeenth century, leprosy was no longer a cause of concern, and although epidemics still threatened the population at regular intervals, health considerations played second fiddle to poverty and to the deviant behavior it spawned. These concerns gave rise to what amounted to a government welfare policy. But the ambiguous reasons concealed behind this welfare program are evident in the fact that charity went hand in hand with maintaining order in the cities. It was in this context that the royal edict of June 1662 created the general hospitals to deal with a category of individuals whose social status was determined by the fact that they were not part of the workaday world. Some fifteen years later the city of Auxerre converted the old leprosarium into the Hospital of Saint Nicolas, made official on 9 March 1678 by letters patent of Louis XIV. "This establishment was intended solely for the sturdy beggars of the city and suburbs, in order to lift them, in the words of the royal letters patent, from the sloth and 'idleness in which they all too frequently wallow, which is the cause of their mendicancy, as it is of all other vices, and in order to render them capable of earning their living by teaching them those crafts for which they show the greatest aptitude. . . .' Later, foundlings, orphans, and abandoned children over seven years of age and born in the city and suburbs were admitted."

The General Hospital at Auxerre was more successful than the leprosarium had been, for on 6 November 1684 the general assembly of the clergy of Auxerre decided to build new quarters on land "along the high road from Paris beyond Saint Simeon's Gate." The buildings were completed within two years, and the poor were moved in on 22 June 1686. The General Hospital continued to grow, and in 1688, 1743, 1756, and 1759 new wings were added, an indication that the number of inmates was continually increasing.

Despite its innovativeness and the facilities at its disposal, the General Hospital did not succeed in solving the problems involved in reabsorbing the mendicant population; numerous royal decrees reminding it of its purpose serve as evidence of this relative failure. The French Revolution dealt a final blow to the General Hospital, for once the Revolution had stated welfare problems in terms of social justice, emphasis was placed upon the dream of wholesale "dehospitalization" and "medicine for the entire social body."[3]

However, although the purely coercive aspect of the general hospitals became quite apparent during the French Revolution, the widespread problem of mendicity, which had increased during this period of economic difficulties (a serious and almost unbroken recession until 1850), remained engrossing. With this problem in mind, Napoleon issued a decree on 5 July 1808 creating new beggars' prisons. But this change in priorities involved words rather than actions. As Flandin, a member of the General Council [of the department of Yonne] later pointed out: "For lack of beggars the buildings reverted to their original use, or at least were put to an analogous use. They were converted into a departmental hospice for the insane and the incurably ill."[4] Indeed, as early as 1817 the General Council requested authorization to convert the beggars' prison into an asylum for "the infirm, orphans, beggars, and madmen." The new "asylum," created on 13 August 1818, housed seventy-two individuals, all of them from the very same categories that earlier had been interned during the *Grand Renfermement* [Great Confinement]: twenty-two beggars, fifteen old people, twelve orphans, sixteen madmen, and seven invalids.

The Care of the Insane in the Department of Yonne between 1830 and 1840

In view of the extreme importance of the law of 1838 for the care of the insane, we shall briefly describe the circumstances leading to that law and the changes occurring at that time in the care of the insane within the department of Yonne.

CARE OF THE INSANE IN FRANCE FROM 1792 TO 1838

After Phillippe Pinel, whose activities brought to an end the "history of madness for the early-modern period," the European public was reminded repeatedly of the inadequate care given the insane. In France, reports by commissions of inquiry, which confirmed these deplorable conditions, brought about a few local improvements (as at La Salpêtrière of Paris) but did not result in legislative measures. The first quarter of the nineteenth century witnessed a rash of inquiries and plans, but the situation as a whole scarcely changed. Europe's renowned alienists—that is, specialists in the treatment of insanity—shared the position taken by J.-E.-D. Esquirol [a French alienist] in his famous memorandum submitted in 1818 to the minister of the interior.[5]

A leader in economic matters, England also led in improving the plight of the insane. Although the inquiry of 1823 ordered by the House of Commons revealed the wretched treatment given the insane, the matter had to be brought up again in 1826. Since the results of the two studies were identical, two laws were eventually passed to permit a general reform in the care of the insane.

As a result of these British inquiries, G.-M.-A. Ferrus [an alienist] and a member of the General Council for Hospices were sent to England. In 1834 Ferrus submitted an extremely favorable report in which he included all the available information on insane asylums. Earlier, in 1833, the minister of the interior had sent the prefects of the various French departments a circular in which he asked fifteen questions concerning the insane. The circular of 29 June 1835, which gave the impression that a decision was imminent, asked the general councils [of the various French departments] to submit to the prefect of their department their ideas "about the manner in which a service to care for indigent madmen can be permanently established." But the failure of these councils to reply made a law necessary.

By the end of 1835 the July Monarchy was at last on firm footing and had assumed all the characteristics that were to remain unchanged until the fall of that regime. After years of economic difficulties and political and social agitation, debates could be resumed. The insane became the topic of discussions throughout France, and the measures to be taken were gradually worked out. The government named Ferrus to the newly created position of general inspector for the care of the insane. In the words of the report by Constans, Lunier, and Dumesnil: "It was at that time that article 6 of the financial law of 18 July 1836 declared that the costs of caring for indigent madmen would be paid from the budgets of the departments, without eliminating the financial obligations of the communities in which the madmen reside or of hospices, where they exist."

A circular dated 5 August of that year explained this arrangement, which, since it was valid only for 1837, was subsequently renewed by another law dated 20 July 1837. Permanent legislation could no longer be postponed, and the government set to work to prepare a legislative bill.

The law of 1838 was not put to the vote until major legislative preparations had been made. Presented to the Chamber of Deputies for the first time on 6 January 1837, it was not ratified by that chamber until 14 June 1838. Although initially distrustful and hostile, almost all opponents were won over during the months of preparation, for in the final ballot 216 votes were tallied in favor of the law and only 6 against. The length of time required to pass the law, the quality of the arguments presented, and the merit of the men preparing the law revealed the deputies' strong desire to enact long-term measures and provide sufficient funds to make satisfactory results possible.

THE SITUATION OF THE INSANE IN THE DEPARTMENT OF YONNE DURING THIS PERIOD

"Each year since 1830 this hospice has aroused the justified concern of the General Council, and in each of its meetings the council has tried to determine what improvements can be made there."[6] A "House of Succor" had existed at Auxerre since 1823 to help the insane of the department. During the 1830s much attention was focused upon the problem of sheltering the insane. By 1833 the General Council had agreed to modify its regulations, which were changed to read as follows:

Article 1. The institution's sole purpose is to admit insane persons and those clearly diagnosed epileptics who have become maniacs. However, the aged and infirm from the old beggars' prison will retain the rights they have acquired.

Article 2. The number of individuals admitted free of charge shall not be less than 90, allocated to the various arrondissements [of the department] according to their population.

Article 3. In addition to those individuals admitted free of charge, paying boarders will be accepted, provided they belong to the category described in article 1.

The General Hospital for the Insane is administered by a commission composed of five members [of the council] and the prefect, who serves as president.

The General Council had become resigned to this arrangement only when confronted by the department's pressing need for a shelter for the insane, who could not be sent to the facilities of other departments.[7] Therefore, after a commission had visited the facility, the council decided to avoid major expenses and add a series of new cells to the garden wing of the insane asylum. "These twenty compartments, recently added to the already existing ones, will meet every need and will also enable the asylum to admit the insane from the five arrondissements. Moreover, the general costs of the institution will remain approximately the same, despite the increased number of inmates; there are real advantages, in addition to the great convenience, in concentrating all the insane in one single department-wide institution." The General Council hoped that expenses would not exceed 7,000 francs. The number of nonpaying patients admitted would gradually increase to a minimum of 110 once the construction program had been completed.

In 1834 the General Council was chiefly preoccupied with this plan for the construction of new cells. In anticipation of its next session, it recommended that the insane be sent to other departments, especially to the institution of

Maréville, near Nancy. That year's meeting concluded with a statement of its current intentions: "Doctor Courot, who proposes that the insane be treated in a rational manner, could not fail to arouse the solicitude of the members of the General Council; but, in addition to the fact that adopting his proposal would completely change the way in which the institution is operated, by transforming it into a mental institution, no approximate estimate was made of the expenses involved in such an innovation. Therefore, without rejecting Monsieur Courot's ideas, the council postponed making any decision on such a serious matter."

In 1836 the General Council approved the acquisition of a plot of ground, although it wanted to be sure "that the already considerable charges paid by the department not be increased by the new quarters now under construction." At that point the circular from the Ministry of the Interior dealing with compliance with article 6 of the financial law of 1837 opened a new period during which the General Council was obliged to heed the orders of the government in Paris and include funds for the insane in its budget. Congratulating themselves for having anticipated the decisions of the lawmakers and for having already met one legal requirement, the council members allocated funds so that the prefect could send the insane to institutions outside the department, since the new cells would not be completed until mid-1837.

Members of the council also found it extremely difficult to determine the amount of money local hospices and the townships in which the insane resided should contribute to the cost of caring for poor madmen; they felt such expenses should be "paid from the national budget." In 1837 the General Council issued a clear statement of its unchanged position: "And if, while giving due praise to the indisputably philanthropic views of Doctor Courot, the council cannot agree with him, it is obviously because that physician has looked at the institution from a purely medical point of view, that is, *the treatment and healing of the individuals admitted to it.* But the General Council never had such an intention. Providing shelter for the mad, especially the poor madmen of the department, is the chief purpose of the institution, and it was in order to be more sure of attaining this goal that it decided to construct twenty new cells. . . ."

However, one year later the law of 30 July 1838 forced the General Council into a one-way path involving the allocation of new funds to meet the requirements of the law concerning the insane. The documentation collected by the prefect showed that in 1839 "about one hundred and twenty individuals, whose madness could be dangerous to public order and the safety of private persons" would be sheltered in the insane asylum at a cost of 365 francs per year for room and board. The insane individual and his family would be obliged to pay in full if the patient's mental condition did not pose a public or private threat; for an indigent patient, half the cost would be met by the department and the other half by the township in which he resided. Aware that the number of insane would increase in the future, the General Council estimated that 3,000 francs would have to be spent on building repairs and 5,000 francs on new furniture, from an annual budget of 43,800 francs for the entire asylum. The council would soon find out that its estimates had been entirely too low.

The law of 1838 had elicited only a few comments during the meetings of the General Council of the department of Yonne, where debates had revolved solely about financial decisions and budgetary plans. Even though the department had by no means been slow to act, major decisions still had to be made before legal requirements could be satisfied. The question of whether private asylums should be preserved, a question that had provoked numerous legislative discussions, never arose at Auxerre.

Dr. Henri Girard's appointment in 1840 placed the institution under the authority of a physician-director. But how did the department of Yonne manage to set up an institution that would be a source of pride for the department and, after 1860, a model for the construction of insane asylums in the department of Seine [that is, Paris and environs]?

Implementation of the Law at Auxerre

THE PHYSICIAN-DIRECTOR'S THEORIES AND
HIS INITIAL MEASURES

In pursuance of the law of 1838, the Ministry of the Interior issued an order on 20 June 1840 naming as chief physician and director of the insane asylum Dr. Henri Girard, then head of the clinic at the School of Medicine at Lyons. Steeped in the great reform movements of the period, Girard did not fail to point out, both in his reports to the central administration and in his newspaper articles, the inadequacies of the institution for which he had just been appointed physician and director. At the same time he began to draw up plans for its reconstruction.

The insane asylum at the time of Dr. Girard's appointment. It is hard to learn much about the institution for the insane of Yonne at the time of the first director's arrival. Between 1829 and July 1840 Dr. Courot had shared with a colleague the responsibilities of official physician for the general hospice for the insane, concurrently with his private practice and his work at the Hôtel-Dieu of Auxerre. He prided himself on having done "special studies at the school of the renowned Esquirol, and an essay on mental illness," and on having carried out major improvements during his eleven years at the Home for the Insane.

In a polemical memorandum dated 1844, to which we shall return later, Courot credited himself with freeing the insane from their shackles; eliminating the movable bracket to which they were attached; suppressing latrines in cells; forbidding the staff to use corporal punishment; submitting to the General Council in 1834, 1837, and again in 1839 memoranda pointing out the needs of the insane; and introducing work programs for both men and women, reading programs, and walks. "But if the state of affairs still was not satisfactory, it was probably the fault of the local administration, for it did not understand that the physician in a home for the insane should be given great authority and it was therefore unable to measure up to its responsibilities." And "lastly, during the entire period of my service, every possible hygienic measure was employed with unqualified success, and I spent an average of two or three hours per day carrying out my major duties. Therefore, in 1842 I was somewhat surprised to read a brochure or notice, which was very inaccurate on this point, signed by Pointe (of Lyons), and an anonymous and no less erroneous comment upon the same matter in issue number 18 of the regional newspaper, *L'Yonne.*"

Indeed, in 1841 Dr. Pointe, a professor of medicine at Lyons, had read a paper before the Society of Medicine of Lyons, describing his visit to the insane asylum of Auxerre in October of that year. The text, which was published the following year, included a retrospective description of the institution at the time of Girard's appointment. Although it is highly probable that this description was inspired by Girard and consequently was partial to him, we shall quote a long passage from this document, the only one available for this particular institution, for it matches quite closely the descriptions of other institutions for the insane made by a number of well-known alienists of the day. (One such example is Esquirol's statement to the Ministry of the Interior in 1818.) In any event, this retrospective picture enables us to grasp Girard's main intentions and his general position concerning the insane.

The slick, humid paving of the courtyards had the grave inconvenience of chilling the lower limbs and consequently of promoting brain congestion; mephitic exhalations rising from holes dug in the ground to bury refuse constituted a permanent source of infection; there were very few trees in the courtyard, and nothing was done to appeal visually to the patients; the courtyard opening into their compartments was enclosed by walls three meters high, and the mad had no view from it; in a word, the interior appearance of the building was more likely to arouse fear and madness than to produce a favorable effect upon the patients' moral state; the fields were planted with grapevines, when they should have been cultivated as gardens, thus enabling the physician to keep more patients occupied.

The damp compartments—badly constructed, poorly lighted, and almost devoid of furniture—totaled *fifty-six;* yet that number must have been considered insufficient, since *twenty-two* more were being built and the grounds had been laid out so as to make the construction of *twenty-two* others feasible in the future. The fifty-six compartments existing in 1839, when the hospital housed no more than fifty madmen, were all occupied at night, and most of them during the day as well.

There were only three bathtubs, carved of stone and fixed into the walls, and one of them, with a shower attachment, was located in a dark cubicle and was a real source of terror for the wretches brought there; it was therefore physically impossible to make use of the one therapy—baths—that is specifically recommended by physicians who have specialized in the study and treatment of mental illness (I am referring in particular to Messieurs Ferrus and Esquirol).

The inadequate dormitories were badly laid out and always open; there was a total lack of water—in summer, at any rate—which meant that it had to be fetched from the river; there was no laundry in the establishment, no drying room. . . .

Such were the institution's facilities. Staff of both sexes received their orders from six nuns belonging to the Sisters of Providence of Evreux.

There is not the least doubt that these nuns, who had directed the institution virtually single-handedly since 1810, were motivated by very praiseworthy zeal and devotion. . . . Eating alone, while the personnel ate in the kitchen, these nuns left the insane unsupervised during that time.

Instead of being separated into distinct categories, the patients were intermingled and mixed in such a way that epileptics would strike terror in those of their companions in misfortune who were prey to mania or melancholy, or who were recuperating. Many of them were constantly shut up in their compartments and as a result were in such a frantic state that no one was allowed to approach them. . . .

Routine and wearisome, life within the institution was completely uncoordinated; the patients generally went to bed too early; they awoke at all hours; and their surveillance was quite poor, since it lacked above all a purpose that could transform it into a powerful tool for healing.

Medical needs were met by two of the most distinguished practitioners of Auxerre. But they did not reside in the institution and took turns for six-month periods; since each had a large practice in town and also was on the staff of the Hôtel-Dieu, these physicians were often inattentive to the needs of a hospice for the insane. Moreover, any efforts on their part to change the internal workings of the establishment were inevitably brought to a halt by resistance from every level of the staff, over whom they had little control.

Under such conditions, and affected by such distressing influences, the insane did not improve but, instead, rapidly reached a state of dementia and eventually became *incurable* or else so frantic that it was dangerous to approach them.

Dr. Girard's psychiatric views.   This young alienist brought with him a whole new doctrine. Medically he adhered to the progressist ideas about the so-called "moral treatment," although he did not espouse the extreme form favored by Dr. François Leuret [an alienist]. Girard's psychiatric views were greatly influenced by the writings of Pinel, Esquirol, and Ferrus. Girard conceived of the asylum as a means of curing the insane by subjecting them to a series of therapeutic measures conducted in a coherent, methodical, and efficient fashion and stressing general therapy rather than such traditional practices as bloodletting or showers. In a publication dated 1843 dealing with the "organization and administration of institutions for the insane,"[8] Girard set forth the basic ideas behind this model institution.

—*Isolation.* Like all alienists of that era of industrialization and urbanization, Girard was absolutely convinced of the need to isolate the insane from other groups confined to institutions, "which of itself represents a whole system, the best all-round system for treating mental illness," according to Falret. The law of 1838 had made it easy to enforce "this strict, unusual, but so often indispensable measure." Material concerns related to isolation included, in Girard's own words: "(1) a suitably chosen location that fulfills the triple requirement involving water, air, and site; (2) buildings constructed according to certain rules; (3) appropriate furnishings; (4) special diet; (5) healthful clothing." Like many of his colleagues, Girard preferred "a vast piece of property that is on a slight elevation, dry, located outside the city, protected from unhealthy odors, noise, and cold, and provided with an abundant water supply."

—*Hierarchic Order.* "The most obvious characteristic of madness is physical and moral disorder, and it is through this disorder that madness becomes noticeable. Therefore the most constant and uniform therapeutic goal must be the reestablishment of order in the exercise of the patient's bodily functions and faculties." Strengthened by these theoretical guidelines, Girard put order into the turbulant and incoherent world of the asylum. "Physical and moral exercise must be subject to a regular schedule, as must the time for waking, going to bed, and eating; the hierarchic order of the staff must be scrupulously observed."

Girard praised the ordinance of 1839 that had permitted the merger of the positions of head physician and director. "I believe it is necessary to construct buildings for the general services in the very middle [of the asylum grounds] and to connect them to the quarters of the physician-director, as if to symbolize the fusion of medicine and administration, which help one another; for in a hospice for the insane the administration is but the application of a carefully worked out system of hygiene." Girard proposed a veritable political vision of the insane asylum: "Using Pinel's apt comparison, I therefore consider a hospice for the insane as a little absolute government or, to be more simple, as a vast organism whose vicious tendencies are corrected by a constantly active mediating force, directed by the central authority."

This activity and this continuous control were possible now that the head physician could devote himself full time to the asylum, now that he had begun to reside there and spend as much time as possible among the patients. But Girard, the omnipotent and omnipresent master of the asylum, in his turn was dependent upon the minister of the interior, who had appointed him and who would determine any future promotions. The following words of Girard are therefore particularly evocative: "The ideas of Monsieur Ferrus are shared by

Dr. Falret, the able physician at La Salpêtrière, who told me during an interview in Paris, 'Give me well-built hospices and a good staff, and from the capital I will be able to direct the institutions for the insane throughout all of France.' "
—*Life in Common and Classification.* During these years solitary confinement was not used within the asylum. As soon as he was appointed, Girard expressed his opposition to the new cells planned by his predecessor. He asserted that the asylum should have the smallest possible number of cells. "This reduction in the number of cells is one of medicine's greatest victories in the battle for understanding mental illness. It dates from Pinel." In the projected rebuilding plan there now were only twenty cells for 300 patients; in other words, one cell for every fifteen patients. "The experience I have acquired during three years in the hospice for the insane at Auxerre fully confirms these facts, and I am happy to state that of 200 insane patients, a mere twelve are locked in cells at night."

Partisan of a comprehensive psychiatric program, Girard felt that architectural planning based upon medical theory should play a major role. Probably as a reaction to the conditions under which the insane had been shut up in the past—the dungeon is the most evocative example—he advocated an architecture "that would keep any idea of confinement from the patient's mind," that would permit air to circulate freely and the eye to look far into the distance, and that would make it easier to classify patients within the methodically and regularly laid out buildings.

Life in common would be the goal "in all the routine practices within the institution, in the workshops, and in such different activities as music, reading, and walks. This is also why the insane eat together, why they sleep together in dormitories as much as possible rather than sleeping in cells." But, in order to forestall the potential difficulties created by this life in common, which under certain circumstances allowed the two sexes to mingle, the positive influence of medical classification had to be allowed full play.

Patients were no longer haphazardly mixed together but were classified in a methodical manner. "In addition to being segregated by sex, the insane are divided into four categories: idiots, senile individuals, and lunatics; insane epileptics; restless maniacs; calm and convalescent maniacs." In this completely hierarchicalized world, the insane constituted a virtual class that was constantly being guided by attendants and physicians so that it might learn to obey the strict rules. "Everyone rises at six o'clock in the summer and at seven in the winter and is required to have left the dormitory one-half hour later. All inmates wear a uniform bearing the initials of the home, facilitating identification should they escape. . . . Each category is under the surveillance of a special attendant, who is aided by a convalescent patient and who is also in charge of taking the insane on their daily walk. There is also a warden for the men and a matron for the women. . . . The utmost order and the greatest regularity reign continually as a result of the unvarying schedule for rising, eating, going to bed, lessons, and all other activities, and it is even evident in the hierarchy of powers exercised by the different employees of the home.''

Girard required the same degree of subordination from the servants, who by then were all lay persons. He had the idea, an innovative one for the period, of requesting the supervisors to submit each morning ''a written report of the behavior of their subordinates, as well as the most noteworthy actions of the insane. . . . A code of rules, which the director strictly enforces, is imposed upon each and every attendant.''

Literally the central figure—and viewed as endowed with great intellectual, and even greater moral superiority—the physician-director reigned over what Pinel had called this ''little absolute government.'' ''The first feeling that the physician tries to inspire in his patients is one of esteem for his person. . . . He often uses the weight of his superior moral power to bend their caprice to his will.'' But in addition to relying upon his personal qualities, Girard appealed to ''the hope of reward and the fear of punishment. . . . The promises of reward, which are the most effective, are those involving liberty and return to the bosom of the family, or a better position within the institution. . . .'' Ordinary punishments included ''tepid baths stretching over a period of four or five hours, brief confinement, the humiliation caused by the equally brief use of the strait jacket, and sometimes, but quite infrequently, cold showers.'' Yet, we must remember that Girard, who on his own territory was the omnipotent and omnipresent master of the asylum, was dependent upon the prefect and upon the minister of the interior, who had appointed him and determined his future promotions.

—*Work.* Convinced of the excellence of Ferrus's ideas, Girard viewed work as one, if not the principal, means of bringing order and calm to the institution. ''Monsieur Esquirol and all physicians today are unanimous in considering work to be one of the most effective means of curing madness; this is no longer a problem to be solved, it is henceforth a scientific truth. At Auxerre work is organized on the broadest possible scale, and I can state that of a population of two hundred inmates, scarcely twenty do not work, and they are paralytics, idiots, or restless maniacs. To this I must add that this procedure has procured order, calm, morality, discipline, and even a reduction in the number of cells being used; all of which have transformed into an ordinary hospital an asylum where agitation and tumult reigned before this practice was put into general use. . . .''

Dr. Girard provided a personal example of the hard-working bourgeois who constantly shouldered new tasks. It is not surprising that under the July Monarchy the ''liberal'' bourgeoisie should consider work a necessary if not always satisfactory step in curing insanity. Certain alienists even went so far as to pity insane nobles, for their social position prevented them from working and therefore from being cured. ''Nonetheless, while proclaiming the beneficial influence of work upon mental derangement, I agree with Monsieur Ferrus that it should by no means constitute the total therapy. Like any idea that excludes all others, such a thought could not enter my mind.''

Agreeing that ''methodical and moderate distractions'' could be useful to the insane, Girard revealed his originality in his systematic use of music as a means of healing the mentally ill. Girard gave the music master a special task in addition to the elementary classes he taught: music was to be incorporated into church services. So, each week the music teacher taught a hymn to those patients whose health permitted it.[9] It may have been no accident that the final pages of Girard's publication were devoted to a discussion of the following question: ''What relationship should exist between church services and the treatment of the insane?'' For it was, of course, understood that ''we need no proof that a chaplain is a necessity at each insane asylum.''

The relationship between the chaplain and the physician-director was determined by the separation between spiritual and temporal functions. But sentences such as the following are even more revealing of Girard's basic position: ''Supervisors in full uniform, helped by the patients, assist the priest at the altar, thus adding the maximum amount of solemnity to the worship service. Was it not through the pomp and prestige of their ceremonies, combined with every imaginable health measure, that the priests of ancient Egypt attained their powerful ascendency? . . . In order to produce a strong and lasting impression among those insane who are capable of witnessing the ceremonies, and in order to inspire a religious feeling among convalescents, I please their senses in order to speak to their intelligence, I make their senses ready to accept the precepts of reason and of a consoling religion.'' The full import of these statements may well be revealed in another of Girard's remarks: ''But in an institution intended for the treatment of madness, experience reveals that religion must in a sense serve a special function.''

—*Economy.*   These new policies at the asylum involved a considerable amount of expense for the department of Yonne. Girard did not miss the opportunity of showing the authorities in charge that he was eager to see philanthropic speeches go hand in hand with profit. ''If you wish to move ahead in the radical reform of insane asylums, the organization and administration of these hospices must be a fusion of medical principles and careful budgeting that involves an optimum use of the money available rather than a tight purse.'' Girard's encounter with Baron Haussmann was to teach him a great deal about this subject.

The first steps.   Within a few months Girard managed to win acceptance for the merit of his ideas, through the gravity and conviction with which he presented them and also through the initial improvements he made at the old General Hospice for the Insane. In the session of 2 September 1840 the General Council expressed its regret at seeing the insane lose the ''very assiduous and benevolent'' care given by the Sisters of Providence of Evreux, who had been administering the institution with such devotion for the previous fifteen years. But above all the council revealed its irritation with the minister of the interior concerning matters over which it had hitherto had exclusive control. ''The council did not note these changes without a pronounced feeling of surprise and regret. . . . It is, of course, aware how advantageous a uniform administrative procedure can be. . . . But is this ordinance above all criticism? Could it not be reproached for having interpreted the law in a manner that is overly favorable to centralization and for having gone beyond the legislators' intentions? Moreover, is not the General Council justified in complaining that the ordinance has assigned it only a very small role in an institution built and maintained with funds from the department, an institution that has already been extremely costly and that threatens to require a larger portion of its income each year?''

Indeed, the care of the insane would henceforth constitute one of the department's major expenditures. Despite its irritation, the General Council accepted the physician-director's proposal that the planned constructions ''be converted from cells to dormitories and dining halls, since the prefect believes that these changes in construction can be made without additional expense.''

During the years 1840–42 the newspapers of the department of Yonne gave their greatest coverage to economic concerns, public schools, the railroad, and the insane asylum. And Girard was well aware of this.[10] Those representatives to the departmental council who appreciated the dynamism and practicality of the physician-director began to see some advantages in this new administrative position, although not all their reservations had been removed. In the meeting of 31 August 1841, ''the General Council was impressed by the favorable results of the reforms made in the organization and administration of the insane asylum. It hastens to point out that Monsieur Girard has turned this institution into a hospice where the wretches it admits are treated with a degree of success that has already inspired the council's great confidence in this physician's methods, and it cannot sufficiently praise his zeal and fervor. . . .''

The council agreed that bathrooms, laundry facilities (rooms for boiling, rinsing, and drying linens), and latrines would have to be built promptly in order not to hamper Dr. Girard's efforts. It requested that the prefect ''have a study made of all the plans as quickly as possible in order to coordinate these constructions with the introduction of the new system within the institution.''

In October Professor Pointe visited the asylum and expressed a desire ''to be shown the improvements in the ways of curing mental illness.'' His account—from which several passages were quoted earlier—reveals the major changes carried out by Girard in just over a year, without the benefit of special funds or new equipment. In short, within a matter of months Girard had managed to transform the General Hospice for the Insane into a true insane asylum by means of strict discipline, methodical classification of patients, and a regime combining communal life with activities involving some degree of work. These were the four basic principles of the so-called moral treatment, in vogue during the first half of the nineteenth century, and Girard was a determined, pragmatic, and methodical proponent of these canons.

During 1842 Girard worked closely with the departmental architect to draw up the general plan requested by the General Council. Almost immediately the results were presented to the public at large in his "General Plan for the Construction of the Departmental Hospice for the Insane," a series of articles published in *L'Yonne* between 22 March and 22 April. In the 15 July issue of that newspaper he adroitly continued to press his point by elaborating on the question, "How do the facilities at homes for the insane influence the treatment of madness?" Here we find a full-page spread with a synoptic chart that compares the material resources of the asylum in July 1840 and in July 1842. By means of this chart Girard demonstrated that his ideas could be realized "with the help of a small subsidy of one franc per day."

Such a position was sure to win the General Council's support. In its meeting of 12 September 1842 the council "noted with interest that despite the increased expenditures of 1841, the care of an insane person costs less than one franc per day. The number of patients has increased to a daily average of 204, with 74,558 patient-days." On 14 September the General Council assumed fiscal responsibility for all the work done by the insane under Dr. Girard's direction, in order to bring water to the institution. "The General Council once again expresses its satisfaction with the favorable results of Girard's program for treating mental illness, the success of which is evident in the increasing number of cures owing to the zeal and self-sacrifice with which Dr. Girard devotes himself to his work, as well as to his experience and understanding." Despite this praise, it failed to allocate funds for items it had considered worthwhile the preceding year.

Next the council studied several plans drawn up by the departmental architect according to Girard's suggestions. It faced a choice: "the total rebuilding of the institution, on the present site or on another more suitable plot to be purchased by the department; or the gradual and successive reconstruction according to an earlier plan that would temporarily preserve the existing buildings and later replace them by other constructions." The first choice, which called for 700,000 francs in construction costs alone, was voted down. The alternative plan was deemed more sensible, although it involved the same expenditures. So the General Council took a middle road that stayed within the departmental budget and involved no irrevocable decisions about the future. It decided that the existing structures would be preserved and that a new building with baths would be built along one side of the northern façade.

It expressed "the hope that the construction would be done with great simplicity, with no exterior decoration, and with a taste that does not preclude elegance despite its lack of ornamentation."

In 1843 the council approved the departmental architect's plans for the new wing, for it was increasingly convinced of the urgent need to render at least some of the hospice buildings suitable for the new methods of treatment. The council "recognizes with satisfaction that steps have been taken to ensure order and economy in the administration of the hospice and that other such measures are in preparation."

The only polemical battle between alienists occurred during 1844. Courot, who had been very irritated by Pointe's pamphlet of 1842 and who was undoubtedly finding it hard to stomach the success of the young rival who had supplanted him, published a memorandum with a very provocative title: "Thoughts on the constructions at the Insane Asylum of Yonne, or Plan according to which 360,000 francs can be saved from a proposed budget of 710,000 francs." The appearance of the memorandum was announced in the 25 July 1844 issue of a new local paper, L'Union. The author of the anonymous article called the director's plans "crazy ideas," since, according to him, the director intended to lead the council members along a dangerous road. "Why vote for the first steps of a plan that will *level everything,* if you don't expect to complete it and see *everything leveled?*" On the other hand, he praised Dr. Courot, whose aim was to preserve the greater part of the existing structures by connecting them to the new constructions and thus save the department money; this plan had been approved by Esquirol.

Girard immediately replied to Courot's memorandum in a brochure entitled "The Insane Asylum of Yonne." With great self-assurance he refuted most of the criticisms and named among his supporters the Royal Academy of Sciences of Lyons,[11] which had given a very favorable reception to his publications, especially to "Concerning the organization and administration of institutions for the insane." In concluding, Girard ironically thanked his colleague "for having shown that his opinions are not so absolutely inflexible that he cannot modify them" (a veiled allusion to the number of new cells to be built).

Despite "A Reply by Monsieur Courot to the Refutation by the Physician-Director of the Insane Asylum of Yonne"—which must have been written very quickly, since it was dated 22 August 1844—Girard won the debate. During the session of 2 September 1844, the commission that the General Council had appointed to study Courot's memorandum advanced virtually the same arguments as Girard's and unanimously declared that there was no reason to modify the general plans that had previously been adopted. On 31 January 1845 Dr. Courot replied to the report about his work submitted by the commission of the General Council of Yonne, but nothing further was said about him, and Girard's competence remained uncontested.

Nevertheless, Girard was forced to request funds continually and to await patiently the new structures that were authorized bit by bit as the years went by. In 1847 the council once again stated that the physician-director's "learning equalled his zeal." But when, on 1 December 1848, Girard earnestly requested that funds be allocated for the construction of a second hospital building, his plans, which would involve a continual flow of new expenditures, elicited refusal and even sharp criticism: "One member states that he opposes the direction that the General Council has taken and seems determined to continue. . . . People want to endow the department with what surely will be one of the finest institutions in France, but no one has given enough thought to the fact that many other institutions exist in this department with needs just as valid as those of the insane. He requests that, while there is still time, the General Council turn aside from the dangerous incline down which the asylum's director—whose zeal, obvious merit, and great capability he acknowledges—will inevitably drag the department by wishing to turn the Asylum of Auxerre into a model institution. . . . Another member seconds this opinion; the project is too vast, it is out of proportion with the department's resources and the institution's needs; the plan was constructed upon faulty foundations; the number of inmates was calculated on the basis of the department's population, without taking into account that most insane people from the well-to-do classes remain with their families and that since each of the buildings is specially designed for a separate type of mental illness, it has been necessary to bring in boarders from other departments in order to fill them."

In the early 1850s many people of Yonne seem to have shared Haussmann's assessment of Girard de Cailleux, found in the Baron's memoirs: "The spirit of initiative and the ardent activity of this physician, an enthusiastic and committed disciple of Esquirol, Ferrus, and Pinel, played a major part in the success of the undertaking; he continued to work with perserverance, tenacity, and patience, as if taking his cue from the daily example provided by his patients—those lucid or rational madmen—with their fixed ideas. So he was jokingly called the 'Madman in Chief.' "[12]

Haussmann and the Completion of the Asylum

An external influence brought a change in the pace of events when forty-one-year-old Georges-Eugène Haussmann became prefect of Yonne on . .22 May 1850. It was his second prefectorial post, for he had entered the administration at a very young age. Upon completion of his law studies he had been named subprefect at Neyrac in 1833, at twenty-four. Seven years later he was transferred to Saint-Girons and in 1842 to Blaye. At thirty-eight he was made an officer of the Legion of Honor, but he had yet to show his full worth.

During the Second Republic he was made a prefect, first in the department of Var and scarcely a year later in Yonne. Eventually he was shifted to Bordeaux and finally to Paris in 1853.

Thus, in 1850 the department of Yonne was administered by a man who was driven by a strong determination to rise in the administrative hierarchy, for Haussmann's stay at Auxerre was part of the social climb that in five years brought him from the small subprefecture of Blaye to the head of the department of Seine. Enterprising prefects of the day felt obliged to shown interest in the construction of buildings for departmental services. It seems likely that Haussmann rapidly realized the advantages to be derived from the building program under way at the Insane Asylum, the equally important penitentiary to be built opposite the asylum, and the Palace of Justice, with its prison for people awaiting trial. In his memoirs Haussmann noted: "The Asylum of Auxerre was in the process of being completely transformed according to a plan inspired by the suggestions of my learned friend, Dr. Ferrus, who was implementing Esquirol's great reform of eliminating padded cells and instituting group activities for the insane."

Haussmann's meeting with Girard led to a rare sort of collaboration that resulted in the realization of innovative institutions that served as models elsewhere. Each man probably recognized the other's high social ambitions and desire to express himself through large building projects and outstanding professional achievements. Later Haussmann wrote that "if the merit of having conceived of the project is not mine, I at least made its realization possible by closely studying every one of its parts, a procedure that permitted me to simplify several steps and markedly reduce its total cost, after long conference sessions with Monsieur Boivin, the departmental architect, and Monsieur Girard de Cailleux, physician and director of the asylum, a very able specialist and a sagacious administrator."

Although new to his post in 1850, Haussmann firmly insisted that the work should be continued as planned: "In my opinion the important task today, a task the General Council cannot avoid accepting, is to bring the men's quarters up to the level of the women's quarters. In comparison with the new buildings, which are in every respect appropriate for their projected use . . ., in comparison with the block of structures that makes the women's section of the Asylum of Auxerre a model for institutions of this sort, the old buildings to which the men have been relegated reveal a combination of the most pernicious conditions, in respect both to hygiene and security and to the separation of the various categories of insane individuals. It is as if someone had intentionally wanted to contrast the new, perfected improvements that have been introduced during recent years with all the distressing and repulsive aspects of the old system."

To find the estimated 280,000 francs that would have to be spent on the asylum, Haussmann proposed a two-fold program to finance departmental buildings. According to him, it was absolutely necessary to find funds, for otherwise the department would take fourteen years to meet the most urgent construction or reconstruction costs. The best solution would be to combine taxes and borrowing: to borrow 840,000 francs for four years and then pay back capital and interest by means of a tax of three centimes added to each of the four collections of direct taxes between 1852 and 1858. His plan was adopted.

The council sessions of 1851 may well have been the most crucial of all for the Insane Asylum. During that session Haussmann presented a long report that contrasted sharply with the reports of his predecessors, both in the quality of its analysis and the perspicacity of its proposals. He acknowledged that he had been obliged to follow the lead of these predecessors during the session of 1850, no matter how irrational it had seemed to him, since he had been new to the job. "Until now no distinction has been drawn between details involving the internal administration of this institution and the small amount of information made available to you about the department's entire program for care of the insane."

Now that the therapeutic approach had been worked out, the session of 1852 was almost exclusively devoted to the financial problems created by compliance with the law of 1838. "The existence of the Asylum of Auxerre is, indeed, extremely imvortant, since it has required and will continue to require great sacrifices on the part of this department." But, Haussmann added, this fact in itself was of secondary importance, for, in the future, even in those departments that lacked asylums and that had to make arrangements with public or private institutions in other departments, "the care of the insane is nonetheless a fundamental branch of the departmental administration."

Unlike all his predecessors, Haussmann began by laying out a comprehensive plan for the insane, giving special attention to the procedures by which patients would be committed under the law of 1838. He reminded the council members of the distinction between forced and voluntary commitment and then observed: "Until now, the distinction between these two categories of inmates, a clear distinction that is established by law, has not been carefully observed in the department of Yonne. Far from it. . . . In actual practice, Yonne has only boarding or indigent patients. Boarders of all categories have entered the asylum through voluntary commitment, while the indigent, whether dangerous or not, were admitted as forced commitments." The question of whether a patient was dangerous remained a crucial one, since it permitted the authorities to determine who would pay for the patient's upkeep.

Haussmann's memoirs give us some idea of the extent of this problem. "But there is a universal tendency to declare even the most inoffensive madmen dangerous so that the local welfare office can be relieved of the cost, and to certify that these wretches are indigents. I had to be very firm in dealing with this two-fold abuse, for the members of the General Council, who in their sessions said I was completely right, were the first to come to my office and brazenly request that the rules protecting the departmental budget be broken."[13] Haussmann wanted this state of affairs settled as soon as possible. He had decided that "in the future . . ., and when someone appeared potentially dangerous, temporary care would be limited to keeping the insane person under surveillance so that he could do no harm. . . ." He reminded the council that, according to his predecessor's decree of 20 August 1839, "when admitting penniless but harmless madmen, preference should be given to those who have a chance of being cured."

Expressing himself in a remarkably modern manner, Haussmann reaffirmed the asylum's mission to provide treatment: "Contrary to the general belief, an insane asylum is not a hospice; it is a hospital. A patient should not be admitted for the rest of his life, but in order to be cured. . . . Harmless incurables should, therefore, not be admitted to the Asylum of Auxerre; and, as far as indigent patients in that category are concerned, if they cannot be sent back to their families, they must be given the help they need and should be sent to hospices at the expense of their townships."

Haussmann sent Dr. Girard to verify cases of dangerous insanity and ordered him "not to worry about the various costs incurred during his travels. Indeed, the results obtained by this precautionary step justify it, for of the ten insane people that I asked Dr. Girard to visit, patients whom perfectly honest physicians had deemed dangerous, only two were found to be so and were placed in the asylum." Of the eight others, one was sent to the hospice in his home town and the seven individuals whom Dr. Girard judged potentially curable were admitted to the asylum as voluntary patients, with the cost paid by their families rather than the department.

Haussmann was quick to quote statistics confirming that these procedures were bearing fruit: "Between 1 January and 30 June last, the stringent procedures I have just outlined led to a reduction in the number of insane paid for by the department and communes from 236 [sic] (157 dangerous and 77 harmless) to 208 (145 dangerous and 63 harmless). Since then, this number has been even further decreased."

In interpreting Haussmann's attitude, we must remember that by 1840 Falret had created a benevolent fund to provide help for sick women not being cared for in La Salpêtrière,[14] and that during some of the 1864 and 1865 sessions of the Medico-Psychological Society a number of alienists, including Girard de Cailleux, recommended early release and supervision outside the asylum. The examinations carried out by Girard at Haussmann's request anticipate an analogous policy adopted by the municipal government of Amsterdam. In 1930 (that is, in the midst of the Great Depression) that city engaged Dr. Querido, a psychiatrist, in order to reduce the number of admissions to the psychiatric hospital run by the city. Haussmann and Girard had come a long way from the traditional view that saw the General Hospital as a depository. For these men, the insane asylum's therapeutic function was closely linked to its economic solvency. Thus, the alienist played an important role in the rapidly evolving capitalist world of the day, for his activities involved both capital and a labor force.

The second part of Haussmann's report on the asylum provides a rather eloquent example of this double emphasis. Work constituted one of Girard's principal therapeutic devices; but it also represented a source of income. "Although the work done by the patients is above all else a therapeutic measure, it does in fact constitute an asset. One of your members was, therefore, correct last year when he noted that it should be included in the bookkeeping." Since most of the work was manual, the bourgeois men who "administered" the Insane Asylum decided, with Haussmann's prodding, to include it in the financial accounting. "No one has ever taken the trouble to find out just how much work was done by the inmates of the asylum, but a ruling that I have ordered to go into effect on 1 January will enable us to make a very rough estimate of this item. A record book has been made for each inmate, and a daily notation is to be made of the number of hours the individual spends working, the sort of work he does, and how well he uses his time. For each quarter, the hours spent working will be classified according to the nature of the work done, and the time will be divided into good, average, and poor hours. The usual working day lasts ten hours, so the salary per hour is one-tenth of the daily wage. We have estimated that men should receive ten centimes per hour and women seven and one-half centimes, if the work is well done; this rate will be reduced by one-third for average work and by two-thirds for poor work."

The asylum was no longer an island unto itself, supporting an idle population on the margins of the economy. At the outset Girard had succeeded in rousing the great majority of his patients and putting them to work. From now on the insane would once again be subject to the laws of the working world, just as the asylum budget had ceased to be autonomous and distinct from the economy as a whole. Even today workshops helping the mentally ill to adjust are based upon the very same principles proposed by Haussmann.

Indirectly introducing a criterion to be used in selecting patients for admission, Haussmann reasserted that since the department and the townships were making considerable sacrifices, nonpaying admission should be limited to those who had recently lost their sanity and showed some chance of recovery. But since, by a happy coincidence, the patient had to work in order to "heal himself"—and balance the budget—the asylum applied the label "incurable" to anyone who was unable to engage in some productive activity. "Whatever the case may be, the current daily expenditure of 1 franc 33 centimes for each third-class boarder would put the asylum into deficit if the institution did not receive almost all the profits from the work done by these boarders."

Continuing to improve the asylum's budget, Haussmann noted that he had been very careful in all the above calculations "to take into account the interest on the capital that forms the asylum's endowment," and that each year, therefore, an unspent sum surely would remain and could be deducted from the subsidy provided by the department.

But the greatest excitement was unquestionably aroused by his proposal to turn over both the men's and women's hospital wings to paying patients, although these buildings had originally been assigned to epileptics. This proposal obliged the General Council to decide whether it would condone speculating in order to reduce the expenses incurred by the department. If, in each section of the asylum, one building were reserved for first-class boarders, the administration could accept requests for admission; and these first-class paying patients "would soon considerably reduce the departmental subsidy paid yearly to supplement the income from boarders." Haussmann proposed that the institution make a profit on the upper classes by asking them "first of all to pay for unusual expenses incurred, such as the replacement of worn-out equipment and the gradual depreciation of the buildings, and then to meet a part of the costs resulting from nonpaying admissions."

Haussmann did not limit his arguments to financial considerations. He declared that the law of 1838 required each department to admit anyone stricken by madness, whatever his personal wealth. "Those departments that create asylums may not be giving enough thought to the general tenor of the law; they rarely try to make these institutions accessible to everyone, for they fail to take into account that people in certain positions have become accustomed to a certain standard of living, although they do realize that such people are able to make economic sacrifices; thus, many families are forced to meet the unlimited demands of private institutions run for a profit. No doubt it is meritorious to show concern for the indigent or poor insane patients; but when, in doing so, we eliminate the more affluent insane, we are failing to comply fully with the requirements of the law of 30 June..1838 and are willingly shoving aside one group in order to care for the other with generosity and ease."

Once again a "lucky" coincidence prompted the commission in charge of the Insane Asylum to agree enthusiastically. When it voiced some hesitations, information was provided to reassure the commission that the places reserved for the indigent insane would not be eliminated in the two newest hospital buildings, that the epileptics could easily be housed in the infirmaries, and that the layout of the asylum, which made any communication between the various sections impossible, would keep this arrangement from being "a cause of either jealousy or irritation among those patients who have been treated less kindly by fortune."

In the ensuing discussions one member of the commission observed that this arrangement was unusual, since within an asylum intended for the indigent, buildings were created that would admit the wealthier insane from other departments. But actually the only open opposition expressed fear of the constant expenses involved. Finally the General Council accepted the proposal of its commission and unanimously approved the measure, which was "fair, appropriate, and advantageous to the department."

In short, Haussmann was trying to show that by launching a rapid construction program at the asylum, the department could implement the law of 1838 and save money in the process, while the hesitation and procrastination shown by the General Council would be more costly in the end. "There is, therefore, no doubt that if we continue to make sure, as I am doing, that the law is soundly interpreted and that the decisions enforcing it are properly carried out, in a very short time the department will have completely redeemed the money it sacrificed . . . and in the near future, once the asylum has been completed, we can justifiably expect the department to offset the deficit it incurs through boarding the indigent insane with the interest earned on the asylum's endowment, so that this deficit can be permanently stricken from the budget. Such a hope is by no means unrealistic, for I have not even included most of one important source of income: the work done by the patients."

No more convincing argument was possible, and Haussmann was justifiably pleased at having made it possible to carry out the plans for the Insane Asylum. In 1851 he had pushed the asylum across a decisive frontier. The administrative building, director's residence, gatekeeper's lodge, and padded cells for violent patients had yet to be built, but loans were now possible. In December 1852, when it made credit available for indispensable work, "the council deem[ed] it appropriate to declare that the time ha[d] come to end the sacrifices that the department [was] making for this institution, and that it [would] not authorize new construction plans." In any event, the administrative decentralization stipulated by the decree of 25 March 1852 had brought unavoidable modifications in the services providing care for the insane.

Without going into the details of the building program, suffice it to say that by 1858 the asylum was considered finished. Girard had successfully completed his vast undertaking, with the aid of the man who by then had been named prefect of Seine. Haussmann wasted no time in summoning Girard to Paris. Indeed, as early as 1853 Girard had been appointed as a substitute to make the inspection rounds for Dr. Ferrus, the inspector general. In its session of 1 September 1860 the General Council announced the departure of the man who now went by the name "Girard de Cailleux." "A change, which we have long expected, has taken place in the personnel of the asylum. Dr. Girard de Cailleux, whose zeal, perserverance, and devotion you have prized for many years and who has been of great help in building our asylum, has been named to the post of inspector for the insane of the department of Seine. He has been replaced by Dr. Renaudin, director of the Asylum of Maréville." As his work progressed, Girard had written articles on the infirmary (1845), the ward for peaceful and melancholy patients (1846), the reservoir and laundry (1848), and so on.

Before turning from Auxerre to Paris, we want to give a description of the asylum for which Girard had worked so zealously and ardently. This complex would serve as a model for the insane asylums of Seine. Here is Flandin's description of 1860:

> In the center is the administrative building, where the general services are located: offices, kitchen, linen supply, pharmacy, etc. . . . Along the sides the buildings housing the insane are laid out symetrically: on one side the men's quarters, on the other the women's. Then, within these groups of buildings, are subdivisions for calm, semicalm, and excited patients. To the rear and parallel to the administrative building are structures for paying boarders, one for men and another for women. In front and to each side of the entrance gate are two lodges, one for the gatekeeper and one for the gardener.
>
> Also incorporated into this plan are the infirmaries, the chapel, and the physician-director's residence (the chaplain lives in town). In front of the buildings for the patients are the water reservoir, the laundry tubs, the boiling room, the baths, and other accessory constructions that I shall not enumerate here. Moreover, there are no surrounding walls, which would make the asylum resemble a convent or a prison. There are merely sunken fences that prevent the inmates from escaping and that calm the imagination by allowing a view of the countryside. . . .
>
> This complex of buildings is situated in the middle of a large plot of ground planted with vines, some of which were uprooted to create a vegetable garden. This garden and the vineyards are cultivated by the inmates themselves, as "a form of medication and a distraction."[15]

At another point Councilman Flandin commented upon the completed asylum: "Need I say that I do not oppose the Insane Asylum, whose creation expresses humane motives and is but the fulfillment of the obligation of Christian charity. . . . In my opinion a half million francs could have been saved on the asylum had the building program been limited to the needs of the department and had people not been carried away by the idea—which has thus far proved a disappointment for the department, if not for the asylum—of making a profit from boarders."

We should perhaps point out that the department of Yonne subsequently constructed a penitentiary. "Opposite the large establishment that the people of Auxerre owe to the intelligent and devoted zeal of Monsieur Girard de Cailleux and that is now being completed, a new departmental prison will be built. . . . Directly opposite the monumental iron gate of the asylum the austere door of the prison will swing open" (as it still does today).

Paris, 1860–70

As prefect of Seine, Haussmann began a reorganization of public care of the insane, which was in a deplorable state. The population had continually grown, and Paris and its adjacent suburbs had increased from 1,002,633 inhabitants in 1836 to 1,226,980 in 1846, and 1,538,613 in 1856.[16] This demogrcphic increase, caused in large part by immigration from rural France, in turn swelled the number of Parisian insane. The annual report that the director of the public welfare office submitted to Prefect Haussmann in 1857 supplies the following statistics for pctients "remaining on 31 December": 2,306 in 1836, 2,888 in 1846, and 3,506 in 1856—an increase of 50 percent over a twenty-year period. Urbanization went hand in hand with an increase in the number of insane.[17]

Yet the institutions admitting them had not evolved during those years. After 1807 La Salpêtrière was the only hospital that would admit mentally ill and indigent women, while their male counterparts had no choice but Bicêtre. As a result, these two hospitals became overcrowded. Private asylums were beyond the means of all but the affluent and could not absorb the excess. Confronted by this state of affairs, in 1844 the department of Seine decided to sign contracts with provincial asylums in order to transfer the incurably insane to those institutions at an advantageous daily rate. (Among these asylums was that of Auxerre, which began taking in such boarders in 1846.) Isolated in distant asylums scattered across France and cut off from their families, the Parisian insane had no hope of being cured and leaving the asylum to which their home department had sent them at its expense.

Dr. Louis-René Semelaigne wrote that "in France, several of the major cities already have model institutions, and similar improvements can be noted abroad. Yet in Paris, by some regrettable anomaly, the hospices of Bicêtre and La Salpêtrière, with their imperfections and lacunae, are failing to keep up with today's scientific progress and achievements. This inertia, in a center from which fertile and innovative ideas usually emanate, cannot long continue. The capital is, so to speak, blushing at itself."[18] The department of Seine's twenty-year delay in complying with the law of 1838 is particularly surprising, since Paris had been the center of an important reform movement that included such steps as Pinel's removal of the chains binding the insane and Ferrus's creation of Saint Anne's Farm. The department had, however, been satisfied to use the existing specialized localities, which were directed by reputable alienists, and had preferred to make do during this period of economic difficulties.

The rapid economic growth after 1851 and the new emphasis upon the circulation of capital permitted Haussmann to begin the immense public works that were to transform Paris. And it was within this same framework, and at Haussmann's urging, that the problem of the insane was studied and solved in a manner that is still employed today. It has become a commonplace to credit Haussmann with Paris as we know it today; but he should also be credited with creating the psychiatric Paris that has come down to us. As he recalled—to his advantage—in his memoirs: "Before the reform that I daringly started, the department of Seine cared for its insane in conditions un-

worthy of such a department, and even profoundly humiliating to its prefect. . . . Unfortunately, the financial troubles that weighed so heavily upon
the budget of the department of Seine did not permit me to broach the matter
openly to the General Council [of Seine] until 1860, when the advance payment made to the Bakers' Fund[19] presented me with an opportunity.''[20]

Indeed, Haussmann launched his plan for psychiatric aid in 1860, when he
created the office of inspector general for the care of the insane of Seine and
named Henri Girard to the post. At Auxerre he had had an opportunity to note
both Girard's abilities as an organizer and his political docility, which had
recently been reinforced when Haussmann helped obtain official recognition
of Girard's new name, "Girard de Cailleux."[21] Haussmann's close col-
laborator was, therefore, devoted to the prefect (to the point that Haussmann's
disgrace was soon followed by Girard's).

A significant change had occurred within a few short years. Discussions
among alienists concerning the model insane asylum no longer had much
political importance. Those representing the state, in this case Haussmann,
could work quickly, since they now had an efficient model that was relatively
easy to reproduce. The earlier period of discussions was replaced by a period
of implementation under the Second Empire.

Haussmann appointed himself president of the special commission he
created on 27 December 1860; the secretary was Girard de Cailleux. This
commission, composed of influential individuals (three senators, one deputy,
one *procureur général,* one councillor of state, the dean of the School of
Medicine [at Paris], and the director of the Public Welfare Administration)
met weekly from February to June 1861. At its final session on 25 November
1861 the vice president, Ferdinand Barrot—senator, former minister of the
interior, and brother of Odilon Barrot—submitted a general report on the
intensive work completed in less than ten months. The institutions planned by
this commission were to serve the insane of Seine for nearly a century.

The time was ripe, so this haste did not indicate rashness. Commission
members had called in such eminent specialists as Moreau and Lelut, but its
basic orientation came from the Haussmann-Girard de Cailleux team, fresh
from its success at Auxerre. The commission also visited the Asylum of
Auxerre on 24 April 1861. In his report Barrot declared: ''The commission
reported that its visit to Auxerre left such a favorable impression that, in one
of its debates, it had felt justified in proposing that an organization along those
lines would be most suitable for the asylums to be created in the department of
Seine.''

The technical data assembled by Haussmann and the commission were
inspired by the principles of mental treatment being worked out during those
years. It was generally agreed that the asylum should be small. Dr. Maximien
Parchappe de Vinay's important book, published in 1858, called for 300 male
and 300 female patients. Since there were approximately 4,000 insane in

Seine, and since the commission believed that this figure would rapidly increase, it planned to construct approximately ten establishments with 600 beds each. Its farsighted master plan took economics, urbanism, and technology into account:

1. Only one institution would be built in Paris proper, on the site of Saint Anne's Farm. It would include a central admissions office (to take over the admissions work done by the central police office), from which the insane would be sent to various asylums as dictated by their particular form of insanity or by available space. A "clinical asylum" would be annexed to this central office.

2. Approximately ten asylums with 600 beds each, all modeled after the asylum at Auxerre, would be built in the nearby suburbs (within a maximum radius of twenty kilometers [12.4 miles], because of horse-drawn vehicles). They would be located along railroad lines, enabling families to visit more easily.

3. Eventually asylums created especially for epileptics and idiots would be constructed.

Girard de Cailleux had made a convincing argument that the planned university "clinic" would train alienists in the new methods of treating the mentally ill, emphasizing the therapeutic role of the asylum. In this way the training of specialists in mental illness could be made more uniform, since a special clinic would make it possible to study the various stages of the most interesting cases. Girard de Cailleux expressed himself as follows in his preface to the commission's report: "This (admissions) office was conceived to arouse as yet dormant vocations and to constitute a training ground for young physicians who will specialize in nervous and mental illnesses. This office should make it possible to establish a methodical classification of abnormal states. And in order to give the student in his final year of medical school and the young physician the opportunity to combine diagnostic studies with the equally important study of the stages of the illness, its treatment, and its termination, as well as the physical disorders that accompany it or result from it, it would be wise to construct adjacent to this office, where facilities have been planned for clinical conferences, a second, rather large clinical asylum housing sufficient patients to permit the serious medical student to watch the various stages of delirium among the men and women he studied and observed during their admission examination."

This institutional system was a totally centralized one whose various cogwheels were directly dependent upon the prefect of Seine. In a way, this organization reflected the insane asylum as it had been created at Auxerre, where complete power lay in the physician-director's hands. Through its organization we can perceive the basic intention of the asylum builders: to place the world of madness under the direct control of one central authority instead of relegating it to dungeons into which no one ever peered. The

Parisian version of the mechanisms that had been created earlier at Auxerre reveals this desire for control and may reflect phenomena involved in the development of capitalist states.

The task of drawing the plans for the first three asylums was assigned to Messieurs Questel, Lequeux, and Leboutteux, architects; but the final decision lay with Girard, who was basking in the power conferred by his long experience at Auxerre, his position as inspector general, and Haussmann's unfaltering support. The very sizable funds that Haussmann made available for the work in Paris made it possible to carry out the commission's plans with great rapidity. The central office opened shortly before the Asylum of Saint Anne, which admitted its first patients in May 1867; then came Ville-Evrard (1868) and Vaucluse (25 January 1869).

But political upheavals just over the horizon ended this ambitious program. Early in 1870 increasingly outspoken opposition forced Emperor Napoleon III to dismiss Haussmann, who was a symbol of the regime; and the proclamation of the Third Republic ended the career of Girard de Cailleux. On 1 October 1870 a decree abolished the post of inspector general for the care of the insane of Seine; and, despite his political connections (including Jules Favre), Girard de Cailleux was informed that his pension would be made available to him. He was forced into retirement at fifty-six, although he made numerous attempts to regain his post.[22]

Conclusion

Thus far we have presented a strictly chronological narrative of the achievements at Auxerre and Paris. The fact that one gave birth to the other enabled us to discuss care of the insane during the period 1840–70. But the progression of events was far from even; the debates that stirred the Chamber of Peers and the Chamber of Deputies in 1838 led to a period of experimentation between 1840 and 1860, which was followed by the assembly-line production of a prototype. And political, social, and ideological factors naturally varied during these three "periods." We shall conclude by attempting to retrace these complex variations.

Before enactment of the law of 1838, the Restoration and the July Monarchy provided brief periods of theoretical research concerning help for the insane, although unanimity was by no means achieved. Of course, Pinel's unshackling of the insane had prompted the initial questions, and the first generation of psychiatrists[23] was seeking to define its mission and its therapeutic procedures (for example, "moral treatment"). Esquirol's influential ideas led to isolating the mentally ill from other patients, although the forms this isolation should take remained the subject of much discussion. The models proposed by Esquirol, Parchappe, and Ferrus remained essentially theoretical ones, and Saint Anne's Farm, created by Ferrus in 1836, did not provide the solution. At that time these discussions were in the main being carried out by specialists and by a large segment of the upper bourgeoisie, which wanted to help the insane.[24]

Not that madmen directly threatened the predominant ideology. But, as Jean Lhomme has shown, when this ideology attained social supremacy, the upper bourgeoisie was obliged to develop a welfare policy whose essential function was to reinforce the bourgeoisie's ideological power.[25] But it soon became evident that the problem of isolating the insane could not be solved within the framework of a welfare policy, if only because of the enormous sums involved. So the upper bourgeoisie, which at that time held the reins of power, tried to have public funds diverted to an undertaking that it had to a large degree instigated. According to the terms of the law of 1838, the state would care for the insane, who thenceforth were under the control of the Ministry of the Interior.

At this point the discussion shifted to the asylums modeled after the prototype of Auxerre. That this asylum was the work of Girard de Cailleux merits some elaboration. Born of a commercial family from Lyons and heir to the famous Count Garat, Girard has appeared throughout our narrative as a perfect example of the bourgeois of the July Monarchy. We cannot go into biographical details here, but we can state that his idea of "moral treatment" was more than a device used by a specialist; it was profoundly rooted in the postulates of the dominant ideology we have just discussed. Therefore, the manner in which the asylum was organized was, from the outset, a caricature of the paternalistic and protectionist reign of Louis Philippe.

The second change in direction—which closed the experimental period initiated by the law of 1838—is incarnate in the strong personality of Baron Haussmann, by then prefect in Paris. Indeed, though Haussmann's presence at Auxerre in 1851 was decisive, Girard was in full charge at that time. He was the specialist and as such made all final decisions.

Things progressed quite differently after 1860, a real turning point in our study. Girard was no longer preeminent; on the contrary, he was now, as Haussmann wrote in his memoirs, merely an "able technician" in the service of a policy that had changed its goals and vocabulary, a policy incarnated by Haussmann just as Girard had been the incarnation of the July Monarchy.

But 1860 was a pivotal point for concerns other than politics. At that time France was experiencing an extremely favorable economic situation and was building a technical infrastructure that enabled it to compete in the brutal world of free trade. As in the case of the Bakers' Fund, large quantities of capital made possible psychiatric projects that would have been unthinkable twenty years earlier. Obviously the Parisian asylums could only be built so rapidly—three in a decade—within the broader context of the Parisian building boom. The available capital was supplemented by a large labor force that had to be given work in order to keep the social difficulties of the liberal Empire from worsening. The economic and social situation, therefore, played a decisive role; indeed, the vocabulary of the charitable bourgeoisie gradually disappeared, until only a remnant remained to embellish the speeches given at dedication ceremonies.

This article confirms Lantéri-Laura's position: "The insane asylum went the way of the railroads; Louis Philippe's regime drew the plans, but the Second Empire and the Third Republic built the tracks and the psychiatric institutions."[26]

Wedged between these two periods, the experimental stage at Auxerre formed a link in the complex chain that stretches from Pinel's initial decision to today's asylums, which we inherited from the Third Republic. We believe that the upper bourgeoisie reacted to the emotions stirred up by the process of isolating the insane and created a welfare policy that it turned over to the state for implementation. The construction of asylums was, therefore, a prefiguration of the "welfare state" and goes a long way toward explaining the "sectorization" found in today's world.

NOTES

1. Michel Foucault, *Histoire de la folie à l'âge classique* (Paris, 1961), abbreviated English translation by Richard Howard, *Madness and Civilization* (New York, 1965).

2. "L'asile départemental d'aliénés," *Almanach de l'Yonne*, 1866, p. 10.

3. In his reports to the Commission on Parisian Hospitals, Pierre-J.-G. Cabanis wrote in 1792: "But this crowding together of people who have no natural link with one another, who remain inert through lack of hope, who are lulled into stunned security and give no thought to the future, who have only artificial and corrupting relationships with their surroundings and the persons upon whom they depend—is not this crowding together, I assert, capable of degrading their intelligence and behavior to the nth degree?"

4. [Louis?] Flandin, "L'asile des aliénés à Auxerre," *Almanach de l'Yonne*, 1865, p. 185.

5. J.-A.-E. Constans, Lunier, and Dumesnil, *Rapport sur le Service des aliénés en 1874* (Paris: Imprimerie Nationale, 1878), pp. 18–37.

6. Debates of the General Council for 1834.

7. "Moved by humane feelings and bowing before the urgent need to open a departmental asylum for the insane who could not find shelter in the general hospice of the chief town near their home, the General Council decided during its last session that it might be possible to place in other institutions outside the department some or all of these unfortunate souls, who are a source of affliction for their families and, all too frequently, a source of fear for their community. Through these deliberations the council made its intentions known to the prefect and a sum of 2,000 [francs] was included in the budget for 1853. The prefect's report, and his correspondence with several of his colleagues, seems to reveal the extreme difficulty if not the outright impossibility of carrying out the council's wishes."

8. Henri Girard de Cailleux, "De l'organisation et de l'administration des établissements d'aliénés," *Annales Medico-psychologiques* 2 (1843): 230–60.

9. Professor Pointe spoke in ecstatic terms about a music lesson he had attended during his visit: "It really was hard to believe we were in a hospice for the insane and among the inmates; yet they were all crazy and almost none of them had the least notion about music, having come from the working or artisanal classes. Some of them had only very recently left the cells in which they had been confined for years on end! They sang several songs, among them a prayer of thanksgiving whose words and music had been composed by the Marquis of Louvois." The latter was a peer of the realm and president of the General Council of Yonne.

10. In 1841 Girard wrote several articles for the local newspaper, *L'Yonne, Journal des intérêts moraux et matériels du département.* On 15 March 1841 he discussed "Work as a means of treating mental illness"; on 30 July and 15 August, "Music viewed as a means of treating mental illness"; on 15 October, "The importance of attendants and their moral and physical influence upon the insane"; and on 15 November, "Financial directors in hospices for the insane." In the last article, he indicated his reasons for writing for the general public: "In the patients' interests, hospices for the insane are a sort of refuge and are closed to the public. The preparation of a moral accounting of how these hospices are administered and the principles according to which they are run therefore becomes the duty of its head and a reassurance for the families concerned. These considerations alone made me decide to make public the ideas guiding their general organization." That same year, in addition to the usual columns on vineyards, agriculture, and forests, the newspaper devoted space to the theatrical scene at Auxerre; to measures taken to combat begging and indigence; to public fountains ("The Town Council is busy trying to find the surest and most economical way to provide the water needed by the inhabitants of each quarter of the city"); to public education ("Every matter involving public education, by its very nature and by the serious thoughts to which it gives rise, is of great social importance"); to the railroad (". . . the formation in Paris of a committee composed of peers of the realm, deputies, and property holders, for the purpose of obtaining a government concession to form a company and build a railroad line from Paris to Lyons via Upper Burgundy"); and to the transformation of the Yonne River into a canal (". . . lacking a railroad, whose completion is so far distant from the plans now being drawn up . . .").

11. A report to the Royal Academy of Sciences and Belles-Lettres of Lyons, based upon Dr. Girard's memorandum and entitled "De l'organisation et de l'administration des aliénés, au nom d'une commission composée de MM. Boullée, Achard-James, et Gauthier," 16 March 1844.

12. Baron Georges-Eugène Haussmann, *Mémoires,* 3 vols. (Paris, 1890–93), 2: 464.

13. Ibid.

14. In Dr. Jules Falret's "Considérations générales sur les maladies mentales," published in 1843, we find: "Above all, women, whose life occupations are confining and disagreeable, even under the most healthful situations, fall victim to these prejudices, these unfair judgments, and for that very reason they can lay first claim to complete redress. . . . In order to remedy to the maximum all these misfortunes, special protection and a charitable organization midway between the hospice and society were organized by my efforts in favor of the convalescent women at La Salpêtrière; they satisfy the most urgent needs of poor women recovering their sanity by offering them shelter, work, and the continued medical advice and religious instruction needed to help them regain their senses and strengthen them against relapses. Then, when the women leave the asylum, they find moral support in each patron or patroness who, after having helped them reenter society, keeps track of their various occupations with true interest."

15. Flandin, "L'asile des aliénés à Auxerre," pp. 184–238.

16. Louis Chevalier, "La formation de la population parisienne au XIXᵉ siècle," *Travaux et Documents,* cahier 10, 1950.

17. Bibliothèque administrative de l'Hôtel de Ville de Paris (B.A.H.V.P.) [Administrative library of the City Hall of Paris].

18. Quoted in G. Daumezon, "Essai d'historique critique de l'appareil d'assistance aux malades mentaux dans le département de la Seine depuis le début du XIXᵉ siècle," *Information psychiatrique* 1 (1960): 5, 29.

19. The Bakers' Fund was established by Haussmann in 1853 to solve the emotion-charged problem of high grain prices resulting from poor harvests. (The disorders of 1847 provoked by such a situation had not yet been forgotten, and 1853 was also a difficult year in this respect.) The principle was a simple one. The fund advanced money to bakers so they could sell bread below cost during years of scarcity; these advance payments were reimbursed during good years. In 1860 Haussmann informed the General Council of Seine that about ten million francs had been repaid into the Bakers' Fund (which had lost much of its prestige when the Emperor decided to open France to free trade); these repayments would make the financing of asylums possible. Some slight of hand was involved in the bookkeeping, but it was relatively easy to transfer the funds allocated in 1853 to the Bakers' Fund (which no longer had any reason for existing) to another account to which members of the General Council might have been more reluctant to allocate such large sums.

20. Haussmann, *Mémoires*, 2: 491.

21. In 1858 Girard wanted to make official the name "Girard de Cailleux," which he had been using since his marriage. After Girard had failed several times to obtain this unjustified request, Haussmann exerted pressure on his behalf and the request was suddenly approved. The correspondence on this issue, which we consulted at the National Archives, leaves no doubt on this point. On 27 January 1860, Haussmann ended a letter to the Keeper of the Seals: "Granting Monsieur Girard's request for this harmless concession, which he feels affects his social position, would be small compensation for the disappointment he experienced last year, but it would nonetheless be a recompense, and I earnestly want it to be granted him."

22. During his years in Paris, Girard de Cailleux's favor with Haussmann had caused his former colleagues to view him as the central government incarnate. We have seen how the physician-director, an omnipotent master within the asylum, was very dependent upon the prefecture and its representative, who by now was Girard de Cailleux. We can therefore perceive that, beyond political quarrels, many other influences surfaced when Girard de Cailleux "retired," and that these influences partially explain the silence surrounding him and his activities after 1870. Yet we are somewhat surprised to note his total "absence" from Constans, Lunier, and Dumesnil's report on the care of the insane submitted in 1874.

23. Psychiatry and dermatology were the first clear-cut medical specializations.

24. On this question we would also like to point out that as early as 1827 benevolent activities led to the creation of English-style *salles d'asile* [shelter rooms], the ancestors of the *classes maternelles* [nursery schools] established during the Third Republic. These innovations were the work of Madame Pastoret and her successor, Madame Millet, and of Jean-Marie Denis Cochin, lawyer, mayor of the twelfth arrondissement of Paris, and majority deputy in 1837. As one might suspect, the motivation was to free a labor force of mothers for the nascent industries and to assume ideological control of children from the proletariat: "These children will in their turn become men. At that time they will constitute among our common people, who are so crude, so prone to debauchery and drunkenness, a new generation that will be noted for its economy, decency, and cleanliness and for its orderly behavior and intelligent work; assuredly that would constitute a true improvement of mankind and a well-placed compassion for his miseries; and it is the poor man's children who will have been raised in this manner, who will have been inculcated with just ideas and honest morals." We have quoted at some length these words of Lord Brougham, founder of the English insane asylums, in order to convey an idea of the goals and tone prevalent among the charitable bourgeoisie, whether they were dealing with poor children or the insane.

25. Jean Lhomme, *La grande bourgeoisie au pouvoir, 1830–80: essai sur l'histoire sociale de la France* (Paris, 1960).

26. G. Lantéri-Laura, "La chronicité dans la psychiatrie moderne," *Annales, E.S.C.* 27 (May–June 1972): 548–68.

7
Delinquency and the Penitentiary System in Nineteenth-Century France

Michelle Perrot

In our day we have taken giant strides toward progress. Punishment must no longer be the only aim of penal law; now that the law has become more prudent and at the same time more humane, it must endeavor not only to obtain the redress to which society is entitled by punishing the guilty but also to find the means of restoring to society members who can usefully serve it.—(Dr. Vingtrinier, Des prisons et des prisoniers)

Blessings bestowed by philanthropists and moralizers: Two young boys died at the Rouen penitentiary, following a rather hearty punishment that consisted of making them stand up for several days in a row in a clock-chamber (presumably to teach them the value of time!); their transgression was laughing during their lesson, laughing! Moreover, they are entrusted to scoundrels who bugger them.—Flaubert, "Lettre à Ernest Chevalier, Rouen, 9 April 1842"

First it was the asylum and now it is the prison, its twin, that has become the object of a historiography increasingly haunted by the nocturnal side of society: disease, madness, delinquency—all of them an exogamic aspect of ourselves, a broken mirror that reflects our image at the outer limit of experience (Michel Foucault) where we can read a culture differently but as clearly as in the accumulated mass of normal events.

In that history the nineteenth century occupies a prominent place. The whole century was pervaded by a two-fold current as by the ground swell of a

Annales, E.S.C. 30 (January–February 1975): 67–91. Translated by Elborg Forster.
This essay was first presented orally at a colloquium on delinquency and social exclusion held on 3 March 1973 at the Ecole Normale Supérieure, Paris. The colloquium was organized by the research group on modern and contemporary history of the Centre National de la Recherche Scientifique (CNRS).

horror novel. The century witnessed the extension of the criminal code, which, in turn, extended the area of criminality. At the dawn of the century, the Napoleonic Code established "the rules of the game in the bourgeois peace,"[1] but that game was soon to become increasingly complex. Industrial enterprises intensified the contacts between various groups and at the same time created a proliferation of norms and prohibitions. Constraining and repressive in many ways, they had rules for everything; by the same token, they manufactured delinquents. It seems to me that a first approach to the subject should be to find out when, how, why, and under what stimulus the relatively simple tree of the original Code branched out to assume the luxuriant thickness we know today; to undertake, in short, the social and economic history of law and jurisprudence.

The extension of the prison was directly related to this development, since imprisonment is at the core of the contemporary penitentiary organization. To be sure, the Ancien Régime had known jails, but they served as depots, warehouses, and way stations leading to other punishments and other places, rather than as long-term abodes and places of penitence; at that time, imprisonment was not the cornerstone of repression. By "inventing liberty" (Starobinski), the French Revolution also gave birth to its opposite. By instituting incarceration as the keystone of the penal system, it began to weave the immense network of institutions—prisons, jails, houses of correction, central and departmental prisons—that eventually was to cover the entire country. The history of this development is a dramatic and profoundly contradictory story. Designed to punish, but also to reintegrate the delinquents into society, "to reform the morals of the inmates so that their return to freedom [would] not be a misfortune to themselves or to society,"[2] the prison eventually had the effect of excluding them from society altogether. Halfway through the nineteenth century the high rate of recidivism, which was to attain more than 50 percent by the end of the century, was already so threatening to the government that it decided to adopt, by the law of 1854, the English model it had so severly criticized earlier, namely, deportation to overseas penal colonies. The Third Republic went even further; the Waldeck-Rousseau Law of 1885, which provided for the banishment of multiple recidivists, expelled the "irretrievables" from French territory. The failure of the prison spelled the triumph of exclusion.

In trying to follow the path of this evolution, the historian of the nineteenth century must cross a rather crowded territory. A great proliferation of outdated criminology must be dealt with,[3] if only to be rejected in the end. There is also an abundance of source material, although it is uneven, not only in kind—great masses of printed sources, very little archival material[4]—but also in subject matter, since these writings dwell at great length on the offenses and the penal institutions but have infinitely less to say about the prisoners. All this makes for an elaborate discourse about crime and penology that masks the absence of the prisoners themselves. We do not hear much from them. Among several hundred books, I count no more than ten written by them. Those who did write were "honorable" prisoners, detained for political reasons or for debts; they were the small fry imprisoned at Sainte-Pélagie, rarely common-law offenders. And with what moderation they wrote. One of them may not have minced his words in depicting the "Inside of Prisons" (1846),[5] but for all that, he did not demand their abolition; being a repentant convert, he only suggested some reforms that would permit the prison to fulfill its function properly. True rebels were rare; at least they did not write.

It is of interest to our study to inquire into the reasons for this silence, regardless of whether it was imposed from the outside or even, at times, freely chosen. Prisoners were hemmed in by a triple layer of walls. The first of these was their illiteracy, which was always higher (by 10 to 15 percent) than that in the population as a whole. Yet, by the last quarter of the nineteenth century, the spread of primary education had changed the prisoners' relation to the written word. Henri Joly made much of the "considerable number of offenders who, with a rudimentary education and without any interest whatsoever in professional literature, nonetheless feel the urge to write for their personal satisfaction and compose drafts of plays and poems,"[6] as well as autobiographies, a certain number of which Joly was able to consult, although they cannot be found today and are probably lost forever. For the institution added a second and very serious obstacle; it stifled the spoken word and buried the written word—if it did not destroy it altogether—in obscure archives that were to remain sealed for a full century. Finally, the shame, the social stigma inflicted by the prison, repressed any desire to give testimony. As early as 1840, Honoré-Antoine Frégier spoke of the "inveterate aversion among all classes of the population for the exprisoner."[7] In a hostile world, only hardened revolutionaries or those condemned to the hardest prison terms dared to speak up. The others, the mass of inmates, tried to hide away in silence; once they were released they had only one obsession: to make the world forget their past in order to "belong."

These prisoners, then, have disappeared from their own history, so that we must follow their traces in what is said about them. To some extent, we can infer their resistance from the various difficulties with which the penitentiary system was beset when it was first established. The prisoners, we are told, were resistant to exhortations; the inmates "made faces as soon as the chaplains had turned their backs."[8] They were also resistant to work, for which they showed, according to Louis-Mathurin Moreau-Christophe, "a profound aversion."[9] "They even look with a kind of pity on those who do work," notes François de Barbé-Marbois, who visited the prisons of Calvados and Manche in 1821.[10] Consider the case of Mathurin Bruneau, an incorrigible liar imprisoned at Mont-Saint-Michel, who was deprived of chewing tobacco in order to make him work in the prison workshop. "He used to take pleasure in spoiling the wood he was given to make clogs; but now he makes good ones."[11] At La Petite Roquette, an institution for juveniles, "a child of fourteen who fell into the category of juvenile delinquent, a lazy and shiftless individual who abhorred work and resisted every means employed to make him do it and acquire a taste for it, boasted to his comrades that he would mutilate himself so that he would henceforth be excused from any occupation. He was as good as his word and resolutely cut off his right index finger. This action deserved to be punished."[12] Only solitary confinement could break his refusal to work.

For nothing caused greater terror than silence and solitude. In order to maintain communication at any price, the prisoners had invented a deceptive private language—"the word become convict" (Victor Hugo)—and an extraordinary art of signs that foiled all attempts at surveillance.[13] To the dreadful solitary confinement (first instituted at Auburn prison), a solitude that brought madness, most prisoners preferred the forced labor camp, which, from the depths of their solitary cells, they came to celebrate like a lost paradise. "At Toulon we had to work hard, that's true enough, but we also did a lot of drinking, and we could talk and laugh all we wanted," a former convict transferred to a Swiss prison of the Philadelphia-type declared nostalgically.[14]

The noisy passing of the chain gang, which, far from showing contrition, actually expressed defiance, was offensive to Bérenger, the inventor of the "paddy wagon."[15] Indeed, that terrible and murderous march created and symbolized, as it were, a subculture that was tolerated in the labor prison but crushed in the prison cell. The terror of imprisonment in a central prison was such that many tried to aggravate their crimes in order to be condemned to forced labor.[16] And when, in 1854, deportation to penal colonies was instituted for long prison terms, more and more criminal acts, notably arson, were perpetrated by prison inmates who wanted to be sent to Cayenne. This went so far that a law, passed in 1880, stipulated that in such cases the sentence would be served "in the same prison where the crime was committed."[17] The prison of the Ancien Régime had not always been very tight, and its inmates were sometimes permitted to slip away.[18] By the end of the nineteenth century, however, it was encrusted with legal provisions, surrounded by physical walls, and closed off from the outside world. It had become as difficult to avoid prison as it was to escape. The dissuasive effect of insurmountable difficulty no doubt explains the decline in attempts at escape.[19]

There is also the matter of collective revolt, but we know little about it. The inventory of series F 16 [in the Archives Nationales] mentions a considerable number of petitions, protests by prison inmates, and foiled conspiracies during the Restoration. In the period that followed, the lack of archival material conveys an impression of calm that is probably deceptive. Various authors speak of periodic, quasi-cyclical outbreaks of restlessness that were quickly squelched by vigilant guards, many of whom were recruited among the

military.[20] Moreau-Christophe evokes "plots, damages, mutinies, and revolts, whose frequent outbreaks make the duties of those charged with pre-
venting them so very onerous."[21] But we hear of nothing that would qualify
as an "event"; rather, it is all a vague background noise, a muted, far-away
rumbling that may have died before it came to fruition; nor do we know
whether to impute this silence to the thickness of the walls, to resignation
within, or to indifference without. Were there many other movements analogous to those of 1885, which had started at the prison workshops of Gaillon
(department of Eure) and spread to a number of other central prisons, eventually becoming so important, massive, and articulate that the press was obliged
to take notice of them?

On the subject of all these forms of resistance—passive, active, individual,
communal—as well as on the modes of adaptation, submission, or even
integration (to what extent was the system able to impose its values, or at least
to instill guilt feelings?) the prison of yesterday is singularly discreet. Yet it is
precisely the real, the daily life of this group—the prisoners—that we must try
to capture at its most hidden level, the level that lies behind and beyond the
serene statements and the conventions of the discourse of the penitentiary. We
are now well aware that there is no such thing as the total absence of a history
of peoples and groups, only the absence of visible traces, which are bound to
come to light as soon as we dig for them more deeply.

Crime, Offense, and the Discourse of
Crime in the Nineteenth Century

A FUNDAMENTAL SOURCE

The *Compte général de l'administration de la justice criminelle*[22] [General
Report of the Administration of Criminal Justice], has been published annually without interruption from 1825 to our own day; it is the basic source for
all criminological studies, one of the great quantifiable series that responds to
the needs of the present-day historian. Existing in a rudimentary form for the
eighteenth century and resumed by the First Consul (circular of 23 January
1801),[23] this publication assumed its definitive form during the Restoration,
owing to the concern aroused by the great increase in delinquency during the
years 1815–18, a concern that also led to the founding of the Société Royale
des Prisons (1819). The work of Guerry de Champneuf, director of criminal
affairs, and Arondeau, department head in the Ministry of Justice, it was
written for magistrates and for "men who like to meditate on matters of
crime." A product of the Enlightenment, it professed a dual purpose. It
wanted to "enlighten justice" and to found a veritable moral science: "Exact
knowledge of the facts is one of the prime needs in our form of government.

Such knowledge makes for enlightened deliberations, which it simplifies and places on a solid foundation by substituting the sure and positive guidance of experience for theoretical vagueness."[24]

Every annual volume consists of two parts. One is a general report on the major features of the situation, which is invaluable for studying the dominant concepts and concerns; the other is a series of tables concerning the facts of crime (the data relating to the assize courts are by far the most developed, while only very summary data are available for courts of correction and the various courts of petty sessions under the jurisdiction of simple police courts). The progressive refinement of the *Compte,* which one can follow from year to year, shows the mounting uneasiness of the state. By 1830–35, however, its main framework was fixed.

Aside from a numerical accounting of the various crimes and offenses, the document yields three major categories of data:

1. For defendants charged with crimes it gives information about age, sex (1826), civil status, residence, place of birth, level of education (1828), occupation according to a detailed nomenclature divided into nine classes (1829), residence in a rural or urban community (1830), social standing according to three criteria (wage earner, self-employed, unemployed) (1830). New tables showing correlations between the nature of the offense and the characteristics of the accused were added constantly.

2. Information concerning repeat offenders, already quite detailed by 1826–28, becomes more and more abundant, in keeping with the ever mounting anxiety they produced.

3. Finally, a whole set of tables concerning the functioning of the judicial system is included. These tables list acquittals and condemnations according to the nature of the crime, the social standing of the defendant, the department, etc.; the nature of the sentences and their length, cases sent to appeal, extenuating circumstances (first admitted in 1832). At first, these data concerned only defendants charged with crimes; by the second half of the century they were also extended to defendants charged with offenses, but the latter were treated in a more summary fashion, owing to their great number (up to 200,000 persons charged with offenses, but only a few thousand charged with crimes).

Many other data are given in the *Compte.* Some of them, such as the alleged motives of crimes, bankruptcies, suicides, are given regularly; others, such as the amount of the gratuity given to prisoners upon release, the statistics of thefts committed in the department of Seine (nature and value of the stolen goods; place, time, and means of the theft, etc.) are given more sporadically. Sometimes one finds marginal notations that stimulate one's imagination: "Three young men of the same village, united in friendship, had planned to assassinate their sweethearts and then to commit suicide. Only one carried out this plan, and his accomplice is listed here."[25]

Beginning in 1850, ten-year summaries are included in the annual reports. Some of the summaries span even longer periods, especially that of 1880 (vol. 55), which is particularly useful since it covers the years 1826–80 and includes the maps and charts prepared for the Penitentiary Exhibition (sic) of 1879.

This series, considered a model of its kind and widely imitated abroad— although for some reason it receives very little attention today—called forth innumerable commentaries in the course of the nineteenth century. It was the main source for the first "moral science" so brilliantly exemplified by the works of Guerry (*Essai sur la Statistique morale de la France,* 1833) and Quételet who, as early as 1826, attached such importance to the use of judical statistics that he devoted an entire book of his famous treatise, *Sur l'homme et le développement de ses facultés; ou, Essai de physique sociale,*[26] to them. The *Compte général* reached its full potential when criminology had become an autonomous science (especially with H. Joly and G. Tarde). It also furnished the raw materials for the famous works of Emile Durkheim (*Le Suicide,* 1894; "Deux lois de l'évolution pénale," in *Année Sociologique,* 1901). The historian who uses it is therefore likely to follow a well-beaten path.

Nonetheless, the present-day historian will do well to be wary of the rather peremptory, indeed triumphant, criminology of this era of positivist science. Guerry, Joly, and their successors had no doubt that there was such a thing as the "facts of crime."[27] To them, the data of the *Compte* were absolute values, and as a result they used the statistics of defendants charged with crimes and offenses not only for studying crimes and offenses, which might possibly be considered legitimate, but also for studying criminals and delinquents. The distinction between alleged (defendants), legal (convicted prisoners), and real criminality, usually taken for granted today, had not yet become part of their thinking.

Such a purely positivistic use of the *Compte* is out of the question today. There are no "facts of crime" as such, only a judgmental process that institutes crimes by designating as criminal both certain acts and their perpetrators. In other words, there is a discourse of crime that reveals the obsession of a society. What we need to know is how that discourse functioned and how it changed, to what extent it expressed reality, and in what ways various influences came to shape it.

SUGGESTIONS FOR A TOTAL READING

The *Compte,* if used wisely, offers a vast field of opportunity to the researcher. As a first approach to a fuller understanding, it may be helpful to consider the following data.

Shifts in the nomenclature of crimes and offenses.   Few changes were made in the list of crimes. The classic major distinction between crimes against persons and crimes against property was supplemented by two subdivisions after 1850, namely, crimes against public order and crimes against morality, these last rising very sharply.

By contrast, the list of offenses was growing constantly, not only because certain acts that had earlier been classified as crimes were now assigned to correctional courts [i.e., courts that dealt with intermediate offenses], but especially because of new additions. Beginning with the Second Empire, we find a profusion of economic offenses (related to checks, commercial companies, loans), all of them involving the kind of "clever cheating" that marks the beginning of "white collar" delinquency. At about the same time, the policing of drinking places also became more complex. The offense of drunkenness, invented in 1873, resulted in an additional 4,000 charges the very next year. By 1880, some 60,714 persons were arraigned before police or correctional courts for intermediate or minor offenses of this kind. This was much less than in England where, as the *Compte* pointed out, 172,589 persons were so charged.

Generally speaking, the Napoleonic Code was continually activated by new deposits, each of which immediately provoked an inflation in delinquency. Withdrawals were much less frequent. Only a major upheaval or a long period of lax enforcement could bring about the legislative measures necessary for the abolition of an offense. In the *Compte* of 1880, the magistrates demanded that loans at interest be striken from the list of offenses, since various legislative bills attempted to establish the legitimacy of such loans. The courts had long ceased to prosecute anything but the most flagrant usury. Surely the time had come to exonerate capital!

The curve of offenses and crimes.   What is the significance of their rise and decline? Consider two opposing examples. The curve of offenses pertaining to forests is a story in itself. On the average, 135,000 persons per year were charged with this offense between 1831 and 1835, although it should be added that this maximum was related to the economic crisis.[28] In 1910, only 1,789 persons were so charged. By the beginning of the twentieth century the forest had ceased to be the traditional food preserve during times of shortage for the community. A rise in the rural standard of living and probably also a decline in the practice of gathering, related to more concentrated land-use and a greater prevalence of private ownership, are partial explanations of this phenomenon. Formerly an eminently popular and collective act, and also the female offense *par excellence* (in 1860 women accounted for one-fourth of those charged), poaching became an individual act—a mutation, incidentally, that is echoed in French literature. The difference between Balzac's band of peasants on the offensive and the marginal and hunted Raboliot described by

Maurice Genevoix in the Sologne of the great bourgeois hunting parties exemplarily illustrates this evolution. In addition, however, the decline in this kind of delinquency also followed the outline traced by the Code. In 1835 the Department of Waters and Forests was granted the option not to prosecute offenses committed in forests owned by the state and by local communities, a decision that resulted in an immediate decline in the number of persons charged. Nonetheless, that number still amounted to 75,000 in 1851–55. Then the law of 18 June 1859 extended the right not to prosecute to all categories of forests. From then on, the number of these offenses declined rapidly and steadily, also eliminating a considerable part of female delinquency.

Thefts and cases involving indecent behavior, on the other hand, showed rising curves, particularly crimes and offenses against children. In 1850, the *Compte* sounded a note of alarm: infanticide had risen by 49 percent between 1826 and 1850, abortion by 50 percent, while rape and indecent assault against children under sixteen had tripled. The summary of 1880 expressed even more alarm and devoted considerable space to the search for "causes," which it found mainly in the promiscuity of the city and the factory. In 1876–80, there were 791 cases of indecent assault against children listed, compared with only 136 in 1826–30; although it should be pointed out that the raising of the legal age of childhood (from 11 to 13 and finally 16 years) partially explains this inflation. Crimes in the narrow sense had actually declined somewhat since the middle of the century (see table 7.1). The Public Ministry expressed misgivings about this decline in the number of charges brought, as well as about the high level of acquittals. Both were apt to convey the impression that the sensibility of the period attached greater importance to virtue than to life.[29]

The methods of repression and their evolution. Here we find some interesting suggestions. First of all, who brought the charges? Increasingly, it was the Public Ministry. In correctional courts, it introduced 30 percent of the cases in 1831–35, and 89 percent in 1876–80. The increasing incidence of offenses of insubordination, especially of outrages against public officials— and these offenses were rarely acquitted—also indicates a strengthening of the judicial system as a tool of the state.

Table 7.1—Number of Infanticides and Abortions Prosecuted, 1831–80

	Infanticides	Abortions
1831–35	471	41
1851–55		172 (maximum)
1856–60	1,069 (maximum)	
1876–80	970	100

The tendency to reduce the role of the jury was part of the same process, for juries were considered too lenient, particularly with respect to the punishment of crimes against persons. The tendency to reduce the role of the jury was implemented by assigning more and more cases to correctional courts; but the apparent leniency of this step actually served to camouflage a desire for greater efficiency. It was a matter of lightening the work load of the assize courts and at the same time of "using a little indulgence to make up for the too numerous chances of impunity" (*Compte* of 1880).

For it was a fact that the magistrates were more severe. Acting as willing tools of the state, most of them had ceased to be purveyors of Enlightenment by the nineteenth century. It is significant that they played a relatively minor role in prison reform or in social reform in general, by comparison with the much more open-minded physicians with whom they often came into conflict. The magistrates were strenuously opposed, for instance, to the law of 30 June 1838, which gave the supervising physicians of prisons the right to transfer mental patients, large numbers of whom were still confined in penal institutions. For a long time, the magistrates refused to accept madness as an extenuating circumstance. Dr. Vingtrinier deplored their attitude: "The corps of magistrates is wrong when it rejects, or only begrudgingly accepts, the psychological and medical statements sometimes made in court by physicians." "The defense," said one president of an assize court, "talked of some kind of illness, dredged up from the murky depth of modern science, in order to excuse the crime."[30] The magistrates refused to accept this minimal, yet fundamental, competition of the asylum. There were times, to be sure, when they had their doubts—and these are reflected in the jurisprudence—when their consciences were torn. This was the case, for example, in 1846–48. The *Compte* of 1850 deplores the magistrates' lack of firmness, showing that they had reduced their sentences in 72 percent of the cases. "This excessive leniency brought about an investigation which, in turn, resulted in the laws of 4 and 9 June 1853."[31] But such moments of weakness, signs of the stirring of a social conscience, seem to have been rare. These magistrates were untroubled defenders of the bourgeois order, and as such they deserve Daumier's caricatures and the young Flaubert's sarcasm.[32]

The percentages of condemnations and acquittals according to the nature of the offense or the offender, the acceptance of extenuating circumstances, the nature and the length of the sentence—all these are so many more or less deferred clues to the penal sensibility of a society, at least that part of it that sat in judgment. In this respect, a history of the repressive measures against abortion would tell us a great deal about the attitude toward life of ordinary people. This history indicates that an act that was no doubt largely condoned by the pervasive Malthusianism of the environment came to be reproved only slowly; it also shows the decisive role of the governing elites in the making of a new "morality," for by the last third of the nineteenth century these elites had become very concerned about France's declining population.[33] While it is true that early in the century abortion was a crime to be tried in assize courts, the small number of cases prosecuted and the high rate of aquittals suggest a certain indifference.

In 1830, four women were tried, three of whom were aquitted; in 1834, five of eight cases were dismissed, and five of twelve defendants were acquitted. Between 1831 and 1880, 40 percent of all cases of abortion ended in acquittal, and in 78 percent of the cases the defendants were given the benefit of extenuating circumstances. The *Compte* of 1880 deplores the laxity of the jury, especially since "in the last few years the practitioners of abortion have developed a scandalous proficiency" (p. xv). It compares infanticides in the countryside, 52 percent of which were committed by illiterate women, with abortion in the city (amounting to 60 percent of all cases), where it was the work of more knowledgeable (only 29 percent illiterates), and hence more depraved, women. The *Compte* called for greater severity. During the years that followed, pressure from the Public Ministry led to some widely publicized trials that were no doubt intended to shake the lethargy of public opinion. Some of the public sessions brought to light a remarkable discrepancy in moral perception. Reporting on the Louviers case, the correspondent of *Le Temps* was amazed at the "nerve" of the abortionist who

freely admitted his shameful profession. . . . He complacently laid out every detail. He told how the idea first struck him when he visited the anatomical exhibits of country fairs. He prided himself on his skill acquired through long experience. He compared his fees to those of his colleagues. He claimed that physicians, pharmacists, and herbalists, in recognition of his incontestable superiority, sent male and female clients to him. After him, the court heard from husbands, who declared that they had taken their wives to his consulting room. They explained their action by saying either that they were guided by the desire to spare their spouse the pain of a pregnancy or that they succumbed to the fear of risking total destitution by permitting their family to grow larger. . . . All these defendants, whether peasants or factory workers, appeared surprised at being prosecuted for acts that they considered altogether natural.[34]

This is an exemplary case of time-lag, which we find at every turn in judicial history. It also illustrates the spurious, or at least eminently social, character of the Code, clearly the expression of the permanent, yet subtly changing, exigencies of a single group.

DELINQUENCY AND ITS DISCOURSE

Property and sexuality. The statistics of crimes and offenses furnish the facts and figures of a two-fold obsession: property and sexuality.[35] In 1835, the defendants arraigned in assize courts were divided as follows: 29 percent were charged with crimes against persons, 71 percent with crimes against property. In the course of the century, these proportions shifted toward a greater percentage of crimes against persons, owing to the increased practice of trying cases involving property in courts of correction. Between 1830 and 1880, courts of correction registered an increase of 238 percent for cases of theft, 323 percent for cases of swindling, and 630 percent for cases of breach of trust. Changes in procedure must therefore not be permitted to obscure the real decline in homicides and the extraordinary increase in all forms of offenses against property.

The character of these offenses tended to change. Offenses committed in rural areas remained predominant until about 1840. Theft was the undisputed king of offenses in the middle of the century, when it attained its highest point as far as the courts of correction were concerned (24,000 cases tried, 42,000 persons charged). While theft in churches declined and while highway robbery ceased almost altogether, having become the preserve of young people who still dreamt of being Mandrin,* all forms of urban theft began to come into their own. Theft committed by domestic servants was severely punished; it was the obsession of Balzac's bourgeois[36] or of those described in [Zola's] *Pot-Bouille*. After 1850, shoplifting, stimulated by the fascination of the female public for department stores, entered the competition,[37] as did petty theft—the much-coveted watch launched many a career of delinquency[38]— and, increasingly, theft of money, usually small sums, since these were the only ones within reach.[39] "The confidence trickster and the pickpocket tend to replace the highway robber."[40] Yet the fact that so many children and vagrants were charged with "pilfering food"[41] affords a glimpse of the cramped horizon of a society of scarcity, and the existence of marginal but persistent hunger.

Beginning in the 1860s, theft was outdistanced by the so-called clever offenses: forgery, influence peddling, fraudulent stock-transactions, breach of trust—all of them perpetrated within four walls and with the utmost politeness. These were the subtle fruits of business acumen, the work of "city-slickers" in the true sense of the word. "The wider distribution of wealth, the increasing prevalence of greed, speculation in the stockmarket, etc., may be sufficient to account for the rise in such offenses," comments the *Compte* of 1880 (p. lxiii).

Thus, the thief and especially the swindler caused much more concern than the assassin in these times of capitalist accumulation. No wonder that the comparison between the naive, impulsive, but fundamentally good-natured murderer of the rural areas and the southern departments and the depraved crook of the industrial areas and the big cities of the North-northeast, the man who manipulated things, was a common theme in the criminological literature

*Louis Mandrin is identified in a translator's note in Chapter 4 of this volume.—Trans.

of the period. "Offenses against property . . . carefully premeditated and committed over and over again, are proof of a distressing perseverence in evildoing and imply both depravity and baseness; they never elicit any sympathy. The swindler, the forger, the fraudulent bankrupt of our northern departments who, with his polite manners and a varying degree of education, coldly accomplishes the ruin of twenty families whose trust he has betrayed, is to our minds more contemptible and more immoral than the illiterate inhabitant of our southern provinces who strikes or even kills his adversary in a fight."[42] Juries were in full agreement with this assessment. In the period 1825–30, they acquitted 50 percent of crimes against persons, but only 31 percent of crimes against property.[43]

Murder reigned supreme in the "gothic" horror novels; it was the mainstay of a serials literature that, until the dawn of the twentieth century, bore the stamp of a rare violence, a violence that seems to have spilled over into popular imagination. But this literature, however important for capturing people's opinions and mental images,[44] should not lead us astray. The shift from a criminality of violence to a criminality of "cunning," as evidenced by the case of Ferri, began in the eighteenth century[45] and continued its long sweep throughout the fluctuations brought about by the economic and political crises of the nineteenth century. Industrialization did not reverse this trend; quite the contrary was true. But its violence was of a different order.

Proceeding in a galloping inflation, crimes and offenses "against morality" were always related to sexuality, which is, in itself, a rather remarkable identification. A few figures will indicate their growth (see table 7.2). This was the heyday of suppressed sexuality, and to a certain extent the judicial statistics permit us to gauge the sexual repression of which the castrating prison was the ultimate, intensified image. All writing on the penitentiary fairly overflows with phallic anxiety; sexual promiscuity, nocturnal masturbation—which was held responsible for the pallor of the inmates—and homosexuality were the obsession of a discourse racked by puritan terror of

Table 7.2—Crimes and Offenses "Against Morality" Prosecuted, 1826–30 and 1876–80

	1826–30	1876–80
Assize courts		
Crimes against morality	305	932
Indecent assaults against children	136	791
Courts of correction		
Indecent acts in public	302	2,572
Adultery	53	131

the flesh. Pederasty above all was condemned as the gateway to crime. According to Joly, all *"antiphysiques"* [sic] were potential delinquents. Being exclusively concerned with matters of morality, the prison vastly intensified the constraints obtaining in the outside world: "Moral offenses are severely punished, especially *theft* and *indecent acts.* Thieves have their heads shaven, they are fettered with chain and ball, and they must wear a green cap with the inscription *thief.*" Sometimes the prison was able to instill the guilt feelings that so many educational institutions were attempting to foster. "As for other crimes, the warden tries as much as possible to avoid making an issue of them so as not to give the other inmates ideas; but if the matter has become known, the punishment meted out to the offender is of an almost exclusively moral nature; the humiliation to which he is exposed is more important than the slight blow he must receive from each one of the inmates in his cell-block."[46]

Deviants.   By setting the norm, the Code also designated the *deviants.* In this respect the data of the *Compte* are inconsistent, since they are much more complete for persons charged with crimes than for persons charged with offenses. Some of the commentaries provide us with a first inkling of what was apt to be suspect and what was apt to be treated leniently.

The early criminology was based on two basic ideas: the constancy and regularity of the "fact" of crime, which was bound to appear year after year since it was subject to its own laws (cf. Guerry and Quételet); and the existence of a more or less pronounced "proclivity toward crime," ranging from the idea of "innate depravity" that was to culminate in Lombroso's "born criminal," to the idea that the influence of the milieu plays a role. If there was such a thing as proclivity, the question was, What makes for the steepest slope? In other words, what drives people to crime? On this point, the discourse is groping and tentative; but at times it does afford a glimpse of its underlying assumptions in the conflicting strands of hypotheses whose stammerings we cannot fully treat here.

One first approach focused on geography. It sought to determine the space of crime in France by outlining a cartography. Guerry, who can be considered the father of social cartography, distinguished between a France of theft, namely the north-northeastern part of the country where delinquency was more prevalent than crime, and southern France, an area that was brutal in dealing with persons but respectful of property. Corsica, violent but virtuous, was very different from northern France and of course Paris, the very capital of depravity. What accounted for this dichotomy? No doubt it was unequal economic development, of which contemporary economists were very well aware.[47] Guerry himself noted that the departments where commerce and industry were most developed were also those where theft flourished. "It is possible," he wrote, "that those departments where the most considerable fortunes are found are precisely those where a certain segment of the population also lives in the most abject poverty."[48] This is a recurrent theme of the contemporary Christian political economy of the aristocratic and rural persuasion (Moreau-Christophe, Villeneuve-Bargemont) as well as of the literature that took a critical view of the economy (Buret, for instance). But Guerry also stressed the "natural influences that hardly anyone seems to take into consideration, although they have a very powerful impact." On his map of criminality he traced a line marking the boundaries of olive cultivation. He also invoked the complex networks of customs that had welded the various regions into distinct entities and the "difference in acquired or original organization which, despite the uniformity of our new administrative subdivisions, still permits us to recognize within the kingdom something akin to several distinct nations, each one of which has its own language, mores, habits, and traditional prejudices" (p. 40), all of which anticipates a rudimentary anthropology of crime.

A second, widely shared approach was of a biological order. It laid the blame on such factors as seasons (summer is the season of crime, winter the season of theft), age and sex, incriminating young men and exonerating women. The *Compte* of 1836 notes that 53 percent of the persons charged with crimes are under thirty years old and strongly recommends the searching out, "in order to combat them, the causes that are such a powerful incentive to crime at a time of life when all honorable resources lie open to those who are willing to take advantage of them" (p. vii). [49] Young men between sixteen and twenty-one accounted for 11 percent of the delinquents in 1831–35, 14 percent in 1876–80. The report of 1909 fixes the level of criminality of the age group eighteen to twenty-one at 3 percent, which is three times as high as for other age groups. Fear of young men came to permeate this society, especially since 581 out of every 1,000 of these young men were charged with theft (statistic of 1876–80) and thus chiefly posed a threat to the sanctity of property. H. Lauvergne speaks of the "vermin of petty thieves between eighteen and twenty-one," who are "veritable ferments of corruption."[50] All kinds of coercive measures were taken to control this menace of juveniles and children; these measures constitute an essential and prolific chapter in the history of the penitentiary. Wavering between close supervision outside the prison (*patronage extérieur*) amounting to a half-hearted attempt at creating a parole system, solitary confinement such as it was instituted at La Petite Roquette ca. 1836, and assignment to work farms of the Mettray type, these measures eventually had the effect of keeping more and more of these roaming youths under lock and key. In the period 1826–30, 98 youths per year were placed in houses of correction; by 1871–75 this figure was 2,813. Consequently, the population of these institutions kept growing ever larger, reaching 5,293 by about 1840, and 22,000 twenty years later.

Women, on the other hand, seem to have been "not punishable," as Michelet wrote. At least, their weight on the scales of Justice became lighter.

Moreover, this figure declined not just in relative, but in absolute, terms (down 28 percent in courts of correction between the beginning and the end of the century), a fact that is related in part to the decrease of offenses involving forests and subsistences, traditionally the most prevalent offenses committed by women in their role as housekeepers and providers of food. In addition, however, women were treated with far-reaching leniency, as evidenced by a high rate of aquittals, even in cases of infanticide and abortion. Women were easily accorded extenuating circumstances, and the courts were reluctant to condemn them to death. (Some sixty persons were executed between 1876 and 1880, but not one of them was a woman). (See table 7.3.)

The reason is that women did not appear to pose a serious threat. Furthermore, their criminality was commensurate with their weakness. A woman's life, after all, was centered on the house, her own or that of her masters; her target was the defenseless child or the feeble old man, her weapon was fire or, better yet, poison. "Arsenic in a cup of tea, a box of poisoned chocolates, . . . these are women's crimes," declares Hercule Poirot.[51]

Crimes and offenses were men's business, manly acts committed in the "asphalt jungle." Does lack of visibility on that stage indicate submissiveness or greater morality on the part of women? Or was this one of the ways of keeping them off-stage? Indeed, is not such leniency altogether suspect? It does seem that denying women their criminal stature was simply another way of putting them down.[52]

This does not mean that the criminological literature considered women innocent. It actually dwelt at some length on the devious, depraved character of female criminality. "The crimes in which the proportion of women is highest are not those that presuppose the least immorality, but those that demand deviousness and cunning rather than strength and daring; these are the crimes that are committed within the household and the family."[53] "Natural affections that have taken a wrong turn and the exaggerated emotions to which women are so often prone seem to be the prevalent cause of crimes against persons committed by them; and the character of the resulting crime is determined by their weakness," wrote Guerry.[54] According to Lucas, "the criminality of women is more dangerous than that of men, because it is more contagious, just as their morality is perhaps more useful because it is more expansive."[55] All authors stressed the hidden, underlying role played by women in crimes committed by men. "Almost all of these crimes were

Table 7.3—Percentage of Women Arraigned, 1826–1902 (selected years)

Year(s)	In Assize Courts	In Courts of Correction
1826–30	19	22
1876–80	16	14
1902	14	

committed for or because of a woman."[56] "Most of the time men steal for them, and the women are aware of it, although they always feign ignorance. Of all the kinds of complicity, this is the most subtle, and the most dangerous to society. . . . The ferocity . . . [of women] surpasses that of men. But the outstanding feature to be revealed in criminal trials is the consummate cruelty and perfidiousness with which they savor their vengeance, the skill with which they make others commit their crimes for them."[57]

Even in our own day, "the prison inmate shares the popular belief that it is woman who has instigated the crime, that she is the cause of all his misfortunes."[58] Woman as man's evil genius; the literature on crime obviously partakes of the myth of the eternal Eve.

Migrations and the cities were suspected very early. As early as 1828 the *Compte* was interested in finding out whether the defendants had left their native department; by 1830 it stated whether they lived in an urban or a rural community. The tranquil department of Corrèze and the utterly depraved department of Seine marked the two extremes of the chain of crime. Yet the material did not quite bear out these suspicions, for the statistics for 1831–80 show that 68 percent of the defendants were born in the department where they had run afoul of the law. Also, the cities came to outweigh the countryside only by the beginning of the twentieth century. (See table 7.4.)

Nonetheless, the *Compte* of 1860 came to the conclusion that "the life of the countryside has a fortunate influence upon morality." This was a classic theory, although it had been contested for some time by industrialists and by those who saw the cities as centers of enlightenment and education for the people. But in the nineteenth century it was revived by a whole movement interested in prison reform (for example, Léon Faucher and Dr. Ferrus) and in social reform in general (for example, de Gérando, de Morogues, Villeneuve-Bargemont, Huerne de Pommeuse).[59] All these reformers repeated what Delille, the poet of physiocracy, had said: "By instilling love for the open country, we will instill love of virture." "In the art of crime, as in all others, those who seek perfection betake themselves to the city, especially to the big city," wrote Lucas, who stressed the contrast between the clever and corrupt "urban race" and "poor country folk." It was also pointed out that the cities fueled not so much the assize courts as the sordid courts of correction; being the haunts of theft and vice, and given to guile more than to crime,

Table 7.4—Residence of Defendants, 1840–1902 (selected years)

Year(s)	Rural Communities (%)	Urban Communities (%)
1840–50	59	37
1851–60	56	39
1876–86	51	49
1902	40	60

230   MICHELLE PERROT

the cities were held responsible for the outstanding forms of modern criminality. Paris alone, which in 1880 furnished one-tenth of the cases brought before
the courts of correction, perhaps did not deserve its somber literary reputation
as the capital of crime as much as that of a Babylon of money and the flesh. It
is interesting to note that the "Parisians" constituted a prison-aristocracy:
"Whenever the prison inmates want to cite an elite population in matters of
criminality, whom do they name? The inmates from Paris. The inmate from
Paris is an unmistakable type. In all the prisons of the kingdom he not only
preserves his identity, for he calls himself and is called the *Parisian,* but he
also preserves his character, his influence, even his walk and his stance. . . .
Among a thousand prisoners, you will always recognize the Parisian by the
way he struts, which makes him the *fashionable* of the prison. But what is the
secret of his renown in prison? It is not that the Parisian institutions are
naturally more conducive to crime; it is just that there the wicked education of
prison life can deploy a more powerful influence, for it can offer more examples, greater skill in teaching, a richer tradition, and a greater variety of
resources than institutions elsewhere."[60]

In the 1880s, yet another category became tainted with suspicion: foreigners. The *Compte* of 1880 compares the level of criminality among foreigners (38 percent) with that among the French (12 percent). The *Compte* of
1894 gives a summary of delinquency by foreigners for the preceding twenty
years, and another such summary is found in the *Compte* of 1902. At that
date, 7 percent of the persons charged with crimes were of foreign origin, with
Italians heading the list. Here is the sign of an anxiety that was to grow ever
deeper in the subsequent years.

But it is time now to turn to those against whom there is actual evidence: the
poor and, above all, the workers. They filled the prisons in such numbers that
the prisons were conceived for them, in terms of their economic and cultural
standards. "The proper prison diet," wrote Faucher, "will be one that is
based on a working-class family diet, albeit at a somewhat reduced level."[61]
By following the changes in prison diet, one would be able to perceive what
was considered to be the minimum intake at any given period. In the same
spirit, Lucas remarked that the industrialized populations of northern France,
"accustomed as they are to the miasma of the workshop, are more easily
acclimatized" to imprisonment than the rural people of southern France.[62] In
a sense, the factory has prepared them.

Oriented more toward biological and moral than toward economic considerations, the discourse of crime attributed only secondary importance to this
latter factor. Nonetheless, it did recognize that economic considerations can
have an impact in a number of ways. The first of these is related to prosperity
or the lack thereof *(conjoncturel)*; the *Compte* of 1880 notes the correlation
between waves of delinquency and the high price of grain (p. viii). "Poverty
has driven large numbers of wretchedly poor workers to theft." It also ac-

knowledges that "the various industrial and commercial crises" had something to do with the steep rise in beggary and vagrancy.[63] Economic factors also shaped the social structure of a criminality that was fueled by the wage-earning class; in 1832, 59 percent of those charged with crimes were wage earners. Industry, whose sole purpose is the creation of things, incited the workers to thievery (raw material, finished articles), and its promiscuous way of life fostered sexual degradation, which is why industrialization was held mainly responsible for indecent assaults upon children. Industrial workers came to replace domestic servants in the ranking of dangerous persons, for even though, in 1880, they represented only 26 percent of the population, they accounted for 34 percent of those charged with crimes. (Persons engaged in agriculture furnished 39 percent, but they represented 53 percent of the population). The *Compte* of 1902 establishes the supremacy of the workers in matters of crime: 47 percent of the persons charged with crimes came from industry and transportation, with railroad workers and dockers most heavily involved in a new kind of meridional violence. "Urban day laborers," we are told—that is, unskilled, unqualified (or disqualified) workers—were those who kept the prisons filled at the dawn of the twentieth century. This was, in short, a subproletariat, distinct from the category of capable "honest workers."

Does this shift in interpretation correspond to a real social change? At the very least, it suggests a hardening of social attitudes. In the first half of the nineteenth century a reformer or a philanthropist might still speak up for the "lower classes," showing that the precariousness of the workers' condition could be a source of delinquency.[64] Later, in the name of a hypothetical equality of opportunity, emphasis was placed either on "innate depravity" or on the individual responsibility of the delinquent. Vagrancy was largely considered to be a "freely chosen condition." The explanatory statement of the Waldeck-Rousseau Law concerning the expulsion of repeat offenders stigmatized "this phalanx of voluntary déclassés, sharpers who ply their loathsome trade."[65] This text is the very sign of a society in the process of rationalization that could no longer tolerate these marginal characters who consistently wasted their time. There was only one way to deal with these "rebels against any kind of work"[66]—as repeat offenders were characterized— and that was—exclusion.

The interaction of the "discourse" and the "fact" of crime constitutes the major difficulty of a study like the present one. Both are real enough, but they are so tightly interwoven that it is probably futile to ask which came first. Historians, then, must steer a safe course between two dangers: on the one hand, the positivistic study of the statistics of crime; on the other, the purely ideological study of the Code and its implementation. For if the offense is defined by the Code, the Code itself is also the expression of something else; while it is, of course, the expression of a social group that tries to come to grips with a reality it attempts to master and to categorize, it is also that of the magistracy, of the state, of public opinion, and so forth. Therefore, the historian must closely follow every change and the processes leading to it in order to understand the role played by the different powers and the influences they exerted on each other.

The Prison as a System of Social Exclusion

If it were possible to find the means of masterminding everything that could possibly happen to a specific group of people, if one could arrange their entire environment in such a way that it produces only such impressions as one wishes to convey, if one could control all their actions and all their contacts, with the result that nothing escapes or counteracts the desired effect, there is no doubt that a system of this kind would be a most effective and useful tool, which governments could apply to various matters of the highest importance.—From the introduction to the French edition of J. Bentham's Panopticon

Jeremy Bentham's *Panopticon* is among the most perfect expressions of the new model of the prison that was being elaborated between 1780 and 1820. Now that the prison had become the focal point of the penitentiary system to the very extent that deprivation of liberty had become its central core, it assumed a three-fold function: it was designed to punish, to protect society by isolating the offender in order to contain the threat of contagion and by instilling dread of his lot in others, and to reform the culprit with a view to restoring him to society *at the level where he belonged.* How and under what influences—of a religious or economic nature—this prototype of totalitarian institutions came to be accepted is a vast question that I shall not attempt to treat here.[67] I shall limit myself to evoking the major phases of the history of the French prison in the nineteenth century, its functioning, and its ambiguous effects.

THE MAJOR PHASES OF THE FRENCH
PENITENTIARY SYSTEM

The triumph of the prison, 1815–48.   Theoreticians had no doubts as to the repressive and educative value of the prison; they only argued, with a great deal of passion, about the best type of prison to be adopted. Should it be the Auburn model, with solitary confinement at night and silent work in groups during the day, whose principal supporters were Charles Lucas and the architect Baltard?[68] Or should it be the Philadelphia model, which called for solitary confinement by night and by day and was vigorously advocated by Beaumont and Frégier; Moreau-Christophe and Tocqueville; Bérenger, the inventor of the paddy wagon; and by Blouet, the builder?

Those who favored the Auburn model clearly had their way until about 1835. But the growth of recidivism soon aroused misgivings. Certain writers criticized the naiveté of the philanthropists of the Société Royale des Prisons (founded in 1819). "Prison has ceased to be a punishment as it were; it affords the criminal asylum, an existence, security, sympathy, and the approbation society denies him," wrote Demetz.[69] Punishment must be rigorous: "Penal justice, after all, is an act of social revenge; social revenge is a legitimate satisfaction; satisfaction means expiation; and expiation means *real* suffering in body and spirit," chimed in Moreau-Christophe, who had long been singing the praise of the cell. The Academy of Medicine contributed its share by certifying that solitary confinement could not lead to madness (Dr. Lélut). A whole series of measures marked the success of those who advocated solitary confinement,[70] culminating in the introduction of a bill providing for the general application of that system in 1844. It seems likely that this law would have been passed if it had not been for the Revolution of 1848.

The great fear of 1848. Stringent repressive measures and deportation under the Second Empire.   Solitary confinement for all inmates was very costly. As early as the 1840s, intense criticism had been leveled against the inefficiency and the high cost of prisons. According to Vingtrinier (1840), "nowadays people would laugh at a man who would talk of improving the physical lot of the prisoners. 'They are too comfortable as it is,' he would be told." Vingtrinier spoke of a "social cancer" costing thirteen million francs a year.[71]

The agitation of 1848 could only reinforce such criticism. The June days so filled the prisons that they reached their high-water mark. At that point they held 50,000 inmates, a threatening flood that the propertied classes saw poised to burst upon their fortunes. The *Compte* of 1850 reflects this fear; it dwells at greater length on the problem of recidivism and chastizes the reprehensible leniency of the magistrates. "All of a sudden," wrote Ernest de Blosseville, a fervent supporter of deportation to the colonies, "public opinion became aroused, for it came to see, as in a flash of insight, the threat to society inherent in a constantly growing number of discharged and recidivist criminals. . . . With instant unanimity that segment of the press that is pledged to uphold civilization demanded that the government disperse and stamp out the menacing assemblage of 50,000 thieves who were being formed into regiments in our prisons under the guise of being corrected by group punishment."[72]

In the history of repression, the Second Empire marks a time of undeniable hardening. It considerably strengthened both urban and rural police forces, which were now more than twice as large as they had been in 1830. "Today very few unlawful acts escape the watchful eye of the Law."[73] The regime tried to reinvigorate an "enervated repression" [sic] when it lectured the magistrates and reduced the role of the jury by expanding the jurisdiction of the courts of correction. Above all, it instituted the central police file *(casier judiciaire)*. With respect to its prisons, it abandoned the system of solitary confinement, which was found to be too costly and too inefficient (Persigny circular of 1853). With the passing of the law of 30 May 1854, it resolutely opted for deportation. Forced labor was to take place "in transatlantic penal colonies;" upon expiration of their term, those convicted to forced labor were to remain in these colonies for a time equal to their sentence if it was less than eight years, and *for the rest of their lives* if it was longer. The passing of this law immediately brought a sharp rise in the number of sentences to more than eight years, designed to bring about permanent deportation. Such sentences, which had been imposed in 55 percent of the cases between 1836 and 1845, were now imposed in 66 percent of the cases.

The triumph of Cayenne was the very symbol of the failure of the prison.

The Third Republic; or, multi-faceted repressive measures. In 1873–75, a major parliamentary investigation attempted to evaluate the penitentiary system. Was this investigation, led by Comte d'Haussonville, an outgrowth of the aristocratic and Christian movement? However that may be, the law of 1875 restored solitary confinement as most conducive to the improvement of malefactors. Between 1872 and 1908, some sixty prisons of this type were to be built.

On the other hand, the Third Republic preserved and strengthened deportation by making it the punishment for repeat offenders. The *Compte* of 1880 expressed shock and dismay at the high rate of recidivism—50 percent of the defendants in assize courts (up to 70 percent charged with crimes involving property) and 41 percent of the defendants in courts of correction. These repeat offenders "obstinately refuse to do work of any kind; and it would seem consistent with principle that such an attitude be treated with increased severity; but unfortunately exactly the opposite is the case." Therefore, the state had to make up for the excessive leniency of the magistracy. "The urgent need for energetic repression with respect to incorrigible recidivists has become obvious."[74] Consequently the Waldeck-Rousseau Law of 27 May 1885 provided for the banishment to penal colonies of repeat offenders. Between 1886 and 1900, there were 9,978 convicts evacuated in this manner. This was a veritable purge, designed to "clear the departmental prisons of their habitual inmates, a step that made it possible to refit these institutions" with cells for "repentant" prisoners.[75]

Thus, the penitentiary system appears to have almost totally forsaken its original objectives. Far from reintegrating, it expelled, evacuated, and repudiated those whom it considered irretrievable. However, this very attitude may also reveal its true, though unstated, purpose, which was to protect the industrial bourgeois society based on property and work. Prison was the specious safety valve of that society.

PRISON AS A FACTOR OF EXCLUSION

The nineteenth century created the "chill of the penitentiary." Step by step, it was building today's prison.

Inside the prison, the system endeavored to break all community, to prevent any form of sociability in order to submit the inmate exclusively to influences from above and to check the "contagion of vice," which it dreaded like a spreading cholera.

The system was based, first and foremost, on "classification." It was necessary to separate the sexes: "The two sexes must never see each other, never hear each other, never, even without seeing each other, so much as attend divine services together."[76] The theoreticians of the penitentiary system were haunted by sexual obsessions; on this point their imagination was overwrought and sick. Lucas spoke of the "conflagration of the senses, kindled by the presence of women," which would produce "consuming flames . . . emanations of desire." "The atmosphere is burning with coquetry and lewdness."[77] Age groups (sixteen marked the end of childhood) also had to be separated. Different grades of morality had to be segregated. Lucas, for example, advocated twelve separate quarters for prisoners awaiting trial alone, depending on the nature of the charges.[78] Other distinctions were made according to the nature and the length of the sentence, the degree of improvement in behavior (different quarters assigned as punishment, for evaluation, as reward, etc.)

Total isolation of the individual was the logical end-result of such subdivision *ad infinitum*. As a first step, the prisoner had to break with his old identity: "He loses his name as he enters and is henceforth designated by a number, so that his presence will leave no trace in the institution."[79] He was made to keep absolute silence; not only was he not permitted to speak to his neighbors, he must not even be able to hear them. "The architect must invent and design the means to absorb all sounds in isolated cells."[80] Only screams would pierce the silence, for it was not undesirable that the prisoner should feel fear. "We do not want the inmates to hear each other speak, but we cannot help it if they hear each other scream."[81] In the complete cell system (of the Philadelphia type), the inmate was denied the very sight of his fellow-prisoners. This resulted in extremely complicated arrangements for airing and exercise, instruction, and especially attending mass. Frégier extolled the merits of a "compartmentalized chapel and the rigorous use of hoods." Should that prove impossible, one would simply have to do without mass. After all, the Catholic Church excused sick persons from divine service, and surely, prison inmates were sick persons. Frégier, a great admirer of La Petite Roquette, wanted the children "encelled" there to wear hoods wherever they went. "This disguise would have nothing to sadden his [the juvenile inmate's] imagination, as long as he knew its purpose."[82]

Those who claimed that such solitude would lead to madness were contradicted by an authoritative statement from the Academy of Medicine. And besides, as Blosseville said, there is nothing wrong with paying for an effective system with a few extra cases of insanity.

This isolation, it was felt, would vouchsafe the total reeducation of the offender, since it removed him from his former associations and subjected him, body and soul, to the authority of the penitentiary, to that central and all-encompassing eye of Bentham's, which, in its ambiguous way, represents both God and conscience. For it was indeed the inner man that the pedagogy of the penitentiary wanted to change, persuaded as it rightly was of the power of ideology. "In our era of civilization, order inside and outside of the prison is most powerfully sustained not so much by material as by moral forces," wrote Lucas, who would have wished to replace prison walls with psychological pressure.

To educate the prisoner was to teach him to restrict his needs: "The greatest service we can render the lower classes is to establish, once and for all, the predominance of essential needs over accessory needs";[83] it is also to force the prisoner to acquire new habits, "the habits of work and saving," by means of compulsory work, the central core of the system, and adherence to a strict time schedule. In this respect the prisons came to elaborate regulations of a positively bizarre meticulousness, ludicrous distortions of these long, empty days in which every activity was clocked to the exact minute. Lucas provided seven minutes for "unexpected needs"; workshop regulations, anticipating the dream of a perfect industrial discipline, prescribed every last motion.[84] There were to be sanctions for work; below a certain threshold, the food ration was to be gradually reduced "down to the bread ration, which alone will remain intact and guaranteed."[85] Above that threshold, a certain sum was to be set aside for the prisoner, either as a nest-egg for the future or as a gratuity for his immediate use, especially in the famous *"cantine"* [snack-bar], which was such a controversial subject in reformer circles. The proper dosage of rewards and punishment was, and still is, the mainstay of this infantilizing discipline.

As for education, it was to be limited to the elementary notions of reading, writing, and arithmetic. Any excess would be harmful. It was important not to "open the resources of intelligence to criminality." For it was known that the Melun prison, where the level of instruction was highest, also had the highest level of recidivism. Consequently, the majority of directors consulted in 1834 declared that they wholeheartedly opposed the organization of primary education. "In the education of the upper classes, intelligence is, after all, a goal and a means to other ends; but one must not make the mistake of treating the lower classes, who must take care of the basic necessities of life, like the upper classes, who are exempt from such concerns. All that is needed among the lower classes is training for a trade, as well as moral and religious instruction, which are necessary to curb their wants and their passions. To add to this intellectual instruction, to instigate and foster, as some propose, their intellectual emancipation, would be to hold out to them the inducements and the joys of science without also affording them the resources and the leisure necessary to attain them."[86] It is not good to instruct the people, but it is necessary to adapt them to the norms of the nascent industrial society: order, work, punctuality, thrift, respect for property. In a text written at the dawn of the century, and remarkable only for its outstanding naiveté, Barbé-Marbois speaks of his astonishment at the "savagery" of the inmates of Coutances, a prison he had visited: "These men are as brutish as savages; and their reasoning also is very much like that of savages: 'We are born to live, and whatever we need to live is ours.' . . . Respect for property can exist only in a very advanced society. We must teach the poor who have no property that work can make up for this lack, and that work is the only means by which they too can acquire property."[87] This, essentially, was the moral lesson to be conveyed by the prison.

This idealized discourse has very little in common with the actual practices that will some day have to be described in their concrete daily manifestations. It was not the regenerated, sober, submissive, and hardworking individual dreamed of in the texts, but a thoroughly ill-adapted man, broken in body and spirit, that the prison returned to society—if, indeed, it did not destroy him. The excessively high mortality of the prisons was denounced by a number of physicians.[88] Even Lucas felt that prison sentences should not exceed ten years; he admitted that it was easier to survive twenty years at forced labor than ten years in a central prison. Prison was a killer. It also stigmatized. Bentham advised that the prisoners' garb should have sleeves of unequal length. In this manner prisoners would be recognized by the difference in skin color if they escaped. Nicole Gérard describes the difficulty in putting on, after "seven years of penance" (the title of her book), the clothes she had worn when she entered prison, noting that their anachronism gave her away.

Thus marked in his body, the ex-prisoner's record subjected him to police surveillance. In 1810, he was assigned to a place of residence; in 1832, he was forbidden to live in certain areas (Paris, Lyons, Bordeaux—all the big cities) and his passport was stamped. In 1850, his name was entered in the central police file (casier judiciaire).

Every testimony confirms that it was extremely difficult for the ex-prisoner to find work. "As soon as the veil covering his status as ex-prisoner is lifted, everyone avoids or flees him; if he works in a workshop, those who a moment earlier had treated him as a comrade will suddenly tolerate his presence only impatiently or begrudgingly; not only does he cease to be their fellow-worker, he is no longer their equal, their fellow man. Order and harmony will only be

restored when he is expelled,'' wrote Frégier.[89] Elsewhere he says: ''As
everyone knows, there exists among all classes of the French population an
inveterate aversion for ex-prisoners.''[90]

Being a man of order, Frégier was glad to see such behavior. But his
attitude is part of a larger context. It raises the fundamental question concerning the relationship between the inside of the prison and the outside world.
What, in that French society, were the boundaries of respectability? And
what, in particular, were the attitudes and feelings of the lower classes with
respect to delinquents and prisoners? How far did social censure extend? What
about solidarity? In this area, it will be impossible to formulate more than a
few disjointed remarks or to hazard more than a few hypotheses.

To begin with, it is a truism to point out that there was no unity among the
lower classes, or even within the working class. There were only social
categories, which, whenever they were undergoing upward mobility, tended
generally to endorse the dominant cultural model. The moralistic attitude of
the journeymen's associations, of the workers subscribing to *L'Atelier* (1840),
of the mutual-aid societies whose statutes excluded not only anyone who had
ever been sentenced but even those who had been found in a state of
drunkenness—this moralistic attitude is well known. But what does it mean?
Who adhered to it?

It is possible, too, that the boundaries within the lower classes shifted in the
course of time. Between 1815 and 1840, there seems to have been a relative
solidarity between the laboring classes and the dangerous classes, since they
were sociologically overlapping.[91] Furthermore, the right to unionize did not
exist, and strikers went to prison. We are told that in 1825, on the occasion of
a union league meeting at Toulon, the workers laughed as they were marched
off to prison and that there was constant communication between the prison
and the town. Popular literature—inexpensive reading material of all kinds
and the first serial novels—celebrated those who defied the law, men like
Cartouche or Mandrin, or a certain Anthelme Collet ''deceased in the forced
labor prison of Rochefort on November 9, 1840, after having long perpetrated
the most extraordinary swindles and the most daring thefts,''[92] much to the
disgust of a literary critic like Nisard, who called for heroes of a different ilk.
Finally, the prison was still surrounded by that halo of religious prestige that is
conferred by passion of any kind. The suffering of the captive sanctified him
and placed him nearer to God.

Moreau-Christophe relates some intriguing aspects of this attitude. In
Dauphiné, ''the lower classes believe that no prayers can be more efficacious
than those of prisoners. Therefore, in all critical situations of life, whenever
people feel the need to ward off a troublesome premonition or to turn away an
impending misfortune, they make their way to the prison.'' There was a
special alms box where one could deposit an offering before ringing the bell.
''Thereupon the prisoners come running to the scene, and one of them intones

the appropriate prayer, which he recites very hurriedly, while the others engage in frequently obscene banter."[93] This account shows all the characteristics of a disintegrating tradition. As for the author, he was outraged in his deepest feelings as a puritan and a reformer. He disapproved of this medieval spectacle. "Those who are guilty must expiate their crime; this expiation must be suffering; and suffering is the punishment." It makes no sense to help them, and even less to ask for their help. Penal institutions must be closed off from the outside world—totally closed.

By the middle of the century (1840–50?), the continued impact of stringent repressive measures, but also the powerful influence of the opinion-making system that had been elaborated over the preceding decades, and whose mainstays were the school system and the large-circulation press,[94] began to show results; the lower classes assumed a moralistic attitude and gradually turned their backs on the denizens of the prisons, who lost what little glory had remained to them and sank deeper into the dreary and lackluster anonymity of petty delinquency. They were ashamed to emerge into the open. The contemptuous notions of "hard-core" and "irretrievable" took the place of romantic sympathy for the defiant or unhappy prisoner. Distinctions originating in the division of labor were applied to delinquency. The laboring classes were differentiated from the dangerous classes. It is no secret that to this day socialist thinking takes a rather dim view of what is called the "subproletariat."

It is a fact that none of the great revolutions of the nineteenth century opened the gates of the prison, not even in 1789 or 1848. Let us reread Michelet: "The prisoners of Saint-Lazare had escaped. Those of the Force prison, detained for debts, were freed. The criminals of the Châtelet wanted to take advantage of the situation and were already beginning to break down the gates. The gatekeeper called on a band of common people that happened to pass by; they entered, opened fire on the rebels, and forced them to return to order."[95] The Republic of 1848 introduced a number of major penal reforms but did little to change the prisons. The decree of 24 March did away with prison workshops, "given the fact that the work of the prisoners has become an object of speculation" and that it "cheapens the price of free and honest labor." Between 1876 and 1914 the problem of prisons was to be dealt with almost exclusively from this angle of competition in the labor market, whenever it was broached by the various labor and union congresses. In 1885, when revolts broke out in the main central prisons, newspapers like Vallès's Cri du Peuple reported the facts with understanding but detachment—and almost invariably on an inside page. By and large, the organized labor movement was not really interested in the problem of the penitentiary.

The only voice to be heard in this semisilence was that of the libertarians, Kropotkin in particular,[96] who formed a fragile bridge between an increasingly organized working-class world that was growing roots of its own and the delinquents who were suspected of being unassimilable parasites. Moreover, by the eve of the war, even that voice was muted by the full weight of the exigencies arising from the movement's having opted for productivity, as no doubt it was bound to do. In the Victorious Revolution envisioned by Pataud and Pouget, common-law prisoners would have to make a choice between full integration into society through work and going into exile; however, those who chose the latter option would be provided with a ''small allowance.'' The imaginary speech to be delivered to the common-law prisoners by the confederated delegates—and they might be likened to commissars of the people—is worth quoting: ''They described the conditions of the new life and explained to them that, since the Revolution had been fought in order to get rid of idlers, parasites, thieves, and criminals of every kind, everyone was henceforth expected to work, and that no able-bodied person could be permitted to shirk this responsibility. Then, speaking to both the guards and the prisoners, they added: 'It is up to you to decide whether you feel capable of adapting to this new life, of making a fresh start. If you do, you will choose an occupation or a craft, and you will be admitted to its union. There you will find only comrades; they will treat you as friends and will ignore—or forget—the man you have been. . . . If this existence of healthy labor, the basis of all well-being, should not be to your liking, you are free to reject the social contract we are holding out to you. In that case, you will be banished from the territory and sent wherever you wish to go. But in order to give you something to fall back on when you arrive there, we shall provide you with a small allowance.''[97]

In the rising industrial society, there was no room for marginal people. Caught in the snares of economic growth, the revolutionaries learned their lesson well. At the dawn of the twentieth century the prison, walled in by contempt—which of all walls is the highest—finally closed in upon the solitude of an unpopular people.

NOTES

The first epigraph is taken from *Des prisons et des prisoniers* (1840), p. 215, by Dr. Vingtrinier, physician in charge of the prison at Rouen. The second epigraph comes from volume 1 of Gustave Flaubert's *Correspondance* (Paris: Gallimard, Collection de la Pléiade, 1973), p. 100.

1. André-Jean Arnaud, *Essai d'analyse structurale du Code civil français. La règle du jeu dans la paix bourgeoise,* preface by Michel Villey, postface by Georges Mounin (Paris: Durand-Auzias, 1973)—a very original work.

2. Jeremy Bentham, *Panopticon; or, The Inspection House,* ed. J. Bowring (New York, 1962). French edition: *Panoptique. Mémoire sur un nouveau principe pour construire des maisons d'inspection, et nommément des maisons de force, imprimé par ordre de l'Assemblée Nationale* (Paris, 1791). [Published under the direction of Dumont, this text is not an exact translation of J. Bentham]. It is a fundamental text, which exerted a profound influence, and should be reprinted.

3. J. Léauté, *Criminologie et science pénitentiaire* (Paris: P.U.F., 1972), conveys a very good impression of this profusion.

4. In addition to the many books and pamphlets produced by the century's heated debate on the penitentiary system, there is also a rich official literature: the *Compte général de l'administration de la justice*, statistics, reports, parliamentary investigations, etc. Of particular interest among these last is the investigation of 1819, which was studied by Catherine Duprat in an as yet unpublished work, as well as that of 1873–75: *Enquête parlementaire sur le régime des établissements pénitentiaires* (8 vols., in 4°, Bibliothèque Nationale [hereafter B.N.] 4° Le 894), a veritable mine of information. The archival material, on the other hand, presents some serious gaps, and at this point there is some doubt whether they will ever be filled. This fact is related, in part, to the chaotic history of the prison administration. A special administrative department, created only in 1845, was part of the Ministry of the Interior until 1911, thereafter of the Ministry of Justice. The situation is even more complicated for the registers kept by the court recorders who until quite recently were not civil servants and consequently were under no obligation to deposit the records regularly—a fact that explains why series U of the departmental archives, which should have received them, are so often spotty. However that may be, series F 16 of the Archives Nationales [hereafter A.N.] contains precious documentation for the period 1791–1838; this series permits the researcher to follow the birth of the new penitentiary system, particularly the organization of the great central prisons like Clairvaux. (See the detailed inventory drawn up in 1916 by Jules Viard, 5 xeroxed volumes covering call numbers 101–1154.) It appears that no records were deposited after 1838; at least the 1962 supplement to the inventory does not mention any. What, then, has happened to the prison archives after 1840? As far as Paris is concerned, no one seems to know. We will have to look further into this situation. By contrast, the series Y of the departmental archives are much better supplied; that of Aube has good documentation for Clairvaux, that of Indre-et-Loire for Mettray, and so forth.

5. Anonymous, *Un détenu: L'intérieur des prisons, réforme pénitentiaire, système pénitentiaire, emprisonnement commun . . .* (Paris: Labitte, 1846).

6. Henry Joly, *Le crime: Etude sociale* (Paris: Le Cerf, 1888), p. 17.

7. Honoré-Antoine Frégier, *Des classes dangereuses de la population dans les grandes villes*, 2 vols. (Paris, 1840), 2: 480.

8. François de Barbé-Marbois, *Visite des prisons des départements du Calvados et de la Manche* (Paris: Imprimerie Royale, 1821), p. 33.

9. Louis-Mathurin Moreau-Christophe, *De la réforme des prisons basée sur le principe de l'isolement individuel* (Paris: Huzard, 1837), p. 455.

10. Barbé-Marbois, *Visite des prisons*, p. 3.

11. Ibid., p. 27.

12. Frédéric-Auguste Demetz, *Lettre sur le système pénitentiaire* (Paris: Fourni, 1837), p. 36.

13. See Frégier, *Des classes dangereuses*, 2: 513; letter from the director of the Lausanne prison.

14. Charles Lucas, *De la réforme des prisons ou de la théorie de l'emprisonnement* (Paris, 1836), 1: 359. This is a classic work.

15. Bérenger, *Des moyens propres à généraliser en France le système pénitentiaire* (Paris: Imprimerie Royale, 1836), p. 45. Many documents on chain gangs can be found in A.N., series F 16, bundles 466–98.

16. Arthus-Barthélémie Vingtrinier, *Des prisons et des prisonniers* (Paris, 1840), p. 218: "Whenever it is obvious that an individual has aggravated his crime in order to be sent to the forced labor prison, he must be punished by being placed in a central prison."

17. *Compte de l'administration de la justice criminelle* (1880), p. 4. During the years 1867–80, 7 percent of the cases of arson prosecuted were perpetrated by prison inmates who wanted to be sent to a penal colony.

18. Cf. Yves Castan, *Crimes et criminalité en France aux XVIIᵉ et XVIIIᵉ siècles*. Cahiers des Annales (Paris: Colin, 1971), p. 130. One little town "did have its own prison, but the prisoner held there systematically dismantled its walls with the full knowledge of the community. It took him more than a day to break out, and although no one provided either help or hindrance, a crowd of onlookers commented on the matter. Nor did the local authorities take sides in the prisoner's struggle against his prison."

19. Here are the statistics of offenders charged with attempted escape from prison: from 1826 to 1830, 275; from 1851 to 1855, 279; from 1871 to 1880, 101.

20. See Jacquinot-Pampelune, *Sur la maison centrale de détention de Melun* (1819), p. 18.

242   MICHELLE PERROT

21. Louis Mathurin Moreau-Christophe, *De la réforme des prisons en France* (1838), p. 310.

22. B.N., Paris, Lf 107, 6, 4°.

23. See Bertrand Gille, *Les sources statistiques de l'histoire de France* (1964), p. 170. The first statistical tables can be found in A.N., Series F 16, 525; the volume for 1850 of the *Compte* contains summaries for the years 1803–25.

24. *Compte* of 1825, p. x.

25. *Compte* of 1830, p. 84.

26. (Paris: Bachelier, 1835), 2 vols. Book 3 (2: 92–242), entitled "Développement des qualités morales et intellectuelles de l'homme," is essentially a commentary on the French *Compte* and the corresponding Belgian statistics.

27. Joly, *Le crime*, (1888); *La France criminelle* (1889).

28. The *Compte* of 1832, p. xiv, states that since 1829, the number of offenses related to forests has almost doubled, "owing to the high price of foodstuffs and especially the commercial crisis which, by closing down so many workshops and manufactories has caused the naturally peaceful and hard-working local populations to turn to the devastation of forests in their desire to find the resources their normal occupations no longer provide." For these problems, see Maurice Agulhon, *La République au village* (Paris: Plon, 1970).

29. These statistics give the average annual figures. The incidence of arson reached its high point in the period 1851–55, when 244 cases were tried—an increase the *Compte* attributed to the growth in the number of insurance companies (19 per cent of the cases were related to the desire to receive insurance payments). Second in the order of motives was revenge on the part of workers, and third, the desire of prison inmates to be sent to a penal colony. It would be possible to undertake a study similar to A. Abbiateci's "Les incendiaires devant le Parlement de Paris au XVIIIe siècle," in *Crimes et criminalité en France XVIIe-XVIIIe siècles*, ed. P. Goubert (Paris, 1971).

30. Vingtrinier, *Des prisons*, p. 98.

31. *Compte* of 1880, p. xlv. Cf. also the *Compte* of 1850, p. xcvii, which denounces the "general tendency to more lenient punishment in today's thinking."

32. Gustave Flaubert, *Correspondance* (Paris: Gallimard, Collection de la Pléiade, 1973) 1: 98. To Ernest Chevalier, 15 March 1842: "The most grotesque aspect of all this is the magistracy that protects public decency and combats any attack on orthodox ideas. In any case, human justice is the most ludicrous thing in the world, as far as I am concerned. . . ." This, to be sure, is a rather hasty judgment; a closer look at the problem will be provided by M. Darmon, *Magistrats dans la première moitié du XIXe siècle* (forthcoming dissertation).

33. Bertillon, in *La dépopulation de la France* (1911) speaks of "criminal abortion," which he condemns in vigorous terms.

34. *Le Temps*, 21 January 1889, cited by Joly, *La France criminelle*.

35. To which we must add, as Maurice Agulhon pointed out during the colloquium, the obsession with violence.

36. According to Balzac, domestic servants were "hired thieves," who should be required to carry a work-book, like the workers. He speaks of the "alarming number of twenty-year-old workers marrying forty-year-old cooks who have become rich through theft." He blames the socialist propaganda: "baneful results of the antisocial doctrines that have been spread about among the lower classes by meddlesome writers." *Oeuvres* (Paris: Gallimard, Collection de la Pléiade), vol. 6., *La Cousine Bette*, p. 274.

37. On this point, see Joly, *Le crime*, p. 157: "As everyone knows, the Parisian department stores are the outstanding places where women commit theft. These stores . . . are now guarded and policed in the most intelligent and humane fashion." Were women the first victims of the consumer society?

38. See the examples given in Joly, *Le crime*.

39. The *Compte* of 1850 lists the thefts of money that were prosecuted according to the sums involved. The maximum lies between 30 and 50 francs.

40. Joly, *Le crime*, p. 157. This situation should be compared with the incidence of theft in eighteenth-century Paris described by P. Petrovitch in *Crime et criminalité*, ed. Goubert, pp. 209 ff. "In 87 percent of the cases, then, crime equals theft." Paris, in short, was ahead of its time and exhibited even then the very profile of criminality that was to characterize the nineteenth

century. See also *Le vol alimentaire à Paris au dix-huitième siècle* (Paris: Plon, 1974), by Annette Farge, which had not yet appeared when this article was written.

41. See for instance, Dr. Vingtrinier, *Des enfants dans les prisons et devant la Justice* (Rouen, 1855).

42. André-Michel Guerry, *Essai sur la statistique morale de la France* (Paris, 1833), p. 44.

43. In 1876–80 the percentages of acquittals were as follows: crimes against persons, 25 percent; crimes against public decency, 21 percent; crimes against property, 15 percent (*Compte* of 1880, p. xxxix).

44. Louis Chevalier, *Classes laborieuses, classes dangereuses* (Paris, 1958). English translation by Frank Jellinek, *Laboring classes and Dangerous Classes in Paris during the First Half of the Nineteenth Century* (New York, 1973).

45. Cf. Petrovitch in Goubert, ed., *Crime et criminalité*, pp. 257 ff; also, Emmanuel Le Roy Ladurie, "La décroissance du crime au XVIIIᵉ siècle," *Contrepoint* 9 (Winter 1973).

46. Jacquinot-Pampelune, *Sur la maison centrale de détention de Melun* (1819), p. 11. A present-day witness says that homosexuality is "not only forbidden by the rules, but also frowned upon by the subculture of the prison": Simone Buffard, *Le froid pénitentiaire* (Paris: Seuil, 1973), p. 44.

47. See, for example, Dupin, *Des forces productives et commerciales de la France* (Paris, 1827).

48. Guerry, *Essai sur la statistique*, p. 42.

49. Cf. also Lambert-Adolphe-Jacques Quételet, "Recherche sur le penchant au crime aux différents âges," *Mémoires de l'Académie de Bruxelles* (1831).

50. Dr. H. Lauvergne, *Les forçats considérés sous le rapport physiologique, moral, et intellectuel, observés au Bagne de Toulon* (Paris, 1841), pp. 255, 260.

51. Agatha Christie, *Hercule Poirot's Holiday*, p. 67.

52. Many explicit texts to this effect could be found. An outstanding example is Restif de la Bretonne, *Les gynographes, ou Idées de deux honnêtes femmes sur un projet de règlement proposé à toute l'Europe, pour mettre les Femmes à leur place, et opérer le bonheur des deux sexes* (The Hague, 1777) [The Gynographers, or exchange of ideas between two respectable women concerning a set of rules to be adopted by all of Europe, which would put women in their place and bring happiness to both sexes]: "Actions based entirely and fully on will, unmotivated by anything but the individual's inner perception, are the exclusive portion of Men. But in our sex, it is not a blemish, but rather a special attribute, to be passive in physical as well as in moral matters. From this it follows that if virtue in a Woman can never be as meritorious as in a Man, a criminal Woman is also less guilty."

53. *Compte* of 1834, p. x.

54. Guerry, *Statistique morale*.

55. Charles Lucas, *De la réforme des prisons ou de la théorie de l'emprisonnement* (1838), 3: 397.

56. Ibid., p. 396.

57. Joly, *Le crime*, pp. 265 ff.

58. Buffard, *Le froid pénitentiaire*, pp. 3, 143.

59. Léon Faucher, *De la réforme des prisons* (Paris, 1838); Ferrus, *Des prisoniers, de l'emprisonnement, et des prisons* (Paris, 1850). The most significant of these works is undoubtedly that of L. F. Huerne de Pommeuse, *Des colonies agricoles et de leurs avantages pour assurer des secours à l'honnête indigence, extirper la mendicité, reprimer les malfaiteurs, et donner une existence rassurante aux forçats libérés, tout en accroissant la prosperité de l'agriculture, la sécurité publique, la richesse de l'Etat* (Paris: Huzard, 1832). [On the advantages of work-farms as a means of offering help to the honest poor, eradicating beggary, controlling delinquents and providing a settled existence to ex-convicts, while at the same time increasing the prosperity of agriculture, public security and the wealth of the State.]

60. Lucas, *De la réforme des prisons*, 2: 38.

61. Cited in ibid., p. 163.

62. Lucas, *De la réforme des prisons*, 2: 176.

63. *Compte* of 1880, p. lix. Since 1826 the number of charges of vagrancy had risen four-fold, charges of beggary had risen eight-fold.

244 MICHELLE PERROT

64. See, for example, Lucas, *De la réforme des prisons*, pp. 50, 82.

65. Cited by Joly, *Le crime*, p. 37.

66. *Compte* of 1880, p. lxxxix. The *Compte* devoted a great deal of space to the problem of recidivism, that "scourge of society," thus preparing the way for the Waldeck-Rousseau Law of 1885.

67. England and especially the United States were the major terms of reference, and puritan influences are usually the first to be cited. The reformers did indeed look for models in the United States, and the entire debate on the penitentiary was centered about Cherry Hill versus Auburn. Nonetheless, the tradition of the Catholic convent was not a negligible factor either. We should not forget the writings of Mabillon, as well as certain experiments carried out in Italy under the pontificate of Clement XI, and especially the famous *maison de force* of Ghent, a full description of which can be found in the book by Vicomte Jean Villain XIV, *Mémoire sur les moyens de corriger les malfaiteurs et fainéants à leur propre avantage et de les rendre utiles à l'Etat* (Ghent, 1775) [Memoir on the Means of Correcting Malefactors and Idlers to Their Own Advantage and of Making them Useful to the State.] Such things as solitary confinement at night, silence, classification, and work were already among the features of this prison-workhouse.

68. Louis-Pierre Baltard, *Architectonographie des prisons* (Paris, 1829) (40 plates).

69. Demetz, *Lettre sur le système pénitentiaire* (1838), p. 3.

70. These measures included the following: in 1836, a circular from Gasparin stating that only floor plans calling for individual cells would be given consideration; another circular made silence compulsory. In 1836, La Petite Roquette, a prison for juveniles, was converted to individual cells. In 1838, a majority of prison boards opted overwhelmingly to adopt solitary confinement at all times. In 1839, a memorandum by Montalivet called for absolute silence in the prison. But a half-century was to elapse before these measures were put into practice, as is shown in the master's thesis by Mme. Boudier, *L'architecture des prisons au XIXe siècle* (unpublished).

71. Vingtrinier, *Des prisons*, p. 19.

72. Ernest de Blosseville, *Histoire de la colonisation pénale et des établissements de l'Angleterre en Australie* (Evreux, 1859). This is a classic of its kind. "All these charitable dreams must be subordinated to the defense and the preservation of society" (p. xxix).

73. *Compte* of 1880, p. llvii.

74. Summary in ibid., p. lxxxix.

75. Ibid., p. xciii.

76. Bérenger, *Des moyens propres à généraliser le système pénitentiaire*, p. 42.

77. Lucas, *De la réforme des prisons*, 1: 89.

78. Ibid., p. 107.

79. Demetz, *Lettre sur le système pénitentiaire*, p. 38. This author also envisions a kind of baptismal ceremony to celebrate the prisoner's resumption of his name upon release from prison.

80. Lucas, *De la réforme des prisons*, 3: 145.

81. Ibid.

82. Frégier, *Des classes dangereuses*, 2: 359.

83. Lucas, *De la réforme des prisons*, 2: 157.

84. Examples of regulations for prison workshops can be found in the parliamentary investigation of the prisons of France of 1819; in Jacquinot-Pampelune, *Sur la maison centrale de détention de Melun* (1819); and in Fresnel, *Considérations qui démontrent la nécessité de fonder des maisons de refuge . . .* (1819), pp. 82–103.

85. Lucas, *De la réforme des prisons*, 2: 242.

86. Ibid., 3: 256.

87. Barbé-Marbois, *Visite des prisons*, p. 18.

88. Villermé, *Des prisons telles qu'elles sont et telles qu'elles devraient être, par rapport à l'hygiène, à la morale et à l'économie* (Paris, 1820); Villermé, "Mémoire sur la mortalité dans les prisons," *Annales d'Hygiène publique*, 1829.

89. Frégier, *Les classes dangereuses*, 2: 448.

90. Ibid., p. 480.

91. This is the main theme of Louis Chevalier's *Laboring Classes and Dangerous Classes*. See, for example, p. 110 of Jellinek's translation: "Crime was no longer closely tied to the dangerous classes, but changed its significance and extended to broad masses of the population, to the greater part of the laboring classes."

92. Charles Nisard, *Histoire des livres populaires* (Paris, 1853), 2: 523.

93. Moreau-Christophe, *De la réforme des prisons*, p. 318.

94. *Le Petit Journal*, created in 1863, was the first to publish a certain type of moralizing serial novel in which the delinquents, usually members of the "lowest class" or of Jewish banking circles, are punished. These serial novels enjoyed great popularity.

95. *Histoire de la Révolution française*, bk. 1, chap. 4.

96. Pierre Kropotkine, *Les prisons*, 2d ed. (Paris: Publications de la Révolte, 1890), p. 59. Some fragments of a press conference held by Kropotkin on 20 December 1887 were republished in *Politique Aujourd'hui*, May 1972, in a special issue on prisons.

97. Pataud and Pouget, *Comment nous ferons la Révolution* (1911), p. 187.